Necroculture

Charles Thorpe

Necroculture

Charles Thorpe
University of California, San Diego
California, USA

ISBN 978-1-137-58302-4 (hardcover) ISBN 978-1-137-58303-1 (eBook)
ISBN 978-1-349-93111-8 (softcover)
DOI 10.1057/978-1-137-58303-1

Library of Congress Control Number: 2016944346

© The Editor(s) (if applicable) and The Author(s) 2016, First softcover printing 2019
This work is subject to copyright. All rights are solely and exclusively licensed by the Publisher, whether the whole or part of the material is concerned, specifically the rights of translation, reprinting, reuse of illustrations, recitation, broadcasting, reproduction on microfilms or in any other physical way, and transmission or information storage and retrieval, electronic adaptation, computer software, or by similar or dissimilar methodology now known or hereafter developed.
The use of general descriptive names, registered names, trademarks, service marks, etc. in this publication does not imply, even in the absence of a specific statement, that such names are exempt from the relevant protective laws and regulations and therefore free for general use.
The publisher, the authors and the editors are safe to assume that the advice and information in this book are believed to be true and accurate at the date of publication. Neither the publisher nor the authors or the editors give a warranty, express or implied, with respect to the material contained herein or for any errors or omissions that may have been made.

Cover illustration: © CoverZoo / Alamy Stock Photo

Printed on acid-free paper

This Palgrave Macmillan imprint is published by Springer Nature
The registered company is Nature America Inc. New York

Contents

1 The Necroculture of Capitalism   1

2 Artificial Life on a Dead Planet   53

3 Speed and Stasis   93

4 The Pornography of Information   153

5 The Tyranny of Negative Freedom   205

Index   261

CHAPTER 1

The Necroculture of Capitalism

THE LIVING AND THE DEAD

In the television series *The Walking Dead*, survivors of an apocalypse take shelter in a prison, while zombies circle the fences looking for a way in.[1] The zombies are shadows cast by a past to which the survivors cannot return but which they cannot escape. The living dead represent the past that, as Karl Marx wrote, "weighs like a nightmare on the brains of the living."[2] The prison that holds us today is what right-wing philosopher Francis Fukuyama called "the end of history," a predicament in which "we cannot picture to ourselves a world that is *essentially* different from the present one, and at the same time better."[3] Fukuyama welcomed the end of history as the victory of capitalism and liberal democracy. But the end-of-Cold-War triumphalism that Fukuyama's book emblematized has disappeared as global capitalism piles crisis upon crisis, and the thinning veneer of democracy reveals callous class rule. This system's continued existence is an *imposed* end of history, achieved by *suppressing* humanity's creative ability to "picture" a better world, to make history, and to remake itself in the process. The end of history is the enforced stasis of a decaying system stubbornly resisting its slow death. Its life support is imperialist war, ecological destruction, police-state surveillance and brutality, the degradation of culture by corporate mass media, and a mass psychology of hopelessness.

The chaos of war, want, and despoliation today is so gratuitous because it stands in such immense contrast to the level of productive, scientific, technological, artistic, and intellectual accomplishment that the human race has achieved. The destructiveness contrasts so painfully with the well-being and creative flourishing of all that our level of economic, technological, and cultural development places within humanity's grasp. The resources and capabilities produced by today's globally integrated productivity are locked up as financial wealth possessed and controlled by a narrow class layer. According to the Credit Suisse Global Wealth Report for 2015, the bottom half of the global population own less than 1 % of total household wealth, while the top 1 % of wealth holders own half of the world's wealth.[4] The mass of dead wealth piled up at the top is the denied potential of humanity and the barrier between present and future. The denied future is a system in which the fruits of human productivity are shared equally, society's creative and productive capacities are consciously applied for the benefit of all humanity, and living human need, not dead mammon, is the goal of production.

Capitalist culture is *necroculture*—a culture that aggrandizes the dead and non-living over the living. Necroculture is the culture of a social world subsumed by capital, one in which relations between human beings have been thoroughly colonized by, and subordinated to, the reproduction of capital. The concept of necroculture, as I use it, draws together Marx's concept of *alienation*, as the domination of living labor by its dead products, with Erich Fromm's psychoanalytic conception of *necrophilia* as the love of death over life.

Fromm interprets Marx's theory of alienation to be essentially about the relationship between the living and the dead. Fromm argued:

> For Marx, capital and labor were not merely two economic categories. Capital for him was the manifestation of the past, of labor transformed and amassed into things; labor was the manifestation of *life*, of human energy applied to nature in the process of transforming it. The choice between capitalism and socialism (as he understood it) amounted to this: Who (what) was to rule over what (whom)? What is dead over what is alive, or what is alive over what is dead?[5]

Capital is the power of the *dead* and of the *past*. It is dead, but draws sustenance, energy, and power from its exploitation of the living. It becomes *living* dead by appropriating the life of the worker. Marx wrote, "Capital is dead labour which, vampire-like, lives only by sucking living labour, and lives the more, the more labour it sucks."[6] Living death describes the occult power of what Marx called the "animated monster" of capital and the degradation and suffering endured by labor caught in its jaws.[7] As it is drained of its energy, creativity, and vitality, labor is transformed from the living into the living dead. The condition of alienation within capitalism is one of *living death*.

The subsumption of life by capital is culturally expressed in fetishistic interest in artificial things—technology and consumer products—to the exclusion and detriment of the living world of nature and human relationships. Obsessed with commodities and technological applications, necroculture treats with indifference the ongoing degradation of the richness of human life and the diversity of the natural world. It combines apocalyptic resignation and apocalyptic longing. It is increasingly evident that the wasteful and exploitative consumer-capitalist way of life must come to an end. But along with avoidance, anxiety, and mute despair, and in the ideologically enforced absence of a conscious alternative, there is a cultural undercurrent of attraction to apocalyptic scenarios as wish-fulfillment fantasy, offering release from the impersonal oppression that weighs on people.

Capitalism gains ideological support from the notion that the "free market" sets the individual free from external constraint (providing freedom in a purely *negative* sense). However, Fromm argues that this freedom from constraint made the individual "alone, isolated," and therefore powerless before "overwhelmingly strong forces outside of himself." With the rise of capitalism, man "became an 'individual,' but a bewildered and insecure individual."[8] Capitalist relations subject the individual to the anonymous demands of the market, and these demands are translated into personal forms of domination, submission, exploitation, and competition.[9] The business owner aims to annihilate the competition; the manager subjugates and exploits the worker, but, in turn, must meet his performance targets and fears his own superiors; the worker is forced to compete against his fellows. Personal relations infected with envy, resentment, aggression, and contempt are overdetermined by an economic system that makes life a struggle of all against all and turns all increases of productive power into human powerlessness.

The negative freedom of the individual under capitalism, therefore, produces insecurity and subjugation to impersonal forces that are hard for the individual to identify and comprehend. Fromm writes, "Aloneness, fear, and bewilderment remain; people cannot stand it forever. They cannot go on bearing the burden of 'freedom from'; they must try to escape from freedom."[10] The fear of freedom may be temporarily assuaged by amassing objects. Fromm writes that in capitalist culture, the individual's self "was backed up by the possession of property. 'He' as a person and the property he owned could not be separated… The less he felt he was being somebody the more he needed to have possessions."[11] Objects become, under capitalism, not only material security but security of the self. Being is subordinated to having, and life made dependent on non-living things. The spontaneity of life is subordinated to the discipline of the market, and the range of human creativity and desire is narrowed down to the drive to accumulate. The flight from negative freedom also, Fromm argues, is the root of the psychological attraction of fascism and other forms of authoritarianism. These forms of politics express the psychological need to submerge the self in a powerful entity.[12]

The "escape from freedom" is linked to a psychology of lifelessness. In his later work, Fromm came to see the fundamental social–psychological problem facing modern society as the choice between *biophilia* and *necrophilia*, or the love of life versus the love of death. Necrophilia, as Fromm uses the term, is "the passionate attraction to all that is dead, decayed, putrid, sickly; it is the passion to transform that which is alive into something unalive; to destroy for the sake of destruction; the exclusive interest in all that is purely mechanical. It is the passion 'to tear apart living structures'."[13] As a "character-rooted passion," it is not instinctual, but specifically human, arising from human existential needs, in response to, and shaped by, a particular social and historical formation.[14]

Necrophilia is not an idiosyncratic perversion, but rather a symptom of a mode of social life. It can take extreme destructive form, or more commonplace form in which life is treated with mere indifference. It is pervasively manifested today in the tendency "to install technical progress as the highest value." This priority expresses "a deep emotional attraction to the mechanical, to all that is not alive, to all that is man-made."[15] Fromm suggests that the attraction to what is artificial and non-living is not fundamentally different from an attraction toward what is dead. Hence, he writes:

> Those who are attracted to the non-alive are the people who prefer "law and order" to living structure, bureaucratic to spontaneous methods, gadgets to

living beings, repetition to originality, neatness to exuberance, hoarding to spending. They want to control life because they are afraid of its uncontrollable spontaneity; they would rather kill it than to expose themselves to it and merge with the world around them.[16]

Fromm perceived that the necrophile orientation was becoming increasingly dominant. The population's passive acceptance of the nuclear arms buildup that threatened their own survival and that of their children and grandchildren indicated that *"people are not afraid of total destruction because they do not love life*; or because *they are indifferent to life*, or even because *many are attracted to death.*"[17] The value-orientation of the necrophile character corresponds to the value-framework of capitalist society. For the necrophile, Fromm wrote, *"things rule man; having* rules *being; the dead* rule *the living.*"[18] This value-framework is what I call necroculture.

Capitalism as Exterminism

E.P. Thompson coined the term "exterminism" to characterize the destructive logic immanent in the production of nuclear weapons. Industries geared toward the production of weapons are "Satanic mills ... grinding out the means of human extermination." Exterminism is production turned into destruction; the products of human ingenuity and labor as "thing[s] of menace," threatening human survival; the increased capacity for social and technical coordination producing systems that defy control.[19]

Destructive production, however, is not confined to the military–industrial complex. With its wasteful production for the sake of profit rather than true human needs, capital puts the whole living world at risk. Not long after Thompson's paper, the German eco-socialist Rudolf Bahro argued that

> exterminism is in no way confined to the danger of nuclear war... Not least, and inseparably connected with the military and economic aggression, exterminism is expressed in the destruction of the natural basis of our existence as a species... The result of our efforts is the destruction of whole species of plants and animals... We poison the atmosphere, heating it up until self-regulation of the climate is destroyed not just locally, but on a world scale. We let loose millions of chemicals on human beings, plants, land and sea, without even being able to assess the consequences.[20]

The incessant push toward the expansion of production meant, Bahro argued, the "industrialisation-to-death of the world."[21]

Thirty years after Thompson and Bahro wrote, the evidence of the exterminist character of capitalist civilization is impossible to avoid. The US bombing and occupation of Iraq have, as James Cogan of the *World Socialist Web Site* puts it, "amounted to a conscious policy of sociocide—the destruction of the very fabric of a society." The war ripped the society into sectarian fragments, smashed the physical and social infrastructure, and left behind a legacy of toxic contamination.[22] The failure of the Copenhagen negotiations in 2009 has left the world plunging headlong toward a likely climactic tipping point in which catastrophic climate change will become unstoppable and irreversible.[23] Drawing attention to the massive global extinction of plants and animals, UN Secretary General Ban Ki-moon wrote that "[c]urrent trends are bringing us closer to a number of potential tipping points that would catastrophically reduce the capacity of ecosystems to provide these essential services."[24] The Deepwater Horizon oil spill in the Gulf of Mexico in 2010 and the Fukushima nuclear power plant disaster in 2011 revealed the fragility and ecologically destructive potential of the energy infrastructure of contemporary capitalism. Both disasters showed the way in which the potential for serious environmental catastrophe is routinely discounted in the calculus of short-term profit.[25]

The relentless pursuit of profit leaves an apocalyptic trail of war and environmental destruction. Beneath the glitter of consumerism is a swamp of toxic pollution. The products that poison the workers who produce them enjoy a brief moment in the limelight of consumer desire before, discarded, they poison the earth. The remnants of each new fad overflow landfills and clog the oceans with plastic debris.[26] The European Union recently announced that it would pay fishermen to collect plastic from the ocean rather than fish.[27] Overfishing has massively reduced fish stocks throughout the world's oceans. As the oceans are depleted of organic life, they are filling with the byproduct of consumer-capitalist production and consumerist lifestyles. Yachtsman Ivan MacFayden describes sailing from Osaka to San Francisco: "After we left Japan, it felt as if the ocean itself was dead... In place of the missing life was garbage in astounding volumes."[28]

Marx observed that capitalist wealth presents itself as an "immense collection of commodities."[29] The corollary of this accumulation of non-living things is the thinning of the living world, and the replacement of life with synthetic waste. As Guy Debord states, "The rate of production of non-life has risen continually on its linear and cumulative course: a final threshold having just been passed in this progression, what is now produced, directly, is *death*."[30]

Releasing the energy of past life, stored in fossil fuels, capitalist production throws the global climate out of equilibrium. Concerted action to stem the emission of carbon into the atmosphere is blocked by the power of capitalist interests invested in the extraction and commodification of fossil fuels. As a result of the political paralysis, some scientists and engineers are now searching for a technological fix in the form of geoengineering. One idea is "solar radiation management," which means attempting to cool the atmosphere by technological means of blocking new energy from the sun reaching the Earth (injecting large quantities of sulfur into the stratosphere or even placing giant solar reflectors in Earth's orbit). The domination of the present by the past is, therefore, evident in the thermodynamics of capitalism. In order for past energy to keep being circulated as commodity, and expended in commodity production, scientists and engineers are today seriously proposing that present energy in the form of solar radiation, our common free gift of the sun, should be filtered and weakened.[31]

The inversion of social priorities and the subordination of life to destructive inhuman systems are most clearly manifested in weapons production. In 2010, world military spending reached $1.6 trillion, comprising 2.6 % of global GDP.[32] This level of destructive expenditure, while people go hungry and while the financial costs of taking action to curb climate change are eschewed, makes military spending a "double curse," according to political scientist Ralph Summy. It means "shunting huge sums of money into a negative project when it is desperately needed for a wide range of positive purposes."[33] John McMurty points out that while the business of war is presented as "defense," society's "*real* systems of self-defence" are systematically run down, "its public infrastructures of hazard and disease control and prevention, universal health care, public education, life-long income-security, social safeguarding and care for the old, the young and the infirm, and regulatory protection of the environmental life-host are in this way downgraded and deprived of their income support."[34]

Mobile financial capital carries out raids on the social body's material sources of sustenance and security. McMurty argues that when capital exits a country "overnight in haemorrhages of investment infrastructure," it effectively "assaults... society's life-defence."[35] The "liberalization" of the Russian economy following the dismantling of the Soviet

Union represented exactly this type of assault, as economic institutions and resources were privatized and plundered, and as employment, medical care, and social services collapsed. Out of the post-Soviet economic and social chaos, organized crime was unleashed with a vengeance.[36] In Mexico, neoliberal reforms have exacerbated poverty and displacement of people, fueling the country's extraordinarily violent drug trade.[37] Mexican drug gangs laundered money through banks such as Wachovia and HSBC. According to former executive director of the United Nations Office on Drugs and Crime, Antonio Maria Costa,

> The penetration of the financial sector by criminal money has been so widespread that it would probably be more correct to say that it was not the mafia trying to penetrate the banking system, but it was the banking sector which was actively looking for capital—including criminal money.[38]

Widespread fraud in selling mortgages and packaging these as financial instruments was a key factor contributing to the economic crisis of 2008.[39] The growing economic criminality stems from the increasingly unproductive nature of capital as it seeks avenues for profit outside a stagnating real economy.[40] As it does so, it becomes more brutally and openly parasitic.

In Russia, the wealthiest fifth of the population have seen their income double since 1991, while the poorest fifth of the population have seen their income fall by 55 %. Between 2002 and 2010, the country saw a population decline of 2.2 million and widespread alcoholism accompanies chronic unemployment among men.[41] Such signs of social disintegration are also evident in the USA. In many poorer counties of the USA, life expectancy is now in decline, especially among women. The *Los Angeles Times* states, "For life expectancy to decline in a developed nation is rare. Setbacks on this scale have not been seen in the U.S. since the Spanish influenza epidemic of 1918."[42] Detroit exemplifies America's urban blight—the city's population has dropped by a quarter over the last decade.[43] Film director Julien Temple depicts a scene as if from a J.G. Ballard novel: "The vast, rusting hulks of abandoned car plants… beached amid a shining sea of grass. The blackened corpses of hundreds of burned-out-houses, pulled back to earth by the green tentacles of nature… Approaching the derelict shell of downtown Detroit, we see full-grown trees sprouting from the tops of deserted skyscrapers."[44]

Referring to America's increasingly obsolete infrastructure, *The Economist* magazine notes that "America, despite its wealth and strength, often seems to be falling apart."[45] This can be seen not only in busted levees and crumbling bridges but also in decayed and dysfunctional schools. Years of disinvestment in education in the USA are being compounded by the economic crisis, with states cutting budgets by laying off teachers.[46] With mass joblessness after the 2008 financial crisis, millions of Americans have faced their unemployment benefit running out, leaving them with nothing.[47] One in five American children live in families that are below the poverty line.[48] The despair and powerlessness of America's poor occasionally breaks into the news when it boils over into violence as when, in December 2011, a Texas mother who was denied food stamps shot herself and her two children.[49] Austerity for the most vulnerable in society is imposed as the corollary of the ready availability of money for war and for the needs of the financial sector.

The exacerbation of social inequalities undermines social cohesion and fosters a culture of selfish individualism, oriented toward competitive conspicuous consumption.[50] The system that produces individuals' inner emptiness encourages them to fill the void with the acquisition of things.[51] In *Society of the Spectacle*, Debord writes, "From the automobile to television, all the *goods selected* by the spectacular system are also its weapons for a constant reinforcement of the conditions of isolation of 'lonely crowds'."[52] Consumerism distorts human need into the need for objects. As various devices become the focus of attention, these channel people's attention away from their fellow human beings, and from the reality of the natural world. The ease of relaxation in front of the television isolates and deadens the mind, inducing a state of passive receptivity to propaganda and advertising; ease of cooking with a microwave means eating processed food packaged in plastic; ease of communicating via computer "social networks" thins out and limits relationships, reducing them to the exchange of sound bites between ghostly images.[53] The direction is toward E.M. Forster's dystopian vision in *The Machine Stops* (1909), of human beings isolated in cells in which they are nourished and nurtured by technology.[54]

However, Forster's short story also shows the vulnerability that accompanies atomization and technological dependency—if the machine mulfunctions, the isolated individual is left helpless. Zygmunt Bauman observes that "the most technologically equipped generation in human history is the generation most haunted by feelings of insecurity and helplessness."[55] The fear of technological catastrophe combines with what Bauman calls "liquid fear," an inchoate anxiety produced by an atomized "liquid" society in which the social safety net is in tatters, community is eroded, and the individual has no one to rely on except himself or herself.

Apocalyptic anxiety is by no means irrational. It corresponds to the reality of a global capitalist system that is corroding social bonds, destroying the planet's ecological integrity, and producing ever more sophisticated means for killing and devastation. The isolation and powerlessness of individuals is a corollary of the autonomous power of systems: financial, technological, and military. What Bauman terms the "Titanic syndrome," a sense of impending disaster, or "horror of falling through the 'wafer-thin crust' of civilization," has to be understood in relation to the way that "civilization" itself has become destructive of life.[56] Whether in the threat of unemployment, financial destitution, or climactic catastrophe, the things that human beings have made react back against us.

The self-defeating character of social activity should be understood as an aspect of alienation, which means that human creativity and activity come to be split off from human beings, and embodied in something alien and hostile. Capital, this alien power, is the product of human labor, but it is labor embodied in objects (especially, money and machines), which the producers do not control and which confront the producers as an external force. Under the domination of capital, the more technologically and organizationally sophisticated human beings become, the more vulnerable they find themselves before the powerful forces that they have unleashed. "The alienation of humankind," Istvan Mészáros writes, "in the fundamental sense of the term, means *the loss of control.*"[57] Marx's theory of alienation, as put forward in the 1844 *Economic and Philosophic Manuscripts*, provides the key to understanding the dynamic destructiveness of capitalist society.

Alienation as Death

Human beings are productive beings. Labor is human life activity, mobilizing human beings' physical energy, conscious understanding, and creativity. For Marx, labor is "*productive* life itself." Labor is an expression of the life of the individual human being, and the life of the human species. Marx writes that "productive life... is life-engendering life."[58] Labor not only satisfies physical needs but is also an expression of species life in the sense of being an expression of what it *is* to be human. Labor reproduces and develops the specifically human character of the species. Labor creates the conditions for the development of higher levels of consciousness and for the progressive realization of human capacities for creativity, self-expression, and freedom. Thus, labor is "life-engendering life" for the individual, society, and species. It is "life-engendering" in the sense that it not only maintains and improves the conditions for physical life, but also actualizes and develops the social and creative character of human life.

Labor is also life in the sense of being a living relationship with nature. Marx writes that "Man *lives* on nature" so that "nature is his *body*, with which he must remain in continuous interchange if he is not to die." Human beings do not come to nature from a position outside. The human interchange with nature "means simply," Marx writes, "that nature is linked to itself, for man is a part of nature." But although *within* nature, human beings interact with the rest of the natural world in a specifically human way. Through labor, human beings physically, intellectually, aesthetically, and spiritually take in, and humanize, "inorganic nature," that is, nature external to the human body.[59] In contrast to animals occupying a particular ecological niche, human beings transcend any particular locale, developing a more global interchange with nature, especially as human understanding develops through modern science.

Unlike the activity of other animals, human life-activity is self-conscious and creative. Marx writes: "[M]an produces even when he is free from physical need and only truly produces in freedom therefrom." Human beings are able to reshape the world creatively and aesthetically, rather than in a merely instrumental way. Human beings form and cultivate inorganic nature in such a way that they can experience themselves in the material world around them, recognizing human nature in nature. Marx writes that, "*in his work upon* inorganic nature, man proves himself a conscious species being."[60] As free, conscious activity, the human transformation of the natural world is an expression, and realization, of what it means to *be* human.

To say that the human being is a *species being* means that any individual's activity always transcends the finite individual. Individual activity is a manifestation of *human* activity, owing to the historical development of human thought and skill, and also contributing to this broader development of humankind. The individual outside society can only be an abstract figment. Marx writes that "the individual *is the social being*. His life... is therefore an expression and confirmation of *social life*."[61] The most private thought is made possible by social structures of cognition and language that articulate the historical self-development of the species.[62] Self-consciousness is social—one relates to oneself through the way in which one participates in, and therefore realizes oneself in, social life. Hence, "man's relation to himself only becomes for him *objective* and *actual* through his relation to the other man."[63]

The ways in which human beings engage with the natural world, and with each other in society, produce different historical forms of human life. Human life takes social forms, which are particular historical manifestations of species being. But species being transcends any of these particular manifestations, since the *potential* of the human species for universality and freedom surpasses what has been possible in any *given* society. Species being is manifested in social being, but transcends any current or hitherto existing social form. What Marx identifies as the essence of the human being, that is, free, conscious life-activity, exists as a potentiality that has been realized only incompletely. As such, it is a future condition and a task which humanity must accomplish. The human species is always, therefore, in the process of making itself—this is what Marx calls "man's establishment of himself by practical activity."[64]

Humanity makes itself by making history. Marx rejected a view of human behavior as determined by a preexisting human nature. History develops *toward* human nature. The "ear" for music or the "eye" for beauty can only develop with the development of music and artistic activity. In this way, "The *forming* of the five senses is a labor of the entire history of the world down to the present."[65] Human nature emerges in a historical process of which human beings are the subjects: "History is the true natural history of man."[66] Marx suggests that history is the continuous process by which the human species gives birth to itself and comes to comprehend itself. He writes, "*[T]he entire so-called history of the world* is nothing but the creation of man through human labor."[67]

If that is so, then the alienation of labor, as a *loss of control* of human beings over their life-activity, means that the historical process of humanity's self-creation is blind and unconscious. This is particularly significant today, when alienated labor involves the mobilization of technology of tremendous power. As is suggested by Thompson and Bahro's notion of exterminism, the alienated development of society's productive forces puts the very survival of humanity at risk. What Marx wrote of the alienated individual is true also of the human species under generalized alienation: "His life appears as the sacrifice of his life… his production as the production of his destruction."[68] The destructive aims of alienated technological capacity thwart the realization of humanity's potential and threaten the physical life of the species. This general thwarting of human potential is inextricable from the crushing of individuals' potential within organizations and technological systems that reduce people to mere cogs in the machinery.

In wage labor, one sells one's capacity to work (including one's physical energy, manual and intellectual skills, knowledge, etc.). Effectively, as Marx writes, the worker is selling "himself and his human identity."[69] Alienated labor actively produces and reproduces the means and conditions of alienation, that is, the means and relations of production. Marx emphasizes that alienation is manifested "within the *producing activity*, itself... If then the product of labor is alienation, production itself must be active alienation, the alienation of activity, the activity of alienation."[70] The longer workers work, the more intensely they work, the more of themselves they give up in the process. Not only the product of their work, but their life-activity itself, becomes something outside them, and hostile to them. Alienation means, therefore, "living of life as the estrangement of life."[71]

The individuals' loss of their own activity is also their separation from the broader world. It is separation from the life of the species, since alienated workers are no longer able to universalize themselves in free, creative activity. It is separation from nature (the "inorganic body"). All these aspects of existence—species life, society, nature—become mere instruments. When workers have no inherent interest in, or commitment to, their work, they will tend to treat their own activity, and the world they encounter through it, as a mere means toward getting through the day and getting paid.

Any human meaning we are able to find in work is *in spite of* its capitalist organization. As human life-activity, labor naturally reflects the diversity of human individuality. Marx writes, "In labor all the natural, spiritual, and social variety of individual activity is manifested." In contrast, he argues, "dead capital always shows the same face and is indifferent to *real* individual activity."[72] Capital actively seeks to repress the diversity of human beings and their activities.

In the pursuit of efficiency, controllability, and speedup, capital imposes simplification and homogenization, together with the fragmentation of tasks. In *The Economic and Philosophic Manuscripts*, Marx pointed to the tendency of capitalist organization to turn work into "mechanically monotonous activity."[73] In his later writings, Marx developed the critique of the capitalist labor process more systematically. Especially important are the concepts of formal and real subsumption that he introduced in a chapter titled, "Results of the Immediate Process of Production," which was not included in the originally published version of *Capital*.[74] Capital formally subsumes labor by rendering it in terms of a measure of time to be exchanged for a wage. Formal subsumption means that work is measured by the abstract mechanism of the clock, and that this abstract measure of duration takes precedence over the content of the task. As Marx said, "Time is everything, man is nothing; he is at the most, time's carcase."[75] But, in real subsumption, this process of abstraction shapes working activity.[76] In the capitalist labor process, labor tends to be routinized and deskilled, complex tasks are broken down into simple components, and wherever possible, these activities are taken over by machines.

In *Capital Volume 1*, Marx vividly describes how the worker within the factory is subsumed into the system of machinery, and subordinated both physically and mentally. Marx describes, in visceral terms, the physical toll on the worker as a living being caught up in a "lifeless mechanism." The factory "exhausts the nervous system... does away with the many-sided play of the muscles, and confiscates every atom of freedom, both in bodily and in intellectual activity."[77] By standardizing and homogenizing labor, factory organization puts the worker in a state of "helpless dependence upon the factory as a whole, and therefore upon the capitalist."[78]

Alienated individuals are unable to participate in a rich and vibrant way in the world. Instead, they find comfort by retreating into the most basic physical needs. Marx describes how

> man (the worker) only feels himself freely active in his animal functions—eating, drinking, procreating... and in his human functions he no longer feels himself to be anything but an animal. What is animal becomes human and what is human becomes animal.[79]

Far from being creative realization of self, work is a grind that leaves itself imprinted in stressed muscles and mind. Non-work time invites sheer physical relief, often through drugs, alcohol, or just sitting in front of the television. "Sunshine in a bag" provides relief from the cold despair of everyday life. "Living for the weekend" means hedonistic self-annihilation.[80]

Marx commented on England's gin shops that "Industry speculates on... *self-stupefaction*—this *illusory* satisfaction of need."[81] Illusory satisfaction is overlaid onto real degradation and pauperization, as the fundamental need of humanity for an environment capable of supporting human life is systematically denied. The destruction of the natural environment was, for Marx, a key aspect of capitalism's "bestial barbarization" of needs:

> Even the need for fresh air ceases for the worker. Man returns to a cave dwelling, which is now, however, contaminated with the pestilential breath of civilization... *Filth*, this stagnation and putrefaction of man—the sewage of civilization (speaking quite literally)—comes to be the *element of life* for him.[82]

Today, the smogs and effluent of nineteenth-century Britain are replicated in the massive pollution accompanying the rise of China as today's workshop of the world, poisoning its workers, polluting the Pacific Ocean, and increasing global atmospheric pollution. The transition to capitalism in China has been accompanied by an upsurge in cancer rates. According to *The Guardian*, "In 2007, the disease was responsible for one in five deaths, up 80 % since the start of economic reforms 30 years earlier."[83]

Marx made the point that the workers of Manchester could only *actualize* a need for a dank cellar dwelling. Of course, the worker *needs* proper shelter, fresh air, and unpolluted food. But this is not what economists call "effective demand."[84] Today, the homeless have no "effective demand" for a home more sturdy than a sleeping bag or a tent. Our human needs for oceans unpolluted with mercury and for a stable climate do not translate into purchasing power, so capital does not recognize these human needs.

Needs are "effective" only if they are supported by money. It is neither the human being nor the human need that is recognized, but money and purchasing power. So money stands in for, and takes over from, the human being. Marx writes:

> That which is for me through the medium of *money*—that for which I can pay (i.e. which money can buy)—that am I, the possessor of money... Thus what I *am* and *am capable* of is by no means determined by my individuality. I *am* ugly, but I can buy for myself the most *beautiful* of women. Therefore I am not *ugly*, for the effect of *ugliness*—its deterrent power—is nullified by money. I, as an individual, am *lame*, but money furnishes me with twenty-four feet. Therefore I am not lame. I am bad, dishonest, unscrupulous, stupid; but money is honored, and hence its possessor. Money is the supreme good, therefore its possessor is good.[85]

In America, the most ruthless businessmen, whether John D. Rockefeller, Henry Ford, Andrew Carnegie, Bill Gates, or Warren Buffet, come to be lauded as "philanthropists," the money they have acquired enabling them now to be generous humanitarians. They seem to say, "I am selfish, but my money is generous, therefore I am generous."[86]

Money has the power to make the selfish man generous, the ugly man attractive, and so on. By the same token, the lack of money denies to people the ability to actualize their real human qualities and thereby negates real human need. An anti-intellectual individual from a wealthy family, George W. Bush, is able to go to Yale University. There are countless people in America who are denied their vocation for study due to underfunded schools, the barrier of the fees charged by universities, and the debilitating weight of student loan debt.[87] Money, therefore, "appears as this *overturning* power... It transforms fidelity into infidelity, love into hate, hate into love, virtue into vice, vice into virtue, servant into master, master into servant, idiocy into intelligence, and intelligence into idiocy."[88]

Against this confounding, overturning power of money, Marx contrasts the truly human relationship. In contrast to abstract exchange mediated by money, the truly human relationship depends on the actual qualities of the human being, manifested in their living being and their orientation to the world. Marx writes:

> If you want to enjoy art, you must be an artistically cultivated person; if you want to exercise influence over other people, you must be a person with a stimulating and encouraging effect on other people. Every one of your relations to man and to nature must be a *specific expression*, corresponding to the object of your will, of your *real individual* life. If you love without evoking love in return—that is, if your loving as loving does not produce reciprocal love; if through a *living expression* of yourself as a loving person you do not make yourself a *loved person*, then your love is impotent—a misfortune.[89]

Love is paradigmatic of the truly human relationship, in that it is based entirely on the expression of what the individual *is* as a human being and the calling forth reciprocally of love in the other individual as a manifestation of their *being*.

If economic life was truly human, then love would be an aspect of production and exchange. Marx describes a truly human relationship between producer and consumer or user: "I would have been the *mediator* between you and the species and you would have experienced me as a redintegration of your own nature and a necessary part of your self; I would have been affirmed in your thought as well as your love."[90] Marx describes reciprocity that, unlike commodity exchange, is not merely the recognition of property by property, but rather is an unmediated relationship among human beings. When I read Marx's writings, his production, which is the objectivation of his self, becomes part of my consciousness and self and also my relationship to humanity. To be productive is both self-creation and creation for other human beings. It expresses and builds both the self of the producer and that of the consumer, and in doing so creates a social bond. When one cooks for another person, *their* enjoyment is part of *one's own* satisfaction in preparing the meal. Truly human production, therefore, involves care for the other person as an essential element. Truly human production validates the producer's humanity by linking the producer as individual with society and species. The sense that truly human production creates not just reciprocity but also wholeness is inherent in Marx's notion that, for the consumer, the producer is "a redintegration of your own nature and a necessary part of your self."[91]

As the Marxist cultural critic Christopher Caudwell notes, the opposition between love and economy is a bourgeois artifact: "To-day it is as if love and economic relations have gathered at two opposite poles. All the unused tenderness of man's instincts gather at one pole and at the other are economic relations, reduced to bare coercive rights to commodities."[92] The idea of production as a loving act is paradoxical only from the point of view of bourgeois relations, which have emptied economic and public affairs of their affective element, instead constraining emotional ties within the private, erotic, and family spheres, which are squeezed from all sides and distorted by the market.[93]

The notion of production as an expression and awakening of love conceptualizes production in terms of being, or lived human existence and experience. *Being* implies a completely different conception of richness than that taken for granted in the *having* mode of capitalist society and formalized in economics. Marx writes, "in place of the *wealth* and *poverty* of political economy comes the *rich human being*." The human being can be rich in needs. This notion is utterly paradoxical in relation to the categories and calculations taken for granted in capitalist everyday life. But, by insisting on it, Marx shows how prevailing notions of wealth and need obscure the living human being. Richness of need makes sense from the perspective of the development of the living human being, because it indicates the developmental character of human sensibilities and capabilities and, corresponding to this, the historical character of needs: "The *rich* human being is simultaneously the human being *in need of* a totality of human manifestations of life—the man in whom his own realization exists as an inner necessity, as *need*." The true needs of human beings arise from our development as social beings, in relationship with other people. Therefore, Marx writes that the "greatest wealth" is "the other human being."[94]

Capitalism's reduction of need to acquisitiveness imposes the logic of material scarcity: it means holding back from life in order to increase one's stock of things, in particular money. The resultant accounting mentality is exemplified by Benjamin Franklin's dictum that "time is money," which Max Weber took to encapsulate the capitalist spirit.[95] It means measuring one's life not in terms of whether the activities in which one is engaged are personally fulfilling, but in terms of the stock of money that one is accumulating. Marx describes this calculus when he writes:

> The less you eat, drink and buy books; the less you go to the theater, the dance hall, the public house; the less you think, love, theorize, sing, paint, fence, etc., the more you *save*—the *greater* becomes your treasure which neither moths nor dust will devour—your *capital*. The less you *are*, the more you *have*, the greater is the store of your estranged being.[96]

Money stores the past estranged labor of others. This money becomes the possessor's being, which now, therefore, exists outside him as an object. *Having* is *estranged being*.

As the representation or embodiment of estranged being, money is abstract power that can buy anything for its possessor, quite independent of the possessor's personal qualities. Marx writes: "The universality of its *property* is the omnipotence of its being. It therefore functions as almighty being."[97] The universality of money derives from its abstractness as quantity separated from any particular qualities. This abstractness is, however, the product of concrete activity: "Money is the alienated *ability of mankind*."[98] Money is universal power because it derives its value from the universal alienation of human capacities, skills, and powers. Money makes "the world upside-down" because it reflects the inversion of subject into commodity-object.[99] In a world dominated by money, "everything is itself something *different* from itself... all is under the sway of an *inhuman* power."[100] A house is not a home but a real-estate investment; education is, in the words of *The Economist* magazine, an "asset that cannot be repossessed." A corporation is a person.[101]

Money is the epitome of the rule of objects over people. For the economists who articulate the value-framework of capitalism, "men are nothing, the product everything"[102] The inversion that money instantiates is fundamentally an inverted relationship between the living and the non-living. This inversion between life and death is suggested when Marx writes that alienated labor is "vitality as a sacrifice of life."[103] Life becomes merely a means for the augmentation of the abstract power of capital (past labor or dead labor). When human activity is subsumed by capital, it becomes "an activity quite alien to itself, to man and to nature, and therefore to consciousness and the flow of life."[104] In capitalist work, fragmented, repetitive, and one-sided, the human being is split off from the diversity and richness of the "flow of life" and is reduced to an "*abstract* existence... as a mere *workman*."[105] The "workman" is an instrument of the accumulation process, rather than a subject freely and actively pursuing individual and collective human goals.

The workman, Marx writes, "may... daily fall from his filled void into the absolute void—into his social, and therefore actual, non-existence."[106] The working day is a "filled void" in the sense that it is filled with activity, but this mechanical activity, however frenetic, is boring and mentally and physically painful, and is resented by the worker. As Marx puts it, instead of work being a "*free manifestation of life* and an *enjoyment* of *life*," under capitalism, "Working is *not* living."[107] This dead time has to be endured on pain of unemployment, loss of livelihood, homelessness, hunger, and, ultimately, death, "the absolute void." The workers' alienated activity is a form of living death in which they remain trapped by the ever-present fear of losing their means of survival.[108]

While workers experience their lived time as living death, non-organic objects—money and commodities—take on the characteristics of life. This imbuing of non-living objects with qualities of life is akin to idolatry or fetishism. Marx described those who regard value as inherent in metal money as "fetish-worshippers."[109] He criticized laws against gathering firewood for giving wood (as private property) a status above human life. In such laws, "the wooden idols triumph and human beings are sacrificed!"[110] The same idolatry of property was evident in the punishment of so-called looters, who were taking what they needed to live in the aftermath of Hurricane Katrina in New Orleans in 2005.[111]

Idolatry grants a dead object power over living human beings. In religion, worshippers give their soul over to the deity; in work, laborers give up their soul to the commodity. Marx wrote in the *Grundrisse* that "living labour appears merely as a means to realize objectified, dead labour, to penetrate it with an animating soul while losing its own soul to it."[112] The relationship between labor and capital is a relationship between the worker as a living being and the commodity as the idolized dead object. The power of money under capitalism represents "the complete domination of dead matter over mankind."[113] Bourgeois class power operates through the fetish, "the rule of the capitalist over the worker is the rule of things over man, of dead labour over the living."[114]

The idea of capitalism as the domination of the living by the dead is most vividly expressed by Marx in the image of the vampire. The metaphor portrays the cruelty and violence inherent in capitalism, which is whitewashed by bourgeois economists. Excavating the brutal origins of capital in primitive accumulation—conquest, expropriation, and the slave trade—Marx concluded with an image of capital as a blood-soaked monster: "[C]apital comes dripping from head to toe, from every pore, with blood and dirt."[115] But Marx's vampire metaphor also expresses the fundamental philosophical tenet that capital is the non-living embodiment of past labor, but derives the attributes of life from this labor.[116] As the productive and creative energies of labor are alienated and transferred to capital, it seems to be capital itself that is productive and creative. Marx writes in the *Grundrisse*: "What was the living worker's activity becomes the activity of the machine. Thus the appropriation of labour by capital confronts the worker in a coarsely sensuous form; capital absorbs labour into itself."[117] As it absorbs labor, capital appropriates for itself the capacities of labor and seems itself to be the source of those capacities: "Thus all powers of labour are transposed into powers of capital."[118]

Capital moves through the transformation M-C-M, in which money is invested in commodity production, and commodities, via the market, are reconverted into money at a profit. In this process, capital appears as "self-valorizing value." Marx writes, "it has acquired the occult ability to add value to itself. It brings forth offspring, or at least lays golden eggs."[119] This is the view of the capitalist investor who experiences his money as, by itself, making money. But what appears to be the self-generating capacity of capital is, in fact, capital's appropriation of surplus labor. So, capital gains its occult "life," its self-generating productive and creative powers, by drawing those powers from living labor.[120]

Labor is denuded of autonomy and meaning, becoming merely energy expended. Workers are drained by the end of the working day or shift and at the end of their working life left nursing their injured body. Capital colonizes the worker's life-time and, within that colonized time, makes the worker's activity its own, subsuming it so that workers cease to express themselves as living beings. In real subsumption, laboring activity comes to be patterned at a minute level according to requirements of capital. Capitalist relations are then embodied in the very sinews of the living worker. Paradoxically, the worker is not only against capital, but also *is* capital. In the capitalist labor process, the worker reproduces himself or herself in the form of a commodity. Glenn Rikowski writes, "Capital is an invasive social force that 'possesses' the human... We are becoming capitalized, which is the becoming of capital within us."[121]

Capital possesses us not only in work, but also in consumption. As human needs are translated into the need for commodities, everyday life is subsumed by capital. Our relationship with the physical world of nature is highly mediated by commodities in, what philosopher Albert Borgmann has called, the "device paradigm" of contemporary consumption.[122] The advertising phrase "there's an app for that" suggests the way in which activities and needs are automatically translated into the demand for technological/commodity "applications." Our human relationships, and our relationship with the natural world, are mediated by devices, and therefore, by commodities. Mark Neocleous writes, "Because capital is dead labour, the desire to live one's life through commodities is the desire to live one's life through the dead."[123]

An extreme manifestation of this fetishistic attachment to the dead over the living was the South Korean couple who allowed their own baby to starve to death while they obsessively tended to a virtual child in a computer game.[124] The commodity spectacle had created an artificial object of desire, with its own artificial needs. The couple, in turn, deeply internalized the false "need" to satisfy these imaginary needs of this figment of the spectacle, while turning away from the real needs of their living child. The commodity, the virtual "baby," was here a monster: its artificial needs were monstrous needs, to which this couple had allowed themselves to be enslaved. Capital has more generally enslaved us to *its* needs, which we, in turn, experience as *our* needs, while we turn away from each other and from the living world. Many people are tethered to their mobile phones, laptops, and notebook computers and, thereby, to work and to the needs of capital. Melissa Gregg describes as "presence bleed" the process by which, through technology, work penetrates and draws in everyday life.[125]

NECROPHILIA AND CAPITALISM

Capital subsumes human life, and in the process transforms it into living death, but as it does so, it puts forward the commodity as an object of fetishistic identification, offering escape from this life-as-death. In Marx's exploration of alienation, Fromm found a dynamic psychology of the escape from life as a fundamental feature of the character structure fostered by capitalism. Fromm writes that a "basic category in Marx's psychology is that of life as against death, not in a biological-physiological sense, but in a psychological one... Perhaps the most decisive question in Marx's psychology is whether a man, class, or society is motivated by the affinity to life or to death."[126] Fromm read the *Manuscripts* as providing a social–psychological analysis of the "ascetic, hoarding character of the bourgeois of the nineteenth century and of the self-indulgent character of those who could afford the luxurious life."[127] Particularly important, for Fromm, is Marx's distinction between *having* and *being*: "[T]he less you are, the more you have." Capitalism encourages an orientation toward *having*, in which the self is identified with the accumulation of objects. In the having mode, Fromm writes, "My property constitutes myself and my identity."[128] As the ability of individuals to express their life and to develop meaningful social relationships is debilitated within capitalism, people turn to the substitutions offered—the objects churned out by alienated production, which seem themselves to bear life and to contain the promise of restoring what is otherwise absent.

Fromm suggests that this acquisitive, hoarding approach to life represents an interest in dead things that derives from the inner deadness of alienation. The hoarding character has been understood classically in psychoanalysis to be reproduced in repression in early child-rearing and to express an obsessive interest in possession and control. Freud argued that gold and money were symbolic substitutions for feces, and miserly hoarding has been understood psychoanalytically as a key expression of anal libido.[129] Fromm, however, argued that the anal character was closely related to what Freud called the death instinct, since feces are the body's waste, dead matter. Fromm writes: "The anal character is attracted by feces as he is attracted by everything that is useless for life, such as dirt, death, decay."[130] It is this interest in what is not alive that is expressed in the hoarding of money and material things.[131]

Fromm acknowledged that the capitalist personality of the twentieth century was different from that of the ascetic nineteenth-century entrepreneur criticized by Marx (and, later, ambivalently admired by Weber). The new hedonistic ethic of consumer capitalism, however, does not supplant, but complements, the asceticism of work and accumulation. Fromm writes:

> Obsessional work alone would drive people just as crazy as would complete laziness. With the combination, they can live. Besides, both contradictory

attitudes correspond to an economic necessity: twentieth-century capitalism is based on maximal consumption of the goods and services produced as well as on routinized teamwork.[132]

Consumer culture has taken alienation deeper to the core of the self, producing, what Fromm called, the "marketing orientation" in which the individual relates to himself or herself "as a thing to be employed successfully on the market."[133] Fromm's insight is even more significant today as service work increasingly commodifies emotion and self-presentation and as social relationships (which, thinned of human content, become "social networks") are subsumed within marketing.[134]

The "hedonism" of consumer culture is far from being an expression of aliveness. Rather, Fromm observed, the commodification of enjoyment reduces experience to increasingly simple stimuli: "What is stimulated are such drives as sexual desire, greed, sadism, destructiveness, narcissism; these stimuli are mediated through movies, television, radio, newspapers, magazines, and the commodity market."[135] Today, we could add the Internet to this list. Beneath the appearance of hedonism is a pervasive and chronic boredom. This is often mingled with depression, which may be masked or even unconscious.[136] The stimuli of consumer culture promise pleasure and escape, but cannot deliver this, except fleetingly: "The person continues to feel 'empty' and unmoved on a deeper level. He 'anesthetizes' this uncomfortable feeling by momentary excitation, 'thrill,' 'fun,' liquor, or sex—but *unconsciously* he remains bored."[137] Bored people go through the motions of living without being engaged and present in their lives. These, for Fromm, are "zombies... people whose soul is dead, although their body is alive... who chatter instead of talk, and who assert cliché opinions instead of thinking."[138] He notes that the bored person often seeks stimuli in "reports of crimes, fatal accidents, and other scenes of bloodshed and cruelty that are the staple diet fed to the public by press, radio and television."[139] To alleviate boredom, people turn to a media culture of sadistic-necrophiliac fascination and enjoyment of violence, mutilation, and death. In addition to the movie audience's passive reception of Hollywood's sexualized violence, there is also the promise of more active participation in violence through videogames centering on gun mayhem and mutilated or exploding bodies.

The "device paradigm" enables a withdrawal from the living world. Direct experience is oriented to technological commodities, which prepackage and simplify our experiences. "In a device," Borgmann argues, "the relatedness of the world is replaced by a machinery, but the machinery is concealed." The device frees the user from "the encumbrance of or the engagement with a context."[140] A key characteristic of "contemporary industrial man," Fromm writes, is "the stifling of his focal interest in people, nature, and living structures, together with the increasing attraction of mechanical, nonalive artifacts." Fromm describes the person for whom "taking pictures has become a substitute for seeing," "the gadgeteer…who is intent on replacing every application of human effort with a 'handy,' 'worksaving' contraption," or people who automatically use the car for any journey, no matter how close their destination. For such people, technology "becomes a *substitute* for interest in life."[141]

People lose themselves in their mobile devices, never fully present in-the-moment with the people and physical environment around them. Fromm describes the type of individual for whom "his machines are just as much the object of his narcissism as he is himself."[142] People today enlist their devices in their narcissistic self-fixation—the "selfie-stick" for taking self-portraits, which can then be displayed on social media. Capital inserts commodities between us, and advertisers tout these gadgets or applications as bringing us together. Society becomes "the network," but the image of social networking hides increasing detachment and withdrawal.[143]

Tech corporations are exploring technologies to seamlessly integrate their products and services into everyday life, to make these a *necessary vehicle* for everyday life (as the car was made necessary in Fordist American suburbia). "Google Glass" (Internet connected eye-glasses) integrates real space with virtual space by providing "data" on the wearer's locale (e.g. shops and restaurants).[144] But this involves placing a data screen between self and world. The wearer can never be entirely present, but is instead always a cognitively distanced observer. Technological "connectivity" represents disconnectedness from the immediacy of experience.[145] It also represents the separation of the self from itself, the separation of cognitive activity from *one's own* mind, as consciousness is more and more seamlessly integrated into the network.

The technological mediation of experience is a vehicle for total commodification. In 2014, Amazon.com brought out a new phone that, according to *The Economist*, would

> provide the user with information about more or less anything the phone sees or hears, be it a song, a television show, a bottle of wine, or a child's toy—including how to buy it from Amazon. If it works as promised, it will turn the whole world into a shop window.[146]

Technology provides the means for the subsumption of human existence, now not only in production, but also in consumption. Capital is ever-present, in all the minutiae of everyday life.

Google Glass and the Amazon phone establish an informational environment that mediates between the human user of the device and the world. Life is encountered both in concrete reality and (at the same time) in the abstract informational space of the web or "cloud." The overlaying of this abstraction onto the concreteness of everyday experience allows the world to be encountered as a collection of commodities. In addition to their concrete presence in front of the individual, things are immediately also encountered as priced items, objects with exchange value in the abstract space of the market. So the human appropriation of the real world, in the sense of its becoming a reality *for* human beings, is also the appropriation of the world and human experience by capital. With one's Amazon phone, what one senses one is able to *have*, by purchasing it in the informational ether. The world is there for one's appropriation, through the power of money.[147]

Technological mediation allows the individual to distance himself or herself from material reality, encountering it, but not being present in it. This form of technological removal of self from world operates in warfare to enable dispassionate killing at a distance. It allows killers to feel absolved of responsibility for the act in which they are involved as mere cogs in a bureaucratic machine. Fromm writes, "In modern aerial warfare destruction has been transformed into an act of modern technical production, in which both the worker and the engineer are completely alienated from the product of their work."[148] This kind of alienated, technicized killing is epitomized today in the Central Intelligence Agency (CIA) apparatus for drone killing.[149] These technicians of death are examples of what Fromm describes as "totally alienated man whose dominant orientation is cerebral, who feels little love but also little desire to destroy," at least, that is, little *conscious* desire.[150] Mass murder is euphemized and sanitized as "collateral damage" from "surgical strikes."[151]

The dominance of instrumental *means*, and inability to articulate *ends* in more than formulaic terms, masks the destructive purposes to which capitalism applies society's productive capacities. This instrumental orientation arises organically from the character of capitalist relations in which the worker has no say about the tasks to which he or she is assigned, and the goals of production are given over to the "hidden hand" of the market. The domination of exchange value over use value, and quantity over quality, entails the subordination of thought and activity to what Fromm calls "the process of *quantification* and *abstractification*."[152] Abstractification is inherent in the transformation of things into money and their evaluation in terms of the balance sheet of profit and loss. Fromm writes that the attitude of abstraction has spread beyond purely economic calculations and has come to define human beings' relationship to the world and to themselves: "[T]he concrete reality of people and things to which we can relate with the reality of our own person, is replaced by abstractions, by ghosts that embody different quantities, but not different qualities."[153] A world of alienated objects, and of actions from which the agent feels morally divorced, is a world in which "nothing is real."[154] Lived reality becomes split off from life-activity, taking the commodified form that Debord termed "spectacle."[155] The alienated products of human activity circulate as tantalizing images. This grand illusion becomes increasingly sophisticated and animated at the same time that nature is drained of aliveness and richness.

Technology under capitalism is developed and employed in an exploitative relationship to nature, just as it is employed in the exploitation of human beings. The reduction of the productivity of nature to a stock of resources for exploitation finds its parallel in the reduction of human productivity to energy in the service of capital. Human need, desire, and culture are reduced to "demand," to be surveilled, quantified, processed, and manipulated within the apparatus of corporate marketing, advertising, and public relations. Living diversity is reduced to standardized, manageable quantities. Treated as a quantity of dead matter, the world becomes that. Fromm observes:

> Death is no longer symbolically expressed by unpleasant-smelling feces or corpses. Its symbols are now clean, shining machines; men are not attracted to smelly toilets, but to structures of aluminium and glass. But the reality behind this antiseptic facade becomes increasingly visible. Man, in the name of progress, is transforming the world into a stinking and poisonous place (and this is *not* symbolic). He pollutes the air, the water, the soil, the animals—and himself. He is doing this to a degree that has made it doubtful whether the earth will still be livable within a hundred years from now.[156]

The technologically processed and packaged world of capitalism is revealed as "only another form of the world of death and decay."[157]

The Living Dead

The image of the vampire served, for Marx, as a way of portraying the predatory violence of capital, but also, as David McNally argues, it was a language with which to "divine the mysteries of capitalist social life." The image of the living dead was one of Marx's literary "strategies for theorizing the doublings and transpositions that occur in a world governed by capital."[158] The "occult" character of the commodity as self-valorizing value, seeming to have its own life, but, in fact, animating itself only through the extraction of labor, is vividly encapsulated in the gothic image of the vampire. Further, the notion of living death points specifically to the contradictory character of the commodity as a non-living thing that is the product of human life-activity and to the antagonistic position of the worker as a living, breathing component of the "lifeless mechanism" of the factory. It points to the worker's contradictory existence as a being with, as Marx explains, "the misfortune to be a *living* capital, and therefore a capital *with needs*."[159] But it also points to the sterility of capital, the fact that it is not alive and can only *possess* life by possessing the worker. Capital can *only* live by sucking living labor, and therein lies its fundamental contradiction, its dependence on an antagonistic force.

Capital's historical decline, driven by the declining rate of profit, is bound up with its attempt to escape from this dependency via automation, an attempt that proves increasingly self-defeating as the growing "organic composition of capital" deprives capital of its external life-source. As in the movie *Daybreakers* (2009), the vampires begin to starve and turn on each other, as they run out of human blood. In the wake of the 2008 financial crisis, as stock market speculation has continued unabated while the real economy and productive investment stagnates, the Bank of England's chief economist Andy Haldane has said that businesses are "almost eating themselves."[160] The totally commodified world of the spectacle is a world of death and decay as capital inflicts ever greater violence on nature and society, but it is also capital that is dying and decaying. The animated corpse of capital stumbles as it decomposes; it becomes more vicious in its quest for blood; its exquisite cloak and seductive features fall away to reveal its true monstrosity. The seductive vampire becomes the repellently rotting zombie.

With capital increasingly assuming an openly parasitic speculative form, the living dead have bubbled to the surface of the cultural imaginary.[161] Recent popular culture shows intense fascination with vampires and zombies, and in both cases there is a strong element of ambivalence in the portrayal, a combination of fear and identification. The sense that *we* are the living dead underpins the ubiquity of vampires and zombies in contemporary popular literature, cinema, and television, and provides the distinctive orientation of contemporary portrayals of these mythic creatures.[162] The vampire is not only a predatory monster to be destroyed, but also a figure in which we recognize ourselves.

Milly Williamson traces the emergence of the "sympathetic vampire," no longer found in gothic castles, but instead making its way in the modern world. The vampire, as a romantic outsider, is a figure of ambivalent attraction, an image resonating with an individualistic culture of consumerism.[163] Rob Latham argues that the vampire has become a symbol of the combination of exploitation and seduction, especially for youth caught up in the culture of consumption. In its narcissistic individualism and predatory attitude, the vampire epitomizes the personality type fostered by consumerism.[164] Identification with the vampire mirrors the consumer's identification with the celebrities and elites, as the attempt to gain individual distinction and status through conspicuous consumption has paradoxically become a mass pursuit. The vampire, as outsider, remains an aristocratic figure, with charismatic aloofness and effortless superiority over the population on which it feeds. But this paradoxically reflects the mass attitude of consumer society, in which, as Steve Hall, Simon Winlow, and Craig Ancrum have explored, everyone is encouraged to engage in "distinguishing the self as a 'cool individual' from others cast as the hapless, moribund 'herd'."[165] Contemporary depictions of the vampire depart, as Mark Edmundson argues, from the tradition in which "one was expected to be fascinated with vampires, to be mesmerized by their glamour, their weird allure. But finally one sided with the middle-class characters who... contrived to drive the stake into Dracula's heart." In this way, "The traditional vampire tales played out the theme of modern revolution. The overthrow and death of the aristocracy was dramatized once more." Edmundson identifies the key break from this tradition occurring in Anne Rice's *Interview with a Vampire*, published in 1976 (and made into a Hollywood movie in 1994) and her subsequent best-sellers written over the course of the 1980s and 1990s. Edmundson observes that "Rice... seems to have sensed the fact that in the age of the Reagan-Bush plutocracy, readers would be more than happy to throw their allegiances to the higher orders." So, in her novels "one is invited to identify with the victimizers, the master race of vampires against the pale, quivering mortals."[166] So, depictions of the vampire mesh with the promotion by Hollywood and mass media of the predatory excesses of the ruling class as models for popular aspiration, the latter epitomized by what Marxist film critic David Walsh calls Martin Scorcese's "celebration" of financial fraudster Jordan Belfort in the 2013 film *The Wolf of Wall Street*.[167]

The zombie has none of the seductive qualities of the vampire. Its monstrosity is openly visible; it is manifestly a walking corpse.[168] Most importantly, the zombie is not representative of the elite or ruling class, but of the mass. The zombie genre in Western popular culture was established by George Romero's low-budget 1968 horror-movie, *Night of the Living Dead*.[169] Romero's zombies are ordinary Americans in a rural small-town setting, and they move *en masse*. In the subsequent genre that Romero inspired, zombies always appear in large numbers. Their appearance is an apocalyptic phenomenon that one has to assume encompasses the world.[170] There are a small number of survivors holding out against an unindividuated horde of zombies.

Although the mythological or folkloric zombie was slave labor, it has now become a symbol of mindless consumerism after Romero portrayed zombies advancing through a shopping mall in his 1978 film, *Dawn of the Dead*.[171] In contrast with the status-figure of the vampire, the zombie represents consumerism as mass conformism. It is an image which collapses the boundary between the movie viewer and the Other, implicating all of us in the official zombiedom of consumer-capitalist society. One of Romero's human survivors explains why the zombies return to the mall: "Some kind of instinct, memory of what they used to do. This was an important place in their lives." Another of the survivors adds, "They're us, that's all."[172]

The image of the zombie-like relentless consumer is horrifically mirrored in consumer stampedes of bargain-hunting shoppers that have occurred at superstores in the USA, the UK, and other countries, in which shoppers and store employees have been injured and even trampled to death.[173] To participate in such a shopping-mall rush is to give oneself over to the pleasure of abdicating individual responsibility in the visceral unity in the crowd, which is unified in its atomization as a mass pursuit of ruthlessly competitive individualism. It is a ritual abandonment of inhibition sanctioned by the consumer society. Self-conscious identification with the zombie is displayed in the so-called Zombie walks, in which hundreds, sometimes even thousands, of people parade through the streets made up as zombies.[174] These events represent a carnivalesque disruption of the banal routine of capitalist urban life, and therefore might be seen as an implicit protest against its automaticity and mindlessness.[175] But imagining oneself as a zombie and making oneself up as such a creature is also an embrace of the disinhibition inherent in mindlessness. The pleasure in being a zombie is the pleasure of escape from a humanness that has become alien. In that sense, it is the pursuit of the individual who "only feels himself freely active in his animal functions": identifying with the mindless hunger of the flesh-eating zombie is a state of self-abandonment *in* alienation similar to the shopping mall stampede or the self-annihilation of "living for the weekend."[176]

There is a scene in *Dawn of the Dead* in which one of the survivors sheltering in the giant shopping mall mistakes a store mannequin for a zombie. The scene makes a connection between the zombie and the commodity on sale as similarly living dead. The store mannequin is a fetish. The religious fetish gains its life from that which is alienated by its worshippers. It becomes alive in their life, as the manifestation of their collective power, which is now separated off in an object. The religious fetish gains life in consciousness, culture, and the social superstructure of rule, whereas the commodity fetish gains its life from the material processes and relations of its production. Its power as fetish, its value, derives from labor expended. In the shopping mall, the commodity appears abstracted from its production, and as valuable in itself; the source of that value is obscured. On the basis of that process, the commodity becomes a modern equivalent of the religious fetish, ascribed the power to give status, membership, and identity. Its symbolic power is a collective representation. The consumer approaches the commodity with something like religious reverence. This new jacket will make me a new person. But what the consumer gives up is not only soul but also body, for, in order to buy the commodity, the consumer must work. In mass consumption, the consumer is the worker, and consumption is umbilically linked to production. The consumer zombie is necessarily also the zombie wage-slave, enslaved to the commodity that they also desire to possess.

The extreme anxiety that the zombie represents is the fear of death, non-being, non-identity, chaos, the "yawning abyss," with which a being conscious of its own mortality is faced.[177] While this anxiety is usually thought of as "existential" in the sense of concerning consciousness and meaning, it is very much existential in a material sense, given that death can only be staved off in the material world of nature, not in consciousness. The commodity as fetish stands between the individual and this abyss in a dual sense. Firstly, and most basically, under capitalism, the essential objects (water, food, clothing, housing, medical care) are commodities. Without them, one dies. Secondly, as culture is commoditized and commodities increasingly mediate human relationships and stand in for any social whole, commodities also become increasingly laden with symbolic meaning and become holders of the symbolic meanings that are projected onto them. So, commodities mediate the relationship of the individual to society, which is the individual's only protection against the abyss of reality faced by a naked, alone, starving, but fully aware and self-conscious, being.[178] This conscious being that is itself a creation of society, as the collective self-making of the human species, cannot exist apart from society.

As the commodity has become the mediator of social bonds, the commodity confers social identity, in what is now a competitive struggle for social recognition, that is, for existence in society, to be socially alive and not dead. Without commodities, individuals are on the edge of dying—the homeless people hiding in plain sight in the dead areas of America's cities, at road intersections or center medians, on empty lots, on pedestrian bridges, in canyons, on the edges of the sidewalk. These people are also *socially* dead. They are unrecognized, or "unseen."[179] Bauman writes:

> They are *failed consumers*, walking symbols of the disasters awaiting fallen consumers, and of the ultimate destiny of anyone failing to acquit herself or himself in the consumer's duties. All in all, they are the 'end is nigh' or the 'memento mori' sandwich men walking the streets to alert or frighten the bona fide consumers.[180]

Those who cannot consume are excluded from identity and membership in the society. The commodity, therefore, is desired as a fetish object that has the power to bestow social identity, protection against being a non-entity, in other words against non-being.[181]

The more money one has, the more one feels safe and remote from suffering and death. Those closer to suffering and death remind you of it and so you do not like to be around them; it feels somehow unsafe; and they, therefore, underneath it all, repulse you.[182] In London, a luxury apartment complex installed beds of 1.5-inch metal spikes in stairwells and doorways to deter people from sleeping rough. As one resident put it, "We used to come back and find drunk homeless people in the doorway, which is not very nice at all."[183] So consumption is a competitive struggle, firstly, not to die, but secondly, not to be a social reminder of death, and therefore socially dead. Bauman suggests that

> [f]or defective consumers, those contemporary have-nots, non-shopping is the jarring and festering stigma of a life un-fulfilled—and of own nonentity and good-for-nothingness. Not just the absence of pleasure: absence of human dignity. Of life meaning. Ultimately, of humanity and any other ground for self-respect and respect of the others around.[184]

To be a fully recognized member of the consumer society is to not fear that you will be beaten to a pulp by a security guard at Whole Foods Market, because you tried to pay with an Electronic Benefit Transfer card (food stamps), an incident that occurred in Oakland California in September 2015.[185] People in poverty frequently find themselves unemployable or consigned to menial and out-of-view jobs, because, as "defective consumers," they are unable to maintain the requisite appearance of affluence. Their missing teeth are too much of a reminder of the ever-present insecurity of life under capitalism.[186] Commodities mediate, and are necessary for, the individual's existence, both materially and in the social imagination. Commodities do indeed have awesome power.

If existence is dependent on commodities, then one's primary relationship to the world must be that of having. Being depends on having. This illogical relationship is in fact the case. The only protection against non-being is money, and money can be lost or stop coming in. So the *having* relation necessarily produces deep insecurity and fear. Fromm observes:

> *If I am what I have and if what I have is lost, who then am I?...* Because I *can* lose what I have, I am necessarily constantly worried that I shall lose what I have. I am afraid of thieves, of economic changes, of revolutions, of sickness, of death, and I am afraid of love, of freedom, of growth, of change, of the unknown... I become defensive, hard, suspicious, lonely, driven by the need to have more in order to be better protected.[187]

While capitalism has taken over the globe, it has, at the same time, fragmented social relationships. The competitiveness of capitalist relations weakens the collective sense of a social whole. The "sacred canopy" becomes thin and full of holes.[188] People turn to fetishism, which proliferates in the form of commodities. However, they are short-lived, flimsy things, and quickly out of date. Debord writes that "the object which was prestigious in the spectacle becomes vulgar as soon as it is taken home by its consumer—and by all other consumers. It reveals its essential poverty (which naturally comes to it from the misery of its production) too late."[189] These objects lose their magic. They provide little shelter from chaos. Others have newer, more prestigious objects, so in the competitive struggle to distance oneself from the smell of death, the individual is always in danger of falling behind. The zombies are always at one's heels.

The zombie apocalypse is the giving way of everyday life to the void. Kyle William Bishop notes that "the primary details in Romero's series of zombie films are in essence bland and ordinary, implying that such extraordinary events could happen to anyone, anywhere, at any time."[90] The zombie is everything that is excluded from the protective shell of everyday life. It is, therefore, a symbol resonating with contemporary "liquid fear." It evokes the feeling of foreboding inhabiting a world that seems inherently incalculable and in which prediction and control over the future appear utterly elusive.[191] The current rash of zombie films that began with Danny Boyle's 2002 *28 Days Later* reflects, in part, the post-9/11 climate of collective paranoia that has fixed on the image of the terrorist.[192] The terrorist and the zombie fulfill the same function as an image providing a focus and representation for inchoate anxiety. In his 2005 return to the genre, *Land of the Dead*, Romero portrays a militarized enclave walled off from a zombified world. Inside the enclave, there is further division, as the rich are sequestered in a luxury high-rise from a slum-dwelling majority. It is a scathing allegory not only for the Bush administration's politics of fear but also, more fundamentally, for the growing class polarization of America, the brutality of which was revealed in the same year by Hurricane Katrina.[193]

The US government's Center for Disease Control (CDC) itself has drawn on the zombie as a symbol for liquid fear, using preparation for a fictive "zombie apocalypse" as template for instilling its doctrine of "preparedness" for its more staple threats of epidemic, terrorism, hurricanes, floods, and earthquakes. The CDC advises:

> Plan your evacuation route. When zombies are hungry they won't stop until they get food (i.e., brains), which means you need to get out of town fast! Plan where you would go and multiple routes you would take ahead of time so that the flesh eaters don't have a chance! This is also helpful when natural disasters strike and you have to take shelter fast.[194]

Bauman writes that we are caught in "fears of a breakdown or a catastrophe that may descend on us all, hitting blindly and indiscriminately, randomly and with no rhyme and reason, and finding everyone unprepared and defenceless."[195] Just as the figure of the zombie encapsulates the dehumanization of the individual in a world in which the dead dominates the living, the zombie apocalypse projects the overarching destructive trajectory of an alienated society in which the growing capacity and sophistication of human productivity manifests itself in more sophisticated means for destroying ourselves.

Many Americans are stockpiling guns and ammunition to prepare for what they see as a coming collapse.[196] *The Walking Dead*, which began in 2010, and Season Five of which opened in 2014 with 17.3 million viewers, foregrounds, in its zombie apocalypse, survivalist cultural themes such as the collapse of urban life and retreat to the rural heartland.[197] At the gun range, the zombie is popular as a shooting target. One can buy rubber zombie torsos that bleed when shot. There is the phobia-inducing clown zombie and the Nazi authority figure zombie. "The Ex" is a sexualized semi-naked female "zombie" with a bloody mouth and blood running down her cleavage. There are terrorist themed zombies with Middle Eastern looking features, or zombies that resemble President Obama.[198] The gun target zombie is a portrayal of one's fears, which can now be shot at. One can expend one's ammunition, but the underlying anxiety represented by these targets cannot be killed with a bullet, and continues to gnaw.

A recent book on personal finance, titled *Zombie Economics*, employs the trope of the zombie apocalypse to put forward, what one reviewer calls, a "survivalist approach to financial freedom."[199] The book, co-authored by CNN economics journalist Lisa Desjardins with broadcaster Rick Emerson, presents maxims of financial prudence, as strategies for survival in an essentially hostile world. The conceit is that the attitudes that will ensure survival in a zombie apocalypse are also the attitudes necessary to getting by in today's recession economy. *Zombie Economics* presents America as a world in which living is reduced to survival, in which one's relationship with other human beings is characterized by suspicion and hostility, in which one has to steel oneself against a threatening external world, and in which the hoarding of material possessions is paramount.

The book opens with a staple zombie movie scenario, a house under siege from "a mass of biting, squirming death." Those inside turn their attention to what they have hoarded: "[T]hey start to count things: the number of potato chip crumbs left inside the bag; the number of water bottles that haven't been drained."[200] The book advises that "[a] zombie economy is infectious, contaminating and threatening everything it touches." Its features are unemployment, debt, "staggering medical bills," loss of means of transportation, and "a self-perpetuating sense of doom." The book advises how to "defend yourself in advance."[201] The experience of living through recession is one of being under attack, both from other human beings and from non-human forces, for example, the bill arriving in the mailbox: "As long as those bills accumulate, stuffed into drawers and stacked into teetering piles of unopened envelopes, your sense of doom and utter hopelessness will only get worse."[202] American life is one of perpetual insecurity—you could lose your job and your health insurance "could vanish overnight."[203] One has to be prepared for such disasters. To stave off doom, one must have a "well-stocked financial arsenal" and learn how to dig "financial trenches."[204] One must keep working stoically, and reject all "fantasies of calling it quits." To be without a job is to be "in the graveyard."[205]

The key message of the book is that life is a struggle of the individual against a hostile world. Interviewing for a job is "fighting hand to hand" against the other applicants.[206] The reader is admonished that "No one is coming to save you."[207] You also must resist the temptation of going to the aid of others. Indeed, friends and relatives with financial problems, who exhibit poor money management, and who might seek your help, are the financially "infected." You cannot help them; instead, you must concentrate on your own survival. If in a relationship with a "financial zombie," you have to realize "You're not dealing with a person, just a disease with a human voice."[208]

The book's zombie imagery is a clever way of marketing a book offering such mundane financial advice as the wisdom of paying bills before unnecessary expenses and not running up credit-card debt. Nevertheless, the imagery captures something of the deeper experience of living in a capitalist society—its insecurity, anxiety, and isolation, the overarching power of non-human things (money and bills) over human beings, and the degradation of human relationships when mediated by money. In capitalist relations, other people are merely sources of financial advantage or disadvantage and, in being reduced to mere means, are rendered objects. No longer experienced as fully alive, they are the living dead.

The book ideologically presents these aspects of capitalist society as the basic, unchangeable reality to which the individual must adapt. What is demanded for survival in the capitalist economy is treated as a set of imperatives by which one must live. There is no sense that this reality can be changed. To think about changing these realities would be so much naïve idealism of the sort that would distract one from the unforgiving demands of the daily struggle and lead one to certain death in the hand-to-hand combat of everyday life. The book portrays the zombification of a world ruled by money and the implicit violence of capitalist everyday life in the form of a manual for living. It is an ideological demand that one accept and adapt to this world. The survivalism of *Zombie Economics* makes explicit the aggression and fear that are always implicit in the competitive struggle of capitalist life.

The "zombies" that Desjardins and Emerson suggest we need to barricade ourselves against are those who have fallen out of financial security. It is only one's savings that prevent one from also succumbing to this fate. To lose financial security is to have nothing but one's own body and one's own labor, to rely on to live another day. This means being in a state of perpetual insecurity, where the loss of a job can lead to total catastrophe—the loss of health insurance, home, the ability to feed oneself and one's family. The "zombie" here is the human being naked before nature, and vulnerable to exploitation by other human beings. It is precisely the condition with which capitalism daily threatens the working class, and into which it frequently plunges them. *Zombie Economics* is a manual for the middle class on protecting themselves against the proletarian condition. Identifying one's security, and indeed one's very humanity, with capital, the reader is encouraged to see those in that condition of naked need as a threat. They want what *you have*. If you lose what you have, you will be just like them. You also will be part of this vast insatiable need, the *hunger* of the zombie.

Capitalism systemically confronts the individual with their own mortality and at the same time promises release from that mortality through possessive identification with non-living objects.[209] The commodity distances the owner from death, but to do so, it must hide its own origins. The commodity's occult life promises its owner escape from mortality. However, this occult life is nothing other than human labor exploited in the process of its production. The elixir of life is the lifeblood of others, and one's own lifeblood as worker. The zombie is the haunting of the commodity by the human life that animates it. The present is haunted by past labor that circulates as the present's animating lifeblood.

Since being depends on having, the individual's existence under capitalism is inherently insecure. The individual is continually confronted by his or her own mortality in the form of scarcity and the fear of losing what they have. The atomized individual competing in the market confronts their mortality alone. The commodities that appear the source of life are no more alive and have no more power than the primitive idol. The movement of the commodity on the market and its correlative life in the spectacle of consumer culture is, as Debord explains, "the autonomous movement of the non-living."[210] But the occult life of commodities is precisely what confronts human beings each day with the precariousness of their existence: the lost retirement savings, the rising price of food, gas, and medical care, the closure of the factory, the downsizing of the office, the loan one can no longer repay, the foreclosed home. It is also what confronts the species and the planet with non-existence—the imperialist drive toward world war, the oceans emptied of life, the inexorable heating up of the planet. Capitalism renders life dependent on the non-living. The zombie, as living dead, is life's interpenetration with death. The zombie is the absolute void present within capitalist everyday life.

Notes

1. *The Walking Dead*, Season 3, AMC, 2012–2013.
2. Karl Marx, "The Eighteenth Brumaire of Louis Bonaparte," in Robert C. Tucker ed., *The Marx-Engels Reader* (New York: W. W. Norton and Co., 1978), 594–617, on 595.
3. Francis Fukuyama, *The End of History and the Last Man* (New York: The Free Press, [1992] 2006), 46. Emphasis in original.
4. Patrick Martin, "Top 1 % Own More than Half of the World's Wealth," *World Socialist Web Site*, October 14, 2015, https://www.wsws.org/en/articles/2015/10/14/weal-o14.html; Daniel Bentley, "The Top 1 % Now Owns Half the World's Wealth," *Fortune*, October 14, 2015, http://fortune.com/2015/10/14/1-percent-global-wealth-credit-suisse/; Jill Treanor, "Half of World's Wealth Now in Hands of 1 % of Population—Report," *The Guardian*, October 13, 2015, http://www.theguardian.com/money/2015/oct/13/half-world-wealth-in-hands-population-inequality-report
5. Erich Fromm, *The Anatomy of Human Destructiveness* (New York: Holt, Rinehart and Winston, 1973), 339, note 14. Emphasis in original.
6. Karl Marx, *Capital Volume 1: A Critique of Political Economy*, trans. Ben Fowkes (New York: Vintage Books, 1977), 342. See also Mark Neocleous, "The Political Economy of the Dead: Marx's Vampires," *History of Political Thought* 24(4) (Winter 2003): 668–684, esp. 679; David McNally, *Monsters of the Market: Zombies, Vampires and Global Capitalism* (Chicago: Haymarket Books, 2011), 113–173.
7. Marx, "Appendix: Results of the Immediate Process of Production," in idem, *Capital Volume*, *1*, 943–1084, on 1007.

8. Erich Fromm, *Escape from Freedom* (New York: Henry Holt and Co., 1969), 120.
9. Fromm, *Escape from Freedom*, 166.
10. Fromm, *Escape from Freedom*, 133.
11. Fromm, *Escape from Freedom*, 120.
12. Fromm, *Escape from Freedom*, 133, 140–177.
13. Fromm, *Anatomy*, 332.
14. Fromm, *Anatomy*, 5, 227.
15. Erich Fromm, *The Revolution of Hope: Toward a Humanized Technology* (New York: Harper and Row, 1968), 42.
16. Fromm, *Revolution of Hope*, 42–43.
17. Erich Fromm, *The Heart of Man: Its Genius for Good and Evil* (New York: Harper and Row, 1964), 56. Emphasis in original.
18. Fromm, *Anatomy*, 339. Emphasis in original.
19. Edward Thompson, "Notes on Exterminism: the Last Stage of Civilization," *New Left Review* 1 (121) (May–June 1980): 3–31, quoting 6, 7.
20. Rudolf Bahro, "Conditions for a Socialist Perspective," in Bahro, *Socialism and Survival: Articles, Essays and Talks, 1979–1982* (London: Heretic Books, 1982), 123–137, quoting 124.
21. Rudolf Bahro, "Who Can Stop the Apocalypse? Or the Task, Substance and Strategy of Social Movements" in Bahro, *Socialism and Survival*, 142–157, on 157.
22. Quoting James Cogan, "Iraq's Tragic Encounter with US Imperialism," *World Socialist Web Site*, December 27, 2011, http://www.wsws.org/articles/2011/dec2011/pers-d27.shtml. (accessed December 27, 2011); Martin Chulov, "Research Links Rise in Falluja Birth Defects and Cancers to US Assault," *The Guardian*, December 30, 2010, http://www.guardian.co.uk/world/2010/dec/30/faulluja-birth-defects-iraq
23. John Vidal, Allegra Stratton, and Suzanne Goldenberg, "Low Targets, Goals Dropped: Copenhagen Ends in Failure," *The Guardian*, December 18, 2009, http://www.guardian.co.uk/environment/2009/dec/18/copenhagen-deal; George Monbiot, "Requiem for a Crowded Planet," December 21, 2009, http://www.monbiot.com/2009/12/21/requiem-for-a-crowded-planet/ (accessed September 2, 2012); George Monbiot, "Climate Change Enlightenment was Fun while it Lasted, but now it's Dead," *The Guardian*, September 20, 2010, http://www.guardian.co.uk/commentisfree/2010/sep/20/climate-change-negotiations-failure; Gustave Speth, *The Bridge at the End of the World: Capitalism, The Environment, and the Crossing from Crisis to Sustainability* (New Haven: Yale University Press, 2008).
24. Ban Ki-moon, "Foreward by the United Nations Secretary General," in Secretariat of the Convention on Biological Diversity, *Global Biodiversity*

Outlook 3 (Montreal: Secretariat of the Convention on Biological Diversity, 2010), 5.
25. Suzanne Goldenberg, "Gulf Oil Spill: Firms Ignored Warning Signs Before Blast, Inquiry Hears," *The Guardian*, May 12, 2010, http://www.guardian.co.uk/environment/2010/may/12/deepwater-gulf-oil-spill-hearing; Suzanne Goldenberg, "BP Cost-Cutting Blamed for 'Avoidable' Deepwater Horizon Oil Spill," *The Guardian*, January 5, 2011, http://www.guardian.co.uk/environment/2011/jan/06/bp-oil-spill-deepwater-horizon; Elaine Grossman, "Japanese Panel Finds Fukushima Accident was 'Manmade' and 'Preventable,'" *Global Security Newswire*, July 6, 2012, http://www.nti.org/gsn/article/japanese-panel-finds-fukushima-accident-was-manmade-and-preventable/; Risa Maeda and Linda Sieg "Japan's Atomic Disaster due to 'Collusion': Panel Report," *Reuters*, July 5,2012,http://www.reuters.com/article/2012/07/05/us-japan-nuclear-report-idUSBRE8640K420120705
26. Juliette Jowit and Justin McCurry, "A Torrent of Plastic: How to Cope?" *The Guardian Weekly*, January 6–12, 2012, 1–2; David Pellow, *The Silicon Valley of Dreams: Environmental Injustice, Immigrant Workers, and the High-Tech Global Economy* (New York: New York University Press, 2002); Elizabeth Royte, *Garbage Land: On the Secret Trail of Trash* (New York: Back Bay Books, 2005).
27. Fiona Harvey, "EU Unveils Plan to Pay Fishermen to Catch Plastic," *The Guardian*, May 4, 2011, http://www.guardian.co.uk/environment/2011/may/04/eu-fishermen-catch-plastic. Cf. Kim De Wolff, *Gyre Plastic: Science, Circulation and the Matter of the Great Pacific Garbage Patch* (Doctoral Dissertation, University of California, San Diego, 2014).
28. MacFayden, quoted in Greg Ray, "The Ocean is Broken," *Yahoo! News* (reprinted from the *Newcastle Herald*), October 22, 2013, http://news.yahoo.com/the-ocean-is-broken-133327474.html
29. Marx, *Capital, Volume 1*, 125.
30. Guy Debord, "A Sick Planet," in idem, *A Sick Planet*, trans. Donald Nicholson-Smith (London: Seagull, 2008), 75–94, quoting 85. Emphasis in original.
31. Adrian Parr, *The Wrath of Capital: Neoliberalism and Climate Change Politics* (New York: Columbia University Press, 2013), 15; Brynna A. Jacobson, "Geoengineering and the Politics of Climate Change," Paper Presented at the Annual Meeting of the American Sociological Association, San Francisco, California, August 16, 2014; Bron Szerszynski, Matthew Kearnes, and Phil Macnaghten, Richard Owen, and Jack Stilgoe, "Why Democracy and Solar Radiation Management Won't Mix," *Environment and Planning A* 45 (12) (2013): 2809–2816; John Shepard et al., *Geoengineering the Climate: Science, Governance and Uncertainty* (London: The Royal Society, 2009). Philip Mirowski, *Never Let a Serious*

Crisis Go to Waste: How Neoliberalism Survived the Financial Meltdown (London: Verso, 2013), 341; Fred Magdoff and John Bellamy Foster, *What Every Environmentalist Needs to Know about Capitalism: A Citizen's Guide to Capitalism and the Environment* (New York: Monthly Review Press, 2011), 122.
32. Sam Perlo-Freeman, Julian Cooper, Olawale Ismail, Elisabeth Sköns and Carlina Solmirano, "Military Expenditure," in Stockholm International Peace Research Institute, *SIPRI Yearbook 2011: Armaments, Disarmament and International Security* (Solna, Sweden: SIPRI, 2011), 157–229, on 157; *SIPRI Yearbook 2011: Armaments, Disarmament, and International Security. Summary* (Solna, Sweden: SIPRI, 2011), 9.
33. Ralph Summy, "The Paradigm Challenge of Political Science: Delegitimizing the Recourse to Violence," In Joseph de Rivera ed., *Handbook on Building Cultures of Peace* (New York: Springer, 2009), 71–87, on 84.
34. John McMurty, *The Cancer Stage of Capitalism* (London: Pluto Press, 1999), 93. Emphasis in original.
35. McMurty, *Cancer Stage*, 93.
36. Nikos Passas, "Global Anomie, Dysnomie, and Economic Crime: Hidden Consequences of Neoliberalism and Globalization in Russia and Around the World," *Social Justice* 27 (2) (2000): 16–44.
37. Peter Watt and Roberto Zepeda, *Drug War Mexico: Politics, Neoliberalism and Violence in the New Narco-Economy* (London: Zed Books, 2012).
38. Quoted in Malcolm Beith, "HSBC Report Shows Difficulty of Stopping Money Launderers," *Daily Beast*, July 19, 2012, http://www.thedaily-beast.com/articles/2012/07/19/hsbc-report-shows-difficulty-of-stopping-money-launderers.html. See also Ed Vulliamy, "How a big US bank laundered billions from Mexico's murderous drug gangs," *The Guardian* April 2, 2011, http://www.guardian.co.uk/world/2011/apr/03/us-bank-mexico-drug-gangs. See also Rajeev Sayal, "Drug Money Saved Banks in Global Crisis, Claims UN Advisor," *The Observer*, December 12, 2009, http://www.theguardian.com/global/2009/dec/13/drug-money-banks-saved-un-cfief-claims
39. Jeffrey Sachs, "World is Drowning in Corporate Fraud," *Commondreams.org*, May 3, 2011, http://www.commondreams.org/view/2011/05/03-8; "Blanket Settlement with J.P. Morgan: a $13 billion Cover-Up," *World Socialist Web Site*, October 21, 2013, http://www.wsws.org/en/articles/2013/10/21/pers-o21.html
40. Barry Grey, "Senate Report on the Wall Street Crash: The Criminalization of the American Ruling Class," *World Socialist Web Site* April 18, 2011, http://www.wsws.org/articles/2011/apr2011/pers-a18.shtml; David North, "The Theoretical and Historical Origins of the Pseudo-Left:

Report to the Second National Congress of the Socialist Equality Party (US)," July 2012, in idem, *The Frankfurt School, Postmodernism and the Politics of the Pseudo-Left: A Marxist Critique* (Oak Park, MI: Mehring Books, 2015), 199–220, on 199–201.

41. Tom Parfitt, "Russia's Rich Double Their Wealth, But Poor Were Better off in 1990s," *The Guardian*, April 11, 2011, http://www.guardian.co.uk/world/2011/apr/11/russia-rich-richer-poor-poorer; Tom Parfitt, "Heartland of Russia in Crisis as Despair and Vodka Take Their Toll," *The Guardian Weekly* April 29, 2011, 3.

42. Noam N. Levey, "Life Expectancy of U.S. Women Slips in Some Regions," *Los Angeles Times*, June 15, 2011, http://articles.latimes.com/2011/jun/15/nation/la-na-womens-health-20110615; Patrick Martin, "Life Expectancy Declining in Many Parts of US," *World Socialist Website*, June 16, 2011, http://www.wsws.org/articles/2011/jun2011/life-j16.shtml

43. Time Newsfeed, "Vanishing City: The Story Behind Detroit's Shocking Population Decline" *Time*, March 24, 2011, http://newsfeed.time.com/2011/03/24/vanishing-city-the-story-behind-detroit%E2%80%99s-shocking-population-decline/

44. Julien Temple, "Detroit: The Last Days," *The Guardian*, March 10, 2010, http://www.guardian.co.uk/film/2010/mar/10/detroit-motor-city-urban-decline; "Detroit in Ruins" *The Observer*, January 1, 2011, http://www.guardian.co.uk/artanddesign/gallery/2011/jan/02/photography-detroit; Joe Kishore and David Walsh, *The Defense of Culture and the Crisis in Detroit* (Oak Park, MI: Socialist Equality Party, 2013).

45. "America's Transport Infrastructure: Life in the Slow Lane," *The Economist*, April 28, 2011, http://www.economist.com/node/18620944; Thomas Geist, "The Detroit Blackout," *World Socialist Web Site*, December 4, 2014, http://www.wsws.org/en/articles/2014/12/04/pers-d04.html

46. Dave Eggers and Nínive Clements Calegari, "The High Cost of Low Teacher Salaries," *New York Times*, April 30, 2011, https://www.nytimes.com/2011/05/01/opinion/01eggers.html?hp

47. Yian Q. Mui, "What Do the Jobless Do When the Benefits End?" *The Washington Post*, February 11, 2014, http://www.washingtonpost.com/business/economy/what-do-the-jobless-do-when-the-benefits-end/2014/02/11/e135d74a-8eb7-11e3-b227-12a45d109e03_story.html; Paul Harris, "Jobless Millions Signal Death of American Dream for Many," *The Guardian*, August 14, 2010, http://www.guardian.co.uk/world/2010/aug/15/jobless-millions-death-american-dream; Dominic Rushe, "America's long-term unemployed: 'For those looking for work, it's very bleak'," *The Guardian* May 3, 2012, http://www.guardian.co.uk/business/2012/may/03/us-long-term-unemployed-obama; Andre Damon and Barry Grey, "Cutting Food Stamps: the Ruthlessness of the

American Ruling Class," *World Socialist Web Site*, October 29, 2013, http://www.wsws.org/en/articles/2013/10/29/pers-o29.html
48. "Child Poverty," National Center for Children in Poverty http://www.nccp.org/topics/childpoverty.html (accessed September 2, 2012).
49. Jim Forsyth, "Woman denied food stamps kills self, shoots children," *Reuters*, December 6, 2011, http://www.reuters.com/article/2011/12/06/us-crime-foodstampoffice-texas-idUSTRE7B51W820111206; Naomi Spencer, "Notes on the Social Crisis in America," *World Socialist Web Site*, December 8, 2011, http://www.wsws.org/articles/2011/dec2011/socr-d08.shtml
50. Richard Wilkinson and Kate Pickett, *The Spirit Level: Why More Equal Societies Almost Always Do Better* (London: Allen Lane, 2009); Steven Hall, Simon Winlow and Craig Ancrum, *Criminal Identities and Consumer Culture: Crime, Exclusion and the New Culture of Narcissism* (Cullompton, Devon: Willan Publishing, 2008).
51. Bruce E. Levine, *Get Up, Stand Up: Uniting Populists, Energizing the Defeated, and Battling the Corporate Elite* (White River Junction, VT: Chelsea Green Publishing, 2011), 72–73.
52. Guy Debord, *Society of the Spectacle* (London: Rebel Press, 1987 [orig.1967]), 28. Emphasis in original. (References to this book will cite numbered theses not page numbers).
53. Levine, *Get Up, Stand Up*, 60–68; Albert Borgmann, *Technology and the Character of Contemporary Life: a Philosophical Inquiry* (Chicago: University of Chicago Press, 1987), esp. 40–48; Sherry Turkle, *Alone Together: Why We Expect More of Technology and Less from Each Other* (New York: Basic Books, 2011).
54. E. M. Forster, "The Machine Stops," (orig. 1909), in Groff Conklin ed., *17 x Infinity* (London: Mayflower-Dell, 1964), 84–117.
55. Zygmunt Bauman, *Liquid Fear* (Cambridge: Polity Press, 2006), 101.
56. Bauman, *Liquid Fear*, 17.
57. Istvan Mészáros, *Marx's Theory of Alienation* (London: Merlin Press, 2005), 8.
58. Karl Marx, *The Economic and Philosophic Manuscripts of 1844*, ed. Dirk Struik, trans Martin Milligan (New York: International Publishers, 1964), 113. Emphasis in original. (Hereafter cited as *EPM*).
59. Marx, *EPM*, 112 (emphasis in original); John Bellamy Foster, "The Dialectic of Organic/Inorganic Relations: Marx and the Hegelian Philosophy of Nature," *Organization & Environment* 13 (December 2000): 403–425; Meszaros, *Marx's Theory of Alienation*, 81.
60. Marx, *EPM*, 113. Emphasis in original.
61. Marx, *EPM*, 138. Emphasis in original.
62. Marx, *EPM*, 137.
63. Marx, *EPM*, 116. Emphasis in original.

64. Marx, *EPM*, 141 (emphasis in original). See also Erich Fromm, *Marx's Concept of Man* (New York: Frederick Ungar, 1961), 32.
65. Marx, *EPM*, 141 (emphasis in original). See also Fromm, *Marx's Concept of Man*, 32.
66. Marx, *EPM*, 182. See also Fromm, *Marx's Concept of Man*, 24–26.
67. Marx, *EPM*, 145 (emphasis in original). See also Friedrich Engels, "The Part Played by Labour in the Transition from Ape to Man," in idem, "The Dialectics of Nature," Karl Max and Frederick Engels, *Collected Works, Volume 25* (New York: International Publishers, 1987), 313–588, on 452–464.
68. Marx, "From Excerpt-Notes of 1844," in *Writings of the Young Marx on Philosophy and Society*, ed. and trans. Lloyd D. Easton and Kurt Guddat (Garden City, NY: Anchor Books, 1967), 265–282, on 272.
69. Marx, *EPM*, 70.
70. Marx, *EPM*, 110. Emphasis in original.
71. Marx, *EPM*, 159.
72. Marx, *EPM*, 66–67. Emphasis in original.
73. Wilhelm Schulz, quoted in Marx, *EPM*, 72.
74. Marx, "Results of the Immediate Process of Production," 1019–1038.
75. Karl Marx, *The Poverty of Philosophy* (New York: International Publishers, 1963), 54. See also Istvan Mészáros, *The Challenge and Burden of Historical Time: Socialism in the Twenty-First Century* (New York: Monthly Review Press, 2008), 47.
76. See also McNally, *Monsters of the Market*, 123–124, 128–129.
77. Marx, *Capital Volume 1*, 548.
78. Marx, *Capital Volume 1*, 547.
79. Marx, *EPM*, 111.
80. Marx, *Capital Volume 1*, 522, note 51; Christine Griffin, Andrew Bengry-Howell, Chris Hackley, Willm Mistral, Isabelle Szmigin "'Every Time I Do It I Absolutely Annihilate Myself': Loss of (Self-) Consciousness and Loss of Memory in Young People's Drinking Narratives," *Sociology* 43 (3) (2009): 457–476; Simon Winlow and Steve Hall, "Living for the Weekend: Youth Identities in Northeast England," *Ethnography* 10 (1) (2009): 91–113. "Sunshine in a bag" is a lyric from "Clint Eastwood" by Gorillaz (EMI Records Ltd., 2001).
81. Marx, *EPM*, 153. Emphasis in original.
82. Marx, *EPM*, 148–149. Emphasis on original.
83. Jonathan Watts, "China's 'cancer villages' reveal dark side of economic boom," *The Guardian*, June 7, 2010, http://www.guardian.co.uk/environment/2010/jun/07/china-cancer-villages-industrial-pollution; Jonathan Watts, "Chemical plant protest highlights China's class divide," *The Guardian* August 18, 2011, http://www.guardian.co.uk/environment/blog/2011/aug/18/chemical-plant-protest-china-middle-class;

David Kirby, "Made in China: Our Toxic, Imported Air Pollution," *Discover Magazine*, March 18, 2011, http://discovermagazine.com/2011/apr/18-made-in-china-our-toxic-imported-air-pollution; Juli S. Kim and Jennifer L. Turner, "China's Filthiest Export," *Foreign Policy in Focus* (January 16, 2007), http://www.fpif.org/articles/chinas_filthiest_export; Dan Shapley, "Your Tuna Is Getting More Toxic," *The Daily Green*, May 1, 2009, http://www.thedailygreen.com/environmental-news/latest/tuna-mercury-47050102#ixzz1bqCiu7oA

84. Rob Reiner, *Law and Order: An Honest Citizen's Guide* (Cambridge: Polity Press, 2007), 5.
85. Marx, *EPM*, 167. Emphasis in original.
86. See also Andre Damon, "The Gates Foundation and the Rise of 'Free Market' Philanthropy," *World Socialist Web Site*, January 22, 2007, https://www.wsws.org/en/articles/2007/01/gate-j22.html; David Walsh, "The Philanthropy of Warren Buffet," *World Socialist Web Site*, June 27, 2006, https://www.wsws.org/en/articles/2006/06/buff-j27.html
87. George Gallanis, "Seven Million Americans in Default on Student Loans," *World Socialist Web Site*, August 26, 2015, http://www.wsws.org/en/articles/2015/08/26/debt-a26.html
88. Marx, *EPM*, 169. Emphasis in original.
89. Marx, *EPM*, 169. Emphasis in original.
90. Marx, "From Excerpt-Notes of 1844," 281. Emphasis in original.
91. See also Erich Fromm, *The Art of Loving* (London: George Allen and Unwin, 1957), 25–26.
92. Christopher Caudwell, "Love: A Study in Changing Values," in idem, *Studies in a Dying Culture* (New York: Dodd Mead and Co., 1938), 129–157, on 157.
93. Caudwell, "Love," 154–155.
94. Marx, *EPM*, 143–144. Emphasis in original.
95. Max Weber, *The Protestant Ethic and the Spirit of Capitalism* (New York: Charles Scribner's Sons, 1958), 48. See also Barbara Adam, *Time and Social Theory* (Cambridge: Polity Press, 1994), 113–114; Barbara Adam, *Timewatch: The Social Analysis of Time* (Cambridge: Polity Press, 1995), 87–91; Barbara Adam, "When Time is Money: Contested Rationalities of Time in the Theory and Practice of Work," *Theoria: A Journal of Social and Political Theory* 102 (December 2003), 94–125, esp. 97–98.
96. Marx, *EPM*, 150. Emphasis in original.
97. Marx, *EPM*, 165. Emphasis in original.
98. Marx, *EPM*, 168. Emphasis in original.
99. Marx, *EPM*, 169.
100. Marx, *EPM*, 156. Emphasis in original.

101. Rowan Moore, "London: The City that Ate Itself," *The Guardian*, June 28,2015,http://www.theguardian.com/uk-news/2015/jun/28/london-the-city-that-ate-itself-rowan-moore; "The Indebted Ones" (Leader comment) *The Economist* (October 29, 2011) 16, 18, on 18; Suzanne McGee, "Corporations, Artificial People, and the Unintended Risks of Hobby Lobby," *The Guardian*, July 6, 2014, http://www.theguardian.com/money/2014/jul/06/corporations-artificial-people-hobby-lobby-rights-power-influence.
102. Marx, *EPM*, 89.
103. Marx, *EPM*, 119.
104. Marx, *EPM*, 122.
105. Marx, *EPM*, 122. Emphasis in original.
106. Marx, *EPM*, 122.
107. Marx, "Excerpt Notes of 1844," 281 (emphasis in original). See also Carl Cederström and Peter Fleming, *Dead Man Working* (Winchester, UK: Zero Books, 2012).
108. Raoul Vanegeim, *The Revolution of Everyday Life*, trans. Donald Nicholson-Smith (London: Left Bank Books/Rebel Press, 1983), 120–123, 176.
109. Marx, *EPM*, 153.
110. "Proceedings of the Sixth Rhine Province Assembly. Third Article. Debates on the Law on Thefts of Wood" Published in *Supplement to the Rheinische Zeitung*, Nos. 298, 300, 303, 305 and 307, October 25, 27 and 30, November 1 and 3, 1842. Trans. Clemens Dutt, http://www.marxists.org/archive/marx/works/1842/10/25.htm
111. Henry Giroux, *Stormy Weather: Katrina and the Politics of Disposability* (Paradigm Publishers, 2006).
112. Karl Marx, *Grundrisse: Foundations of the Critique of Political Economy*, trans. Martin Nicolaus (New York: Penguin Books, 1973), 461; quoted also in Neocleous, "The Political Economy of the Dead," 680.
113. Marx, *EPM*, 102.
114. Marx, "Results of the Immediate Process of Production," 990; quoted also in Neocleous, "Political Economy of the Dead," 680.
115. Marx, Marx, *Capital Volume 1*, 926; quoted in Neocleous, "The Political Economy of the Dead," 668.
116. Neocleous, "The Political Economy of the Dead," 679.
117. Marx, *Grundrisse*, 704.
118. Marx, *Grundrisse*, 701.
119. Marx, *Capital Volume 1*, 247–257, quoting 255. See also McNally, *Monsters of the Market*, 132, 145.
120. McNally, *Monsters of the Market*, 151–156.
121. Glenn Rikowski, "Alien Life: Marx and the Future of the Human," *Historical Materialism* 11(2) (2003): 121–164, on 158.

122. Albert Borgmann, "The Moral Complexion of Consumption," *Journal of Consumer Research* 26 (4) (March 2000): 418–422.
123. Neocleous, "The Political Economy of the Dead," 683.
124. Mark Tran, "Girl Starved to Death While Parents Raised Virtual Child in Online Game," *The Guardian*, March 5, 2010, http://www.guardian.co.uk/world/2010/mar/05/korean-girl-starved-online-game
125. Melissa Gregg, *Work's Intimacy* (Cambridge: Polity, 2011), 2–3, 14–15.
126. Erich Fromm, "Marx's Contribution to the Knowledge of Man," in idem, *The Crisis of Psychoanalysis: Essays on Freud, Marx, and Social Psychology* (New York: Henry Holt and Co., 1970), 62–75, on 72. Fromm should say "not *only* in a biological-physiological sense." For the working class, alienation is indeed biological: it is about whether they eat, have a roof over their heads, medical care, and so on. To be estranged from one's labor is to be estranged from one's biological ability to live, which now depends on an alien power. This is combined with the psychological aspects of alienation.
127. Fromm, "Marx's Contribution to the Knowledge of Man," 73.
128. Erich Fromm, *To Have or To Be?* (London: Continuum, 2010), 63. See also Zygmunt Bauman, *Consuming Life* (Cambridge: Polity Press, 2007), esp. 57.
129. Sigmund Freud, "Character and Anal Eroticism," in Peter Gay ed., *The Freud Reader* (New York: W. W. Norton and Co., 1989), 293–297, on 296–297.
130. Fromm, *Anatomy*, 462. See also Fromm, *Heart of Man*, 54–55.
131. Fromm, *To Have or To Be?*, 63–64.
132. Erich Fromm, *The Sane Society* (New York: Holt, Rinehart and Winston, 1955), 141–142.
133. Fromm, *The Sane Society*, 141–142.
134. Cf. Cederström and Fleming, *Dead Man Working*, 31–42.
135. Fromm, *Anatomy*, 240–241.
136. Fromm, *Anatomy*, 242–251, esp. 248–249 for unconscious depression. See also Bruce E. Levine, *Surviving America's Depression Epidemic: How to Find Morale, Energy, and Community in a World Gone Crazy* (White River Junction, VT: Chelsea Green Publishing, 2007).
137. Fromm, *Anatomy*, 245. Emphasis in original
138. Fromm, *Art of Loving*, 105.
139. Fromm, *Anatomy*, 248.
140. Borgmann, *Technology and the Character of Contemporary Life*, 47.
141. Fromm, *Anatomy*, 342–343.
142. Fromm, *Anatomy*, 352.
143. Natalie Gil, "Loneliness: a Silent Plague that is Hurting Young People Most," *The Guardian*, July 20, 2014, http://www.theguardian.com/life-andstyle/2014/jul/20/loneliness-britains-silent-plague-hurts-young-people-most

144. http://www.google.com/glass/start/what-it-does/. Accessed December 17, 2013.
145. Turkle, *Alone Together*; Mark C. Taylor, *Speed Limits: Where Time Went and Why We Have So Little Left* (New Haven: Yale University Press, 2014), 216–218.
146. "Relentless.com," *The Economist*, June 21, 2014, 23.
147. Neither Google Glass nor the Amazon phone were market successes. This, perhaps, suggests that these devices represent a degree of technological subsumption to which people are still resistant. But everyday life is increasingly mediated by devices, in many different and changing forms. Taylor Hatmaker, "Google Explains Why and How Glass Failed," *The Daily Dot*, March 17, 2015, http://www.dailydot.com/technology/google-glass-failure-astro-teller/; Ben Fox Rubin and Roger Cheng, "Fire Phone One Year Later: Why Amazon's Smartphone Flamed Out," *CNET*, July 24, 2015,http://www.cnet.com/news/fire-phone-one-year-later-why-amazons-smartphone-flamed-out/
148. Fromm, *Anatomy*, 346.
149. Jennifer Robinson, "'Bugsplat': The Ugly US Drone War in Pakistan," *Al Jazeera English*, November 29, 2011, http://www.aljazeera.com/indepth/opinion/2011/11/201111278839153400.html; "Pakistanis Protest 'Playstation' Project," *RT*, June 6, 2011, http://rt.com/news/drone-us-pakistan/
150. Fromm, *Anatomy*, 348.
151. Carol Cohn, "Sex and Death in the Rational World of Defense Intellectuals," *Signs* 12 (4) (Summer 1987): 687–718; Henry T. Nash, "The Bureaucratization of Homicide," in E. P. Thompson and Dan Smith eds, *Protest and Survive* (Harmondsworth, Middlesex, England: Penguin Books, 1980), 62–74
152. Fromm, *The Sane Society*, 111 (emphasis in original). On abstraction, see also McNally, *Monsters of the Market*, 128–131.
153. Fromm, *The Sane Society*, 114.
154. Fromm, *The Sane Society*, 120.
155. Debord, *Society of the Spectacle*.
156. Fromm, *Anatomy*, 350. Emphasis in original.
157. Fromm, *Anatomy*, 351.
158. McNally, *Monsters of the Market*, 118, 120; see also ibid., 116.
159. Marx, *EPM*, 120. Emphasis in original.
160. Quoted in Ferdinando Giugliano, "BoE's Haldane Says Corporations Putting Shareholders Before Economy," *The Financial Times*, July 25, 2015, http://www.ft.com/intl/cms/s/0/7d347016-32f4-11e5-b05b-b01debd57852.html#axzz3kXAH9XrX. See also Nick Beams, "The Rot at the Heart of the American Economy," *World Socialist Web Site*, August

4, 2015, https://www.wsws.org/en/articles/2015/08/04/pers-a04.html. On the declining rate of profit, see Andrew Kliman, *The Failure of Capitalist Production: Underlying Causes of the Great Recession* (London: Pluto Press, 2011); Chris Harman, *Zombie Capitalism: Global Crisis and the Relevance of Marx* (Chicago: Haymarket Books, 2010), esp. 195–201, 231–236.
161. Henry A. Giroux, *Zombie Politics and Culture in the Age of Casino Capitalism* (New York: Peter Lang, 2011); McNally, *Monsters of the Market*, 163–171; Jean Comaroff and John Comaroff, "Alien-nation: Zombies, Immigrants and Millennial Capitalism," *The South Atlantic Quarterly* 101 (4) (Fall 2002): 779–805, esp. 781.
162. Robert Latham, *Consuming Youth: Vampires, Cyborgs, and the Culture of Consumption* (Chicago: The University of Chicago Press, 2002), 71; Tim Kane, *The Changing Vampire of Film and Television: A Critical Study of the Growth of a Genre* (Jefferson, NC: McFarland and Co., 2006), esp. 88–127; Fred Botting, "Zombie Death Drive: Between Gothic and Science Fiction," in Sara Wasson and Emily Alder eds., *Gothic Science Fiction 1980–2010* (Liverpool: Liverpool University Press, 2011), 36–54, on 49–50.
163. Milly Williamson, *The Lure of the Vampire: Gender, Fiction and Fandom from Bram Stoker to Buffy* (London: Wallflower, 2005), 2; Milly Williamson, "Let Them All In: The Evolution of the 'Sympathetic' Vampire," in Leon Hunt, Sharon Lockyer, and Milly Williamson, *Screening the Undead: Vampires and Zombies in Film and Television* (London: I. B. Tauris, 2014), 71–92.
164. Latham, *Consuming Youth*, 26–95. The still relevant classic is Christopher Lasch, *The Culture of Narcissism: American Life in an Age of Diminishing Expectations* (New York: Warner Books, 1979).
165. Hall, Winlow and Ancrum, *Criminal Identities and Consumer Culture*, 97.
166. Mark Edmundson, *Nightmare on Main Street: Angels, Sadomasochism, and the Culture of Gothic* (Cambridge, MA: Harvard University Press, 1997), 43.
167. David Walsh, "The Wolf of Wall Street: Why Should We Admire Such Figures?" *World Socialist Web Site*, December 30, 2013, https://www.wsws.org/en/articles/2013/12/30/wolf-d30.html
168. Kyle William Bishop, *American Zombie Gothic: The Rise and Fall (and Rise) of the Walking Dead in Popular Culture* (Jefferson, NC: McFarland and Co., 2010), 110.
169. Bishop, *American Zombie Gothic*, 96; Ben Hervey, *Night of the Living Dead* (Houndmills, Basingstoke, UK: Palgrave MacMillan, 2008). On the zombie's roots in Haitian folk culture and on earlier cinematic portrayals, see Shawn McIntosh, "The Evolution of the Zombie: The Monster that

Keeps Coming Back," in Shawn McIntosh and Marc Leverette eds., *Zombie Culture: Autopsies of the Living Dead* (Lanham, MD: The Scarecrow Press, 2008), 1–17.
170. Bishop, *American Zombie Gothic*, 101.
171. Bishop, *American Zombie Gothic*, 130; Matthew Bailey, "Memory, Place and the Mall: George Romero on Consumerism," *Studies in Popular Culture* 35 (2) (Spring 2013): 95–110; Stephen Harper, "Zombies, Malls, and the Consumerism Debate: George Romero's *Dawn of the Dead*," *Americana: The Journal of American Popular Culture* 1 (2) (Fall 2002), http://www.americanpopularculture.com/journal/articles/fall_2002/harper.htm; Matthew Bailey, "Dawn of the Shopping Dead," in Robert Smith? ed., *Braaaiiinnnsss! From Academics to Zombies* (Ottawa: University of Ottawa Press, 2011), 195–207.
172. https://en.wikiquote.org/wiki/Dawn_of_the_Dead_(1978_film), accessed September 7, 2015. See also Kim Paffenroth, "Zombies as Internal Fear or Threat," in Stephanie Boluk and Wylie Lenz, *Generation Zombie: Essays on the Living Dead in Modern Culture* (Jefferson, NC: McFarland and Co., 2011), 18–26, on 19.
173. Robert McFadden and Angela Macropoulos, "Wal-Mart Employee Trampled to Death," *New York Times*, November 28, 2008, http://www.nytimes.com/2008/11/29/business/29walmart.html?pagewanted=all; Colleen Curry, "Black Friday Turns Dark as Twitter, Websites Track Injuries, Fights, Deaths," *ABC News*, November 29, 2013, http://abcnews.go.com/US/black-friday-turns-dark-twitter-websites-track-injuries/story?id=21048805; Mark Oliver, "Slowly but Steadily, Madness Descended," *The Guardian*, February 10, 2005, http://www.theguardian.com/business/2005/feb/10/money.uknews; "Black Friday Stampede at UK Shopping Centre," http://news.bbc.co.uk/2/hi/middle_east/3618190.stm
"Three Die in Saudi Shop Stampede," *BBC News*, September 1, 2004, http://news.bbc.co.uk/2/hi/middle_east/3618190.stm
174. "Mexico City Claims Zombie Walk World Record," *BBC*, November 27, 2011, http://www.bbc.co.uk/news/world-15911862; "Zombie Attack: Leicester City Council Overrun by 'Undead'" *BBC*, June 18, 2011, http://www.bbc.co.uk/news/uk-england-leicestershire-13823427
175. Jennifer Rutherford, *Zombies* (London: Routledge, 2013), 27–28; Sasha Cocarla, "Reclaiming Public Spaces through Performance of the Zombie Walk," in Smith ed., *Braaaiiinnns: From Academics to Zombies*, 113–131, esp. 114; Simon Orpana, "Spooks of Biopower: The Uncanny Carnivalesque of Zombie Walks," *TOPIA: Canadian Journal of Cultural Studies* (25) (Spring 2011), 153–176; Carmen Leigh Kuhling, "Zombie banks, zombie politics and the 'Walking Zombie Movement': Liminality and the post-crisis

Irish imaginary," *European Journal of Cultural Studies* (2013); Markus Wessendorf, "Zombie Walks and Zombie Economics," *Journal for Contemporary Drama in English* 1 (1) (2013): 92–102; Brendan Riley, "Zombie Walks and the Public Sphere," *Transformative Works and Cultures* 18 (2015), http://journal.transformativeworks.org/index.php/twc/article/view/641/508

176. Cf. Jen Webb and Sam Byrnand, "Some Kind of Virus: The Zombie as Body and as Trope," *Body & Society* 14 (2) (2008): 83–98, on 89.
177. Quoting Søren Kierkegaard, *The Concept of Dread* (Princeton: Princeton UP, 1957), 55. See also Peter L. Berger, *The Sacred Canopy: Elements of a Sociological Theory of Religion* (New York: Anchor, 1990), 26–27 and 39; Charles Thorpe, "Death of a Salesman: Petit-Bourgeois Dread in Philip K. Dick's Mainstream Fiction," *Science Fiction Studies* 38(3) (November 2011): 412–434.
178. Cf. Ajit Varki and Danny Brower, *Denial: Self-Deception, False Beliefs, and the Origins of the Human Mind* (New York: Twelve, 2013).
179. Using a term from China Mieville's novel *The City & the City* (London: Pan Books, 2009).
180. Bauman, *Consuming Life*, 124. Emphasis in original.
181. Zygmunt Bauman, "The London Riots: On Consumerism Coming Home to Roost," *Social Europe*, August 9, 2011, http://www.socialeurope.eu/2011/08/the-london-riots-on-consumerism-coming-home-to-roost/; David Moxon, "Consumer Culture and the 2011 'Riots'," *Sociological Research Online* 16 (4) (2011), http://www.socresonline.org.uk/16/4/19.html
182. Ernest Becker, *Escape from Evil* (New York: The Free Press, 1975), 85–86.
183. Quoted in Paul Stuart, "Luxury Apartment Complex in London uses Spikes to Deter Homeless," *World Socialist Web Site*, June 14, 2014, http://www.wsws.org/en/articles/2014/06/14/spik-j14.html
184. Bauman, "The London Riots."
185. Julia Carrie Wong, "Violent 'Altercation' at Oakland Whole Foods; Witness Says Black Customer Bloodied After Attempting to 'Buy Groceries with his EBT Card,' *SF Weekly*, September 4, 2015, http://www.sfweekly.com/thesnitch/2015/09/04/violent-altercation-at-oakland-whole-foods-witness-says-black-customer-bloodied-after-attempting-to-buy-groceries-with-his-ebt-card
186. See Linda Tirado, *Hand to Mouth: Living in Bootstrap America* (New York: Berkeley Books, 2015), 37–46.
187. Fromm, *To Have or To Be*, 89. Emphasis in original.
188. Berger, *The Sacred Canopy*, 22.
189. Guy Debord, *Society of the Spectacle*, 69.
190. Bishop, *American Zombie Gothic*, 112.

191. Christine Schaefer, "World War Z: Monsters of this Society's Own Making," *World Socialist Web Site*, October 25, 2007, http://www.wsws.org/en/articles/2007/10/mons-o25.html; cf. Bill Durodié, "Fear and Terror in a Post-Political Age," *Government and Opposition* 42 (3) (2007): 427–450.
192. Kyle William Bishop, "Dead Man *Still* Walking: Explaining the Zombie Renaissance," *Journal of Popular Film and Television* 37 (1) (2009): 16–25.
193. Terence McSweeney, "*The Land of the Dead* and the Home of the Brave: Romero's Vision of a Post-9/11 America" in Jeff Birkenstein, Anna Froula and Karen Randell, *Reframing 9/11: Film, Popular Culture and the "War on Terror"* (New York: Continuum, 2010), 107–116, esp. 111–112; Tony Williams, "Land of the Dead," *Rouge* 7 (2005), http://www.rouge.ccm.au/7/land_of_the_dead.html
194. http://blogs.cdc.gov/publichealthmatters/2011/05/preparedness-101-zombie-apocalypse/. Dated May 16, 2011. Accessed December 20, 2011. See also Steven Morris, "When Zombies Attack! Bristol City Council Ready for Undead Invasion," July 7, 2011, http://www.guardian.co.uk/society/2011/jul/07/when-zombies-attack-bristol-city-council-undead-invasion/
195. Bauman, *Liquid Fear*, 18.
196. "Preparing for the Apocalypse: I will Survive," *The Economist*, December 20, 2014, http://www.economist.com/news/christmas-specials/21636611-when-civilisation-collapses-will-you-be-ready-i-will-survive
197. Rick Kissell, "AMC's 'Walking Dead' returns to Record 17.3 million viewers," *Variety*, October 13, 2014, http://variety.com/2014/tv/ratings/amcs-walking-dead-returns-to-record-17-3-million-viewers-1201328583/
198. Katie McDonough, "Bra-clad Zombie Ex-Girlfriend Target Bleeds when you Shoot it," *Salon.com*, April 1, 2013, http://www.salon.com/2013/04/01/bra_clad_zombie_ex_girlfriend_target_bleeds_when_you_shoot_it/; Benny Johnson, "National Rifle Association Bans Bleeding 'Obama' Target, Others Remain," *Buzzfeed*, May 5, 2013, http://www.buzzfeed.com/bennyjohnson/national-rifle-association-bans-bleeding-obama-target-others#.sbodrZ1o9; Stan Alcorn, "What Happens When a Gun Accessories Company Makes Bleeding Ex-Girlfriend Shooting Target," *Co.Exist*, October 25, 2013, http://www.fastcoexist.com/1682024/what-happens-when-a-gun-company-makes-bleeding-ex-girlfriend-shooting-target
199. Lisa Desjardins and Rick Emerson, *Zombie Economics: A Guide to Personal Finance: How to Slay Your Bills, Decapitate Debt, and Fight the Apocalypse of Financial Doom* (New York: Avery, 2011), quoting front cover blurb.
200. Desjardins and Emerson, *Zombie Economics*, 2.

201. Desjardins and Emerson, *Zombie Economics*, 4–5.
202. Desjardins and Emerson, *Zombie Economics*, 10.
203. Desjardins and Emerson, *Zombie Economics*, 100.
204. Desjardins and Emerson, *Zombie Economics*, 52, 167.
205. Desjardins and Emerson, *Zombie Economics*, 67–68.
206. Desjardins and Emerson, *Zombie Economics*, 122.
207. Desjardins and Emerson, *Zombie Economics*, 89.
208. Desjardins and Emerson, *Zombie Economics*, 154–155.
209. Cf. Becker, *Escape from Evil*, 73–90.
210. Debord, *Society of the Spectacle*, 2.

CHAPTER 2

Artificial Life on a Dead Planet

Animated Technology and Reified Life

Philip K. Dick's science fiction masterpiece, *Do Androids Dream of Electric Sheep?* presents a future in which most of Earth's species have been wiped out by radioactive fallout and the human survivors are fleeing a ravaged Earth. Survival on the inhospitable terrain of other planets is made possible by android slave labor. For those who cling on in Earth's decaying cities, possession of a live animal is highly coveted, due to the fragility of biological life on the planet and the scarcity of animal life. The majority who cannot pay the premium for a live animal accept, as second best, an android replica of a sheep, snake, or an owl.[1]

Science fiction frequently couples artificial life with ecological devastation, violence, and the destruction of human life. Movies like *The Terminator* or *The Matrix* present an eviscerated Earth covered in scrap metal and stalked by machines, and scenarios of biotechnological experimentation gone awry have been the premise in recent films such as *I am Legend* and *28 Days Later*. These films reflect a cultural undercurrent of

---

This chapter is re-published, with permission, from Angharad N. Valdavia and Kelly Gates eds, The International Encyclopedia of Media Studies, Volume VI: Media Studies Futures (Chichester, West Sussex, UK: Wiley-Blackwell, 2013). Copyright, 2013 Blackwell Publishing Ltd. All rights reserved.

unease that contrasts with the techno-hype current in our universities and among our policymakers.

Margaret Atwood's novel *Oryx and Crake* portrays a world in which, as the Earth's species face extinction, corporate laboratories are turning out new genetically engineered life-forms, such as pigs with human internal organs.[2] The corporations also are boosting demand for their pharmaceutical products by surreptitiously producing new diseases. Atwood combines imagery of sterility, extinction, and death with the portrayal of the uncontrollable overflowing of bizarre new life-forms. Life takes new forms, but in ways that offer bleak prospects for the continuation of *human* life.

As Daniel Dinello has argued, such science fiction visions of technology out of control can no longer be dismissed as mere sensationalism or paranoia.[3] Rather, these fictional scenarios can sensitize us to dynamics that are institutionally embedded and have political and economic power, but which are also the source of pervasive social anxiety. Such dystopian and pessimistic forms of science fiction offer a useful counter to the breathlessly optimistic, utopian language in which technologies such as nanotechnology and robotics are framed by their proponents.[4] What, then, is the critical significance of these couplings of artificial life with the destruction of life? Do these combined images reflect real-world developments? If this is a warning, is it about technology itself, or about a more fundamental dynamic in our social relations and social organization?

Today, the destruction of ecosystems and species by deforestation, chemical pollution, and the effects of climate change is indeed being accompanied by a parallel process of the creation of artificial forms of life. We currently face the evisceration and breakdown of all the systems that sustain life on this planet—from the oceans, to the soil, to the atmosphere. But as capitalist industry devastates the existing natural world, capitalist-aligned technoscience brings into being new forms of autonomous or "lifelike" technologies.

In his famous missive in the year 2000, "Why The Future Doesn't Need Us," computer scientist Bill Joy used the term "GNR technologies" to designate the converging fields of genetics, robotics, and nanotechnology—scientific fields that produce technologized forms of life or lifelike technologies. Joy warned that what is new in such technologies is the potential for "uncontrolled self-replication," which poses the "risk of substantial damage in the physical world."[5] In the mid-twentieth century, philosopher and sociologist Jacques Ellul used the concept of "the self-augmentation of technique" to designate the way in which large-scale modern technological and instrumentally rational systems (such as nuclear power) build their own internal momentum and escape social control.[6] What is striking today is the fact that this autonomy of technology is no longer merely metaphorical, designating a loss of control by human beings over our collective creations. The goal of science and engineering in the GNR fields is to produce technological forms that are literally and concretely autonomous, that is, robots that act independently of human command, or new manipulated or synthesized living things–technologies that appropriate the ability of living things to reproduce and multiply.

In an essay discussing the meaning of the android in his fiction, Dick observed that "the greatest change growing across our world these days is probably the momentum of the living toward reification, and at the same time a reciprocal entry into animation by the mechanical."[7] This offers a profound insight into contemporary capitalist technoscience. The reification of the living as resource or commodity and the transformation of living organisms into productive machines are accompanied by the animation of the non-living. Life is reified, as it is subsumed within commodity relations and the cash nexus. The living world is integrated within capitalism as a stock of resources to be exploited and as a sink for pollutants. The consequent intense exploitation and waste is largely responsible for the unprecedented human degradation of the natural world and assault on the conditions for life that we are witnessing today. This degradation of the natural world combines with the intensified subsumption of nature and of life itself within capital—the transformation of the living world so as to shape the reproductive capacities of the living according to the timescales and efficiency norms of capitalist production. The result of these processes is a vast simplification in the natural living world: the degradation of the earth's ecosystems, the loss of biodiversity, and the imposition of standardized agro-business monoculture. As in Atwood's *Oryx and Crake*, this destruction of natural diversity is accompanied by at least the promise of a proliferation of new forms of life, engineered or synthesized living organisms and lifelike machines. A dead planet and artificial life, therefore, represent twin trajectories of contemporary capitalism.

From Abstract Labor to Abstract Life

In order to make sense of the contemporary interpenetration of life and technology, we must come to grips with how life is used and transformed within our productive and social relations. Karl Marx argued that the capitalist mode of production means the domination of living labor by its alienated, dead products. As he put it in *Capital Volume 1*, "Capital is dead labour which, vampire-like, lives only by sucking living labour, and lives the more, the more labour it sucks."[8] The workers' labor is transformed into an independent power, standing over and against them. In capital, the living is transformed into the dead, and what is dead takes on power over what is living.[9]

Capitalism also involves the domination of the living in a broader sense. In the *Economic and Philosophic Manuscripts*, Marx wrote that alienated labor makes nature into "an alien world inimically opposed" to the worker.[10] Through alienated labor, human beings do not engage nature as a life-giving milieu with which their labor is interconnected. Rather, nature is constructed as a set of resources to be exploited. The aim of this exploitation is not the immediate satisfaction of human needs, but rather the augmentation of capital as self-valorizing value. Marx wrote that as nature is appropriated through alienated labor, "it more and more ceases to be *means of life*."[11] I want to suggest that this alienation of nature and of life today has two aspects. One is the degradation of the life-supporting abundance of the natural world through extraction, exploitation, and waste, resulting in the mounting global ecological crisis.[12] The other is the production of life that is interpenetrated with capital and, hence, takes the form of capitalized life or living capital.[13]

The subsumption of life by capital parallels, and is related to, the subsumption of labor. Labor is formally subsumed under capital when it takes the form of commodified labor capacity; in other words, when it becomes *wage labor*. Labor comes under real subsumption when capital assumes direct control over the labor process, transforming working activity so that it takes on a specifically capitalist character. In numerous passages, Marx described how mechanization represents a transformation of labor such that the worker's life-activity is appropriated and subsumed by capital in the form of technology. The machinery develops complexity and takes on a central power in the production process as the worker's activity is simplified and fragmented.[14] Hence, according to Marx, "What was the living worker's activity becomes the activity of the machine."[15]

The reification of labor as a commodity is experienced by the worker as estrangement from their living activity, as their work is regulated, standardized, and disciplined. What Harry Braverman described as the "degradation" of work accompanies and is a condition of the augmentation of the capacities of machinery in the productive process.[16] Marx argued that, under capitalism, value is derived from "abstract human labour," that is, labor as a general capacity abstracted from such concrete actions as weaving or tailoring.[17] It is also implied by Marx's theory of real subsumption that capital tends to reconstruct labor as an activity, so that differentiating qualities are increasingly lost. The specifically capitalist labor process is one in which work is simplified and rendered abstract in practice, as the organizing intelligence in the labor process passes from the worker to capital itself expressed in the system of machinery.

The tendency in Taylorism, automation, and later twentieth-century developments in computerization is toward the loss of differentiating qualities from work. Hence, the mid-twentieth century saw the rise of the "mass worker" whose working activity "meets Marx's definition of 'abstract labour'–labour which is independent of the particular concrete form it takes at any given time."[18]

Continuous with modern capitalism's tendency toward abstract labor is a tendency toward abstract life. This means the decontextualization, reification, and commodification of the productive and reproductive capacities of living things.[19] Sociologists William Boyd, W. Scott Prudham, and Rachel Schurman argue that an *analogy* can be drawn from Marx's concepts of the formal and real subsumption of *labor* to the formal and real subsumption of *nature*. Under formal subsumption, nature is transformed into a set of resources and commodified. But the "natural schedules of biological or geophysical (re)production," the available natural stock of these resources, and their geographical location are confronted by the capitalist as exogenous brute facts.[20] This is the case in extractive industries such as mining and logging. In contrast, "[t]he real subsumption of nature refers to systematic increases in or intensification of biological productivity" through inputs such as fertilizers and growth hormones or through the manipulation of the genetic program.[21] Under real subsumption, capital imposes a specifically capitalist mode of (re)production, speeding up natural processes or altering them to increase reliability, predictability, efficiency, and control.

Boyd, Prudham, and Schurman are too cautious, however, in referring to the relationship between the real subsumption of labor and that of nature as merely *analogous*. These are not mere analogies but are actually historically and practically interrelated developments. Marx treated the organization of labor and the organization of nature as interrelated aspects of the capitalist production process. Just as labor is transformed, through its combination and mechanization, nature is transformed as "gigantic natural forces... [are] pressed into the service of production."[22] The pioneer of Marxist environmental critique, John Bellamy Foster suggests a close *actual* relationship between the real subsumption of labor and nature as interconnected developments within monopoly capitalism. The scientization of production was closely related to the concentration of capital in oligopolistic enterprises. The application of science in the chemical and electrical engineering industries meant a new level of capital intensiveness that gave advantage, through economies of scale, to large firms. Foster argues that the scientization of production under monopoly capitalism "was aimed at extending both the division of labor and the division of nature, and in the process both were transformed."[23] The real subsumption of both labor and nature tended toward simplification and homogeneity: "[C]omplex, highly skilled labor was to be reduced to its simplest most interchangeable–and hence cost-efficient–parts. . . . As labor became more homogeneous, so did much of nature, which underwent a similar process of degradation."[24]

Modern sciences of genetics and bioengineering have pioneered the control of life, for example, in the production of standardized organisms, such as particular varieties of mice or fruit fly, for use as experimental models.[25] Today, such scientific techniques are harnessed closely to capitalist production, so that the control of life through genetic engineering and biotechnology allows the intervention in reproductive processes so as to configure these for efficient commodity production. In this process, life is rendered abstract. Particular qualitative differences (e.g. between species) are overcome as genes are moved around and spliced between organisms and as, in synthetic genomics, the disassembly of life into its most basic components facilitates the assembly of new forms of life as patented living commodities. Sociologist Finn Bowring argues that "modern biotechnology. . . allows human beings to disregard animals' natural form of life." At its most extreme, "its goal is to transform the natural world into a universe of functional bio-machines."[26]

As well as in genetic engineering and "synthetic biology," abstract life is expressed in what John Johnston calls the "machinic life" of robotics and computational artificial life.[27] While synthetic genomics attempts to create "programmable" biological organisms, bringing the logic of engineering into the biological realm, the fields of machinic life may be seen as an attempt to relocate the reproductive capacities of life in the inorganic domain of metallic robots and computers. In new fields such as bionanotechnology, we can see practical efforts to break down the boundaries between what practitioners refer to as "hardware," "software," and "wetware," and indeed to merge the so-called hard artificial life of computing and robotics with the so-called wet artificial life of synthetic biology.

Robotics pioneer Rodney Brooks suggests that the melding of flesh and machine is pervasive in contemporary culture: "Researchers are placing chips in animal, and sometimes human, flesh and letting neurons grow and connect to them. The direct neural interface between man and machine is starting to happen. At the same time, surgery is becoming more acceptable for all sorts of body modifications." As the robotics revolution becomes integrated with the biotechnology revolution, he argues, "Our machines will become much more like us, and we will become much more like our machines."[28]

In these discourses and accompanying practices, life is thereby abstracted not only from particular organisms and ecologies, but also from the organic altogether; life becomes instead a set of abstract functions that may be expressed in either animal or machine, or in their combination. The constitution of abstract life tends toward the *conceptual* abstraction from qualitative differences between the organic and the non-organic and toward their *practical* reconstitution.

The technological convergence between the sciences of automation, information, and biological control, signaled by acronyms such as "GNR," suggests the convergence between abstract labor and abstract life. Such ideas are part of the discourse of capitalist techno-futurism, a way of promising continued progress and the continual reinvention of capital.[29] A recent advertisement for the Lexus automobile forecasts: "Someday nanotechnology will be used to turn plants into [automobile] components."[30] The dream of total automation and the workerless factory, central to the techno-utopian fantasies of robotics and nanotechnology pioneers, combines with visions of the total control of the reproductive capacities of living organisms. Such techno-futurist visions are not idle fantasies but are pursued in the projects of universities, spin-out firms, and industrial research laboratories. What such visions and projects augur is the emancipation of capital from its dependencies on human and biological life exogenous to it through the appropriation of life for capital itself. "Thus all powers of labour" *and*, we should now add, *of life*, "are transposed into powers of capital."[31]

A Dead Planet

We are currently undergoing what scientists dub the "sixth extinction," the sixth mass extinction event in the world's history—and the first one that is caused by human activity.[32] Plant and animal species are vanishing at 100 to 1000 times the natural "background" extinction rate. In their 2007 survey of species, the International Union for the Conservation of Nature found that 39 % of the species they surveyed were threatened with extinction: "[O]ne in three amphibians, one quarter of the world's pines and other coniferous trees, one in eight birds and one in four mammals."[33] The Zoological Society of London (ZSL) reported in 2008 that the world's population of wildlife has fallen by between a quarter and a third since 1970. Populations of marine species decreased by 28 % in just 10 years (1995 to 2005) and that of ocean birds by 30 % since the mid-1990s.[34] The editor of the ZSL report, scientist Jonathan Loh, described the decline as "completely unprecedented in terms of human history. You'd have to go back to the extinction of the dinosaurs to see a decline as rapid as this."[35] This massive loss of species is caused by a combination of the destruction of natural habitat, overexploitation, pollution, the spread of invasive species, and, increasingly, the effects of climate change.

Ocean ecosystems are under severe pressure caused by exploitation and pollution, leading to a dramatic decrease in the diversity and complexity of ocean life. According to marine ecologist Jeremy Jackson:

> Synergistic effects of habitat destruction, overfishing, introduced species, warming, acidification, toxins, and massive runoff of nutrients are transforming once complex ecosystems like coral reefs and kelp forests into monotonous level bottoms, transforming clear and productive coastal seas into anoxic dead zones, and transforming complex food webs topped by big animals into simplified, microbially dominated ecosystems.[36]

Overfishing has led to the plummeting of fish stocks. Descriptions from the pre-industrial era portray an abundance of ocean life that is now hard for us to imagine. Callum Roberts, professor of marine conservation at York University, remarks that, "[w]e have come to accept the degraded condition of the sea as normal. People. . . dismiss as far-fetched tales of giant fish or seas bursting with life."[37] An article in *The Economist* notes that

> the fish that once seemed an inexhaustible source of food are now almost everywhere in decline: 90 % of large predatory fish (the big ones such as

tuna, swordfish and sharks) have gone, according to some scientists. In estuaries and coastal waters, 85 % of the large whales have disappeared, and nearly 60 % of the small ones. Many of the smaller fish are also in decline.[38]

Effects of overfishing are compounded by global warming. Coral reefs are bleached and dying: "Perhaps only 5 % of coral reefs can now be considered pristine, a quarter have been lost and all are vulnerable to global warming."[39] There are ever more algal blooms appearing in the oceans and ever more and ever larger "dead zones" caused by algal blooms—areas of ocean depleted of oxygen and therefore sea life. These had been known to occur as the result of fertilizer runoff from agriculture. They are now occurring more frequently, independently of fertilizer runoff, apparently from global warming causing shifting ocean currents to bring nutrients up from the depths to the surface, leading to growth of algae. In 2006, the UN Environment Program said that the number of such dead zones had grown by a third in the space of two years.[40] According to a Pulitzer Prize-winning *Los Angeles Times* story, the algal blooms are "distress signals from an unhealthy ocean. Overfishing, destruction of wetlands, industrial pollution and climate change have made the seas inhospitable for fish and more advanced forms of life and freed the lowliest–algae and bacteria– to flourish."[41] The complex ocean ecosystem, once capable of sustaining abundant and diverse life, is being transformed into an eviscerated environment sustaining only simplified and less diverse organisms.

In recent years, there have been a number of both disturbing and poorly understood cases of the crashing of wildlife populations. Scientists do not fully understand what is causing the Colony Collapse Disorder affecting honeybee populations in the USA and Europe, but it seems to be the result of a "synergistic" combination of stresses such as chemical pollution, parasites, pathogens, and lack of food.[42] It is similarly unclear what is behind the fungal infection known as "white nose syndrome" that is killing vast numbers of bats in North America.[43] Along with factors such as disease and habitat destruction, chemical pollution is thought by scientists to be a contributor to the sharp decline of amphibian populations, with 32 % of the world's amphibian species now threatened.[44] A recent study suggests that deformities found in increasing numbers of frogs in the USA are "caused by a synergism between parasitic infection and exposure to low levels of agricultural chemicals."[45] Professor of ecology Joseph M. Kiesecker speculates, in line with this, that chemical pollution may be "changing the environment in ways that increase disease prevalence."[46]

Soil erosion is a silent crisis facing global agriculture. As environmental journalist Stephen Leahy states, "[I]n the past 40 years alone, 30 % of the planet's arable land has become unproductive due to erosion, mainly in Asia and Africa. At current erosion rates, soils are being depleted faster than they are replenished."[47] According to Lester Brown, director of the Earth Policy Institute research group, deforestation and overgrazing in Africa are contributing to dust storms that "are slowly draining the continent of its fertility and biological productivity."[48]

Deforestation, in particular the destruction of the rainforests, is a major cause of biodiversity loss and a contributor to climate change and is caused by logging, clearance for agriculture, mining and industrial development, and dam projects.[49] Deforestation of tropical forests and primary forests increased in the first five years after the millennium, compared with the 1990s (though the Brazilian government recently announced plans to reduce the rate of deforestation). According to the environmental news site *Mongobay.com*, "each day at least 80,000 acres (32,300 ha) of forest disappear from Earth."[50]

Climate change caused by greenhouse gas emissions (and intensified by deforestation) adds to and compounds problems of the alteration and depletion of life-sustaining systems and the extinction of species.[51] Research by National Aeronautics and Space Administration (NASA) scientist James Hansen reveals that the planet has undergone warming of 0.6 °C (1.08 °F) since 1970, and the ten hottest years occurred between 1997 and 2008. This warming is due to accelerate, with devastating consequences. As Hansen puts it, these changes place the world in "imminent peril."[52] In 2004, a group of zoologists and biodiversity scientists wrote to *Nature*, predicting "on the basis of mid-range climate-warming scenarios for 2050, that 15–37 % of species in our sample of regions and taxa will be 'committed to extinction'."[53] In 2007, the Intergovernmental Panel on Climate Change warned that 20 to 30 % of plant and animal species would be at increased risk of extinction if average global temperatures were to increase by 2.7 to 4.5 °F.[54] On January 28, 2009, Al Gore testified to the Senate Foreign Relations Committee that if carbon emissions were unchecked, global average temperatures could rise by 11 °F over the next century. With increased desertification and crop failure cutting food supplies, as well as the melting away of glaciers threatening water supplies for irrigation and drinking water, such a development would bring "a screeching halt to human civilisation and threaten the fabric of life everywhere on Earth."[55]

Already, climate change is producing serious water shortages. According to the Working Group on Climate Change and Development, the melting of Andean glaciers "forces people to farm at higher altitudes to grow their crops, adding to deforestation, which in turn undermines water resources and leads to soil erosion and putting the survival of Andean cultures at risk."[56] In 2008, the executive director of the UN Environment Program warned that climate change may lead to severe droughts and water shortages such that parts of the world may have to be abandoned by humans.[57] So, the creation of oceanic dead zones is paralleled on land by desertification—complex life-sustaining ecosystems are replaced by simplified ecologies incapable of supporting human life.

The evisceration of ecosystems is connected with a more general process of homogenization. Bio*diversity* is lost, and wild species give way to domesticated monocultures of industrialized farming. The destruction of the wild accompanies and furthers the global expansion and dominance of a globalized corporate culture in which all differences are assimilated to a common commodity form. The loss of habitat for wild species is accompanied by the loss of diversity of human cultures. As journalist Terry Glavin points out, a corollary of the extinction of species is the destruction of indigenous peoples and the extinction of their cultures and languages.[58] The complexity both of nature and of human cultures is being diminished, giving way to monoculture. The environmental crisis manifests a powerful tendency toward *simplification*.[59]

We are seeing not only the extinction of wild species, but also a dramatic decline in the diversity of domesticated plants and animals. Glavin writes, "[B]y the beginning of the twentieth century, about 4000 breeds of animals had been domesticated, but by the end of the century, 618 of those distinct breeds were extinct and another 475 were threatened with extinction." It is estimated that the diversity of major livestock breeds is diminishing at about 5 % per year. There has also been a dramatic reduction in genetic diversity in all major food crops over the course of the twentieth century. What Pat Mooney, executive director of the Rural Advancement Foundation International, calls a "plague of sameness" attacking the world's plants has accelerated with contemporary agrobusiness and biotechnology. The tendency toward sameness was exacerbated by the industrialization of agriculture promoted in the post–World War II "Green Revolution," which increased and concentrated the corporate control of agriculture.[60]

Industrial agriculture imposes standardization and monoculture, abstracting the reproduction of plants and animals from the interconnected processes of natural ecosystems. Sociologist Barbara Adam describes how industrial agriculture abstracts not only from place, but also from time. Technoscientific and industrial techniques detach agriculture from the natural rhythms that traditionally linked the patterns of farming to those of the natural world:

> Despite this inescapable tie of (almost all) life forms to the earth's rhythmicity and seasonality, attempts are being made to transcend that context-bound temporal characteristic and incorporate agriculture more fully within the industrial way of doing things: improve productivity, efficiency and profitability by creating sheep that 'produce' lambs twice a year, crops that grow in extended seasons, apples that keep for an extra couple of months.[61]

A similar process of abstraction is indicated by the distinction drawn between farming and agriculture by biologists Richard Lewontin and Jean-Pierre Berlan: "Farming is producing wheat; agriculture is turning phosphates into bread."[62]

Agriculture relies increasingly on industrial inputs of fertilizer, pesticide, and machinery. In many cases, industrialized agriculture involves the total abstraction of the organism from the environment. Foster gives the example of cattle "removed from pasture and raised in feedlots." Under these industrial conditions, "their natural waste, rather than fertilizing the soil, becomes a serious form of pollution."[63] Industrial raising and slaughter of animals exemplifies the linkages between the real subsumption of labor and the real subsumption of life. In the mechanized chicken processing plant, one can see the relationship between the standardization of non-human animals as commodities and the routinization and control of human labor.[64]

The intimate historical and material relationship between the real subsumption of labor and the real subsumption of life is also indicated by Barry Commoner's 1976 analysis of the economic roots of the energy crisis of that decade. Commoner pointed out that the extreme energy-dependence of our economic and social activities was a relatively recent phenomenon: "[T]here have been sweeping changes in the technology of agricultural and industrial production in the last thirty years."[65] New technologies integrated into mass production after World War II massively increased the environmental impacts of the modern economy. The economy became more dependent on oil with highway building and increased use of automobiles and trucks for transportation. Petrochemical products became much more widely used in industry, agriculture, and consumer products. The vast quantities of non-biodegradable, and often toxic, synthetic products produced and used in the post-war period marked this, Commoner argued, as the "Synthetics Age." The combined capital intensiveness and energy intensiveness of the new industrial system was driven by attempts to integrate science into the production process so as to subsume both nature and labor. The new highly energy-dependent petrochemical agriculture was aimed at overcoming the barriers to profitability posed by natural growth cycles and local ecological conditions, harnessing nature to industrial patterns and products. Industry itself was becoming more capital- and energy- intensive in the ongoing quest to replace labor with automatic machinery. Commoner argues that the overriding obsession with increasing the productivity of labor led to a capital- and energy-intensive apparatus of production, one which is highly wasteful and inefficient in its use of natural resources.[66] Commoner points to the relationship between the real subsumption of labor via mechanization and the degradation of the environment.

Drawing on Commoner's analysis, Foster argues that the post–World War II system of mass production and industrial agriculture is "counter-ecological." The system is predicated on the *denial* of the ecological principle that "everything is connected to everything else." The standardized, simplified ecosystems of industrial agriculture are expressions of the way in which industrial agriculture binds life to the abstract value of money. In contrast to the interconnectedness of living things within natural ecosystems, in capitalist agriculture, as Foster puts it, "the only lasting connection between things is the cash nexus."[67]

We are frequently left with the remnants of formerly vibrant ecosystems—parks and zoos rather than genuine wilderness and wildlife. As wilderness is eliminated through deforestation, as the fabrics of ecosystems are ripped apart, and as biodiversity of both wild and domesticated nature is lost, species are preserved in a "living dead" form in zoos and national parks. Glavin writes that "living dead" is "a term biologists have begun to use to describe those species that are not expected to escape extinction without significant human intervention, such as captive breeding. Among the world's endangered mammals, birds, and reptiles, already 1500 species are expected to be wholly dependent upon captive breeding by 2050." The surviving members of these species live an abstracted existence in parks or zoos; they become specimens. As Glavin puts it, "[T]hey will not be 'wild' animals at all. They will be functions of artificial selection. They will live on in zoos, and perhaps some large parks. . . They will live in a simulacrum of the real world." The boundary between the natural and artificial is broken down as the survival of these specimens comes to depend on interventionist programs of captive breeding. Such programs are promoted in terms of the pervasive ideology of techno-salvationism: "The alchemies of cryogenics, transgenetic manipulation, and the emerging biotechnologies that zookeepers are developing raise the very real possibility that many of the 'living dead' species of the world will never become extinct, at least not in the way that geneticists or taxonomists use the term." In the USA and Britain, zoos and natural history museums are preserving genetic information on endangered species as "frozen arks." As Glavin points out, given the destructive trajectory of modern societies, the notion that such projects constitute an "ark" and that there will, at some point in the future, be wild habitats into which these species can be restored seems "utopian." Instead, the most that such projects seem to promise is merely the indefinite maintenance of the "living dead" status of such species.[68]

Species are extracted from decimated ecosystems and preserved as specimens in zoos, and their sperm, embryos, tissue, and DNA are preserved. Already, the reproduction of these endangered species is increasingly indebted to techniques such as artificial insemination. Glavin writes, "Semen is being extracted from anesthetized tigers and stored away in frozen test tubes. The fertilized embryos of endangered gaurs are being implanted in Holstein cows. Horses are giving birth to zebras."[69] So, alongside the abstract existence of these species as "specimens," there is a further abstraction at work, accomplished by the new capabilities of genetic engineering. These species are preserved as abstract life. The preservationist project becomes linked to the technological control of abstract life in which qualitative differences between organisms and species are overcome. As Glavin puts it, "it is about the bleeding away of differences in the living world, and of differences between captivity and freedom, between the real and the fabricated."[70]

Artificial Life

Animal specimens are being abstracted, for their own protection, from ecosystems that are being destroyed. At the same time, genetic engineering is producing new animal strains, which themselves are seen to represent risks to natural ecosystems and which therefore must be segregated. An example is the controversial transgenic AquAdvantage salmon, developed by the company AquaBounty to be faster-growing than natural varieties of salmon currently used in aquaculture. Transgenic salmon are controversial because of worries about the potential for their escape from aquaculture nets into the wild and the possibly disastrous effects of their breeding with wild salmon. The production of transgenic salmon would be continuous with the dynamics of capitalist industrialized agriculture whereby natural processes are overcome in the cause of the enhancement of productivity; reproductive capacities of life are mobilized, but reconfigured to fit with capitalist dynamics.[71] This poses the problem of the relationship between this manufactured life-form and the broader natural environment. The risks are unknown, and the existence of such life in the natural environment takes the form of a "real-world experiment."[72] Risk is contained by the sequestration of the new organism from the ecosystem. The AquAdvantage salmon is designed to be sterile, with sterility protecting not only the intellectual property of the biotech corporation but also the environment.[73] Yet, the sterility of all individuals in a population may not be guaranteed, so there is also the problem of the containment of the creatures from the environment. For the protection of the natural environment, either by sterility or by spatial segregation in "escape-proof facilities," these creatures may have to be kept in abstraction from the ecosystem.[74]

"Life" is today radically abstracted, resituated, and reconfigured. The term "artificial life" is used with broad connotations in this chapter to denote the manifold ways in which modern technosciences, including genetic engineering, computing, robotics, and nanotechnology, are technologizing biological life and creating new forms of autonomous, self-replicating, and, hence, "lifelike" machines. But "artificial life" is also a term of art, and one of the most radical challenges to existing conceptual and ontological barriers between life and technology has come from the new technoscientific field that takes the name of "Artificial Life" (AL). Thomas Ray, a pioneer of the field, defines its goal as "understanding biology by constructing biological phenomena out of artificial components, rather than breaking natural life forms down into their component parts. It is the synthetic rather than the reductionist approach." The umbrella incorporates hardware (robotics, nanotechnology), software ("replicating and evolving computer programs"), and wetware ("replicating and evolving organic molecules").[75] AL seems, however, to be mainly associated with the "software" aspect in which Ray himself specializes, and which is associated with the complexity and computational sciences of the Santa Fe Institute in the USA.[76] The thrust of the project is the computer simulation of the self-organizing, replicating, and reproductive capacities of living things and ecological systems. These simulations inevitably raise the problem of the relationship between the simulated and the real: the philosophical question underlying much of the interest in AL is whether this "life on screen" is not merely "like" a living system but is an alternative *instance* of life.[77]

Although Ray emphasizes that AL is synthetic, not reductionist, it nevertheless follows the logic of abstract life. Ray writes:

> Our concepts of biology, evolution, and complexity are constrained by having observed only a single instance of life, life on earth. A truly comparative biology is needed to extend these concepts. Because we cannot observe life on other planets, we are left with the alternative of creating Artificial Life forms on earth. I will discuss the approach of inoculating evolution by natural selection into the medium of the digital computer.[78]

Stefan Helmreich writes that AL may be seen as the consolidation of theoretical biology, artificial intelligence (AI), and robotics. But he argues that the project derives much of its character from theoretical physics: "This shapes... its claims to be a biology that will be true anywhere in the universe, just as physics is true everywhere in the universe."[79] AL operates with a conception of life that is abstracted from any given existence, form, or environment. From the initial abstract, universalistic, theoretical physics–influenced concept of life, there follows the thought that life could evolve beyond the merely incidental biological forms of plants, animals, and micro-organisms.

Techno-futurist literature often posits a movement from biological to technological evolution. Hans Moravec, artificial intelligence researcher of Carnegie Mellon University, is a key proponent of a kind of cosmic transhumanism in which living intelligence evolves beyond the organic to inhabit machines, and ultimately to inhabit the universe itself, as intelligence takes on new manifestations in post-terrestrial, post-Darwinian life. "We are," he says, "in the process of inspiriting the dead matter around us. It will soon be our honor to welcome some of it to the land of the living." Moravec fantasizes about the diversity of this post-human and post-terrestrial intelligent life, evolving over the next millennium from his own and his colleagues' attempts to instill intelligence in non-organic matter.

As "ex-human" life, derived from these experiments, evolves to inhabit outer space, this new extra-terrestrial ecology will become "much more diverse than Earth's biosphere, shaped by discoveries and inventions yet to be made and thus hard to conceive."[80]

The prediction of a new diversity of AL is also put forward by Rodney Brooks, the director of the Massachusetts Institute of Technology (MIT) Artificial Intelligence Laboratory. He foresees a "Cambrian explosion" of robotic life, a new complexity and diversity in artificial intelligence and robotics reminiscent of the rapid proliferation of complex biological organisms about 530 million years ago. Indeed, Brooks saw his laboratory's creation of "Genghis," an insect-like robot, in which the interaction of simple components yielded complex behavior that gave the appearance of intentionality, as the beginning of his laboratory's own "Cambrian explosion."[81]

Brooks insists that the robots that he is producing, which are able to act somewhat autonomously in unstructured environments, "are not just robots. They are artificial creatures."[82] Brooks' vision is shared by scientists working on the Symbrion Project at the University of the West of England (UWE) in Bristol. The project involves the construction of motorized robots, each approximately the size of a sugar cube, which are able to communicate with one another and to "assemble themselves into much larger machines to carry out specific tasks when required." According to Alan Winfield of UWE, these robots will "not only… cooperate, they'll self-assemble and self-organise into artificial organisms."[83] Like Brooks' insect-like robots, these are also modeled on an ant or termite colony, each organism relatively simple but together forming swarms that can manifest adaptive behavior.

There is a growing interest in designing robotics to mimic the natural world. Researchers at Tufts University are attempting to develop a robot that mimics the motion of caterpillars. A *New York Times* article reports:

> In trying to reproduce the caterpillar, the Tufts researchers are taking part in one of the biggest trends in robotics and locomotion studies, which are increasingly taking inspiration from the world of biology. Joseph Ayers of Northeastern University in Boston has created an artificial lobster. Ian Walker of Clemson University in South Carolina has a robotic arm that draws its inspiration from the elephant's trunk and the octopus's arm. There are robotic salamanders, snakes, cockroaches, fish and geckos.[84]

Such robots frequently have military applications. The MIT-linked defense robotics firm Boston Dynamics produces robots that mimic animal motion, such as the four-legged "Big Dog" that can carry supplies over rugged terrain. A collaboration between College of Pennsylvania, Carnegie Mellon University, Stanford University, University of California at Berkeley, Lewis and Clark College, and Boston Dynamics has produced the "bioinspired" RiSE robot, capable of climbing vertical walls, a project that obviously has surveillance and military applications.[85] iRobot, the private firm founded by Brooks, has also become a major manufacturer of robots for war.[86]

The development of animal-mimicking robots is paralleled by the technologization of animals. There is a trend, particularly in military and security research, to use animals as instruments. Scientists at Los Alamos have used Pavlovian conditioning to train bees to detect explosives. A newspaper article on this development features pictures of bees restrained in "specially designed harnesses" at the laboratory.[87] This denaturing of the animal, as it is placed under laboratory controls and divorced and deprogrammed from its natural behavior, aims at turning the animal into a technological tool. The hope is to integrate the bee into a device. The research scientist leading the project claims that "the bees could be carried in hand-held detectors the size of a shoe box, and could be used to sniff out explosives in airports, roadside security checks, or even placed in robot bomb disposal equipment."[88]

Genetic engineering aims at an even more fundamental technologization and control of living creatures. The production of transgenic animals collapses barriers between life and technology and between species, but also merges what were previously distinct sectors of production: agriculture, pharmaceuticals, and the industrial production of materials. In February 2009, the US Food and Drug Administration (FDA) approved the safety of ATryn, an intravenous anti-clotting drug produced in the milk of genetically engineered goats.[89] The Canadian firm Nexia Biotechnologies has created a goat that produces spider silk protein in its milk. As the company's CEO puts it, the genetically altered goats are "cheap factories" for the company's product, an ultra-strong material that they have dubbed "BioSteel."[90]

The technologization of animal life is carried forward by the new potential for the standardization of animals through cloning. Cloning represents an extension of the simplification of nature that one finds in agricultural monoculture, and the key application of cloning is in agriculture. The *New Scientist* notes that "cloning. . . offers a much more precise way of making genetically engineered animals. Traditionally, transgenic animals were made by injecting gene copies into a new embryo–an inefficient and chaotic process. Genes can land anywhere in the genome, disrupting other genes. Now researchers can insert DNA at a precise position into a single adult cell, and then clone it to create the desired animals."[91] So, cloning is a radical extension of engineering control over life and therefore of the capitalist subsumption of life, rendering life compatible with industrial norms of precision, standardization, and regularity.

Synthetic biology represents a still more radical development beyond genetic engineering. In a paper published in *Science* in early 2008, the J. Craig Venter Institute announced that its scientists had created a synthetic chromosome, synthesizing from laboratory chemicals the genome of the bacterium *Mycoplasma genitalium*.[92] This synthesis of DNA was a step toward Venter's "ultimate goal of inserting the synthetic chromosome into a cell and booting it up to create the first synthetic organism."[93] In 2010, Venter confirmed that his team had accomplished this next step, thereby making a "synthetic cell."[94]

Computing imagery (such as "booting it up") signifies the technologization of the organism and the ambition toward predictability and control.[95] William Boyd argues that there is an affinity between the conceptual modes through which biological technosciences approach life and the capitalist dynamics involved in the manipulation of life—scientific reductionism facilitates commodification. He argues that "the metaphor of life as code... has come to provide much of the foundation for efforts to 'improve' biological systems by intervening directly in the genetic program itself. Codes... can be cracked, programmed, and reprogrammed."[96] Nobel laureate Hamilton Smith, who led the scientific team at the J. Craig Venter Institute, likened the production of the artificial genome to finishing the operating system of a computer: "By itself, it doesn't do anything, but when you install it on a computer, then you have a working computer system. It's the same with the genome: the genome is the operating system for a cell and the cytoplasm is the hardware that's required to run that genome."[97] The understanding of life in terms of hardware and software is bound up with the practical goal of the computer-assisted design of life: Venter called his new cell "the first self-replicating species that we have on the planet whose parent is a computer."[98]

Synthetic biology follows an engineering paradigm, and there are striking similarities with Taylorism. Just as Taylorism involves the initial analysis of the worker's living activity, the analytical breaking down of that activity into its constituent parts, and the re-engineering of the work process, similarly synthetic biology involves the breaking down of the complexity of life into relatively simple components with the aim of re-building these components. Like capitalist mass production, synthetic biology operates via the assembly of standardized or replaceable parts. A key tool of synthetic biology is known as the "BioBrick," which consists of fragments of DNA. An article in the popular science magazine *BBC Focus* explains:

> Scientists can clip DNA segments from nature, or they can order them. [University of California scientist Chris] Voigt prefers to order them, sending instructions listing what DNA he wants to a company, which will then synthesise the strings of genetic material for him. In this case, the company copies segments of existing DNA using a polymer chain reaction (PCR) machine and puts them together in the required sequence. Alternatively, researchers can buy ready-made parts, known as BioBricks. The synthesised parts are made in a similar way, but researchers choose what they want from the BioBrick library. The parts will arrive suspended in a liquid and are then added to bacteria cells, such as *E. coli*. The bacteria is zapped with electricity to create pores in the cell walls, a technique which allows the DNA to filter inside.[99]

The BBC article emphasizes that this use of standardized parts reflects an engineering orientation and points out that "a number of this new breed of biologists have come from an engineering rather than a life sciences background."[100]

The production of abstract life means intervention aimed at overcoming the complexities and interdependencies of the natural world, as the following quote in the BBC article makes clear:

> Professor Tom Knight, senior research scientist at MIT, draws a parallel with a joke often told to illustrate the differences between scientists and engineers. A scientist goes into her lab and carries out an experiment. When she gets the result, she discovers that the system she is studying is twice as complicated as she thought. "Great," she thinks to herself, "I get to write a paper on that." An engineer goes into her lab and carries out the same experiment. But this time, when the results come back and she sees that the system is twice as complicated as she'd predicted, she says to herself: "Now how do I get rid of that?" "I'm firmly in the 'how do I get rid of that' category!" says Knight.[101]

Synthetic biology is an assault on complexity not only analytically, but also in practice, as it seeks to package nature into standardized components to aid production of standardized engineered-but-living products.

Drew Endy, another MIT scientist working in synthetic biology, explains that the goal is to build predictability into biological processes: "We can probably engineer biology in such a way to produce components that are insulated from one another, that are designed to be easy to put together and then behave in ways that you expect."[102] As science journalist Alok Jha states, "[I]f biology is to truly turn into a technology, engineers need to develop standard biological components that they can simply plug into their application–something available in all other forms of engineering."[103] *The Economist*, which has published a number of cautiously optimistic articles about this new technoscientific field, notes that "[s]ynthetic biologists plan to. . . industrialise the process in a way that will let people order biological parts as routinely as they order electrical components. If this vision is realised (and there is still a long way to go) biotechnology will become a true branch of engineering."[104]

Synthetic biology operates with abstract life–life broken down into components that can be treated as engineering tools. This abstraction is also abstraction from ecosystems and geography—the appropriation of the productive capacities of nature and their re-situation in a technological/industrial setting. In this way, the obstacles posed for capitalist production by natural scarcities, timescales, and geographies may be overcome. *Financial Times* journalist Clive Cookson writes, "[W]ithin a decade some researchers believe that bacteria, for example, could be designed that would mass-produce drugs that currently have to be painstakingly harvested from rare plants."[105]

Scientific reductionism and technological standardization are linked together in a process of the commodification of the living. As Nikolas Rose has written with regard to the development of the "molecular" approach to biomedicine:

> Molecularization strips tissues, proteins, molecules and drugs of their specific affinities–to a disease, to an organ, to an individual, to a species. It confers a new mobility on the elements of life. They can be de-localized–moved from place to place, from organism to organism, from disease to disease, from person to person.[106]

These processes of reduction and manipulation are linked to what Rose calls "a new political economy of life in which. . . biopolitics has become bioeconomics."[107] Epistemological reduction of the living to the level of the molecule combines with an engineering ethos that aims toward efficiently reordering life for the purpose of making it optimally productive.

The engineering paradigm in biology is merging with nanotechnology as a project of technologizing life and animating technology. Bionanotechnology is predicated on the notion that DNA molecules, proteins, and enzymes are already "machines" or "self-assemblers" found in nature, which can themselves manipulate matter at the nanoscale. The UK Biotechnology and Biological Sciences Research Council (BBSRC) defines bionanotechnology as

> a multidisciplinary area that sits at the interface between engineering, biological and the physical sciences... The range of topics within bionanotechnology is broad and includes examples in which biological components may be used to facilitate new technologies (e.g. the reconstruction of biomolecular systems as machines or motors), as well as those in which new technologies are used in the study of biological systems.[108]

The aim is to harness natural processes occurring at the nanoscale for a variety of applications from medicine to "molecular computing" to the manufacturing of materials. The linking of biotechnology with nanotechnology is associated with hope of unifying biology with industry, harnessing natural reproduction to the production of medical and industrial technologies and consumer goods.

Although bionanotechnology is in its infancy and nowhere near the production of industrial-scale quantities of materials, there are hopes for the possibility of scaling up.[109] Nadrian Seeman, New York University chemist, has pioneered attempts to harness the self-assembly of DNA molecules to make complex self-assembled structures, leading ultimately to the ability to manufacture fibers or electronic devices. An article in the *Christian Science Monitor* describes him as the "Henry Ford" of nanotechnology, for his attempts to develop the production of molecular machines to industrial levels of efficiency and mass production. According to the article,

> Nadrian Seeman sees a future filled with extremely small factory workers... He and a Chinese team at Nanjing University have built a nanoscale factory worker. The tiny machine is made of DNA, the molecule that governs the way cells make proteins... Seeman 'programs' his tiny machine by stringing the right combinations of DNA–much in the way computer engineers use binary code... [He can] arrange pieces and form specific molecules with some precision–similar to the way a robotic automobile factory can be told what kind of car to make.[110]

Commenting on the potential feasibility of Seeman's vision of molecular mass manufacture, British nanotechnology scientist Richard Jones notes that

> molecular biology is being quickly industrialised; now adverts in the journal *Nature* compete to offer custom synthesis of DNA for as little as 80p per base. You simply send them the sequence you want and the money, and a couple of weeks later a little trace of DNA comes back. At the laboratory level, we have at least one demonstration that we can use the full power of self-assembly to make, not a single soft machine, but billions of them all at once.[111]

The potential applications for bionanotechnology techniques are already entering into the imagination of new avenues for business (as in the Lexus advertisement quoted earlier). Cookson writes in the *Financial Times*: "The fusion of nanotechnology and biology may also allow us to grow products such as solar collectors and liquid crystal displays from living material."[112]

A key feature of techno-futurist discourse is the image of the displacement of the factory and thereby the emancipation of production from its dependence on potentially antagonistic human labor. Seeman's "extremely small factory workers" signify an escape from dependence on human labor by harnessing the fundamentals of life. In nanotechnology guru Eric Drexler's visions of the future, the workers are self-assembling nanobots or "molecular assemblers."[113] Ray Kurzweil draws on these ideas in a way that exemplifies how nanotechnology visions express the desire to meld production with life. In the idea of self-assembly, the productive apparatus of capitalism is imbued with life: "Self-assembly allows improperly formed components to be discarded automatically and makes it possible for the potentially trillions of circuit components to organize themselves, rather than be painstakingly assembled in a top-down process. It would enable large-scale circuits to be created in test-tubes rather than in multibillion-dollar factories."[114]

At the same time as life is reified, transformed into a mechanism or object, capital is strangely imbued with lifelike qualities. Drexler explicitly puts forward nanotechnology as a project which liberates capital from the productive and reproductive powers of both labor and nature, instead vesting those powers in technology and, hence, in capital itself. In *Engines of Creation*, Drexler writes:

Assembler-based systems, if properly programmed, will themselves *be* productive capital. Together with larger robotic machines, they will be able to build virtually anything, including copies of themselves. Since this self-replicating capital will be able to double many times per day, only demand and available resources will limit its quantity. Capital as such need cost virtually nothing.[115]

Nanotechnology, as "self-replicating capital," represents the emancipation of capital from contradictions and limits. Nanotechnology is the material realization of the ideal of productive capital, or in Marx's terms, of capital as "self-valorizing value."

Melinda Cooper argues that the combination of economic crisis and a growing recognition of ecological limits, expressed most influentially in the Club of Rome's *Limits to Growth* report of 1972, was the impetus toward the development of the bioeconomy. The promotion of commercial biomedicine and bioengineering was, Cooper argues, in opposition to the tropes of stagnation and limits that pervaded the political economy and culture of the 1970s. Biotechnology, since highly dependent on venture capital, was economically linked to the financialization of the economy, the expansion of debt, and the uncoupling of the financial sector from the "real economy." It was a focal point for fantasies of the dematerialization of capitalism and the overcoming of all limits. These futures were founded on the assumption that "while industrial machines are subject to the laws of depletion and diminishing returns, life at its most 'lifelike' obeys a law of self-organization and increasing complexity. Where industrial production depends on the finite reserves available on planet earth, *life, like contemporary debt production, needs to be understood as a process of continuous autopoiesis, a self-engendering of life from life, without conceivable beginning or end.*"[116] Biotechnology was linked to the promise of self-reproducing capital and never-ending growth.

During the financial crisis of 2008, the surge of speculative money into commodities (combined with other factors including the taking over of agriculture by biofuel crops) led to a spike in food prices.[117] At the height of the crisis, techno-salvationism reared its head, with genetic modification and other technoscientific innovations put forward as the solution to food scarcity. As food prices surged, the *Financial Times* called for a "second 'green revolution' " arguing for new investment in raising agricultural productivity through advanced technology.[118] The chairman of Nestlé took the opportunity of high commodity prices to make the case for overcoming European resistance to agricultural biotechnology: "You cannot today feed the world without genetically modified organisms."[119] As the world appeared headed for 1970s-style stagflation, Jeffrey Sachs asserted that new technologies offered a way out of both the food crisis and the broader economic crisis. Sachs argued for massive investment in sustainable technologies such as solar power, electricity storage and transmission, hybrid engines, carbon capture, cellulose-based ethanol, "safe nuclear power," new drought-resistant crop varieties, and new irrigation techniques that "can help impoverished farmers move from one subsistence crop to several high-value crops year round." He opined that "countless other technologies on the horizon can reconcile a world of growing energy demands with increasingly scarce fossil fuels and rising threats of human-made climate change."[120] This new techno-salvationism offers to overcome the problems generated by past development and by earlier failed technological fixes. Climate change has exacerbated the depletion of world food stocks. But the legacy of the Green Revolution has also added to the problem, since it led to the development of agriculture that was highly dependent on energy and petrochemical inputs and water. The new "green revolution" means using biotechnology, including genetic modification, to try to increase yields despite shortages of water and the growing cost of energy and petrochemical inputs.[121] Techno-enthusiasts become more insistent about the "imperative" for such technological fixes in proportion with the irrational, crisis-ridden nature of the prevailing economic system and its destructive relationship to the natural world.[122]

As the world's politicians appear paralyzed in the face of global warming, techno-salvationism is rampant in this area. The Bush administration backed a range of technological fixes to the crisis, including "giant mirrors in space or reflective dust pumped into the atmosphere."[123] Private corporations are seeking to profit from developing "geoengineering" solutions to climate change. Proposals have included spreading iron filings on the ocean surface to encourage plankton and sequester carbon dioxide.[124] There have been protests against an Indian and German expedition to the Antarctic to engage in experimentation involving the spreading of 20 tons of iron sulfate over a 300-sq-km area in the Southern Ocean.[125]

The environmental imbalance produced by carbon pollution creates a potentially lucrative demand for technoscientific products and expertise, and there are companies waiting to take advantage of such opportunities. Modern industrial civilization is doing away with the relatively stable and benign climate that has existed for 10,000 years since the last Ice Age. As the environmental journalist Fred Pearce puts it:

> It is arguable that this rather benign world has been the main reason why our species was able to leave the caves and create the urban, industrial civilisation we enjoy today. Our complex society rests on our being able to plant crops and build cities, knowing that the rains will come and the cities will not be flooded by incoming tides. When that certainty fails. . . even the most sophisticated society is brought to its knees. But there is now a growing fear among scientists that, thanks to man-made climate change, we are about to return to a world of climactic turbulence, where tipping points are constantly crossed.[126]

The life-sustaining environment that was a taken-for-granted common good can no longer be taken for granted, and the maintenance of equilibrium in the atmosphere and ecosystem becomes potentially an artificial technological accomplishment. As our life on Earth becomes increasingly precarious, it becomes also increasingly artificial.

Even the problem of algal blooms in the oceans, caused by pollution and climate change, has become a focus for technosalvationist hopes. The problem was highlighted when 32 % of the 50-sq-km area off the coast of Qingdao, devoted to Olympic sailing during the Beijing Olympics, was covered in algae. However, as well as raising awareness about the danger to ocean life caused by the industrial transformation of the environment, the algae also led to technovisionary speculation about the possibility of new biofuels. A *Financial Times* article noted: "But the crazy growth rates of algae under favourable conditions–doubling their mass every day or two–is one reason why they are seen as an attractive future prospect by the biofuels industry.".[127] An economic system that requires "crazy growth rates" finds a match in an equally virulent and invasive species. Not content with existent green algae, bioscientists are seeking to engineer new varieties that may be more efficiently harnessed to capitalism's energy requirements: algae for biofuels is one of the potential applications that Craig Venter promises for synthetic life.[128]

The notion of a technological fix to environmental problems is also dear to the hearts of nanovisionaries. Drexler's nanotechnology manifesto, *Engines of Creation*, contains a chapter on "The Limits to Growth," which presents the nanosphere as holding the solution to problems of resource limits: "When we develop pollution-free nanomachines to gather solar energy and resources, Earth will be able to support a civilization far larger and wealthier than any yet seen. . . The potential of Earth makes the resources we now use seem insignificant by comparison."[129] Historian

W. Patrick McCray argues that the techno-futurist thought of Eric Drexler and Ray Kurzweil was developed in reaction against the 1970s' discourse of "limits to growth." In opposition to the image of Earth as a closed system, in which resources were being rapidly depleted, and the law of entropy applied, techno-futurists like Drexler looked to the infinities of outer space. Before transferring these fantasies of superseding limits into the realm of nanotechnology, Drexler was an enthusiast for space colonies.[130] Access to resources beyond Earth remains central to Drexler's vision: "Yet Earth is but a speck... The resources of the solar system are truly vast, making the resources of Earth seem insignificant by comparison."[131] Similar extraterrestrial fantasies are found in the writings of technovisionaries such as Kurzweil and Moravec.

In Moravec, techno-futurist fantasies of artificial intelligence extending out beyond Earth into the universe combine with a romantic-primitivist critique of industrialism. Moravec's narrative begins with a loss of Eden and develops toward technological salvation. "A thousand centuries ago," he tells us, "the world was fully automated. Our ancestors were supported by the maintenance-free, self-operating machinery called Nature. But, in an Adamic bargain predating Faust, they meddled with the mechanism. By tilling and planting, they magnified the machinery's productivity but trapped themselves in a routine of heavy, unpleasant labor."[132] From agriculture developed urban civilization and modern industrial society. Unchanged biologically from our Stone Age ancestors, we are today born into a highly technologized, unnatural environment. There is a mismatch between the human organism and the industrial urban environment that "induces alienation in the midst of unprecedented physical plenty."[133] Since Moravec conceives of alienation in biological and essentialist terms, he can suggest that the problem is destined to be overcome by transcending and eliminating the biological human organism. "Technological evolution" will again restore us to our natural state of idleness as machines take over work, and "intelligence" will take flight from our unwieldy bodies to inhabit realms beyond Earth itself.[134]

Kurzweil's fantasy of "the Singularity," similarly to Moravec, denies limits by imaginatively escaping from the constraints of Earth as the relevant environment. In Kurzweil, the rejection of spatial limits (of Earth) and of temporal limits (via radical life extension) is achieved ultimately through decorporealization. When minds can be uploaded as information to computational hardware, then at that point the longevity of one's mind file will not depend on the continued viability of any particular hardware medium (for example, the survival of a biological body and brain). Ultimately, software-based humans. . . will live out on the Web, projecting bodies whenever they need or want them, including virtual bodies in diverse realms of virtual reality. . . and physical bodies comprising nanobot swarms and other forms of nanotechnology.[135]

Following abstract labor and abstract life, these fantasies involve a further abstraction: human existence is decorporealized and abstracted as "intelligence" and therefore delinked from its material ecological basis. Kurzweil's fantasy of endless growth deals with the problem of ecological limits just by denying the salience of ecology, seeking what he calls "transcendence" in a decorporealized, informatic consciousness.[136] But the fantasy of transcendence arrives at a state of incorporeal oneness with the universe that seems to be close to religious notions of the afterlife.[137] This artificial life of uploaded, incorporeal intelligence seems to be a form of death.

Artificial Life/Dead Planet

Artificial life and a dead planet are twin expressions of a world built on the basis of alienated labor. The alienation of one's own living activity produces an alienated relationship with the broader world of the living. The degradation of labor is implicated in the degradation of life. The imposition of capital's framework of value devalues the particularities and qualitative potentiality of the individual human being.[138] The broader living world of nature is also deprived of value, as that which cannot be rendered in cash terms no longer *has* value; hence, much of the Earth becomes a sink for pollution and other "externalities" of capitalist production. The standardization and disciplining of human productive activity is accompanied by the standardization and control of the reproductive processes of natural organisms. The living is reified, then, *symbolically* in terms of the way in which it is valued—quality being reduced to quantity—and *practically*, as both human activity and nature more broadly are degraded, standardized, and routinized, becoming increasingly *thing-like*.

As Philip K. Dick perceived, the reification of the living is accompanied by the animation of the non-living. The routinization of work makes mechanization possible, and subsequently is further imposed through mechanization. The sophistication of the capabilities of computers and automatic machinery develops in tandem with the abstraction and simplification of ever-broader swathes of human activity. The standardization, fragmentation, and control of living organisms are achieved by the granting of increasingly lifelike qualities and capacities to the non-living. So, we have technologized life and lifelike or "living" technology.

Drexler's designation of this living technology as "self-replicating capital" and "productive capital" is an analytical insight, the critical implications of which he himself cannot develop. The infusion of capital with life is accompanied by salvationist rhetoric in techno-futurist thinkers like Drexler, Moravec, and Kurzweil and is fundamental to their images of endless expansion and technological progress. As Cooper has argued, the technologization of life through biotechnology has been crucial as a way of maintaining the idea of the progressiveness of capitalism, against the challenge posed both by the threat of economic stagnation and by environmental consciousness of "limits to growth." Although seemingly far-fetched, the technological salvationism of thinkers like Drexler, Kurzweil, and Moravec expresses assumptions that are, in fact, pervasive in the ideology of modern technoscience. Today, as political or regulatory solutions to climate change are stymied by entrenched capitalist interests and by the anarchic international system of nation-state competition, hopes for a solution are increasingly vested in a technological fix, through geoengineering, however fantastical such technological solutions appear.[139] What geoengineering augurs is potentially the radical technologization of the planet's geophysical processes (solar reflectors in space, etc.). This would mean that the Earth itself becomes a capital-intensive system, requiring huge investments of capital to maintain its life-supporting systems. The common milieu of life, making possible all production and reproduction, is thus potentially transformed into an artificial milieu, dependent on and intertwined with capital. At the macro-scale of the Earth system, as well as the micro-scale of the genetic code, the reproduction of life is appropriated by, and subordinated to, the reproduction of capital.

The reification of the living and the animation of the non-living tend toward the environmental degradation of Earth so that life is no longer self-sustaining. For equilibrium, sustenance, and the promise of a future, the technovisionaries encourage us to look instead to the powers of capital, expressed in technological miracles of geoengineering, life in outer space, or uploadable intelligence. The renewal of capital as self-replicating, productive, self-valorizing value takes over from the renewal of life. Or, rather, the renewal of capital becomes the precondition for the renewal of life. Marx wrote in Volume 3 of *Capital*:

> With the development of relative surplus-value in the actual specifically capitalist mode of production, whereby the productive powers of social labour are developed, these productive powers and the social interrelations of labour in the direct labour-process seem transferred from labour to capital. Capital thus becomes a very mystic being since all of labour's social productive forces appear to be due to capital, rather than labour as such, and seem to issue from the womb of capital itself.[140]

As the powers of the living are annexed to technology, an asymmetric symbiosis with capital is increasingly imposed on the living world. Capital becomes the artificial womb for life. The condition of "living dead species" abstracted from their living milieu, surviving in an artificially preserved commodified form, comes to characterize life in general. Marx described capitalism as an inversion through which living labor is appropriated for the augmentation of dead labor, and dead labor rules over the living. The capitalist "vampire" sucks the living activity of the worker (and, we should add, of the broader natural world), and from this it appropriates and takes on the characteristics of life. Living death describes the character of capital itself as self-valorizing value. As labor and life are subsumed by capital, this condition of living death is also generalized. This is the meaning of artificial life on a dead planet.

Notes

1. Philip. K. Dick, *Do Androids Dream of Electric Sheep?* (London: Orion Books [1968] 1999), esp. 15.
2. Margaret Atwood, *Oryx and Crake* (New York: Anchor Books, 2003).
3. Daniel Dinello, *Technophobia: Science Fiction Fisions of Posthuman Technology* (Austin, TX: University of Texas Press, 2013).
4. Dinello, *Technophobia*, 1–17. Obviously, techno-enthusiasm has characterized much of the science fiction genre (e.g. Isaac Asimov and Arthur C. Clarke), and the technofuturist discourse of robotics and nanotechnology enthusiasts often references or overlaps with such techno-optimist science fiction. See Colin Milburn, *Nanovision: Engineering the future* (Durham, NC: Duke University Press, 2008), esp. 39–58.
5. Bill Joy, "Why the Future Doesn't Need Us," *Wired*, *8* (4) (April 2000). Retrieved from http://www.wired.com/wired/archive/8.04/joy.html?pg=1&topic=&topic_set=

6. Jacques Ellul, *The Technological Society* (New York, NY: Vintage Books, 1964), 85.
7. Philip K. Dick, (1995). "Man, Android, and Machine," in *The Shifting Realities of Philip K. Dick: Selected Literary and Philosophical Writings*, ed. Lawrence Sutin (New York, NY: Vintage Books [1976] 1995), 211–232, on 212.
8. Karl Marx, *Capital, Volume One*, trans. B. Fowkes (New York, NY: Vintage Books, 1977), 342.
9. Erich Fromm, *The Anatomy of Human Destructiveness* (New York, NY: Holt, Rinehart and Winston, 1973), 339, note 14; Mark Neocleous, "The Political Economy of the Dead: Marx's Vampires," *History of Political Thought*, 24 (4) (2003), 668–684; John Bellamy Foster and Brett Clark, "The Paradox of Wealth: Capitalism and Ecological Destruction," *Monthly Review*, 61 (6), 1–18.
10. Karl Marx, *Economic and Philosophic Manuscripts of 1844*, trans M. Milligan (New York, NY: International Publishers, 1964), 111.
11. Marx, *Economic and Philosophic Manuscripts*, 109. Emphasis in original.
12. John Bellamy Foster, *The Vulnerable Planet: A Short Economic History of the Environment* (New York: Monthly Review Press, 1994); James Gustave Speth, *The Bridge at the End of the World: Capitalism, the Environment, and Crossing from Crisis to Sustainability* (New Haven, CT: Yale University Press, 2008), 17–66.
13. Edward Yoxen, "Life as a Productive Force: Capitalising the Science and Technology of Molecular Biology," In Les Levidow and Bob Young eds., *Science, Technology and the Labour Process, Marxist studies, Volume 1* (Atlantic Highlands, NJ: Humanities Press, 1981), 67–122; Glenn Rikowski, "Alien life: Marx and the future of the human," *Historical Materialism*, 11 (2) (2003), 121–164.
14. Karl Marx, (1973). *Grundrisse: Foundations of the Critique of Political Economy*, trans. Martin Nicolaus (Harmondsworth, England: Penguin Books, 1973), 693; see also Finn Bowring, "From the Mass Worker to the Multitude: A Theoretical Contextualization of Hardt and Negri's Empire," *Capital and Class*, 83 (2004), 101–132, esp. 103–104.
15. Marx, *Grundrisse*, 704.
16. Harry Braverman, *Labor and Monopoly Capital: The Degradation of Work in the Twentieth Century* (New York: Monthly Review Press, 1974).
17. Marx, *Capital*, 150.
18. Bowring, "From the Mass Worker to the Multitude," 106; see also Michael Hardt and Antonio Negri, *Empire* (Cambridge, MA: Harvard University Press, 2000), 292.
19. The concept of abstract life is implied also by Melinda Cooper's discussion of organ transplantation as an abstraction of the "livable time of the

organ" from the body: Melinda Cooper, *Life as Surplus: Biotechnology and Capitalism in the Neoliberal Era* (Seattle, WA: University of Washington Press, 2008), 126. The idea that abstract life is closely related to abstract labor is also, I think, implied by Eugene Thacker's analysis of "biomaterial labor" and of biotechnology's "economic uses of 'life itself'": Eugene Thacker, *The Global Genome: Biotechnology, Politics, and Culture* (Cambridge, MA: The MIT Press, 2005), 202.
20. William Boyd, W. Scott Prudham, and Rachel A. Schurman, "Industrial Dynamics and the Problem of Nature," *Society and Natural Resources* 14 (2001): 555–570, 563.
21. Boyd, Prudham and Schurman, "Industrial Dynamics," 564.
22. Marx, *Capital*, 775.
23. Foster, *Vulnerable Planet*, 110.
24. Foster, *Vulnerable Planet*, 111.
25. Robert E. Kohler, R. E. (1994). *Lords of the Fly: Drosophila Genetics and the Experimental Life* (Chicago, IL: University of Chicago Press, 1994); Karen Rader, *Making Mice: Standardizing Animals for American Biomedical Research, 1900–1955* (Princeton, NJ: Princeton University Press, 2004).
26. Finn Bowring, *Science, Seeds, and Cyborgs: Biotechnology and the Appropriation of Life* (London: Verso, 2003), 134, 143.
27. John Johnston, *The Allure of Machinic Life: Cybernetics, Artificial Life, and the New AI* (Cambridge, MA: The MIT Press, 2008).
28. Rodney Brooks, *Flesh and Machines: How Robots Will Change Us* (New York, NY: Pantheon Books, 2002), x, 11.
29. Cooper, *Life as Surplus*.
30. Lexus, "Hello Someday" advertising campaign, October 2009.
31. Marx, *Grundrisse*, 701.
32. Richard E. Leakey and Robert Lewin, *The Sixth Extinction: Patterns of Life and the Future of Humankind* (New York, NY: Doubleday, 1995); Niles Eldredge, 1998. *Life in the Balance: Humanity and the Biodiversity Crisis* (Princeton, NJ: Princeton University Press, 1998); Anil Ananthaswamy, "Earth Faces Sixth Mass Extinction." *New Scientist* March 18, 2004, http://www.newscientist.com/article/dn4797-earth-faces-sixth-mass-extinction.html
33. Michael Novacek, "It Happened to Him. It's Happening to You," *Washington Post*, January 13, 2008, http://www.washingtonpost.com/wp-dyn/content/article/2008/01/11/AR2008011101994_pf.html; Jean-Michel Severino and Peter Seligmann, "Conservation with a Human Face," *Project Syndicate* (2008), http://www.projectsyndicate.org/commentary/severino6; Ananthaswamy, "Earth Faces Sixth Mass Extinction."
34. "Wildlife Populations 'Plummeting'," *BBC News*, May 16, 2008, http://news.bbc.co.uk/2/hi/uk_news/7403989.stm

35. ZSL Institute of Zoology, "Biodiversity Plummeting," Zoological Society of London, Institute of Zoology, *Science News*, May 16, 2008, May 16, http://www.zsl.org/science/news/biodiversity-plummeting,458,NS.html
36. Jeremy B. C. Jackson, "Ecological Extinction and Evolution in the Brave New Ocean," *Proceedings of the National Academy of Sciences*, 105 (1) (August 12, 2008), 11458–11465, http://www.pnas.org/content/105/suppl.1/11458.full
37. Quoted in John Vidal, "Last Chance for the Oceans?" *The Guardian Weekly*, November 7, 2008, 25–27, on 26.
38. John Grimond, "Troubled Waters," *The Economist*, January 3, 2009, 3–4.
39. Grimond, "Troubled Waters," 4.
40. "UN: Ocean Dead Zones 'Increasing Fast'," *MSNBC World News* October 23, 2006, http://www.msnbc.msn.com/id/15329993/; Grimond, "Troubled Waters," 4; Ker Than, "Global Warming to Create 'Permanent' Ocean Dead Zones?" *National Geographic News*, January 28, 2009, http://news.nationalgeographic.com/news/2009/01/090128-ocean-dead-zones.html
41. Kenneth R. Weiss, "Dark Tides, Ill Winds," *Los Angeles Times*, August 1, 2006, http://articles.latimes.com/2006/aug/01/local/me-ocean1
42. Debora MacKenzie, "Honeybees under Attack on all Fronts," *New Scientist*, February 16, 2009, http://www.newscientist.com/article/mg20126954.600-honeybees-under-attack-on-all-fronts.html; "Scientists Untangle Multiple Causes of Bee Colony Disorder," *Environment News Service*, July 29, 2009, http://www.ens-newswire.com/ens/jul2009/2009-07-29-094.asp
43. Elizabeth Kolbert, "The Sixth Extinction?" *The New Yorker* (May 25, 2009): 53–63, on 60–62.
44. "Worldwide Amphibian Declines: How Big is the Problem, What are the Causes and What Can be Done?" *Amphibiaweb*, January 22, 2009, http://amphibiaweb.org/declines/declines.html
45. Bette Hileman, "Frog Deformities Explained," *Chemical and Engineering News* (July 15, 2002), http://pubs.acs.org/cen/critter/frogs1.html
46. Quoted in Hileman, "Frog Deformities"; See also James P. Collins and Martha L. Crump, *Extinction in our times: Global Amphibian Decline* (Oxford: Oxford University Press, 2009), esp. pp. 8, 99–100, 101–104, 198–199.
47. Stephen Leahy, "Peak Soil: The Silent Global Crisis," September 14, 2008, http://stephenleahy.net/2008/09/14/peak-soil-the-silent-global-crisis/; see also Ian Sample, "Global Food Crisis Looms as Climate Change and Population Growth Strip Fertile Land," *The Guardian*, August 13, 2007, http://www.guardian.co.uk/environment/2007/aug/31/climatechange.food

48. Quoted in John Vidal, "Dust Storms Spread Deadly Diseases Worldwide," *The Observer*, September 27, 2009, http://www.guardian.co.uk/world/2009/sep/27/dust-storms-diseases-sydney
49. "Amazon Carbon Sink Effect 'Slows'," *BBC News*, March 10, 2004, http://news.bbc.co.uk/2/hi/americas/3499500.stm; "Amazon Destruction Accelerating," *BBC News*, May 19, 2005, (2005, May 19), http://news.bbc.co.uk/2/hi/americas/4561189.stm; Fred Pearce, "Global Meltdown," *The Guardian*, August 30, 2006, http://www.guardian.co.uk/environment/2006/aug/30/society.climatechange
50. "A World Imperiled: Forces Behind Forest Loss," *Mongobay.com*, circa 2009, retrieved December 15, 2009, from http://rainforests.mongabay.com/0801.htm;
   see also "70% deforestation cuts for Brazil," *BBC News*, December 2, 2008, http://news.bbc.co.uk/2/hi/science/nature/7759192.stm
51. J. Alan Pounds and Robert Puschendorf, "Ecology: Clouded Futures," *Nature*, 427 (January 8, 2004): 107–109; "Climate Change Will Significantly Increase Impending Bird Extinctions," *Science Daily*, December 7, 2007, http://www.sciencedaily.com/releases/2007/12/071206094116.htm
52. Quoted in Robin McKie, "Climate Guru Calls for 'Drastic Action'," *The Guardian Weekly*, January 23, 2009, 8.
53. C. D. Thomas, A. Cameron, R. Green, M. Bakkeness, L. J. Beaumont, Y. C. Collingham, . . S. E. Williams, "Extinction Risk from Climate Change," [Letter to the editor] *Nature*, January 8, 2004, http://www.nature.com/nature/journal/v427/n6970/full/nature02121.html
54. Philip Bethge, "Polar Bears for the South Pole? Biologists Debate Relocating Imperiled Species," *Spiegel Online*, November 23, 2007, http://www.spiegel.de/international/spiegel/0,1518,519271,00.html
55. Quoted in Suzanne Goldenberg, "Gore Urges Action on Stimulus Plan's Environmental Provisions," *The Guardian*, January 29, 2009, http://www.guardian.co.uk/world/2009/jan/28/al-gore-senate-stimulus-environment
56. Quoted in John Vidal, "Cities in Peril as Andean Glaciers Melt," *The Guardian* (August 29, 2006), 19.
57. Juliette Jowit, "Drought Will Create 'Economic Deserts'," *The Guardian Weekly* (November 7, 2008), 11.
58. Terry Glavin, *The Sixth Extinction: Journeys Among the Lost and Left Behind* (New York: Thomas Dunne Books, 2006); Daniel Nettle and Suzanne Romaine, *Vanishing Voices: The Extinction of the World's Languages* (Oxford: Oxford University Press, 2000).
59. Tom Wessels, *The Myth of Progress: Toward a Sustainable Future* (Burlington, VT: University of Vermont Press, 2006).

60. Glavin, *Sixth Extinction*, 214, 219; on 'Green Revolution,' see 217–223.
61. Barbara Adam, *Timescapes of Modernity: The Environment and Invisible Hazards* (London: Routledge, 1998), 141.
62. Quoted in Foster, *Vulnerable Planet*, 117.
63. Foster, *Vulnerable Planet*, 122.
64. Roger Horowitz, "Making the Chicken of Tomorrow: Reworking Poultry as Commodities and as Creatures, 1945–1990," In S.R. Schrepfer & P. Scranton eds., *Industrializing organisms: Introducing evolutionary history* (New York, NY: Routledge, 2004), 215–235, esp. 228–229.
65. Barry Commoner, *The Poverty of Power: Energy and the Economic Crisis* (New York, NY: Bantam Books, [1976] 1979), 211.
66. Commoner, *Poverty of Power*, 187, 212.
67. Foster, *Vulnerable Planet*, 120–121.
68. Glavin, *Sixth Extinction*, 20–21, 24–25, 38–39. See also Katherine Harmon, "Endangered species get iced in museum DNA repository," *Scientific American* (July 8, 2009), http://www.scientificamerican.com/article.cfm?id=endangered-species-dna
69. Glavin, *Sixth Extinction*, 39.
70. Glavin, *Sixth Extinction*, 30–31.
71. Bowring, *Science, Seeds, and Cyborgs*; D.D.T. Kelso, "The Migration of Salmon from Nature to Biotechnology," In R.A. Schurman & D.D.T. Kelso eds., *Engineering trouble: Biotechnology and its discontents* (Berkeley, CA: University of California Press, 2003), 84–110, on 93.
72. Les Levidow and Susan Carr, "GM Crops on Trial: Technological Development as Real-World Experiment," *Futures*, 39 (4) (2007): 408–431.
73. Kelso, "Migration of Salmon," 89.
74. Kelso, "Migration of Salmon," 101.
75. Thomas Ray, "An Evolutionary Approach to Synthetic Biology: Zen and the Art of Creating Life," In C.G. Langton (Ed.), *Artificial life: An Overview* (Cambridge, MA: MIT Press, 1995), 179–209, on 179–180.
76. Stefan Helmreich, *Silicon Second Nature: Culturing Artificial Life in a Digital World* (Berkeley, CA: University of California Press, 1998).
77. Sherry Turkle, *Life on Screen: Identity in the Age of the Internet* (New York, NY: Simon and Schuster, 1995), 154–158.
78. Ray, "Evolutionary Approach," 179.
79. Helmreich, *Silicon Second Nature*, 47.
80. Hans Moravec, *Robot: Mere Machine to Transcendent Mind* (New York: Oxford University Press, 1999), 111, 146–147.
81. Brooks, *Flesh and Machines*, 51.
82. Brooks, *Flesh and Machines*, 11.

83. Ian Sample, "'Sugar-Cube' Robots Could Team Up and Change Shape," *The Guardian* (March 13, 2013), http://www.guardian.co.uk/technology/2008/mar/13/robots.artificialintelligenceai/print
84. John Schwartz, "Creating Versatile New Robots to Mimic the Motions of Nature," *New York Times* article, reprinted in *The Observer* (Sunday, April 8, 2007), 6.
85. See Boston Dynamics, http://www.bostondynamics.com/ and the RiSE Project, http://kodlab.seas.upenn.edu/~rise/newsite/index.php?leaf=1
86. P. W. Singer, *Wired for War: The Robotics Revolution and Conflict in the Twenty-First Century* (New York, NY: Penguin, 2009), 111.
87. "Bomb Squad: Bees Trained to Sniff out Explosives," *The Guardian* (December 2, 2006), 27.
88. "Scientists Train Bees to Sniff out Bombs," *MSNBC* (November 28, 2006), http://www.msnbc.msn.com/id/15938954/
89. Jordan Lite, "FDA Approves Blood-thinner Atryn Made from Genetically Engineered Goats," *Scientific American* (February 9, 2009), http://www.scientificamerican.com/blog/post/fda-approves-blood-thinner-atryn-ma-2009-02-09/?id=fda-approves-blood-thinner-atryn-ma-2009-02-09
90. Quoted in Karen Barad, *Meeting the Universe Halfway: Quantum Physics and the Entanglement of Matter and Meaning* (Durham, NC: Duke University Press, 2007), 469 note 26; "GM Goat Spins Web-based Future," *BBC News* (August 21, 2000). http://news.bbc.co.uk/2/hi/science/nature/889951.stm
91. Peter Aldhous, and Andy Coghlan, "Ten Years On, Has the Cloning Dream Died?" *New Scientist* (July 1, 2006), 8–10.
92. Alok Jha, "Biologist Claims Significant Step Towards Artificial Life," *The Guardian*. (January 25, 2008), http://www.guardian.co.uk/science/2008/jan/25/genetics.science/print; "Patent Pending," *The Economist* (June 14, 2007), http://www.economist.com/sciencetechnology/displaystory.cfm?story_id=E1_JPPPQDR
93. Synthetic Genomics, "Venter Institute Scientists Create First Synthetic Bacterial Genome," Press Release, January 24, 2008, http://www.jcvi.org/cms/research/projects/synthetic-bacterial-genome/press-release/
94. Gary Robbins, "First Synthetic Cell Created by Scientists," *San Diego Union-Tribune* (May 21, 2010), 1–2.
95. Adam M. Hedgecoe, "Transforming Genes: Metaphors of Information and Language in Modern Genetics," *Science as Culture*, 8 (2) (1999): 209–229, esp. 217–218.
96. William Boyd, "Wonderful Potencies? Deep Structure and the Problem of Monopoly in Agricultural Biotechnology," in Rachel A. Schurman & D.D.T. Kelso eds., 1993, 24–62, on 31.

97. Quoted in Jha, "Biologist Claims Significant Step."
98. Quoted in Robbins, "First Synthetic Cell," 1.
99. Sanjida O'Connell, "Design for Life," *BBC Focus* (July 2006), 47–52.
100. O'Connell, "Design for Life," 49–50.
101. O'Connell, "Design for Life," 50.
102. Quoted in Alok Jha, "From the Cells Up," *The Guardian* (March 10, 2005), http://www.guardian.co.uk/science/2005/mar/10/science.research/print
103. Jha, "From the Cells Up."
104. "Playing Demigods," *The Economist* (August 31, 2006), http://www.economist.com/node/7854771
105. Clive Cookson, "A World Without Armies where Robots have Rights and Obligations." *Financial Times* (December 20, 2006), 3.
106. Nikolas Rose, "Molecular Biopolitics, Somatic Ethics and the Spirit of Biocapital," *Social Theory and Health* 5(1) (2007): 3–29, on 6–7.
107. Rose, "Molecular Biopolitics," 17.
108. Biotechnology and Biological Sciences Research Council, "BBSRC Priorities," BBSRC (UK) (c. 2009). Retrieved October 20, 2009, from http://www.bbsrc/ac.uk/funding/bbsrc_priorities.pdf
109. Richard Jones, *Soft Machines: Nanotechnology and Life* (Oxford: Oxford University Press, 2004), 125.
110. Jesse Emspak, "Nanotechnology May Have Found its Henry Ford: Tiny DNA Robots Could be the Future of Assembly Lines," *Christian Science Monitor* (March 27, 2009), http://www.csmonitor.com/Innovation/Pioneers/2009/0327/nanotechnology-may-have-found-its-henry-ford
111. Jones, *Soft Machines*, 125.
112. Cookson, "A World Without Armies."
113. Eric Drexler, *Engines of Creation: The coming era of nanotechnology* (New York: Anchor Press, 1986), 14, 54–58; Ray Kurzweil, *The Singularity is Near: When Humans Transcend Biology* (New York: Penguin Books, 2005), 228–230.
114. Kurzweil, *Singularity*, 115.
115. Drexler, *Engines of Creation*, 94. Emphasis in original.
116. Cooper, *Life as Surplus*, 38. See also Kaushik Sunder Rajan, *Biocapital: The Constitution of Postgenomic Life* (Durham, NY: Duke University Press, 2006).
117. Raphael Minder, "India Blames Finance Markets for Rises," *Financial Times* (May 6, 2008), 2; Javier Blas and Guy Dinmore, "Rich Nations Attacked over Biofuels," *Financial Times* (June 4, 2008), 2; Jonathan Watts, "Food Supplies at Risk from Price Speculation, Warns Expert," *The Guardian* (August 19, 2009), http://www.guardian.co.uk/environment/2009/aug/19/food-supply-risk-speculators

118. Javier Blas, "The End of Abundance," *Financial Times* (June 2, 2008), 11.
119. Quoted in Raphael Minder, Andrew Bounds, and Jenny Wiggins, "Nestlé Urges EU to Soften GM Line," *Financial Times* (June 23, 2008), 6.
120. Jeffrey Sachs, "Stagflation is Back: Here's How to Beat It," *Fortune* (June 9, 2008), 29–31, on 31.
121. Alan Beattie, "Seeds of Change: Africa Seeks to Engineer an Agricultural Revolution," *Financial Times* (June 3, 2008), http://www.ft.com/cms/s/0/ba4377d4-30c4-11dd-bc93-000077b07658.html#axzz1Td26Iwnd
122. John Vidal and Felicity Lawrence, "Britain Must Launch GM Food Revolution says Chief Scientist," *The Guardian* (January 6, 2010), http://www.guardian.co.uk/environment/2010/jan/06/gm-food-revolution-government-scientist
123. David Adam, "US Answer to Global Warming: Smoke and Giant Space Mirrors," *The Guardian* (January 27, 2007), http://environment.guardian.co.uk/print/0,,329698233-121568,00.html; William Broad, "How to Cool a Planet (Maybe)," *New York Times* (June 27, 2006), http://www.nytimes.com/2006/06/27/science/earth/27cool.html
124. Etc. Group, *Gambling with Gaia*. Communique #93 (January 2007), http://www.etcgroup.org/en/materials/publications.html?pub_id=608
125. Amit Bhattacharya, "Antarctic Mission Runs into Protest," *Times of India* (January 14, 2009), http://timesofindia.indiatimes.com/Antarctic_mission_runs_into_protest/articleshow/3974980.cms
126. Fred Pearce, "Global Meltdown," *The Guardian* (August 30, 2006), http://www.guardian.co.uk/environment/2006/aug/30/society.climatechange
127. Clive Cookson, "Curse and Blessing of Blooming Algae," *Financial Times* (July 13, 2008), 3.
128. "Craig's Twist," *The Economist* (July 18, 2009), 82–83.
129. Drexler, *Engines of Creation*, 162. Drexler is also an enthusiast for cryogenic freezing as "insurance" against loss of species (ibid., 123).
130. W. Patrick McCray, "Of Futures and Fringes: California's Technological Enthusiasts, 1970–1990," Paper Presented at the Science Studies Colloquium, University of California, San Diego, April 20, 2009; Drexler, *Engines of Creation*, 165.
131. Drexler, *Engines of Creation*, 162.
132. Moravec, *Robot*, 127.
133. Moravec, *Robot*, 7.
134. Moravec, *Robot*, 9.
135. Kurzweil, *Singularity*, 325.
136. Kurzweil, *Singularity*, 388.

137. Robert M. Geraci, "Apocalyptic AI: Religion and the Promise of Artificial Intelligence," *Journal of the American Academy of Religion*, 76 (1) (2008): 138–166.
138. Istvan Mészáros, *The Challenge and Burden of Historical Time* (New York, NY: Monthly Review Press, 2008), 47.
139. Richard York, Brett Clark, and John Bellamy Foster, "Capitalism in Wonderland," *Monthly Review*, 61 (1) (2009), 1–18, esp. 14–15.
140. Karl Marx, K. (1967). *Capital: A Critique of Political Economy. Volume III: The Process of Capitalist Production as a Whole* (New York: International Publishers, 1967), 827.

CHAPTER 3

Speed and Stasis

THE TEMPORALITY OF TECHNO-FUTURISM

Brian Aldiss's short story "Supertoys Last All Summer Long" (first published in 1969) tells of a robotic boy desperate, but unable, to please his narcissistic human "mother," and terrified of the truth that he himself is not a "real" person. This depiction of inner isolation is set in a world of consumerist simulacra, in which time is at a standstill: a house which is an electronically generated "mirage" of a Georgian mansion, a simulated garden in which "it was always summer" and the trees were "in perpetual leaf."[1] The mother's restless self-absorption is expressed by Aldiss as a state in which, "Time waited on her shoulder with... manic sloth."[2] Alongside lived stasis, there is the movement of technology and business. The narrative switches to the corporate executive husband's speech announcing new, advanced forms of humanoid robots made with "synthetic flesh": "For the future, we plan more models... of more advanced design, true bio-electronic beings." He confidently sets out the future as a series of technological inevitabilities: "Not only will they possess their own computers, capable of individual programming: they will be linked to the Ambient, the World Data Network." These technological advances, he asserts, hold the promise of future human happiness, including the overcoming of the loneliness that haunts everyday life: "Thus everyone will be able to enjoy the equivalent of an Einstein in their own homes. Personal isolation will then be banished for ever!" The emptiness of these promises is obvious as Aldiss snaps the reader back to the inertia of the home and the unbearable gulf between the boy and his mother: "Her face was blank... He did not move; she did not move."[3]

In Stanley Kubrick and Steven Spielberg's film *A.I.*, based loosely on Aldiss's story, is a scene in which the android boy, David, sits trapped underwater in his "amphibicopter" amidst the ruins of Coney Island, New York. He emerges two thousand years later, physically and mentally unchanged, from what has now become glacial ice. In this future setting, long after the demise of the human species, far-advanced robots have evolved from human beings' more primitive experiments in robotics and artificial intelligence. The film rushes the time frame forward via a scene of absolute stillness, with David frozen in permanent childhood.[4]

The combination of the driving forward of technological change into an open future with stasis or entrapment in an eternal present is characteristic of advanced capitalism. It is a feature of lived experience and of capitalist ideology that is also part of everyday life (e.g. through media and the consumer spectacle). The individual is assailed with new products, versions, "updates," "upgrades," and technological and biomedical "breakthroughs." The worker and consumer must keep up to date with, adapt to, and "stay on top of" these changes. One must be "flexible," updating one's skills to keep up with "changes in the labor market" and new technologies at work. Change is progress; new technologies are better, faster, and more capable than old ones. There is no sense or point in opposing such change. In practical terms, it will mean being "left behind," being out of work, and being cut off. In ideological terms, it would mean being an irrational Luddite.

And yet, this perpetual motion becomes monotonous. The next must-see film or must-have item is not so different from the last, but each has its brief moment when it is the absolute goal of consumption (corresponding to Warhol's 15 minutes of fame of the modern celebrity).[5] The pushing forward of capitalist production with ever-new products is, for the consumer, a race forward and the endless repetition of the same activity of consumption. Similarly, the necessity for workers (especially in the contemporary post-Fordist "flexible" labor market) to upgrade and update themselves by acquiring new skills all too often is a way not of improving their standard of living, but just maintaining it, or just surviving. The movement from one temporary job to another gives everyday life a quality of what Ivor Southwood calls "non-stop inertia."[6] Hartmut Rosa presents a similarly paradoxical characterization of contemporary life: the "frenetic standstill."[7]

Running to stand still is inherent to capitalism. As Marx emphasized, capitalism is unique as a social system that must produce continual and radical change, and continually transform the means of production, in order to maintain its functioning. A slowdown in growth (let alone its elimination or reversal) is a disaster for the capitalist economy. In order to preserve itself as a system—in order to keep social relations as they are—capitalism must run forward, revolutionizing production in the process. Herbert Marcuse wrote: "Underneath its obvious dynamics, this society is a thoroughly static system of life: self-propelling in its oppressive productivity."[8]

Ideologically, capitalism is presented by its defenders as "the end of ideology" and, more recently, "the end of history," the most rational and most free society possible. Historical alternatives, especially Communism, are supposedly revealed as mere mistakes or deviations from the true path of capitalist modernization. It is entailed by the end of history thesis that this condition must last forever (unless derailed by some apocalypse threatening humanity itself). Continual change in production and consumption is matched by the declaration of the impossibility of fundamental progressive change in social relations. Slavoj Žižek notes that contemporary culture suggests no limits to personal freedoms that can be satisfied by commodities and technology: "'[N]othing is impossible': we can enjoy sex in all its perverse versions, entire archives of music, films and TV series are there to download, space travel is available to everyone (at a price)." However, when it comes to "socio-economic relations, our era... has... accepted the constraints of reality—read: capitalist socio-economic reality—with all its impossibilities."[9] The economic and institutional context must remain perpetually frozen in neoliberal capitalism. Debord wrote: "Nothing stops for the spectacle; this condition is natural to it, yet completely opposed to its inclination."[10] The "inclination" of the spectacle is to hold things as they are, to suggest that each product is "eternal," to suggest that it itself—capitalism—is eternal. But in order to hold social relations still, to preserve itself, it must produce change.

Marx referred to capital as "the moving contradiction."[11] Each moment of capitalism is bursting with contradictions that produce instability—the antagonisms inherent in capital's exploitation of labor and in the competitive dynamic of the market. Since each moment is potentially explosive, capitalism must continually escape by "fleeing forward into the future," as Nick Dyer-Witheford puts it.[12]

Capitalism's compulsive technological development—Schumpeter's "creative destruction"—is reflected ideologically in technological futurism. This is the framework of thought based on the idea that there will be future technological solutions to whatever problems exist in the present and that technology is, by itself, bringing closer future well-being, for example, the end of hunger, the end of disease, the end of death. In this way, capitalism tries to race forward out of its present crises, not only technologically, but also ideologically, as techno-futurists ask us to take our eyes off the present and refocus on "tomorrow's world."

What unites techno-futurist manifestos like nanotechnology pioneer Eric Drexler's *Engines of Creation* (1986), roboticist Hans Moravec's *Robot: From Mere Machine to Transcendent Mind* (1999), and computer engineer and inventor Ray Kurzweil's *The Singularity is Near* (2005), is a common vision in which humans are destined to merge with machines or be supplanted by machines.[13] These are not idle fantasies, but rather are linked to well-funded practical efforts to develop autonomous robots, intelligent computer systems, and nanoscale manufacturing. While more specialized scientists may distance themselves from the fantastical visions of these thinkers, radical visions of the future have nevertheless been highly significant in constituting fields such as nanotechnology and in attracting funding by claiming status as "cutting-edge."[14] In early 2009, Kurzweil established the Singularity University in California, offering courses in artificial intelligence, nanotechnology, and biotechnology. These are fields which Kurzweil believes are already converging with each other, and the development of which will ultimately make possible the merging of human and machine and the takeover of technological creativity and development by machinic intelligence, an event which he calls "the Singularity." The institution is backed by Google, which, in 2012, appointed Kurweil as director of engineering, and NASA has allowed it to use its Ames Research Center in Moffett Field, California. The expensive courses are geared toward the interests of the high-tech elite of Silicon Valley. As *The Guardian* puts it, "The idea is that these people are in place for when this Singularity happens and they almost self-fulfill this prophecy."[15] Kurzweil's ideology of the Singularity taps into the techno-enthusiast culture of Silicon Valley. As well as the "university," his Singularity Institute for Artificial Intelligence in San Francisco also has connections with Silicon Valley and e-commerce. *Time* magazine notes:

"It counts among its advisers Peter Thiel, a former CEO of Paypal and an early investor in Facebook." (Thiel also founded the defense/intelligence agency contractor Palantir Technologies and has been a major financial donor to the right-wing libertarian politician Ron Paul). The institute's "Singularity Summit" includes venture capitalists such as Thiel, as well figures from high-tech business, academia, and media.[16]

Support from corporations or government agencies such as the Defense Advanced Research Projects Agency (which has funded Moravec's research) means that these technological visions are backed by material power.[17] When MIT roboticist Rodney Brooks writes that his prototypes are "a long awaited and necessary step towards the ultimate dream of self-evolving machines," one wonders *whose* dream this is.[18] What allows a small technical cadre to pursue these extravagant dreams? David Noble observes that technical intellectuals court the dominant powers because "it is the access to that power, with its huge resources, that allows them to dream... and the reality of that power that brings their dreams to life."[19]

Techno-futurist dreams have an important ideological function today when there is increasing societal consciousness of the destructive ecological consequences of capitalist growth. In contrast to this growing consciousness of limits, techno-futurists assert the possibility of endless growth, through the mastering of the nanoscale allowing radical new manipulations of matter, the alteration of human existence through the uploading of minds to machines, and the colonization of outer space.[20] Implicit, and sometimes explicit, in this discourse is the continued progressiveness of capitalism. Tomorrow's world, in capitalist ideology, will be technologically advanced, but socially it will be like the present. This is the meaning of David Noble's statement that "Modern Americans confront a world in which everything changes, yet nothing moves": technological change without movement in a historical sense.[21]

However, there is continuing contradiction inherent in the attempt to hold things still within a system that, precisely in order to do this, cannot hold still. Techno-futurism is an ideological attempt to overcome this contradiction by constructing progress as technological development, entirely decoupled from human activity and from history. Drexler, Moravec, and Kurzweil project linear time as the deterministic self-development of technology. The relationship between past, present, and future is traced by technology itself, and the future is being delivered through the acceleration of technological momentum. Techno-futurists describe this seemingly transcendental process of technological change with quasi-religious awe.

Linear Time and the Technological Imperative

Techno-futurism begins from the assumption that technology is an autonomous force in the world. This assumption is explicit in *What Technology Wants*, a book published in 2010 by the "new economy" enthusiast and founding editor of *Wired* magazine, Kevin Kelly. Kelly argues that technology, like life, follows a "self-propelling," evolutionary trajectory.[22] The "cyclotron of social betterment," Kelly writes, "is propelled by technology... each rise in social organization throughout history was driven by an insertion of new technology."[23] But who, or what, does the inserting of technology? Here, Kelly's thought takes a mystical turn. At times, his technological determinism is framed within a kind of high-tech animism, in which technology is not only autonomous, but also in a sense alive, and perhaps a supernatural power. He writes of technology as "a force—a vital spirit that throws us forward or pushes against us. Not a thing but a verb." Kelly struggles for words to express this riddle. Later in the book, he speculates in theological terms: "The ongoing self-organized mutability of life, evolution, mind, and the technium is a reflection of God's becoming, God-as-Verb unleashes a set of rules that unfold into an infinite game, a game that continually loops back into itself." Getting nowhere with these speculations, he sums up "God or not, self-creation is a mystery."[24]

In Kurzweil's *The Age of Spiritual Machines* (1999), a flow chart depicts a series of processes: biological evolution, the development of the human species, the emergence of technology out of biological evolution, and the way in which "technology begets computation." The chart is superimposed on an illustration showing the Milky Way, a cell, the evolution of the human species, industrial technology (an axle and gear wheel), and the personal computer. The implication is that technology emerges out of the cosmos itself. Human beings are a stage in this process of emergence, but the entire process is the expression of more fundamental principles expressing the evolutionary emergence of order out of chaos. The axle intrudes into the center of the picture, the power source unseen, suggesting a cosmic engine driving universal "acceleration."[25]

Kurzweil's later book, *The Singularity is Near*, likewise presents technology as a "continuation" out of biological evolution, and his theory of technological evolution is illustrated with an array of graphs plotting developments such as the rate of adoption of new technologies, the miniaturization of components, and the increasing speeds and falling costs of computing technologies.[26] History is subsumed into these trajectories: for example, "Countdown to Singularity" plots "events" from the Cambrian explosion to the emergence of *Homo erectus*, spoken language, art, early cities, writing, printing, industrial revolution, telephone, electricity, radio, and computer. The overarching principle of "continual acceleration" is shown in the "shorter time to the next event." It was "two billion years from the origin of life to cells," but only "fourteen years from the PC to the World Wide Web."[27] "It's really amazing how smooth these trajectories are," marvels Kurzweil.[28]

He regards these trajectories as law-like. In his discussion of nanotechnology, he asserts "The inevitability of a transformed future," describing nanotechnology as the "inevitable end result of the ongoing miniaturization of technology of all kinds."[29] Kurzweil understands human history, for example, the emergence of art and urbanization, as consisting of moments within the overall trajectory, from the biological to the technological. Particular social transformations can be understood as deriving from these technological trajectories. Both Kurzweil's technological determinism and his capitalist triumphalism are evident in his account of the collapse of the Soviet Union:

> It was not Boris Yeltsin standing on a tank that overturned the 1991 coup against Mikhail Gorbachev, but rather the clandestine network of fax machines, photocopiers, video recorders, and personal computers that broke decades of totalitarian control of information. The movement toward democracy and capitalism and the attendant economic growth that characterized the 1990s were all fueled by the accelerating force of these person-to-person communication technologies.[30]

Kurzweil's technological determinism is based on a view of technology as its own agency: it was not human beings, but machines that overturned the Soviet Union. The Fukuyamian end of history was never really history at all, but trajectory.

In lieu of human agency and history, "change" itself becomes a force in the world. According to Hans Moravec, "Progressive change sculpted our universe and our societies." History is the revelation of this principle of "universal change," which is manifested in the discovery of linear time: "[O]nly very recently has human culture seen beyond the short cycles of day and night, summer and winter, birth and death, to recognize it. No sooner was universal change noted in the traces of history than its accelerating pace becomes discernible in a single lifetime."[31] In this ideological framework, linear time expresses the autonomous and independent trajectory of technology. It is technology itself that is taking us into this open future, and the future is described in technological terms. A study by the US Congress's Joint Economic Committee, "Nanotechnology: The Future is Coming Sooner Than You Think," states:

> Enhanced abilities to understand and manipulate matter at the molecular and atomic levels promise a wave of significant new technologies over the next five decades. Dramatic breakthroughs will occur in diverse areas such as medicine, communications, computing, energy, and robotics. These changes will generate large amounts of wealth and force wrenching changes in existing markets and institutions.[32]

What produces change is not people, but "enhanced abilities" manifested in science and technology. The problem people face is to adapt to the "wrenching changes" produced by these impersonal and abstract "abilities."

We are told that there is no point in resisting such change. Setting out their program for future human immortality in their book, *Fantastic Voyage*, Kurzweil and his co-author Terry Grossman disparage as "regressive" Francis Fukuyama's concerns that biotechnological enhancement will eliminate human nature. "Ultimately," Kurzweil and Grossman say, "such opposition will end up being mere stones in a torrent of innovation, with the continued flow of progress passing around these barriers."[33] In *The Age of Spiritual Machines*, Kurzweil asserts that technological progress cannot be stopped: "The Law of Accelerating Returns forbids it!"[34] When computer scientist Bill Joy warned about the dangers inherent in the self-replicating capacities of genetically engineered life-forms, and new forms of robotics and nanotechnology, Moravec's response was the bald assertion that "We will turn into robots. It's both inevitable and desirable." The process of change is "bigger than we are. We are merely components within it."[35]

Drexler's manifesto for nanotechnology is shot through with the assertion of imperatives and expresses a view of technological development as independent of human agency. Drexler sees technological development as evolution, and he frequently resorts to biological metaphors, for example, marveling at the speed with which "technologies grow and spawn."[36] Biological and technological evolution share a tendency toward increasing complexity— "the emergence of ever more complex and capable forms of life... [and] the emergence of ever more complex and capable forms of hardware."[37] The notion of evolution in Drexler's work entails necessity. Technological determinism results from the survival of the fittest, and the Darwinian struggle is continued in market competition:

> The global technology race has been accelerating for billions of years. The earthworm's blindness could not block the development of sharp-eyed birds. The bird's small brain and clumsy wings could not block the development of human hands, minds, and shotguns. Likewise, local prohibitions cannot block advances in military and commercial technology.[38]

Nature and society are antagonistic settings of a universal technological arms race. On this view, it is necessary to stay competitive, keep up to date, or be wiped out.

In order to understand cultural change, Drexler reaches for Richard Dawkins' notion of replicating patterns or "memes" (which neatly fits with Drexler's own fascination with self-replicating machines). Drexler writes that "[j]ust as genes propagate themselves in the gene pool by leaping from body to body... via sperms or eggs, so memes propagate themselves in the meme pool by leaping from brain to brain via a process which, in the broad sense, can be called imitation." This account denies history as a human process. Drexler's agents are replicators—genes and memes, to which he aims to add his nanotechnological replicating machines. Humans are reduced to biological components that are themselves products of these more basic agents: "Genes built brains skilled at imitation."[39] Or human beings appear as cheerleaders for, and facilitators of, this impersonal process of technological evolution: "A new space program has risen from the ruin of the old. A new generation of space advocates, engineers, and entrepreneurs now aims to make space the frontier it should have been from the beginning—a place for development and use, not for empty political gestures." To the extent that there are anything like human historical actors in Drexler's account, these are human beings who are aligned with the technological imperative, and who represent or are allied with capital.[40]

Drexler combines a general view of technological development as an autonomous process with a specific agenda for the development of technologies that are literally autonomous. The "engines of creation" that he foresees and advocates are nanoscale "assemblers," machines on the scale of molecules that would have the ability to replicate and assemble into larger machines in infinitely complex patterns. These self-replicating machines would represent an entirely new mode of automation, autonomously building objects atom by atom. Drexler portrays the development of these assemblers as the next stage of technological evolution. Already, he suggests, industrial automation is leading toward machines that make machines: "Advances in automation will lead naturally toward mechanical replicators, whether or not anyone makes them a specific goal. As competitive pressures force increased automation, the need for human labor in factories will shrink."[41] Truly autonomous self-replication will come from machines at the molecular scale, machines that resemble cells or "instead resemble factories shrunk to cellular size."[42] These "replicating assemblers," he argues, "will copy themselves by the ton, then make other products such as computers, rocket engines, chairs, and so forth... They will indeed be engines of abundance."[43]

These self-replicating machines would be the concrete realization of technology as a force independent from human agency. This is also the realization of the drive to emancipate capital from its dependence on human labor. Drexler claims that "Since this self-replicating capital will be able to double many times per day, only demand and available resources will limit its quantity. Capital as such need cost virtually nothing."[44]

The future Drexler envisages is one of frictionless capitalism with no labor costs or labor conflict and no tax since "governments with their own replicators and raw materials will have less reason to tax people." Resource scarcity will also have been conquered since "assemblers will be able to make almost anything from dirt and sunlight." The resources of space will be at our disposal with "rubble from asteroids" and "assemblers in space [that] will run off cheap sunlight."[45]

Moravec creates a similar image of the takeover of production by machines, tapping the cornucopia of outer space, and the unfettered movement of technology and capital:

> No less than today's organizations, fully automated companies will compete with one another... To robots built for it, outer space will offer unprecedented energy, materials, room, and perhaps freedom from taxation for these activities—a tremendous competitive advantage. Sooner rather than later, automated industry will grow away from earth.[46]

The passage reveals how Moravec's technological thinking is rooted in existing capitalist structures. The fruit of automation will be the merger between corporate monopoly and machine, that is, "fully automated companies." Human beings meanwhile will be passive consumers of the products of these "robot industries" and will gradually become marginal or obsolete, unless humans transform themselves to keep up with the ever-evolving AI: "Just possibly, human personalities could participate in some way in the mainstream of this future activity, either under the wings of superintelligent hosts, or by being transformed into a compatible form—surely becoming very unhuman in the process."[47] In Moravec, the open-ended future of linear time is an epic tale in which capital itself is the hero, and human beings play a supporting role, destined to be pushed aside unless they remake themselves as technology-capital.

Moravec connects this vision of becoming capital with a utopian language of transcending capitalism. Autonomous technology leads to capital without capitalists: "Like humans pushed out of labor markets by cheaper and better robotic workers, owners will be pushed out of capital markets by much cheaper and better robotic decision makers. The evaporation of ownership will end capitalism, but capital enterprises will thrive as never before."[48] Moravec's vision here resonates with the technocratic utopianism of Henri de Saint-Simon and Thorstein Veblen, but he envisages the perfection of economic rationality taking the form of machinic rather than human intelligence. Rather than *having* capital, Moravec's utopia is one in which we *are* capital. Although he calls it "capitalism's end," it is more the absolute dominance of capitalism, in which real subsumption has pulled in humanity and life as a whole, so that capital now takes on the attributes of life: "The dynamics of capitalism will be replaced by the dynamics of biological reproduction. The ultimate payoff for success in the marketplace will no longer be monetary return on investment, but reproductive success."[49]

This utopia of total roboticization represents the apotheosis of the capitalist ideology of technical progress, which Noble has dubbed "progress without people."[50] As progress is reduced to the perfection of technology, human beings become the alienated spectators of this technical self-perfection and the self-augmentation of capital. For humans to participate in the linear time of technical progress, they must themselves become machinic capital.

Kurzweil predicts that "By the time of the Singularity, there won't be a distinction between humans and technology."[51] "We are going to merge with our technology," he emphatically asserts.[52] In Kurzweil's imagined future, the contents of human brains will be uploadable to computers, allowing the storage as data of "a person's entire personality, memory, skills, and history." The mind will be "reinstantiated" in a "powerful computational substrate."[53] As the mind is shifted from biological brain to computer hardware, the body will also be transformed. Kurzweil asserts that "We Are Becoming Cyborgs" and states that "By the 2030s we will become more non-biological than biological."[54] Ultimately, we might not need physical bodies. Our brains-in-computers would need only the semblance of corporeality, "virtual bodies in completely realistic virtual environments."[55] Alternatively, we could have bodies vastly different to the current biological form. These might be "nanotechnology-based physical bodies" that form "foglets" melding into their surroundings. Through these formless forms, we could so control our environment that the distinction between physical and virtual reality would become moot: "They're called 'foglets' because if there's a sufficient density of them in an area, they can control sound and light to form variable sounds and images. They are essentially creating virtual-reality environments externally (that is in the physical world) rather than internally (in the nervous system)."[56]

In Kurzweil's utopia, nature becomes entirely plastic—the plaything of these transhuman minds. His reductionist form of materialism ends in a kind of idealism, in which boundaries between mind and world, virtual and real, are broken down as the world becomes infinitely manipulable according to the desires of his posited transhumans. He writes:

> [T]he longevity of one's mind file will not depend on the continued viability of any particular hardware medium (for example, the survival of a biological body and brain). Ultimately software-based humans will be vastly extended beyond the severe limitations of humans as we know them today. They will live out on the Web, projecting bodies whenever they need or want them, including virtual bodies in diverse realms of virtual reality, holographically projected bodies, foglet-projected bodies, and physical bodies comprising nanobot swarms and other forms of nanotechnology.[57]

As the world becomes infinitely malleable, the boundary between the thinking and desiring subject and the world breaks down. Mind is transferred to computer. This computer is not a discrete device; rather, Kurzweil talks about "the computational potential of an Earth-size planet and computers on the scale of solar systems, of galaxies, and of the entire known universe."[58] Bodies would similarly dissipate into real or virtual swarms spreading out into the universe.

Kurzweil's progress without people merges the human being into machine and ultimately dissolves the machine into the universe. His linear trajectory ends in a vision of cosmic oneness. The denial of the human subject in the impersonal deterministic trajectory of technology opens the way for a peculiarly inhuman utopianism. This denouement was already contained in, and follows from, Kurzweil's technological determinist premise. The human being as subject is ruled out from the beginning, replaced with the impersonal trajectory of natural and technological evolution. The science-fiction image of the dissolution of the human being into information/matter is just the imaginative portrayal of what is more abstractly assumed as the premise of Kurzweil's technological philosophy.

Escape Velocity

Techno-futurist discourse intersects with the "new economy" jargon that accompanied the dot-com bubble in the late 1990s. In the 1990s, the transformation of industrial capitalism into an "information economy" was presented as holding the key to prosperity. The pundits of the "information age" assured us that, in this "new economy," there would be no boom and slump. The dematerialization of economic goods meant liberation from scarcity. In his 1998 information economy manifesto, *New Rules for the New Economy*, Kelly announced that "[p]lentitude, not scarcity, governs the network economy." Since information can be infinitely copied, "[w]hatever can be made, can be made in abundance."[59] Furthermore, networks offered the promise of unlimited growth "as the number of nodes in a network increases arithmetically, the value of the network increases exponentially." The scope and value of the network "escalates rapidly." The network economy offers the prospect of an "amazing boom."[60] This optimism was informed by the idea that the problems of industrial capitalism—resource scarcity, pollution, and labor conflict—would be overcome in the immaterial realm of information. In this new economy, we would be "living on thin air," in the words of British "knowledge economy" cheerleader Charles Leadbeater.[61]

This promise of abundance was linked with speed. Information technology allowed, what Bill Gates called, "business at the speed of thought." Gates extolled information as the corporation's "digital nervous system." Rapid feedback from sales to production would help the company to have good "reflexes," allowing it to adapt to unforeseen market shifts or crises.[62] Information technology would help reduce time to market, making product cycles more rapid.[63] According to Kelly, new technologies would allow communication, transactions, and the process of innovation to take place in less and less time. One had to keep up with change, and embrace "flux," in order to survive what Kelly called the "tornado of innovation."[64] Kelly writes, "The network economy is so primed to generate self-making newness that we may experience this ceaseless tide of birth as a type of violence."[65] But any attempt to hold things still threatened stagnation: "When flux is inhibited, slow death takes over... If you can stand the turmoil, flux triumphs."[66]

"Flux," "change," and "acceleration" cannot be resisted. The only response is to give oneself over to these forces. But the promise put forward by the techno-futurists is that this technological trajectory is in itself a form of liberation. This is suggested by the notion of "escape velocity," which has become a key motif in techno-futurist literature. The concept refers to the speed at which an object is able to break free from a gravitational field. When a rocket reaches "escape velocity," it can leave the Earth's orbit. Moravec uses the term as the title for the first chapter of his 1999 book, in which he writes of the "accelerating" process of "universal change": "By almost any measure—energy, information, speed, distance, temperature, variety—the developed world is growing more capable and complex faster than ever before... Today the pace strains the limits of human adaptability.... the acceleration continues, as machines take over where humans falter." The outcome is "self-accelerated computer evolution" in which automation speeds innovation, yielding further advances in automation, leading ultimately to the merging of human and machine.[67]

The term is also employed by Aubrey de Grey, a British theorist in the field of gerontology, who claims that aging and senescence will be overcome by modern medicine, making immortality possible. De Grey calls "longevity escape velocity" the "threshold rate of biomedical progress that will allow us to stave off aging indefinitely." He explains, "If we can make rejuvenation therapies work well enough to give us time to make them work better, that will give us enough additional time to make them work better still."[68] If sufficient new therapies are introduced rapidly enough, one just has to stay alive long enough to benefit from each new breakthrough in order to stay alive forever.

Mark Dery took the "escape velocity" metaphor as title for his insightful 1996 study of cyberculture, in which he explored the ideas of Moravec and other "transhumanists," and cultural currents in performance art, music, and science fiction that treated new technologies as an escape from the body. Dery wrote that "cyberculture is approaching escape velocity in the philosophical as well as the technological sense. It resounds with transcendentalist fantasies of breaking free from limits of any sort, metaphysical as well as physical."[69] The notion of achieving escape velocity, a point at which one is released from constraint, gives an apocalyptic and redemptive significance to technological momentum.

Drexler writes, giddily, about the "sheer speed of thought" that artificial intelligence will be able to obtain. "In an hour," a sophisticated form of artificial intelligence would be able to complete "the work of centuries." "[A]utomated engineering systems will move technology forward with stunning speed" as intelligent machines build still more intelligent machines.[70] These developments "will speed our advance toward the limits of the possible."[71]

Society needs to adapt to this increasing pace of development: "To prepare for the assembler breakthrough, society must learn to learn faster."[72] But in Drexler's view, technology obviates the need for structural social change. Redistribution of wealth is misguided and, Drexler suggests, harmful. With the unlimited abundance that technology promises, there is simply no need for redistribution:

> The history of human advance proves that the world game can be positive-sum. Accelerating economic growth during recent centuries shows that the rich can get richer while the poor get richer... Space resources and replicating assemblers will accelerate this historic trend beyond the dreams of economists, launching the human race into a new world.[73]

Escape velocity is, in Drexler's thought, not a metaphor, but literal. The escape from limits, promising total plenitude, derives ultimately from the escape from Earth. Contrary to theorists of "limits to growth," Drexler denies that we are close to using up the Earth's resources. But the real source of wealth lies beyond Earth: "The resources of the solar system are truly vast.... The resources of our galaxy make even our solar system seem insignificant by comparison... The resources of the visible universe make even our galaxy seem insignificant by comparison." Therefore, "opening space will burst our limits to growth, since we know of no end to the universe."[74]

But why this need for escape? What is left unsaid by Drexler is that, if one accepts inequality, "accelerating economic growth" is absolutely necessary so that "the rich can get richer," without the poor being driven into destitution. Without redistribution, the *only way* to maintain reasonable levels of well-being (and prevent the antagonisms of an unequal society from exploding) is through growth. So, acceleration becomes a requirement of "escape" from the antagonism and crisis that are otherwise endemic to an unequal society.

Similarly to Drexler, Moravec portrays technological advance gathering speed before blasting us to the far reaches of outer space. The history of technology is a dynamic in which "The innovations of professional thinkers… accelerate innovation itself. The result is a process far, far faster than biological evolution."[75] Like Drexler, Moravec asserts that the speed-up will become more pronounced as innovation is taken up by machines themselves: "Evolution of full machine intelligence will greatly accelerate." Machines, he claims, will "eventually surpass us in everything."[76] Advanced robots "will be like nothing the world has seen. As they design their own successors, the world will become ever stranger."[77] Moravec welcomes this alien world as he looks toward overcoming all limits. Similarly to Drexler, Moravec indicates outer space as allowing escape from the problems that currently bedevil society. Environmental problems, for example, will be overcome as new technologies, made possible by advanced robotics, allow polluting industries "to be moved to outer space."[78]

Moravec also sees room for escape from ecological limits by manipulating matter at the smallest possible scales. Nanotechnology and robotics come together in Moravec's idea that, instead of "energy- and chemical-intensive industrial separation and shaping processes," armies of robots will "will achieve the same end much more efficiently by tirelessly sorting and rearranging matter on a tiny scale with myriads of microscopic fingers."[79] If the nanoscale of the molecule or atom is exhausted, Moravec suggests that more resources will become available as science delves deeper into the composition of matter, even perhaps escaping the "limits" of matter: "[P]hysical theory already hints at ways of transcending the confines of ordinary matter." Moravec suggests that future machinic intelligences, or "Exes" as he calls them, might find ways to harness the energy of the new particles that physicists are discovering in the subatomic realm, or even be able to harness antimatter: "[A]ntimatter is the most concentrated possible form of energy and will be found in Ex battery packs everywhere."[80]

Moravec imaginatively describes technical possibilities at the extremes of physics. But his social imagination is constrained within the confines of capitalist individualism, a form of life that he projects into the far reaches of the universe. Harnessing antimatter, nuclear fusion, and as-yet-undiscovered subatomic particles would be "just the ticket for an upwardly mobile Ex."[81] In describing what is technically possible, his prose takes flight in imaginative leaps. But when it comes to questions of justifying these technical goals, explaining why we should pursue such possibilities, he sinks into utter banality. He tells us that advances toward intelligent robots "can make the world a nicer place to live."[82]

Despite such bland assurances, Moravec's quest for technological perfection and his account of technological evolution also encode a Social Darwinist worldview in which those who cannot keep up with the pace of technological advance, or who do not choose to become robotic superbeings, are merely obsolete. Questioned by Dery about whether his imagined futures had room for those today on the "lower rungs of the socioeconomic ladder," Moravec replied that questions of the "socioeconomic implications" of his scenarios were "largely irrelevant":

> It doesn't matter what people do because they're going to be left behind, like the second stage of a rocket. Unhappy lives, horrible deaths, and failed projects have been part of the history of life on Earth ever since there was life; what really matters in the long run is what's left over. Does it really matter to you today that the tyrannosaur line of that species failed?[83]

The economically deprived are like dinosaurs, now-extinct evolutionary precursors to *Homo sapiens*, or, in Moravec's mind, a parallel case, indigenous cultures wiped out by "progress": "You see, many cultures are gone; the Maori of New Zealand are gone, as are most of our ancestors or near relatives—*Australopithecus*, Homo erectus, Neanderthal man."[84]

The "rocket" of technical progress, therefore, introduces a separation between the enhanced and unenhanced, leaving the rump behind. In Moravec's outlook, those left behind, destined to go extinct, simply do not "matter." The only individuals who do "matter" are those whose trajectories mesh with the overall impersonal trajectory of "progress," those who have achieved escape velocity and who are departing on the rocket ship of progress. To worry about those left behind is to lose sight of the big picture:

> I think you can wallow in compassion and really screw up the bigger things, an example being the current U.S. welfare system, which I think had much too much compassion for individual cases and in so doing totally wrecked the inner city family by creating the wrong incentives. My own politics are

basically libertarian because I like to see as much happen as possible, and giving people maximum freedom to try things without having to have the approval of everybody else is the most fruitful way to get the most results in the shortest time.[85]

The "culture of dependency" arguments of the American Right fit into Moravec's worldview as evidence that compassion for mere "individual cases" is not *efficacious* in terms of the "bigger things." Moravec's so-called libertarianism is likewise framed by a concern with instrumental efficacy. His notion of freedom means "freedom to try things," which is valuable because it achieves "results." Freedom is thereby equated with technique. It points to his own freedom as an engineer to pursue his technological visions without interference. If left alone to pursue his technical visions, he will "get results."

Freedom, in this sense, is detached from a humanistic conception of individual will. Freedom just means instrumental efficacy—the capacity to achieve what is technically, or physically, possible to achieve. Yet, this conception of freedom is not entirely "post-human," for it also indicates the freedom of certain human beings. When Moravec speaks of "giving people maximum freedom to try things," he is referring to engineers like himself. The autonomy of the engineer from social constraint is ultimately realized in the autonomy of the machine from human constraint.

Kurzweil explicitly projects artificial intelligence as the extension and realization of the engineer or scientist, arguing that when artificial intelligence takes over from human scientists, intelligence and, therefore, technological innovation will expand without limit: "But what would 1,000 scientists, each 1,000 times more intelligent than human scientists today, and each operating 1,000 times faster than contemporary humans … accomplish? One chronological year would be like a millennium for them."[86] Although technocratic thought has promoted a vanguard of perfectly rational scientists and engineers as the implementers of the internal logic of science and technology, Kurzweil seeks to eliminate the human altogether.

The technocratic ideal of the perfectly rational scientist is realized and perfected in Kurzweil's image of an abstracted post-human "intelligence." Just as Moravec valorizes technical capacity as freedom, for Kurzweil the exponential increase in intelligence is an end in itself. The ultimate product of these super-intelligent beings would be more super-intelligence: "They would change their own thought processes to enable them to think even faster."[87] Progress is accelerating, but progress also *equates with* acceleration. Kurzweil's futurism is aimless. Having no particular goal, it is the celebration of the self-reinforcing escalation of technical capacity—accelerating acceleration.[88] Kurzweil's terminology requires similarly escalating hyperbole. He writes that the Singularity "represents the nearly vertical phase of exponential growth that occurs when the rate is so extreme that technology appears to be expanding at infinite speed."[89]

Exponential growth is the fundamental concept of Kurzweil's *The Singularity is Near*. His key idea is that technology develops in an exponential, not linear, pattern. In contrast to "steady" linear growth, exponential growth "becomes explosive." This explosive growth can be seen in the rate at which major "paradigm shifts" occur, in particular, the invention of fundamentally new types of technology: "My models show that we are doubling the paradigm-shift rate every decade."[90] The corollary of infinite speed-up is infinite expansion. For Kurzweil, like Drexler and Moravec, expansion into outer space allows endless growth: "[O]nce we bump up against the limits of matter and energy in our solar system to support the expansion of computation, we will have no choice but to expand outward as the primary form of growth."[91]

In Kurzweil's view, the ecological problems of contemporary society have their solution in further technological escalation.[92] Hunger has its solution in cloning technologies that offer the possibility of "creating meat and other protein sources in a factory *without animals* by cloning animal muscle tissue."[93] Nanotechnology promises applications for removing toxins or purifying water. In the future, Kurzweil envisages nanorobots dealing with nuclear waste. "Self-assembling electronic devices" will use less energy to manufacture and produce less toxic waste than today's factories.[94]

Technology also, according to Kurzweil, allows acceleration out of economic problems: "Note that the underlying exponential growth in the economy is a far more powerful force than periodic recessions. Most important, recessions, including depressions, represent only temporary deviations from the underlying curve... The world economy is continuing to accelerate."[95] Economic cycles represent "minor deviations" from an upward trend of growth and, as this continues, recessions are likely to have less and less effect on standards of living.[96] Continual expansion in productivity will be matched by "the inherently insatiable needs and desires of human consumers."[97]

Kurzweil champions the replacement of humans by machines as the key to productivity growth. Machines are not only cheaper over the long run, but more flexible and reliable than people: "once a skill is mastered by a machine, it can be performed repeatedly at high speed, at optimal accuracy, and without tiring."[98] In a discussion in which the human is progressively eliminated from *doing*, humanity is reintroduced as the recipient of this productivity. The human being, expelled from production, becomes pure consumer, the "insatiable need" required by the infinite and accelerating output of commodities.

In order to consume insatiably, people must always feel themselves to be lacking. What is it that they lack? If one adopts Kurzweil's world view, human beings are always deficient, and therefore lacking, to the extent that they are not machines. Kurzweil predicts that "[m]achines will be able to reformulate their own designs and augment their own capacities without limit." If machines that can be infinitely upgraded are the ideal, then human beings, as biological entities, will always fall short. Kurzweil notes that "[b]iology has inherent limits." "The architecture of the human brain," he tells us, "is... profoundly limited."[99] It follows from Kurzweil's view of the machine and the body that there will always be a perfect symmetry between the augmentation of production and the development of new consumer needs. For, with each step forward by machinery or artificial intelligence, the existing biological human being (or what is left of the biological human being) becomes correspondingly inadequate. This inadequacy mandates further remodeling and enhancement of the human being to bring us into alignment with the technological ideal. Kurzweil sees human bodies as faulty, poorly developed instruments in need of upgrading: "Our version 1.0 biological bodies are likewise frail and subject to a myriad of failure modes, not to mention the cumbersome maintenance rituals they require."[100] Given the limits of biology, inadequacy will continue to be the lot of human beings until the biological body is reduced to nothing.

When performance is pursued for its own sake, technology becomes the ideal, and the human is forever an unfinished artifact until we ourselves become technology. Technology, writes Kurzweil, is starting to allow us to "reprogram our biology to achieve the virtual elimination of disease, dramatic expansion of human potential, and radical life extension." Nevertheless, "no matter how successfully we fine-tune our DNA-based biology, humans will remain 'second-class robots,' meaning that biology will never be able to match what we will be able to engineer."[101]

IMMORTALITY AS THE ETERNAL PRESENT

Kurzweil's description of his own refusal to accept the aging process makes clear his view of the body as an instrument, whose functioning is to be optimized and maintained similarly to technological equipment: "Whereas some of my contemporaries may be satisfied to embrace aging gracefully as part of the cycle of life, that is not my view. It may be 'natural,' but I don't see anything positive in losing my mental agility, sensory acuity, physical limberness, sexual desire, or any other human ability. I view disease and death... as problems to be overcome."[102] Kurzweil is explicit about the parallel with machinery: "My view is that I am *reprogramming my biochemistry* in the same way that I reprogram the computers in my life."[103] He goes on to present his own health regimen as a model, for example, his "aggressive" use of vitamin supplements (taking 250 pills a day), and his diet and exercise regime.[104] As he does so, he provides us with detailed specifications for his body and its current performance: height, weight, percentage of fat, cholesterol levels, lipid levels. He announces that, although he is 56 years old, he has the "biological age" of a 40 year old. Kurzweil's quest for eternal youth (or at least eternal middle-age) involves intense self-monitoring. He subjects himself to a regular battery of tests. He tells us that "[i]n addition to routinely testing many blood levels, I have had a virtual colonoscopy and a lower-body CAT scan of my organs, which were normal. My thallium stress test, a test of cardiac function, was normal. My blood pressure is in an acceptable range. Extensive cancer screens are all negative. My prostate specific antigen (PSA) is low and stable at 0.4 ng/ml (nanograms per milliliter)." He carefully controls his diet, monitoring the number of calories and grams of carbohydrates and protein he consumes per day.[105] This self-surveillance entails a high degree of narcissistic preoccupation with one's own body. It also reflects the alienation of the body, which is externalized from the self, as it is treated as a technological object.[106]

While Kurzweil pays minute attention to his body's functioning, he regards the body as non-essential: immortality requires media less fragile than the biological body. Kurzweil's aim to "live long enough to live forever" means hopping technological bridges to longevity from today's biomedicine to tomorrow's biotechnology, nanotechnology, and artificial intelligence, a process which envisages the body being increasingly reconstituted as technology, and ultimately surpassed by technology.[107] True immortality will follow from the ability to detach self from body, transferring the person as pure information to computer hardware or networks of computers. It will become possible, Kurzweil suggests, to store oneself as a "mind file," transforming oneself into software that can be indefinitely transferred to new forms of computer hardware as these develop. When one machine becomes outmoded, the self can be uploaded to the new model. As a result, "the longevity of one's mind file will not depend on the continued viability of any particular hardware medium."[108]

In this scenario of continual uploading, as the information-self leaps forward with ever-new advances in technological media, the self becomes coextensive with the open-ended future of technology's linear time. Kurzweil refuses to "embrace… the cycle of life," wanting, instead, to stretch life out into an open-ended future. However, this merging of individual lifespan and linear time means that there is no longer any historical development *beyond* the life of an individual. Linear time is submerged in the stasis of an eternal present.

Drexler is a proponent of radical life extension and enthusiastically explores what he calls "biostasis," which involves keeping people in frozen state or preserved "in a tank of liquid nitrogen surrounded by equipment," until such time as future technologies can "stop and reverse" aging. Drexler imagines a scenario in which "At last, the sleeper wakes refreshed to the light of a new day—and to the sight of old friends."[109] If enough people opted for biostasis, then one could enjoy the future not in a "world of strangers" but with "the smiles of familiar faces." Drexler conveys the sense that, although technology would have progressed in leaps and bounds, in human terms little need have changed. The "gamble" of using biostasis is an assessment not only of whether the technology will work and whether future dwellers will want to wake up time travelers from the past. It is also a gamble on whether the future will be worth waking up to. Things could change for the worse—the human race could be wiped out in the intervening years; the best Drexler hopes for is the maintenance of the social and political accomplishments of America at the time of writing, in the mid-1980s. America's "free society" is, on this view, the end of history.[110] But Drexler's interest in society and politics does not go beyond the notion that "freedom" is a necessary condition for technological innovation: "Assume that human beings and free societies will indeed survive… If so, then technology will continue to advance." He cautions against skepticism about these conditions just because such skepticism would be dysfunctional for these technological programs: "[T]o assume failure would discourage the very efforts that will promote success."[111]

Drexler suggests that the will to push technology forward depends on the belief that history will be held still.

"Long Life in an Open World" is Drexler's slogan for his conception of the life-extending power of nanotechnology. The "open world" signifies Drexler's vision of outward expansion beyond Earth and beyond the solar system. But it also signifies the temporal openness of linear time, the open future implied by unlimited technological development and economic growth. The question of "long life" in relation to this "open world" is the relationship between individual time and societal or species time. Yet, Drexler's techno-futurism decouples linear time from human agency, history, and species being. The "open world" becomes a movement of technology, not of society. The problem, then, is how the individual is to relate to, and find meaning in, this impersonal trajectory. Techno-futurist thought decouples technology from the social and, therefore, constructs the human relationship with technology in terms only of the individual. But from the perspective of an atomized individual, any timescale transcending that of the individual's own life must be strictly meaningless. The openness of linear time can only make sense and be valued, for such an individual, if their individual life is extended so as to participate directly in this linear movement of technology.

Progress becomes meaningful for the individual by being coupled with what Drexler calls "progress in life extension." Drexler encapsulates this logic of individualism when he writes:

> The prospect of personal deterioration and death has always made thoughts of the future less pleasant. Yet with at least a hope of a better future and time to enjoy it, we may look forward more willingly. Looking forward, we will see more. Having a personal stake, we will care more.[112]

Advocating "biostasis," or cryonic freezing of people to be awakened at some point in the future, Drexler writes, "By broadening the path to long life, the biostasis option will encourage a more lively interest in the future."[113] Drexler assumes that "care" for, or "lively interest" in, the future requires a "personal stake" and that this stake means the possibility of oneself being present at that future date.

Whereas liquid nitrogen is the medium for Drexler's frozen bodies, cyberspace is Moravec's medium for the freezing of time. An inspiration for much of Kurzweil's theorizing, Moravec envisages replacing human organs with electronic components, the transplantation of human minds "from our original biological brain into artificial hardware," and the melding of minds in the "linked realities" made possible by "cyberspace."[114] Moravec imagines immortality as the resurrection in cyberspace not only of human minds but of history itself:

> Entire world histories, with all their living, feeling inhabitants, will be resurrected in cyberspace. Geologic ages, historical periods, and individual lifetimes will continuously recur as parts of larger mental efforts, in faithful renditions, in artistic variations, and in completely fictionalized forms.[115]

Cyberspace becomes a sacred space of eternal return.[116] However, it also seems to be the apotheosis of post-modern pastiche in which past styles are continually resurrected in the form of simulacra.[117] Moravec writes that "[t]o a simulated entity, the simulation *is* reality and must be lived by its internal rules." In this simulated world, modernity's linear time will have come almost to a standstill, as novelty is abolished: "Single original events will be very rare compared to the indefinitely multiple cyberspace replays."[118]

In cyberspace, Moravec tells us, "Most things that are experienced—this very moment, for instance, or your entire life—are far more likely to be a Mind's musings than the physical processes they seem to be. There is no way to tell for sure," and an unnerving corollary of participating in this informatic consciousness will be "the suspicion that we are someone else's thought... a bit role in a cyber deity's thoughts."[119] Cartesian skepticism has no limit in cyberspace; in this nebulous realm of shared informatic consciousness, there might be no grounds on which to establish the subject of "cogito ergo sum."

Techno-futurist fantasies of immortality derive from the attempt to reconcile the linear time of technological development and capitalist growth with the lived time of the atomized and narcissistic individual who has no ability to identify with future generations and thereby to reconcile himself or herself to being superseded in time. Progress can be made meaningful for such an individual only by promising the extension of his or her lifespan. This promise of immortality means merging the individual with the linear trajectory of technology. It reaches its logical conclusion in the scenario of uploaded consciousness in which the individual, as a bounded entity, is dissolved. So techno-futurist individualism seems to follow the fate of individualism in consumer capitalism, in which the elevation of the principle of individual choice to a supreme value enmeshes the individual a simulated world in which genuine autonomy corrodes.[120]

Moravec unflinchingly follows the implications of the uploading scenario through not only the loss of individuality, but also the fact that the consciousnesses thus created can hardly be called human. The disembodied mind floating free in cyberspace would be very different from the embodied minds of human beings. Human minds, with thought processes rooted in physicality, would have trouble navigating an immaterial information environment:

> Since physical intuitions are probably not the best way to deal with most information, humans would still be at a disadvantage to optimized artificial intelligences... [T]he bodiless mind... would be hardly human. It will have become an AI.[121]

So, technology becomes the ideal not only for the body but also for the mind itself. The mind, conceptualized as "intelligence," is just as instrumentalized as the body, and liable to remodeling in accordance with the technological ideal of the computer. Techno-futurism's alienation of the body is, then, just part of an extreme alienation from humanity itself. Adopting the standpoint of the technological ideal allows Moravec to be contemptuous of such base and limited entities as human beings: "the immensities of cyberspace will be teeming with unhuman superminds, engaged in affairs that are to human concerns as ours are to those of bacteria."[122] In techno-futurism, the human subject dissolves altogether, as each aspect of humanity is found wanting and replaced by technology. As the human subject is lost, the subject that reveals itself, replacing humanity, is the machine.

In the capitalist workplace, the embodied human being is integrated into a technological apparatus. Human activity, or labor, is measured, monitored, assessed, and reorganized for maximally efficient performance. The ideal is an inhuman standard of performance, and the tendency is to replace the worker with an entity that does not resist, does not need sleep, and has no dependents. The machine is the ideal of pure performance.[123] The drive toward maximum efficiency and power inexorably leads to making the human being into a machine, or doing away with the human being in favor of machines.[124] To be maximally productive, efficacious, and dependable is to remake oneself as a piece of technology. The techno-futurist ideal in this way expresses the ideal of capitalist work. The ideal worker is like a piece of technology and is ultimately not a human worker at all.

The worker under capitalism becomes human capital and, as such, is under constant pressure to update their skills and augment their capacities.[125] The pressure to commodify the self is, perhaps, greatest for the professional-managerial stratum for whom tasks at work are not rigidly circumscribed and whose judgment, outlook on life, and presentation of self are key aspects of their value as labor.[126] Erich Fromm was referring to this stratum when he wrote of the "marketing character" for whom "everything is transformed into a commodity—not only things, but the person himself, his physical energy, his skills, his knowledge, his opinions, his feelings, even his smiles."[127] In addition, whereas the lower level worker (whether on the assembly line, cash register, or call center) experiences the technology of the workplace as a brute external reality that constrains him or her, it is possible for the managerial stratum, particularly senior engineers, to view this technology as an expression of their own efficacy and power. In his study of the culture and ideology of computing, David Golumbia writes that "Psychologically, the signal experience of working with computers for the power elite is that of *mastery*."[128] The complete identification of self with technology is conditioned by the reduction of human beings to machines within capitalist production and the way in which the capitalist division of labor makes it possible for some strata to experience that reduction of human to machine as an expression of their own efficacy. Fromm suggested that the managerial "marketing character" would seek to become "cybernetic man."[129]

Identification with technology is a key element of the culture of consumerism. In capitalist consumption, human needs are translated into the need for commodities. The desire for health and well-being is translated into the purchase of supplements and devices. The sense of self as a unique individual is expressed through the purchase of particular commodities, which the individual feels reflects his or her self-image and which, in turn, flatteringly reflect their advertising imagery back onto the individual. Purchasing commodities and identifying the self with these objects is part of the process of making oneself into a desirable or marketable commodity.[130] This acquisitive individualism is competition to outdo others with indicators of status. It is anti-social, not only because it pits people against one other in a contest for the status, but also because it puts the individual in a relationship primarily with objects rather than with other people. Rather than fulfilling individual needs through social cooperation, consumer capitalism undercuts the impulse to cooperate by harnessing individuals' needs to particular commodities. It creates a world of atomized individuals—their homes are filled with devices, they are always in need of new purchases as fashions change, new models become the objects of desire, and planned obsolescence takes its course. Devices mediate the individual's relationship with the world.[131]

Approaching the world through devices and identifying one's self in a possessive mode with the devices one owns leads to judging oneself as a device, subject to failure, and in need of upgrading. As Fromm notes, there is no end to this consumption. No matter how much people buy, "they still feel poor because they cannot keep up with the pace of production or the mass of goods produced." This pursuit of consumption leaves the individual feeling anxious and impotent: "This situation promotes passivity as well as envy and greed and, ultimately, a sense of inner weakness, of powerlessness and inferiority."[132] These feelings spur yet more consumption.

Capitalist relations abstract the individual from ties of community and tradition and create a desocialized atomic individual. However, this individual cannot survive in isolation. Standing in a competitive relationship with other people, the individual's necessary dependency increasingly takes the form of dependence on objects. This dependence on objects is then recast as narcissistic self-affirmation: through these objects the individual experiences prowess and is affirmed as unique, powerful, and worthy of admiration. As Fromm put it, "[H]uman beings, in the state of their greatest real *impotence, imagine* themselves in connection with science and technology to be *omnipotent.*"[133] The whole within which the individual is submerged is not a human whole made up of social relationships. Rather, it is composed of objects, namely, commodities, devices, and the money that buys them. Individuals locate themselves within this whole, which is not society, but capital.

Identification with capital, however, makes the finitude of the individual's own life hard to accept. The atomized and narcissistic individual is unable to sustain deep emotional attachment to a larger social group as an entity that transcends the individual in space and time and reproduces itself into the future.[134] Instead, capitalist production's linear trajectory is the transcendent, ongoing reality within which the individualistic consumer locates his or her own existence. The consumer can buy into this trajectory through purchasing the latest products. But, as Fromm perceives, it is not possible for the individual to keep up fully with "the pace of production."[135] One can never have enough, and production races on oblivious of the death of any individual.

The techno-futurist quest for life extension is an attempt to open out the lifespan of the individual so as to be continuous with the linear temporality of capitalist production. But, as Moravec makes absolutely clear, the logical result of this quest is losing both individuality and humanness, merging oneself into the flow of technology. Production without people is eventless. In Moravec's utopia of cyberspace, instead of "single original events," there will be "indefinitely multiple cyberspace replays." Linear time without history collapses in on itself, giving way to stasis. This stasis is a capitalist heaven in which capital has escaped all contradictions and subsumed reality.

The Opium of the Capitalists

Fromm argued that the marketing character had developed a "cybernetic religion," a modern paganism in which "[m]an has made himself into a god because he has acquired the technical capacity for a 'second creation' of the world, replacing the first creation by the God of traditional religion.... We have made the machine into a god and have become godlike by serving the machine."[136] Fromm was not talking about an explicit set of beliefs, but rather a deep orientation that was much more significant as a source of motivation and perception. The prevailing spirit of advanced capitalism, Fromm suggested, was the worship of technology and the desire to associate oneself with technological power. In techno-futurist thought, this prevailing spirit finds its explicit expression, taking the form of what Keith Ansell-Pearson has called "a new theology of capital."[137]

Techno-futurism is an extreme scientism, in the sense of treating science as superior to all other forms of knowledge and culture and as holding the answers to all human problems. It treats human action in terms of an extreme instrumentalism, measuring all activity in terms of efficient performance. But techno-futurist texts also veer into metaphysical speculation. While presenting his case for life extension through biostasis, Drexler pauses to consider possible religious objections to freezing and reviving the body: what happens to the soul? The soul could be thought of, he suggests, as "the pattern of mind, memory, and personality [which] leaves the body at death, carried by some subtle substance." In that case, he reassures believers, resuscitating a frozen body would "presumably require the cooperation of the soul to succeed."[138] The question of the soul arises also in Kurzweil's conception of "spiritual machines." From machine consciousness, Kurzweil moves into a discussion of the potential for artificial intelligence to develop religious feeling. He imagines that "Twenty-first-century machines—based on the design of human thinking—will do as their human progenitors have done—going to real and virtual houses of worship, meditating, praying, and transcending—to connect with their spiritual dimension."[139] Drexler pays lip service to the soul, in anticipation of a religious backlash against his nanotechnological utopia; Kurzweil melds high technology with a New Age outlook in which "Just being—experiencing, being conscious—is spiritual." Robotic consciousness, then, brings robotic "spirituality."[140]

Beyond these kinds of metaphysical speculations, techno-futurism also has more structural affinities with religion—its interest in immortality and in the apocalyptic notion of transcending the limits of the existing world into a new, and more perfect, world of machinic life.[141] The quasi-religious apocalyptic character of ideas like Kurzweil's "Singularity" has been commented on often, and some analysts have gone so far as to call "transhumanism" a "new religious movement."[142] While transhumanism has attracted devotees, it seems premature to call the phenomenon a "movement." It is primarily an ideological outgrowth of America's technical intelligentsia, pursuing to an extreme the fetishism of technology that, while usually formulated less extravagantly, is deeply embedded within the culture of capitalist technoscience. It is this fetishism that gives techno-futurism its quasi-religious character. As Ludwig Feuerbach showed, religion projects human qualities onto an entity, posited as external to humanity, which is then fetishistically treated as the source of these qualities (e.g. in the notion that God is love). Marx showed how commodity fetishism under capitalism operates similarly, as the human labor that produces capital is obscured, and the commodities circulating on the market seem to have a life of their own separate from, and superior to, labor.

Marx wrote, "Thus at the level of material production, of the life-process in the realm of the social... we find the *same* situation that we find in *religion* at the ideological level, namely the inversion of subject into object and *vice versa*."[143] In religion, humans are dominated by the creations of the human mind; in commodity fetishism, this inversion operates not only ideologically but also materially, as people are dominated by the things they produce. The workings of the market appear as transcendent laws, rather than as aspects of human activity. The mystification of the process of production also gives the commodity what Marx referred to as its "mysterious" quality, as an entity that, although non-living, appears both active and powerful.[144] In contemporary consumer culture, this mysteriousness is an aspect of the strange attraction aroused by commodities. Debord wrote of consumers' "mystical abandon to the transcendence of the commodity." "The fetishism of commodities," he observed, "reaches moments of fervent exaltation similar to the ecstasies of the convulsions and miracles of the old religious fetishism."[145]

Technology fetishism is another facet of commodity fetishism. As its relationship with labor is obscured within the social-economic relations of capitalism, technology takes alienated form as capital. Marx writes, "The transposition of the social productivity of labour into the material attributes of capital is so firmly entrenched in people's minds that the advantages of machinery, the use of science, invention, etc. are *necessarily* conceived in this *alienated* form, so that all these things are deemed to be *attributes of capital*."[146] Technology, as capital, appears as a power that is separate and autonomous from human beings. Techno-futurism exalts this autonomous power, proclaiming it as humanity's salvation. The "'cybernetic religion' of the marketing character" is commodity fetishism.[147]

The identity between commodity fetishism and technology fetishism can be seen in Kurzweil's statement that "It's the economic imperative of a competitive marketplace that is the primary force driving technology forward and fueling the law of accelerating returns." The autonomy of technology, expressed in Kurzweil's law of accelerating technological development, is rooted in the autonomy of economic forces as a set of impersonal imperatives. The forces for which Kurzweil speaks are nothing other than the alienated products of human action. Having reified the market as an "imperative" or "force" separate from human action, Kurzweil then naturalizes capitalist competition in Darwinian terms: "Economic imperative is the equivalent of survival in biological evolution."[148] Capital is ascribed life, and Kurzweil's account becomes one of the evolution of capital in the form of technology.

This technological evolution takes over from biological evolution as the Singularity approaches. The evolutionary development of capital, in Kurzweil's eschatology, is moving toward a higher intelligence, and a higher state of being, a technological nirvana. In this state, technology merges with the universe. As computing requires vaster and vaster resources, it will require converting matter and energy into computing resources, a process that will expand out from Earth to the solar system and beyond. Kurzweil writes:

Once a planet yields a technology-creating species and that species creates computation (as has happened here), it is only a matter of a few centuries before its intelligence saturates the matter and energy in its vicinity, and it begins to expand outward at at least the speed of light... Such a civilization will then overcome gravity (through exquisite and vast technology) and other cosmological forces—or, to be fully accurate, it will maneuver and control these forces—and engineer the universe it wants. This is the goal of the Singularity.[149]

The idea of "saturat[ing]" the universe with intelligence means that Kurzweil's Singularity is not only the merging of human and machine as artificial intelligence, but is also the merging of this artificial intelligence with the *universe itself*. What Kurzweil calls the "the Destiny of the Universe" is its awakening to consciousness through its saturation with artificial intelligence, or its transformation into a computer of infinite extent.[150]

Kurzweil presents the mechanisms of market competition and technological development as drivers of a process that has cosmic significance, ending in the overcoming of all difference as mind merges with matter throughout the universe. Moravec's vision of technological transformation ends in a similar state of cosmic oneness. This nirvana is the overcoming of linear time.

Moravec presents high technology as offering the way out of modern alienation. He describes the reaction of Davi Kopenawa, a Yanomami tribesman, visiting the USA: "If I had to live in your cities for a month, I'd die." "Kopenawa has a point," says Moravec: "The world we inhabit is radically different, culturally and physically, from the one to which we adapted biologically." We are adapted to a world of small-scale communities and "chipped silicon" (e.g. flint arrow heads) and not to a world of cities and silicon chips. Moravec writes: "The mismatch between instinct and necessity induces alienation in the midst of unprecedented physical plenty."[151]

Moravec uses the term "alienation" to refer to discontents of boredom and anxiety. According to him, these stem from the contradiction between human beings' stone-age biology and industrial culture. This is very different from the Marxist conception of alienation as a feature of social relations in which human beings (workers) lose control of their product and productive activity. If one regards alienation in the Marxist way, as a social relationship, then the way to overcome it is through transforming these relationships. The view of alienation as a lack of fit between biology and culture points to two possible solutions. One is a return to a more natural simplicity, as advocated by romantics like Henry David Thoreau and, in more radical form, by contemporary "primitivists" like the anti-technological anarchist John Zerzan.[152] The other is to update biology, or leave it behind, so as to fit the human with ever-advancing technological culture. Moravec rules out any attempt to stem what he portrays as technology's inexorable advance.[153]

One should not attempt to place limits on technological development, Moravec argues, because hopes for a more communal and natural way of life will instead be achieved by letting technological evolution take its course. The abundance provided by an automated economy will reduce social problems: "Modern tensions may subside when robot labor gives us a work-free life and the freedom to abandon the cities." The stresses of city life feature prominently in Moravec's understanding of alienation. His automated future is deurbanized as well as deindustrialized. For Moravec, robotics seems to promise a restoration of Eden. Total automation "paradoxically... will provide the means to restore humanity and nature to an imitation of the wild past."[154]

Conceiving of nature as a "mechanism," Moravec argues that the more mechanized we become, the more natural our lives will be:

> A thousand centuries ago, the world was fully automated. Our ancestors were supported by the maintenance-free, self-operating machinery called Nature. But, in an Adamic bargain predating Faust, they meddled with the mechanism. By tilling and planting, they magnified the machinery's productivity but trapped themselves in a routine of heavy, unpleasant labor.[155]

Automation will restore a state of a self-sustaining abundance, freeing human beings from the need for work. This, Moravec suggests, is an outcome of technology's inevitable progress: "Despite occasional setbacks, the trend is accelerating. After millennia lived by the sweat of our brow, we are at last providing more and more with less and less work."[156]

Moravec's utopia arises without struggle or contradiction. Where he acknowledges inequality—"[i]nstitutions like slavery, feudalism, and capitalism lifted a small minority out of the drudge on the backs of the rest"—it is to suggest that such things will necessarily be overcome by automated abundance and universal leisure. Automation has displaced manual labor in agriculture and factories. It is now displacing office workers. As Moravec portrays this trend, "Humans have been upwardly mobile in the jobs pyramid, but will soon be squeezed out of the apex!"[157] Once there is no more work to do, there will be no more inequality. Utopia is the outcome of a "trend" that Moravec treats as essentially separate from human action. He portrays this trend both as the logic of technology and as arising from the pressure of the market. Either way, the trend is expressed as an imperative: "Rising productivity is a business imperative as long as customers choose better goods at lower prices. Output per worker must increase, and so the amount of essential labor decreases."[158]

The combined action of the market and the self-augmentation of technology is taking us toward a post-work utopia, but this is only one point along technology's path. Beyond the abolition of work is the overcoming of biological humanity altogether, which, for Moravec, is the ultimate overcoming of the discrepancy between biology and culture. He sets out the stages in technology's linear development as follows:

> Advancing automation and a coming army of robots will displace labor as never before. In the short run this threatens unemployment and panicked scrambles for new ways to earn a living. In the medium run, it is a wonderful opportunity to recapture the comfortable pace of a tribal village while retaining the benefits of technological evolution. In the long run, it marks the end of the dominance of biological humans and the beginning of the age of robots.[159]

Moravec portrays the advance of automation as a "flood" gradually taking over ever-greater areas of human activity, starting with things like arithmetic at which humans are comparatively "weak" and eventually arriving at areas like "social interaction" at which humans have excelled. "Advancing computer performance," he writes, "is like water slowly flooding this landscape."[160] He predicts that "[w]hen the highest peaks are covered, there will be machines that can interact as intelligently as any human on any subject. The presence of minds in machines will then become self-evident."[161]

Moravec welcomes this "flood" which overcomes all differences between human and machine and between life and technology. In the medium run, it takes us to an Edenic state of plenty. But even this is only a temporary Eden: "The garden of earthly delights will be reserved for the meek, and those who would eat of the tree of knowledge must be banished. What a banishment it will be! Beyond Earth, in all directions, lies limitless outer space, a worthy arena."¹⁶² Paradoxically, strength here means giving oneself up to the flood of technology, a dissolution of self in the "waters" of technology.

As he takes us to the merger of human and machine, and the awakening of machinic intelligence, the agents are no longer human beings as such, but rather take increasingly ethereal forms:

> Bits of a single body may be distributed over distances: a camera here, an arm there, a controlled vehicle anywhere, all in communication. Although an Ex may occupy a macroscopic volume overall, its parts can be microscopic... Exes will contain and control, perhaps via light beams that both power and communicate, vehicles and manipulators smaller than dust motes. An Ex may often be surrounded by an illuminated cloud that does its bidding as if by magic.¹⁶³

From such nebulous forms, Moravec foresees super intelligences merging with the cosmos itself. For example, "a neutron star could possibly be shaped... into a mind... Like sages on remote mountaintops, isolated, immobile Exes trapped in neutron stars may become the most powerful minds in the galaxy."¹⁶⁴

Moravec formulates a technological animism in which matter, as information, can be understood as expressing mind: "[T]he thermal jostling of the atoms in a rock can be seen as the operation of a complex self-aware mind." Advanced artificial intelligences "may be able to spot fully functioning intelligences in the complex chemical goings on of plants, the dynamics of interstellar clouds, or the reverberations of cosmic radiation."¹⁶⁵ As mind and matter merge, ultimately the discreteness of entities in physical space ends altogether in what Moravec calls "The Age of Mind": "Physical activity will gradually transform itself into a web of increasingly pure thought."¹⁶⁶

The concepts of "information" and "intelligence" form the stepping stones upon which Moravec crosses from scientific materialism to absolute idealism. Robots "may simply seem to vanish, leaving behind a universe indistinguishable from that before their arrival."¹⁶⁷ A pristine universe will, in fact, be a giant system of cognition, absorbing all activity and experience. As discussed above, time is also dissolved in this oneness, since Moravec imagines history being perpetually replayed as simulation within cyberspace. In cyberspace, spirit takes priority over matter. The advance of technology takes us toward the triumph of idealism, as reality is subsumed within universal mind. Moravec writes: "This line of thought, growing out of the premises and techniques of physical science, has the unexpected consequence of demoting physical existence to a derivative role."[168]

Drawing on physicists John Barrow and Frank Tipler's cosmological speculations, Moravec suggests that the destiny of artificial intelligence's "inspiriting" of matter is the development of a self-aware universe or "cosmic mind," which is "subjectively eternal," creating and recreating itself through self-interpretation, memory, and contemplation: "As it contemplates, effects from the universe's past converge on it. There is information, time, and thought enough to recreate, savor, appreciate, and perfect each detail of the moment. Tipler and Barrow suggest that it is this final, subjectively eternal act of infinite self-interpretation that effectively creates our universe."[169] To characterize this dialectical eternal moment, the implosion/explosion and death/birth of the universe, Tipler and Barrow invoke Jesuit philosopher Teilhard de Chardin's notion of the "Omega Point." For De Chardin, the universe's evolution toward ever higher levels of complexity and consciousness is a movement of God's creation toward God, Omega being the point of universal oneness with God, or "God-Omega."[170] The notion of the Omega Point transcends time. As Moravec puts the idea, "We truly exist because our actions lead ultimately to this 'Omega Point.'"[171]

In his sole-authored book *The Physics of Immortality*, Tipler follows De Chardin in suggesting that the Omega Point is the personal God, and he argues that he has provided a physical justification for belief in the afterlife.[172] While Moravec does not adopt this kind of theistic language, there is an underlying similarity in the eschatological direction of his thought. AI and cyberspace function as a form of afterlife for Moravec. He suggests that after death we might "find ourselves reconstituted in the minds of superintelligent successors, or perhaps in dreamlike worlds (or AI programs)."[173]

While Kurzweil expresses skepticism about the idea of a personal God, and rejects a notion of God as Creator, he sets out a conception of the evolution of the universe toward complexity and consciousness that bears striking similarity with De Chardin's Omega Point:

> Evolution moves toward greater complexity, greater elegance, greater knowledge, greater intelligence, greater beauty, greater creativity, and greater levels of subtle attributes such as love. In every monotheistic tradition God is likewise described as all of these qualities... So evolution moves inexorably

toward this conception of God, although never quite reaching this ideal. We can regard, therefore, the freeing of our thinking from the severe limitations of its biological form to be an essentially spiritual undertaking.[174]

Intelligence will "transcend" the human body to inhabit machines and to reach out into the universe itself. Like De Chardin and Moravec, Kurzweil sees technology as having a cosmic destiny, giving consciousness to the universe: "Our civilization will... expand outward, turning all the dumb matter and energy we encounter into sublimely intelligent—transcendent—matter and energy. So in a sense, we can say that the Singularity will ultimately infuse the universe with spirit."[175]

In techno-futurists' apocalyptic speculations, the linear time of technology and capitalist growth moves toward a nirvana in which mind and matter, consciousness and the universe, have become one.[176] Moravec's book opens with the claim that "Progressive change has sculpted our universe and our societies." It closes with Hamlet's paradoxical soliloquy,

To die, to sleep;

To sleep: perchance to dream: ay, there's the rub;

For in that sleep of death what dreams may come.[177]

Modern linear time ends in the afterlife of AI dreams.

Debord writes that the commodity spectacle "is the nightmare of imprisoned modern society which ultimately expresses nothing more than its desire to sleep. The spectacle is the guardian of sleep."[178] The ideological message of the techno-futurists is that market competition, driving the augmentation of technology, will overcome all contradictions and limits. The infinite expansion of capital will bring about earthly paradise, and beyond that catapult us toward a cosmic nirvana. As capitalist competition transforms itself into technological evolution, this evolution is bound in the direction of the oneness of this technology with the universe itself. Techno-futurism extrapolates the "end of history" posited by the ideologues of capitalist globalization into an Omega Point of the triumph of capital. God-Omega is, as Debord defined the spectacle, "the moment when the commodity has attained the *total occupation* of social life."[179]

In this techno-apocalyptic scenario, difference collapses into oneness: humans are merged with machines, mind merges with matter, and AI merges with the universe. In this scenario, linear time is also overcome, as in Moravec's notion that the past would replay itself interminably within cyberspace. Linearity collapses as acceleration turns inward rather than outward. The explosion of technology is transformed into an implosion, compounding everything together so that individuality and discreteness are lost.[180] However, this is nothing other than capital's real subsumption, projected at the scale of cosmos. The subsumption of humanity by technology–capital proceeds outward, colonizing and absorbing the universe within capital, which reaches its highest stage as it becomes immaterial, in Moravec's notion of the universe as cyber simulation. The outward expansion of capital is accompanied by the intensification of exploitation. The explosion of capital as it absorbs space is accompanied by the implosion of everything within capital, as it intensively exploits and transforms what it has absorbed. Techno-futurism is the exaltation of the expansion of capital, its colonization of the living, and its appropriation of the qualities of life. It is a philosophy of the expansion and evolution of capital as living dead, taking into itself more and more of reality, until it reaches the Omega Point of the total capitalization of existence. This final state of subsumption of the world by capital *is* death. The universal acceleration celebrated by techno-futurism is a race to oblivion.

Fromm argued that the cybernetic religion has become increasingly "malignant": destructive aspects of technology are coming to the fore as it becomes increasingly clear that society is not able to exert control over technological development, in other words, as the *alienated* character of technological development becomes more and more apparent. Fromm writes that, "technique, once a vital element of creation, shows its other face as the goddess of destruction (like the Indian goddess Kali), to which men and women are willing to sacrifice themselves and their children. While consciously still hanging onto hope for a better future, cybernetic humanity represses the fact that they have become worshipers of the goddess of destruction."[181]

As a member of the Army Science Advisory Group, Kurzweil advises the US Army on research priorities. Since he joined Google, the company purchased the military robotics firm Boston Dynamics.[182] In *The Singularity is Near*, Kurzweil includes a panegyric on the "movement toward precision intelligent warfare" resulting from the military application of artificial intelligence technology.[183] Like earlier generations of scientists who justified chemical warfare as "a higher form of killing," and biological warfare as killing "without the distressing preliminaries," Kurzweil champions the use of artificial intelligence and robotics in the battlefield as "precise" instruments that would lead to "fewer casualties."[184] Kurzweil illustrates his argument with a chart showing declining numbers of war deaths among US troops from the Civil War up until the current war in Iraq (the chart ends in 2004). Just as the US military has since the Vietnam War ceased to count casualties among the troops or civilians of its adversaries, Kurzweil presents data only for the US side, but gives assurance that the "trend is similar for collateral casualties."[185]

Kurzweil quickly moves on from his superficial reassurances on the cleanness of the new methods of warfare, to the real thrust of his enthusiasm, which is for sheer performativity and power. The US Army's program on Future Combat Systems "represents a pervasive focus of military systems toward remotely guided, autonomous, miniaturized, and robotic systems, combined with robust, self-organizing, distributed, and secure communications." He quotes the US Army's director for research as saying that Future Combat Systems will be "smaller, lighter, faster, more lethal, and smarter." Kurzweil writes that new uniforms employing nanotechnology will "enable combatants to greatly increase their physical strength." The "advanced armor materials and... intelligent systems" give the Abrams tank "a remarkable survival record." "The trend toward unmanned aerial vehicles (UAVs)... will accelerate." Development times for such new technologies are being reduced. The military will employ "self-organizing swarms of small robots." "Want to find a key enemy? Need to locate hidden weapons? Massive numbers of essentially invisible spies could monitor every inch of enemy territory, identify every person... and every weapon and even carry out missions to destroy enemy targets." The military is moving from "dumb missiles" to "smart weapons." Kurzweil's *Singularity* is the saturation of warfare with "intelligence": the era of cyberwar. He writes, "By the late 2030s and 2040s, as we approach human body version 3.0 and the predominance of nanobiological intelligence, the issue of cyberwarfare will move to center stage. When everything is information, the ability to control your own information and disrupt your enemy's communication, command, and control will be a primary determinant of military success."[186]

Warfare, then, follows the more general trajectory that Kurzweil sets out, from roboticization to dematerialization. The "military assault" becomes, as Paul Virilio has written, "shapeless in time and space, absolutely vaporous."[187] This dematerialization and the compression of space and time create a reality infused not only with intelligence but also with intelligent warfare. In cyberwarfare, eliminating space and time, all of reality can be immediately targeted and disrupted. What elsewhere appears as a heaven of ethereal super minds is manifested here as a hell of what Virilio has called "pure war," a reality permeated by war in which there is nowhere to hide.[188]

As Fromm perceived in Filippo Tommaso Marinetti's *Futurist Manifesto* (1909), the "religion of speed" is also the worship of power.[189] Kurzweil's breathless account of the possibilities of battlefield swarm intelligence and cyberwarfare mesh with the US military's projected image of technological power. An online recruitment advertisement for the Air Force boasts, "It's Not Science Fiction: It's what we do every day." Its slogans, such as "Remotely Piloted Aircraft: Power from Above" or "Space Command: The ultimate high ground," trumpet what the US military calls its "full spectrum superiority."[190] This means, as Virilio has noted, "total war is now directed not so much against the enemy's war machines as against the *atmospheric ecosystem* of the target country."[191] The recruitment advertisement, like Kurzweil's prose, assumes among its audience an identification with the agents of this power.

Kurzweil's militarist orientation reflects the close relationship between the scientific field of AI and the military.[192] This link between AI and militarism has been strengthened in the last decade, as the "War on Terror" has been a massive boon to the robotics and AI field, with the US military employing thousands of robots and unmanned aerial vehicles (UAVs) in its campaigns in Iraq, Afghanistan, Pakistan, and elsewhere in the Middle East and Africa.[193] Companies like iRobot, spun out from MIT, are major producers of robots for today's wars.[194]

Robotics has its workplace applications in the replacement of workers by machines, and a major impetus for scientific research on human–machine interaction is to develop machines and expert systems to mechanize the service sector. The industrial application of robotics and AI in the real subsumption of labor is complemented by its military application in achieving full spectrum dominance. Just as techno-futurism adulates capitalist speed-up and intensification, its fantasies of limitless expansion also mesh with capital's appropriation of resources and markets through imperialism. Despite his rhetoric of "transcendence," Kurzweil's support for US militarism connects his technical expertise instead with the neoconservative attempt to freeze history in a "New American Century."[195] Far from moving us toward an open future, the artificial intelligence embodied in the Packbots and Predator drones in Iraq and Afghanistan is part of a project of maintaining US hegemony and preserving petrochemical-based accumulation through oil imperialism.[196]

Against techno-futurist imaginaries of plenty and harmony stands the chaos and destructiveness of technological advance within capitalism. Technological acceleration is also the cascading of technological accidents such as Deepwater Horizon and Fukushima. Virilio suggests that the accident is becoming normalized, with disasters continually replayed as spectacle on 24-hour news and as the fabric of everyday life is interlaced with fear of the next catastrophic accident. As accidents are becoming normal and pervasive, and (ever since the development of nuclear weapons and nuclear power) global in their consequences, the technological trajectory is toward the "global accident."

This global accident is already unfolding in the form of global warming. Chris Harman has aptly described witnessing the world's momentum into deepening climactic disaster as "watching a car crash in slow motion, with the driver aware of disaster ahead but ploughing on regardless."[197] Global warming is not an aberration or breakdown but is, rather, integral to industrial capitalist economic growth and the way in which the technological transformation of the world at a global scale collides with capital's inability to regulate itself on that scale. The capitalist world system is fundamentally antagonistic and tending toward war. Since the declaration of the "War on Terror," a state of perpetual war has become normalized and technological advance is continually upgrading the war machine's capacity for destruction. In such ways, the accident is, Virilio argues, "integral" to the process of technological acceleration: "The ecological, economic and political or integral accident has thus become an element that rises above and beyond war. War or politics become facets of the integral accident."[198]

Globalization of capital now means capital pushing against the limits of the planet's resources and ecological stability. Technological acceleration means intensification of exploitation, transforming from explosion into implosion. We are living inside this accident, and everyday life takes on the character of this implosion. Virilio writes, "*Everything, right now!* Such is the crazy catch-cry of hyper-modern times, of this hypercentre of temporal compression where everything crashes together."[199] Living within this implosion is claustrophobic—consciousness and aspirations are compressed into the confines of the existing capitalist order that is presented as being without alternatives. The consumer-capitalist ideology that one can have "everything right now" also means there is nothing but the *now*. Techno-futurism's celebration of speed within the confines of its assumption of the eternal naturalness of capitalist relations also makes this a form of imagination that is trapped, and entrapping, within the present. Instead of transcendence, it produces paralysis. Virilio writes, "too much speed... and you get inertia."[200] The accident in which we are living is the collision of technological acceleration with the inertia of capitalist relations.[201]

CAPITAL'S IMPLOSION AND HISTORICAL TIME

The techno-futurists argue that technology is taking us toward a better (indeed, magical) future, in an essentially uninterrupted trajectory of exponential acceleration, yielding greater productivity, greater prosperity, and ultimately producing fundamental transformations in the conditions of existence. These changes, the techno-futurists predict, will liberate humanity from want, toil, and eventually from the burdens of earthly existence. These transformations are propelled by an evolutionary dynamic, which, these writers suggest, is expressed in capitalist market competition.

The image of smooth, uninterrupted progress is an effect of the underlying technological determinism in these writers' conceptualization of change.[202] This determinism is, in turn, an expression of commodity fetishism and, as such, masks the human activity and social relations from which technological and market dynamics derive. These social relations within capitalism are not smooth, but contradictory and antagonistic. And the character of acceleration under capitalism is correspondingly contradictory.[203] Where the techno-futurists see only speed, there is also stasis. Acceleration collides into stagnation.

A contradictory feature of late capitalism is the combination of acceleration in the tempo of everyday life, with underlying economic stagnation. The "overworked American" has seen their real wage stagnate since the early 1970s. Despite new globalized networks of production and consumption and the introduction of new information technologies, the overall secular trend for the world economy has been prolonged stagnation in terms of economic growth, labor productivity growth, rates of profit, and rising unemployment and underemployment.[204] This long-term stagnation has been accompanied by economic turbulence. In the 1960s, the notion that capitalism had overcome boom and slump was accepted, as if this was a fundamental historical break, by the Frankfurt School, including Fromm and Marcuse, and by the New Left. But this dynamic has returned with a vengeance, with numerous finance-driven bubbles since the 1980s.

Techno-futurist rhetoric of acceleration and exponentiality fed, and, in turn, saw apparent confirmation in, the speculative mania of the dot-com bubble that burst in 2000.[205] Kurzweil, in particular, continues to write in his 2005 book as if the bubble never burst, promising "accelerating returns" and repeating the New Economy mantra that "this time it's different":

> Contemporary economic theory and policy are based on outdated models that emphasize energy costs, commodity prices, and capital investment in plant and equipment as key driving factors, while largely overlooking computational capacity, memory, bandwidth, the size of technology, intellectual property, knowledge, and other increasingly vital (and increasingly increasing) constituents that are driving the economy.[206]

His language of infinite expansion, acceleration, and the melting of production into the thin air of information fits perfectly with an era of financial speculation in which mobile financial capital seeks to outrrun the underlying problems of the real economy. Kurzweil's own business activities combine his technological faith with speculative investment. In 1999, he set up a company called "FatKat" (Financial Accelerating Transactions from Kurzweil Adaptive Technologies), which makes software for investment decision-making, and in 2005 he set up two hedge funds using the FatKat name.[207] While economic "cycles" may continue, Kurzweil suggests that new technologies, allowing greater responsiveness to market trends, "have diminished the impact of this cycle" so that "'recessions' are likely to have less direct impact on our standard of living."[208]

In fact, the bursting of the dot-com bubble has been followed by far deeper global recession since 2008, following the bursting of the housing market bubble. As John Bellamy Foster and Fred Magdoff put it, "financial explosion" is followed by "financial implosion."[209] In addition to more than 15 % of the US population now living below the poverty line, the crisis has had a dramatic human toll worldwide. In the late summer of 2011, the UN warned "of huge job losses, a rise in the number of people afflicted by chronic undernourishment and the 'extraordinary price' being paid by children and other vulnerable groups as mass austerity programs constrict the developing world."[210] A once-again ebullient stock market, buoyed by the flow of money from the US Federal Reserve, maintains the "standard of living" of the financial elite, while the conditions the UN warned about are the lived reality of the working class worldwide.[211]

Techno-futurism is the transcendence, without negation, of capitalism.[212] It seeks to transcend the contradictions inherent within capitalism, not in order to end capitalism, but in order to preserve it. Techno-futurism thereby functions ideologically to legitimize the intensification of capitalist exploitation, while obscuring the way in which this intensification is producing crisis. The speed-up created by new technologies has intensified work and contributed to the "flexibilization" and increasing precariousness of labor markets and fueled the demand for the instantaneity of "network time," breaking down boundaries around the working day, pressurizing and degrading family life, and straining the social bond. The mobility of capital, enhanced by information technology, causes greater economic turbulence.[213] The barrage of the mass media, new interactive media spectacles, and the flow of new gadgets accompanied by advertising and media hyperbole contribute to the subjective sense of accelerating change. Everyday life becomes a struggle to keep up with accelerating temporal demands. These stresses of everyday life, intensified by technology, go hand in hand with stagnation and crisis tendencies at the macro-scale of the economy. Everyday life is characterized by the acceleration of insecurity.

Kurzweil's "technological fix" approach to economics points to a peculiar feature of techno-futurist thought more generally. While Drexler, Moravec and Kurzweil's conceptualization of technological dynamism operates within a political framework (usually tacit, but sometimes explicit) of market libertarianism, they give very little attention to the market *per se*, and to money in particular. Capital appears in their analyses in the form of technology, or fixed capital. They primarily tout the direct benefits of technology in terms of its use value. In doing so, they obscure the distinction between use value and exchange value, and the dialectical tension between them. But this contradiction is central to understanding the dynamics of capitalism, for example, how economic crisis can follow from increases in productivity.[214] This distinction is further occluded by the assimilation of market competition to evolutionary natural selection. Moravec and Kurzweil imagine technologies developing so as compete with one another no longer through the medium of the marketplace (i.e. through money) but directly as competing forms of life. The "owners" of capital are, in this view, pushed aside by capital itself, which, henceforth, becomes self-directing and self-augmenting.[215] Moravec envisages technologies competing for dominance in colonization of the universe. Since this competition is ecological, money is rendered superfluous. Technologies compete as use values—the most efficient, the best technology in the sense of use values wins. So, market relations of competing exchange values are assimilated to relations of use value. In this way, techno-futurism looks toward the transcendence of capitalism's contradictory relationship between use value and exchange value, not through breaking with capitalism, but rather through the evolution of capital.

The notion that humans will merge with machines, and that the development of technology is a form of evolution, collapses the distinction between capital and labor. Living labor is fully subsumed within capital, which takes on the characteristics of life. In this way, real subsumption of labor gives capital the ability to be self-augmenting value. However, this is a contradictory process. Marx saw that it was a tendency of capital to replace labor with machinery. It is in the interests of individual capitals to reduce labor costs, and discipline labor, through increasing mechanization. Other capitals are compelled by market competition to follow this example. However, Marx reasoned that since exploitation of labor is the source of surplus value (i.e. profit), then the increasing capital intensiveness of the production process (the rising "organic composition of capital") would in the longer term undermine the basis for profitability for capital as a whole.[216] Capital is dependent on living labor at the same time that it stands in an antagonistic relationship with labor. Techno-futurism's image of the merger of human with machine, and the creation of living technology, projects the overcoming of this contradiction. However, it does so without seeking or imagining any break with capitalism itself.

Moravec's "capitalism's end" is the result of an evolutionary development in which capital *realizes itself* as self-valorizing value. This ultimate *end* of technology making itself is, in fact, pre-supposed at the *beginning* of the techno-futurists' argument, since their account of technology leaves aside the crucial fact that technologies are the product and embodiment of human labor. The techno-futurists "transcend" the dialectic between capital and labor merely by denying labor. Their mystification of technology is an intellectual reflection of the commodity fetishism that arises from market relations. Through the denial of labor as a material force, the techno-futurists' non-dialectical, reductionist materialism reifies human material activity as "technology" and human creativity (abstracted from material practice) as "intelligence." Then, the techno-futurists talk about this abstracted "intelligence" being vested in, and taken over by, "technology." They then project the development of technology as the conquest of materiality by "intelligence," leading to what Moravec calls "the Age of Mind." In this way, their materialism becomes idealism.

The underlying idealism of 'knowledge economy' rhetoric is made apparent in Leadbeater's notion of "living on thin air." This is taken further in techno-futurism, as the notion of "intelligence" allows the development of technology to be abstracted from material conditions, contradictions, and scarcities. The fecundity of ideas, the process by which idea can beget idea *apparently* separately from any material basis, and without constraints of scarcity, is translated by techno-futurists into the fecundity of an abstract "intelligence" operating through self-replicating capital. In this way, techno-futurism recapitulates the religious promise that spirit itself can nourish (the magical trick whereby Christ fed the five thousand). Thus, the link between religious mysticism and commodity fetishism becomes overt in techno-futurism. It brings together technological determinism and idealism in its denial of capitalism's dialectical contradictions, most importantly, the dialectic between labor and capital.

Techno-futurism is premised on the occlusion of labor as an active, historical force. Marx says in *The Poverty of Philosophy*, "[M]en make cloth, linen, or silk materials in definite relations of production... [T]hese definite social relations are just as much produced by men as linen, flax, etc." When Marx wrote in that essay that "[t]he hand-mill gives you society with the feudal lord; the steam-mill, society with the industrial capitalist," he was not putting forward technological determinism, but rather was condemning Proudhon's idealist reification of "impersonal reason" and explaining his own conception of the *active, historical* character of human production.[217] Both the steam mill *and* industrial capitalist society are the products of human labor, and there can be no making industrial capitalist relations without making industrial capitalist technology. But that is quite different from, and opposed to, the treatment of technological change as an automatic process that drives human history.[218] Marx's dialectical conception of history, premised on the active, historical character of human production, has nothing in common with determinism. In contrast, denial of the *active, historical* character of human labor is the common denominator in both technological determinism and idealism. Techno-futurism's image of the self-creation of intelligent machines fuses idealism with technological determinism and carries on this obfuscation of the transformative, historical power of labor. Its ideological purpose is to mask the contradictions present in every moment of capitalism, and to portray the future as following a unilinear track. By obscuring labor, techno-futurism operates ideologically to hide the real historical agency capable of transcending capitalism—the working class.

The techno-futurists present the "transhuman" future pointed to by capitalism's technological trajectory as a harmonious transcendence of a flawed human condition. The only element of truth in this portrait is the notion of that capitalist development points toward a future that is dehumanized. To avoid this accelerating race to oblivion is to negate the conception of time as a smooth "trajectory," whether linear or exponential. Technological development is the outcome of human activity that not only manifests objective conditions, but also opens up new possibilities and paths for future action.

Techno-futurists falsely present technological possibilities as imperatives, masking their historical character. Instead, the historical moment contains contradictory forces and competing possibilities. Moishe Postone writes that Marx sought "to uncover a growing disparity between what is and what could be, one that constitutes the objective/subjective conditions of possibility of a different ordering of social life."[219] What István Mészáros means by the "challenge and burden of historical time" is precisely the dialectic between the burden of objective conditions and the challenge of human potential. This potential contains far greater possibilities than those available to the individual in their own lifetime. This gap creates a dialectic of value and counter-value, whereby it becomes possible to negate the objective conditions of the present of the lived individual by reference to the positive potentialities of the human future.[220] Techno-futurism's construction of an eternal present (the immortality project) and collapse of the future into the present (the language of acceleration and imperative) ideologically masks this dialectic. While imaginatively exploring what is technologically possible, techno-futurism transforms possibility into imperative. The techno-futurists' technological imagination is distorted by their lack of social imagination, causing them to project the present, with its "objective" existing constraints, into the future, while erasing the contradictory forces existing in the present and obscuring the possibilities of humanity's future.

Techno-futurism constructs a contradictory eternal present in conjunction with capitalist-technological linear time, producing a temporality that is an implosive acceleration into the present. In this, it reflects late capitalism's illusory end of history. The eternal present of late capitalist, or "post-modern" culture, does not overcome but instead exists in contradiction with the linear time of capitalist production. In capital, the past, in the form of dead labor, dominates the present (living labor, or life activity), and suppresses present life in the service of future accumulation. The acceleration and consequent precariousness of everyday life are manifestations of the increasingly intense subordination of the present to linear time. This present, dominated by the momentum of capitalism's linear time, takes the form of Virilio's integral accident. This implosion of acceleration into the present may yield total destruction, the general accident: economic crisis, ecological disaster, military Armageddon. Alternatively, the contradictions of the late capitalist present can explode into a renewal of history as class struggle, negating capitalism's premature and illusory "end of history."

Foster writes, "The out-of-control destruction that now characterizes the capital system on a world scale, and imperils all life on the planet, has its dialectical antithesis in the potential for an acceleration of history, through the activation of a genuine, mass-based revolutionary struggle."[221] To overcome the social stasis of capital's iron cage is also to counteract the speed with which capital drags human life along the path of the inhuman determinisms of market forces and alienating technology. We are trapped in a capitalist present that dulls historical consciousness at the same time that it reifies the past into the determinisms of "economic growth" and "market forces." The preservation of capitalism means suppressing the ability of human beings to make history and upholding the power of the past embodied in "circumstances" that the vast mass of human beings cannot and do not choose.[222] In contrast, revolution awakens the vitality of the present as it actively creates the future. "In bourgeois society," Marx and Engels wrote, "the past dominates the present; in Communist society, the present dominates the past."[223]

Notes

1. Brian Aldiss, "Supertoys Last All Summer Long," in idem *Supertoys Last All Summer Long and Other Stories of Future Time* (New York: St. Martin's Griffin, 2001), 1–11, on 1, 9.
2. Aldiss, "Supertoys," 2.
3. Aldiss, "Supertoys," 6–7.
4. *A.I. Artificial Intelligence* (Steven Spielberg, 2001); Roger Ebert, "A.I. Artificial Intelligence," *RogerEbert.com*, http://rogerebert.suntimes.com/apps/pbcs.dll/article?AID=/20110707/REVIEWS08/110709988/1023. Accessed 9/20/15; "A.I. Artificial

Intelligence," *Wikipedia*, https://en.wikipedia.org/wiki/A.I._Artificial_ Intelligence. Accessed 9/20/2015.
5. See Guy Debord, *Society of the Spectacle* (London: Rebel Press, 1967), 69.
6. Ivor Southwood, *Non-Stop Inertia* (London: Zero Books, 2011). See also Robert Hassan, "Network Time," in Robert Hassan and Ronald E. Purser eds, *24/7: Time and Temporality in the Network Society* (Stanford: Stanford Business Books, 2007), 37–61, esp. 55.
7. Hartmut Rosa, *Social Acceleration: A New Theory of Modernity* (New York: Columbia University Press, 2013), 15, 272.
8. Herbert Marcuse *One-Dimensional Man* (Boston: Beacon Press, 1964), 17.
9. Slavoj Žižek, "A Permanent Economic Emergency," *New Left Review* 64 (July-August 2010), 85–95, on 93.
10. Debord, *Society of the Spectacle*, 71.
11. Karl Marx, *Grundrisse*, trans. Martin Nicolaus (Harmondsworth: Penguin, 1973), 706. See also Endnotes "The Moving Contradiction: The Systematic Dialectic of Capital as a Dialectic of Class Struggle," *Endnotes* 2 (April 2010), http://endnotes.org.uk/articles/5; Nick Beams, "The Significance and Implications of Globalisation: A Marxist Assessment," *World Socialist Web Site*, January 4, 1998, https://www.wsws.org/en/articles/1998/01/glob-j04.html
12. Nick Dyer-Witheford, *Cyber-Marx: Cycles and Circuits of Struggle in High-Technology Capitalism* (Urbana: University of Illinois Press, 1999), 67.
13. I focus on these thinkers and the following texts, because I regard them as classics of the genre, setting out the foundations and common assumptions of techno-futurist thought. Kurzweil's writings, in particular, synthesize the ideas of others, including Moravec and Drexler, and through his notion of the "Singularity" Kurzweil constructs an overarching transhumanist program. The texts I focus on are Eric Drexler, *Engines of Creation* (Garden City, New York: Anchor/Doubleday, 1986); Hans Moravec, *Mind Children: The Future of Robot and Human Intelligence* (Cambridge, MA: Harvard University Press, 1988); Hans Moravec, *Robot: Mere Machine to Transcendent Mind* (New York: Oxford University Press, 1999); Ray Kurzweil, *The Age of Spiritual Machines: When Computers Exceed Human Intelligence* (New York: Penguin, 1999); Ray Kurzweil, *The Singularity is Near: When Humans Transcend Biology* (New York: Penguin, 2005). Drexler more recently published an update on the progress of nanotechnology, titled *Radical Abundance: How a Revolution in Nanotechnology Will Change Civilization* (New York: Public Affairs, 2013). I will focus, however, on his earlier book, which he notes "served as the flashpoint for all that followed" (ibid., 10).

14. Cynthia Selin, "Expectations and the Emergence of Nanotechnology," *Science, Technology, and Human Values* (March 2007) 32 (2): 196–220; W. Patrick McCray, "Will Small be Beautiful? Making Policies for our Nanotech Future," *History and Technology* 21(2) (2005): 177–203. For a critique of techno-utopianism in computing and IT, see Langdon Winner, "Cyberlibertarian Myths and the Prospects for Community," *ACM SIGCAS Computers and Society* 27(3) (Sept. 1997): 14–19.
15. Ian Sample, "Ray Kurzweil to Head Futurology School Backed by NASA and Google," The Guardian, February 3, 2009, http://www.theguardian.com/science/2009/feb/03/nasa-google-futurology-kurzweil-singularity; Alok Jha, James Randerson, and Ian Sample, "The Singularity University: 'They almost self-fulfil that prophecy'," (audio-recorded discussion) *The Guardian*, February 8, 2009, http://www.theguardian.com/science/audio/2009/feb/09/singularity-university-ray-kurzweil
16. Lev Grossman, "2045: The Year Man Becomes Immortal," *Time*, February 10, 2011; The Singularity Summit Program, 2011, http://www.singularitysummit.com/program. Accessed October 3, 2011; David Weigel, "Ron Paul's Billionaire," *Slate Magazine*, February 20, 2012, http://www.slate.com/articles/news_and_politics/politics/2012/02/investor_peter_thiel_is_the_billionaire_behind_ron_paul_s_presidential_campaign_.html; Wikipedia page for Palantir Technologies, http://en.wikipedia.org/wiki/Palantir_Technologies. Accessed June 2014.
17. Moravec has received funding from NASA, the Office of Naval Research (ONR), and DARPA: http://www.kurzweilai.net/hans-moravec. Accessed June 20, 2014.
18. Rodney Brooks, "From Robot Dreams to Reality," *Nature* 406 (August 31, 2000), 945–947, quoting 947. Brooks was a speaker at Kurzweil's Singularity Summit in 2007: http://itc.conversationsnetwork.org/shows/detail3400.html#. Accessed October 3, 2011.
19. David Noble, *Forces of Production: A Social History of Industrial Automation* (Oxford: Oxford University Press, 1986), 44.
20. W. Patrick McCray, *The Visioneers: How a Group of Elite Scientists Pursued Space Colonies, Nanotechnologies, and a Limitless Future* (Princeton: Princeton University Press, 2012).
21. David Noble, *America by Design: Science, Technology and the Rise of Corporate Capitalism* (New York: Oxford University Press, 1977), xvii. See also Rosa, *Social Acceleration*, 259–276, 313.
22. Kevin Kelly, *What Technology Wants* (NY: Viking, 2010), 11. See also Jaron Lanier, *You are Not a Gadget: a Manifesto* (New York: Vintage Books, 2011), 5.
23. Kelly, *What Technology Wants*, 39.
24. Kelly, *What Technology Wants*, 41, 355.

25. Kurzweil, *The Age of Spiritual Machines*, 26–27.
26. Kurzweil, *Singularity*, 35–110, esp. 48–50, 57–66.
27. Kurzweil, *Singularity*, 17.
28. Kurzweil, quoted in Lev Grossman, "2045: The Year Man Becomes Immortal," Time, February 10, 2011, http://www.time.com/time/printout/0,8816,2048138,00.html
29. Kurzweil, *Singularity*, 407.
30. Kurzweil, *Singularity*, 406.
31. Moravec, *Robot*, 1.
32. Joint Economic Committee, United States Congress, *Nanotechnology: The Future is Coming Sooner than You Think: A Joint Economic Committee Study*, March 2007, http://www.house.gov/je Quoting abstract on title page.
33. Ray Kurzweil and Terry Grossman, *Fantastic Voyage: Live Long Enough to Live Forever* (Emmaus, PA: Rodale, 2004), 8.
34. Ray Kurzweil, *The Age of Spiritual Machines*, 130; quoted also in Robert M. Geraci, *Apocalyptic AI: Visions of Heaven in Robotics, Artificial Intelligence, and Virtual Reality* (New York: Oxford University Press, 2010), 29.
35. Moravec, quoted in "Valley to Bill Joy: Zzzz" *Wired* 04/05/2000, http://www.wired.com/science/discoveries/news/2000/04/35424
36. Drexler, *Engines of Creation*, 30–32, quoting 30.
37. Drexler, *Engines of Creation*, 30.
38. Drexler, *Engines of Creation*, 32.
39. Drexler, *Engines of Creation*, 35.
40. Drexler, *Engines of Creation*, 85.
41. Drexler, *Engines of Creation*, 54–55.
42. Drexler, *Engines of Creation*, 56.
43. Drexler, *Engines of Creation*, 63.
44. Drexler, *Engines of Creation*, 94.
45. Drexler, *Engines of Creation*, 95.
46. Moravec, *Robot*, 10–11.
47. Moravec, *Robot*, 11–12.
48. Moravec, *Robot*, 133.
49. Moravec, *Robot*, 133.
50. David Noble, *Progress Without People: New Technology, Unemployment, and the Message of Resistance* (Toronto, Ontario: Between the Lines, 1995).
51. Kurzweil, *Singularity*, 40.
52. Kurzweil, *Singularity*, 298.
53. Kurzweil, *Singularity*, 198–199.
54. Kurzweil, *Singularity*, 309.

55. Kurzweil, *Singularity*, 199.
56. Kurzweil, *Singularity*, 199, 310.
57. Kurzweil, *The Singularity*, 325.
58. Kurzweil, *The Singularity*, 136; see also 349–353.
59. Kevin Kelly, *New Rules for the New Economy: 10 Radical Strategies for a Connected World* (New York: Penguin, 1998), 39.
60. Kelly, *New Rules*, 23.
61. Charles Leadbeater, *Living on Thin Air* (London: Penguin, 2000).
62. Bill Gates, *Business @ the Speed of Thought: Using a Digital Nervous System* (New York: Warner Books, 1999), quoting 23, see also 151, 181.
63. Gates, Business, 143, 149, 154.
64. Kelly, *New Rules*, 113.
65. Kelly, *New Rules*, 112.
66. Kelly, *New Rules*, 109–110.
67. Moravec, Robot, 1.
68. Aubrey de Grey and Michael Rae, *Ending Aging: The Rejuvenation Breakthroughs that Could Reverse Human Aging in Our Lifetime* (New York: St. Martin's Press, 2007), 330, 413. De Grey spoke at the Singularity Summit in 2009: http://vimeo.com/7339349. Accessed October 3, 2011. See also http://www.singularitysummit.com/summit/past_summits, accessed October 3, 2011.
69. Mark Dery, *Escape Velocity: Cyberculture at the End of the Century* (New York: Grove Press, 1996), 8.
70. Drexler, *Engines of Creation*, 79–80.
71. Drexler, *Engines of Creation*, 77.
72. Drexler, *Engines of Creation*, 217.
73. Drexler, *Engines of Creation*, 98.
74. Drexler, *Engines of Creation*, 162.
75. Moravec, *Robot*, 7.
76. Moravec, *Robot*, 25.
77. Moravec, *Robot*, 110.
78. Moravec, *Robot*, 9.
79. Moravec, *Robot*, 9–10.
80. Moravec, *Robot*, 159–160.
81. Moravec, *Robot*, 160.
82. Moravec, *Robot*, 13.
83. Moravec, quoted in Dery, *Escape Velocity*, 307.
84. Moravec, quoted in Dery, *Escape Velocity*, 307.
85. Moravec, quoted in Dery, *Escape Velocity*, 307.
86. Kurzweil, *Singularity*, 24.
87. Kurzweil, *Singularity*, 24.

88. The term "accelerating acceleration" was used by Buckminster Fuller: Thomas T.K. Zung, *Buckminster Fuller: an Anthology for the New Millennium* (New York: St. Martin's Press, 2001), 300.
89. Kurzweil, *Singularity*, 24.
90. Kurzweil, *Singularity*, 10–11.
91. Kurzweil, *Singularity*, 351.
92. Cf. Ivan Illich, *Tools for Conviviality* (New York: Harper and Row, 1973), 8–9.
93. Kurzweil, *Singularity*, 224. Emphasis in original.
94. Kurzweil, *Singularity*, 252.
95. Kurzweil, *Singularity*, 99.
96. Kurzweil, *Singularity*, 106.
97. Kurzweil, *Singularity*, 102.
98. Kurzweil, *Singularity*, 26.
99. Kurzweil, *Singularity*, 27.
100. Kurzweil, *Singularity*, 9.
101. Kurzweil, *Singularity*, 205–206. He acknowledges the point as owing to Moravec.
102. Kurzweil and Grossman, *Fantastic Voyage*, 139–140.
103. Kurzweil and Grossman, *Fantastic Voyage*, 141. Emphasis in original.
104. Kurzweil, *Singularity*, 211.
105. Kurzweil and Grossman, *Fantastic Voyage*, 140–143, quoting 143.
106. See Christopher Lasch, *The Culture of Narcissism: American Life in an Age of Diminishing Expectations* (New York: Warner Books, 1979), 98.
107. Kurzweil and Grossman, *Fantastic Voyage*, 1–32 (quotation is from book subtitle and title of first chapter); Kurzweil, *Singularity*, 198–203, 324–330.
108. Kurzweil, *Singularity*, 325.
109. Drexler, *Engines of Creation*, 133–138, quoting 136, 138.
110. Drexler, *Engines of Creation*, 144–145. On Drexler's libertarian political leanings, see McCray, *The Visioneers*, 173.
111. Drexler, *Engines of Creation*, 145.
112. Drexler, *Engines of Creation*, 126.
113. Drexler, *Engines of Creation*, 146.
114. Moravec, *Robot*, 169–170.
115. Moravec, *Robot*, 167–168.
116. Mircea Eliade, *The Myth of Eternal Return*, trans. Willard R. Trask (New York: Pantheon Books, 1965); Margaret Wertheim, *The Pearly Gates of Cyberspace: A History of Space from Dante to the Internet* (NY: W. W. Norton and Co., 1999), 256.
117. Frederic Jameson, *Postmodernism, or, The Cultural Logic of Late Capitalism* (Durham, NC: Duke University Press, 1991).

118. Moravec, *Robot*, 168. Emphasis in original.
119. Moravec, *Robot*, 168. Cf. Philip K. Dick, *The Three Stigmata of Palmer Eldritch* (London: Orion Books, 2003 [orig. 1964]).
120. Cf. Lasch, *Culture of Narcissism*, 133.
121. Moravec, *Robot*, 172.
122. Moravec, *Robot*, 172.
123. Bruce Berman, "Artificial Intelligence and the Ideology of Capitalist Reconstruction," *AI & Society* 6 (1992): 103–114, on 111.
124. Paul Virilio, "From Superman to Hyperactive Man," in idem, *The Art of the Motor*, trans. Julie Rose (Minneapolis: University of Minnesota Press, 1995), 99–132, esp. 104.
125. Glenn Rikowski, "Alien Life: Marx and the Future of the Human" *Historical Materialism* 11 (2) (2003): 121–164; Glenn Rikowski, "Education, Capital and the Transhuman," in Dave Hill, Peter McLaren, Mike Cole, and Glenn Rikowski eds., *Marxism Against Postmodernism in Educational Theory* (Lanham, MD: Lexington Books, 2002), 111–143.
126. C. Wright Mills, *White Collar: The American Middle Classes* (Oxford: Oxford University Press, 1956); Jeff Schmidt, *Disciplined Minds: A Critical Look at Salaried Professionals and the Soul-Battering System that Shapes Their Lives* (Lanham, MD: Rowman and Littlefield, 2000).
127. Fromm, *Anatomy*, 349; see also Fromm, *To Have or To Be?*, 122–125. However, this alienated presentation of self is increasingly demanded of minimum-wage workers in the service industry, not only the "middle class." See Linda Tirado, *Hand to Mouth: Living in Bootstrap America* (New York: Berkeley Books, 2014), 19–20.
128. David Golumbia, *The Cultural Logic of Computation* (Cambridge, MA: Harvard University Press, 2009), 185 (emphasis in original); see also 200.
129. Erich Fromm, *The Anatomy of Human Destructiveness* (New York: Holt, Rinehart and Winston), 349.
130. Erich Fromm, *For the Love of Life*, trans. Robert and Rita Kimber (New York: The Free Press, 1986), 19; Zygmunt Bauman, *Consuming Life* (Cambridge: Polity Press, 2007), 57.
131. Albert Borgmann, *Technology and the Character of Contemporary Life: a Philosophical Inquiry* (Chicago: University of Chicago Press, 1987).
132. Fromm, *For the Love of Life*, 20.
133. Fromm, *To Have or To Be?*, 125. Emphasis in original.
134. Lasch, *Culture of Narcissism*, 351.
135. Fromm, *For the Love of Life*, 20.
136. Fromm, *To Have or To Be?*, 124, 125.
137. Keith Ansell-Pearson, *Viroid Life: Perspectives on Nietzsche and the Transhuman Condition* (London: Routledge, 1997), 2. See also David

F. Noble, *The Religion of Technology: The Divinity of Man and the Spirit of Invention* (New York: Penguin Books, 1999), esp. 143–171.
138. Drexler, *Engines of Creation*, 138.
139. Kurzweil, *The Age of Spiritual Machines*, 153; quoted also in Geraci, *Apocalyptic AI*, 133.
140. Kurzweil, *Spiritual Machines*, 153.
141. Robert M. Geraci, "Apocalyptic AI: Religion and the Promise of Artificial Intelligence," *Journal of the American Academy of Religion* 76(1) (March 2008): 138–166, esp. 146.
142. Amarnath Amarasingam, "Transcending Technology: Looking at Futurology as a New Religious Movement," *Journal of Contemporary Religion* 23(1): 1–16; Geraci, *Apocalyptic AI*, 13. See also Slavoj Zizek's discussion of "techno-digital apocalypticism (whose main representative is Ray Kurzweil)" in idem, *Living in the End Times* (London: Verso, 2011), 336–347, quoting 336. On Moravec, see Noble, *Religion of Technology*, 161.
143. Marx, "Results of the Immediate Process of Production," 990. Emphasis in original.
144. Marx, "Results of the Immediate Process of Production," 1056.
145. Debord, *Society of the Spectacle*, 67.
146. Marx, "Results of the Immediate Process of Production," 1058.
147. Quoting Fromm, *To Have or To Be?*, 124.
148. Kurzweil, *Singularity*, 96.
149. Kurzweil, *Singularity*, 364.
150. Kurzweil, *Singularity*, 361. See also Geraci, *Apocalyptic AI*, 35–36.
151. Moravec, *Robot*, 3, 6–7.
152. John Zerzan, *Future Primitive: And Other Essays* (New York: Autonomedia, 1994).
153. Moravec, *Robot*, 8.
154. Moravec, *Robot*, 8–9, 136.
155. Moravec, *Robot*, 127.
156. Moravec, *Robot*, 127.
157. Moravec, *Robot*, 127–128.
158. Moravec, *Robot*, 130.
159. Moravec, *Robot*, 131.
160. Moravec, *Robot*, 70.
161. Moravec, *Robot*, 72.
162. Moravec, *Robot*, 143.
163. Moravec, *Robot*, 150.
164. Moravec, *Robot*, 162.
165. Moravec, *Robot*, 199.
166. Moravec, *Robot*, 164–165.

167. Moravec, *Robot*, 165.
168. Moravec, *Robot*, 194.
169. Moravec, *Robot*, 111, 202. See also John D. Barrow and Frank J. Tipler, *The Anthropic Cosmological Principle* (Oxford: Clarendon Press, 1986).
170. Pierre Teilhard de Chardin, *The Phenomenon of Man* (New York: Harper & Brotehrs, 1959), 287; D. Gareth Jones, *Teilhard de Chardin: An Analysis and Assessment* (London: The Tyndale Press, 1969), 47. See also Eric Steinhart, "Teilhard de Chardin and Transhumanism," *Journal of Evolution & Technology* 20(1) (December 2008): 1–22, http://jetpress.org/v20/steinhart.htm; Oliver Krueger, "Gnosis in Cyberspace? Body, Mind and Progress in Posthumanism," *Journal of Evolution & Technology* 14 (August 2005), http://www.jetpress.org/volume14/krueger.pdf
171. Moravec, *Robot*, 202.
172. Frank J. Tipler, *The Physics of Immortality* (New York: Doubleday, 1994).
173. Moravec, *Robot*, 210–211.
174. Kurzweil, *Singularity*, 389. See also *ibid.*, 15, 390.
175. Kurzweil, *Singularity*, 389.
176. See also Geraci, *Apocalyptic AI*, 31.
177. Moravec, *Robot*, 1, 211.
178. Debord, *Society of the Spectacle*, 21.
179. Debord, *Society of the Spectacle*, 42. Emphasis in original.
180. Dery, *Escape Velocity*, 225. Compare the notion of "a dialectic of implosion and explosion" that Douglas Kellner discerns in Paul Virilio's writings: Kellner, "Virilio, War, and Technology: Some Critical Reflections," http://www.uta.edu/huma/illuminations/kell29.htm (accessed September 20, 2011). See also Virilio, *Open Sky* (London: Verso, 1997), 86; Mark Featherstone, "Virilio's Apocalypticism," *CTheory*, September 16, 2010, http://www.ctheory.net/articles.aspx?id=662#_ednref23. Accessed September 21, 2011
181. Fromm, *To Have or To Be?*, 125.
182. Catherine Cadwalladr, "Are Robots About to Rise? Google's New Director of Engineering Thinks So…" *The Guardian*, February 22, 2014, http://www.theguardian.com/technology/2014/feb/22/robots-google-ray-kurzweil-terminator-singularity-artificial-intelligence
183. Kurzweil, *Singularity*, 330.
184. Robert Harris and Jeremy Paxman, *A Higher Form of Killing: The Secret Story of Gas and Germ Warfare* (London: Chatto and Windus, 1982); Brian Balmer, "Killing 'Without the Distressing Preliminaries': Scientists' Defence of the British Biological Warfare Programme," *Minerva* 40 (1) (2002): 57–75; Kurzweil, *Singularity*, 330.

185. Kurzweil, *Singularity*, 331. Cf. Mary Kaldor, *New and Old Wars: Organized Violence in a Global Era* (Cambridge: Polity Press, 2006), esp. 2–3; John Pilger, *The War You Don't See* (Dartmouth Films, 2010).
186. Kurzweil, *Singularity*, 331–335.
187. Paul Virilio, *Popular Defense and Ecological Struggles* (New York: Semiotext(e), 1990), 72.
188. Paul Virilio, *Popular Defense and Ecological Struggles*, 68, 102; Virilio, *The Information Bomb*, trans. Chris Turner (London: Verso, 2005), 145.
189. Erich Fromm, *The Anatomy of Human Destructiveness* (New York: Holt, Rinehart and Winston, 1973), 344–345. See also Filippo Tommaso Marinetti, "The New Religion-Morality of Speed," in Hartmut Rosa and William E. Scheuerman, *High-Speed Society: Social Acceleration, Power, and Modernity* (University Park, PA: The Pennsylvania State University, 2009), 57-59.
190. http://www.airforce.com/?m=2011EAYouth&pl=Lastfm&med=display. Accessed September 21, 2011; Wikipedia entry on "Full Spectrum Dominance," http://en.wikipedia.org/wiki/Full_spectrum_dominance. Accessed September 21, 2011. Cf. Sam Wallace, "The Proposed Ban on Offensive Autonomous Weapons is Unrealistic and Dangerous," Kurzweil Accelerating Intelligence, Blog, August 5, 2015, http://www.kurzweilai.net/the-proposed-ban-on-offensive-autonomous-weapons-is-unrealistic-and-dangerous. (Accessed November 8, 2015).
191. Paul Virilio, *Strategy of Deception*, trans. Chris Turner (London: Verso, 2000), 14. Emphasis in original.
192. Berman, "Artificial Intelligence and the Ideology of Capitalist Reconstruction," 108–109; David F. Noble, "Command Performance: A Perspective on Military Enterprise and Technological Change," in Merritt Roe Smith ed., *Military Enterprise and Technological Change: Perspectives on the American Experience* (Cambridge, MA: MIT Press, 1985), 329–346.
193. Willie Osterweil, "The Drone of Permanent War," *Dissent* (March 21, 2012), http://www.dissentmagazine.org/blog/the-drone-of-permanent-war; Charles Sheehan, "Robotics Research Gaining in Prestige," Associated Press, April 9, 2004, http://www.redorbit.com/news/technology/54974/robotics_research_gaining_in_prestige (accessed September 21, 2011); Xan Rice, "US drone bases in Africa to focus on al-Qaida targets and Somalia," *The Guardian*, September 21, 2011, http://www.guardian.co.uk/world/2011/sep/21/us-drone-bases-africa-somalia?INTCMP=SRCH; Geraci, *Apocalyptic AI*, 162.
194. P. W. Singer, "Military Robots and the Laws of War," *The New Atlantis* 23 (Winter 2009): 25–45; Singer, *Wired for War: The Robotics Revolution*

and *Conflict in the 21ˢᵗ Century* (London: Penguin, 2009), 21–25. Boston Dynamics is another MIT spin-out http://en.wikipedia.org/wiki/Boston_Dynamics. Accessed September 21, 2011; Will Knight, "Google's Latest Robot Acquisition is the Smartest Yet," *MIT Technology Review*, December 14, 2013, http://www.technologyreview.com/video/522696/googles-latest-robot-acquisition-is-the-smartest-yet/

195. Thomas Donnelly, Donald Kagan, and Gary Schmitt, *Rebuilding America's Defenses: Strategy, Forces and Resources for a New Century* (Washington, DC: The Project for a New American Century, September 2000).
196. John Bellamy Foster, *Naked Imperialism: The U.S. Pursuit of Global Dominance* (New York: Monthly Review Press, 2006), esp. 19, 84–85, 92–93, 103–106, 107–120.
197. Chris Harman, *Zombie Capitalism: Global Crisis and the Relevance of Marx* (Chicago: Haymarket Books, 2010), 310.
198. Paul Virilio (interviewed) in John Armitage, *Virilio Now: Current Perspectives in Virilio Studies* (Cambridge: Polity Press, 2011), 36.
199. Paul Virilio, *The Original Accident*, trans. Julie Rose (Cambridge: Polity Press, 2007), 100.
200. Virilio, *The Original Accident*, 100.
201. Hartmut Rosa suggests a "dialectical relationship between acceleration and inertia": Rosa, *Social Acceleration*, 226; see also 90–93, 277–298.
202. Cf. Bob Siedensticker, *Future Hype: The Myths of Technology Change* (San Francisco: Barrett-Koehler Publishers, 2006), esp. 72–76; David Edgerton, *The Shock of the Old: Technology and Global History Since 1900* (Oxford: Oxford University Press, 2007).
203. David Harvey, *The Condition of Postmodernity: An Inquiry into the Origins of Cultural Change* (Oxford: Wiley-Blackwell, 1991), 230.
204. Robert Brenner, *The Economics of Global Turbulence* (London: Verso, 2006), 1–9; Harman, *Zombie Capitalism*, 231–238; John Bellamy Foster and Fred Magdoff, *The Great Financial Crisis: Causes and Consequences* (New York: Monthly Review Press, 2009), 128–134; Nikos Passas, "Global Anomie, Dysnomie, and Economic Crime: Hidden Consequences of Neoliberalism and Globalization in Russia and Around the World," *Social Justice* 27 (2) (2000): 16–44, on 24.
205. On the "New Economy" enthusiasm of Federal Reserve Chairman Alan Greenspan, see Brenner, *Global Turbulence*, 294–295. For a discussion of the financial crisis in terms of Virilio's theory of the accident, see Arthur and Marilouise Kroker, "City of Transformation: Paul Virilio in Obama's America," *CTheory* (October 30, 2008), http://www.ctheory.net/articles.aspx?id=597. Accessed September 30, 2011.
206. Kurzweil, *Singularity*, 96.

207. http://en.wikipedia.org/wiki/FatKat_(investment_software); FatKat Investment Fund, LP and FatKat QP Investment Fund, LP; SEC Filing (2005) for FatKat Investment Fund, LP: http://www.sec.gov/Archives/edgar/vprr/06/9999999997-06-000333; SEC Filing (2005) for FATKAT QP INVESTMENT FUND LP: http://www.sec.gov/Archives/edgar/vprr/06/9999999997-06-000198
208. Kurzweil, *Singularity*, 106.
209. Foster and Magdoff, *The Great Financial Crisis*, 120. See also Hillel Ticktin, "A Marxist Political Economy of Capitalist Instability and the Current Crisis," *Critique* 37 (1) (2009): 13–29.
210. Larry Elliott, Liz Ford, and agencies, "Warning on Human Cost of Crisis," *The Guardian Weekly* (30 September, 2011), 1; Thomas Gaist, "US Census Report Shows Entrenched Poverty and Declining Living Standards," *World Socialist Web Site*, September 18, 2013, http://www.wsws.org/en/articles/2013/09/18/cens-s18.html
211. Barry Grey, "Economy Slumps, Wall Street Booms," *World Socialist Web Site*, June 20, 2014, http://www.wsws.org/en/articles/2014/06/20/pers-j20.html
212. Cf. Moishe Postone on post-modernism as "a sort of premature post-capitalism" in Postone, "Theorizing the Contemporary World: Robert Brenner, Giovanni Arrighi, David Harvey," in Robert Albritton, Robert Jessop, and Richard Westra eds., *Political Economy and Global Capitalism: The 21st Century, Present and Future* (London: Anthem Press, 2007), 7–23, on 22.
213. István Mészáros, *The Challenge and Burden of Historical Time: Socialism in the Twenty-First Century* (New York: Monthly Review Press, 2008), 159–178; Mark C. Taylor, *Speed Limits: Where Time Went and Why We Have So Little Left* (New Haven: Yale University Press, 2014), 227–265.
214. Tony Smith, "Technological Dynamism and the Normative Justification of Global Capitalism," in Albritton et al., *Political Economy and Global Capitalism*, 25–42, on 38.
215. Moravec, *Robot*, 133.
216. Harman, *Zombie Capitalism*, 70; Beams, "Significance and Implications of Globalisation"; Andrew Kliman, *The Failure of Capitalist Production: Underlying Causes of the Great Recession* (London: Pluto Press, 2012).
217. Karl Marx, "The Poverty of Philosophy," in David McLellan ed., *Karl Marx: Selected Writings* (Oxford: Oxford University Press, 1990), 193–215, on 202. See also Donald MacKenzie, "Marx and the Machine," *Technology and Culture* 25 (3) (July 1984): 473–502. It is indicative of how this passage from *The Poverty of Philosophy* has been misunderstood that Kevin Kelly cites it in support of his own simplistic technological determinism (*What Technology Wants*, 40).

218. See also George V. Plekhanov, *Fundamental Problems of Marxism* (New York: International Publishers, 1969), 68–69.
219. Postone, "Theorizing the Contemporary World," 17.
220. Mészáros, *Challenge and Burden*, 37–38.
221. John Bellamy Foster, "István Mészáros, Pathfinder of Socialism," *Monthly Review* 61 (09) (February 2010), http://monthlyreview.org/2010/02/01/istvan-meszaros-pathfinder-of-socialism
222. "Men make their own history, but they do not make it just as they please; they do not make it under circumstances chosen by themselves, but under circumstances directly encountered, given, and transmitted from the past": Karl Marx, "The Eighteenth Brumaire of Louis Bonaparte," in McLellan ed., *Karl Marx*, 300–325, on 300.
223. Karl Marx and Frederick Engels, "The Communist Manifesto," in McLellan ed., *Karl Marx*, 221–247, on 233. See also Erich Fromm, *Marx's Concept of Man* (New York: Frederick Ungar [1961] 1971), 40.

CHAPTER 4

The Pornography of Information

THE PORNOGRAPHY OF REPRESENTATION

In her groundbreaking study, *The Pornography of Representation* (1986), Susanne Kappeler argued that pornography is a structure of representation in which women are rendered objects for the gaze of the male subject. Man-as-subject and woman-as-object are constructed in opposition to one another within this structure: "The objectification of woman is a result of the subjectification of man."[1] This simultaneously subjectifying and objectifying structure of representation, inherently violent in its reduction of a human being to an object of the gaze, action, and power of another, encodes and solidifies the social structures of hierarchy and domination in which it is embedded. Representing, Kappeler insists, is not an activity that stands outside and documents the exertion of power; it is itself an act of domination. She demonstrates this intersection of representation with domination through a discussion of a news report of the torture and murder of a black Namibian farm worker, Thomas Kasire, by a white farmer and his friends. The killing was motivated by the farmer's suspicion that his employee was part of the SWAPO (South Western African People's Organisation) resistance movement. The perpetrators took photographic souvenirs of the torture and humiliation of the victim—the news report showed an image of Kasire, with his ear cut off, a chain around his neck, and a white arm holding the chain. In another image, Kasire was forced to give a clenched fist SWAPO salute while enduring abuse. Kappeler argues that the taking of photographs was integral to the abuse of Kasire. Photographing the victim was not an external documentation of what was happening to Kasire but was part of the process of dehumanizing and reducing him to an object.[2] The objectification of the victim is also their annihilation as a subject. The victim is dead in the sense that there is no subject position for them to take up: they are rendered as, and made into, a lifeless thing. The authors of the image, the audience, and the viewers of the image who are drawn into this audience, are rendered as subjects in that process.

Kappeler's analysis is essential for understanding the meaning of the more recent Abu Ghraib torture photographs. Notorious photographs show Private Lynndie England and US prison officer and Army reservist Specialist Charles Graner grinning and giving the thumbs up next to naked, hooded Iraqi inmates. Similarly to Kappeler's example of the torture of Thomas Kasire, photography was integral to the abuse of detainees in the US jail in Iraq in 2003. The photographs show, for example, men hooded, with wires applied to their bodies, forced to adopt stress positions; naked men, hooded with a grinning female soldier pointing at their genitals; hooded, naked men piled on top of each other, their genitals and buttocks exposed to the camera; naked men cowering before dogs; a hooded man kneeling with his head in the crotch of another hooded, naked man; a man with a bloodstained bandage on his face stretched out on a plastic sheet, wrapped in clear plastic, with American soldiers smiling giving a thumbs up sign. Prisoners were subjected to sexual assault, including rape, forced nakedness, beatings, sexual humiliation; being forced to lie in urine or feces; being urinated on and spat on; being forced into humiliating positions such as crawling; being intimidated by dogs and bitten by dogs; and being forced to sit and walk like a dog and bark like a dog. An as-yet unreleased photograph is said to show a female prisoner being raped by one of the guards.[3]

Prisoners' accounts refer to photography as a routine part of the abuse. For example, Kasim Mehaddi has described having his clothes taken away, having female underwear placed on his head, being beaten and "Grainer [*sic*] and the other two soldiers were taking pictures of every thing they did to me… I saw [name blacked out] fucking a kid, his age would be about 15–18 years. The kid was hurting very bad and … I saw [name blacked out], who was wearing the military uniform putting his dick in the little kid's ass… And the female soldier was taking pictures."[4] Abdou

Hussain Saad Faleh was made to stand hooded on a box with wires on his fingers, toes, and penis, and a soldier "came with a loudspeaker and he was shouting near my ear and then he brought the camera and he took some pictures of me, which I knew because of the flash of the camera."[5] Another former detainee describes a litany of abuse including beatings, humiliation, and sodomy and other sexual abuse, and says, "And they were taking pictures of me during all these instances."[6]

Journalist Mark Danner suggests that the practices at Abu Ghraib were related to the psychological goals of torture in breaking down prisoners' will and sense of self. Danner argues that the practices at Abu Ghraib are understandable in this light as "staged operas of fabricated shame."[7] He writes:

> Whatever those taking them intended to do with the photographs, for the prisoners the camera had the potential of exposing his humiliation to family and friends, and thus served as a "shame multiplier," putting enormous power in the hands of the interrogator.[8]

The objective image produced by the camera preserves the victim's object status, symbolically holding them in jail as long as the pictures exist.

The Abu Ghraib photographs juxtapose the Americans' absolute license against the Iraqis' abject helplessness. Kappeler points to the way the subjectivity of the abuser and witness is constructed as the opposite of the abused: "How can the subject be sure that he is high if no one is low, how can he know he is free if no one is bound?"[9] In this symbolic way, the degradation of the prisoners could be understood as part of the reassertion of American power after 9/11. When George W. Bush said that the 9/11 attacks were carried out by those who "hate our freedoms," the national ideology of American freedom was set in opposition to the "other" of this freedom.[10] Iraqis, rounded up without cause and incarcerated in Abu Ghraib, became this other, whose symbolic annihilation as subjects correspondingly affirmed the subject position of the American victors.

Not only the sexual aspects of the abuse at Abu Ghraib but also this juxtaposition of subject and object link the abuse photographs to pornography. Military historian Joanne Bourke describes the images as "a pornography of pain" that is "fundamentally voyeuristic in nature. The abuse is performed for the camera. It is public, theatrical, and elaborately staged."[11] Bourke suggests that these images were "trophies." They were "snapshots taken by people who were pleased by what they were seeing."

The gratification gained from the photographs within the culture of the jail is suggested by the use of the images as the screen saver on a military intelligence computer. Bourke argues that "creating a spectacle of suffering was part of a bonding ritual. Group identity as victors in an increasingly brutalised Iraq is being cemented."[12] The Western public viewing these images in the news and online, however troubled they may be individually by the images, are nevertheless drawn into what Bourke calls the "pornographic gaze" as subjects viewing the Iraqis as objects.

The photographing of Palestinian prisoners by Israeli armed forces operates similarly to demarcate subject and object. A female Israeli soldier, Eden Abergil, posted on the social networking site, Facebook, images of herself posing alongside blindfolded Palestinian prisoners. She labeled the folder containing the photos "Army—the best time of my life."[13] Journalist Diaa Hadid describes the photographs as follows: "In one, she is sitting legs crossed beside a blindfolded Palestinian man who is slumped against a concrete barrier. His face is turned downwards, while she leans toward him with her face upturned. Another shows her smiling at the camera with three Palestinian men with bound hands and blindfolds behind her."[14] Posts by Abergil's friends included jokes and innuendos, for example, "You're the sexiest like that." Abergil responded, "I wonder if he's got Facebook!... I have to tag him in the picture."[15] A further scandal was caused by the posting on the online video-sharing site Youtube of a video of a male Israeli soldier belly dancing next to a blindfolded Palestinan woman prisoner.[16] Such images ridicule the prisoners and represent the pleasure of the Israeli soldiers in their power over the Palestinians. The prisoners are blindfolded, but the posing soldiers, those behind the camera, and the online viewers of the photographs or videos witness, and contribute to, their humiliation.

Abergil's post, in which she pretends to wonder whether the prisoner has Facebook, points up the difference between this photographic situation and the "social network" in which people participate as equals. This is not a free participant, but is being held captive, blindfolded, and anonymous. This is not a co-equal subject, but an object who is having things done *to* him or her. In contrast, those posting comments are participating as subjects, sharing what Jonathan Glover calls the "cold joke" of the kind often shared among those committing atrocities, the kind of joke that is accompanied by "contemptuous laughter."[17] The laughter of Abergil and her friends is a laughter full of contempt for the Palestinians, expressing joy in their humiliation and objectification. The photographs should be understood as themselves constituting a cold joke, emphasizing, as Glover puts it, "the difference between 'us' and 'them'."[18] Palestinian Authority spokesman Ghassan Khatib states that the photographs show "the mentality of the occupier… to be proud of humiliating Palestinians."[19]

Kappeler reminds us that "Social relationships are relations between subjects… The roles are reciprocal, the situation is one of intersubjectivity."[20] The social networking site used by Abergil and her friends is based on a relationship between peers, a network of free individual users or communicators. The cold joke at the expense of the photographed Palestinian prisoners is the contrast between their position and that of the free and equal members of the network. The joke depends on recognition that the Palestinians are excluded from the relationships of the network. Their object position is signified and actualized by their place in the photograph and the circulation of their image through the network. The Palestinian prisoners became the objects of exchange through which Abergil and her friends displayed and affirmed to each other their own subject positions by contrast with the objects of their Occupation and domination.

More recently, in Germany, Abu Ghraib-like photographs and videos have been found on the cell phones of security guards working for a private company that operated a detention camp for refugees. A video shows one man being forced to lie on a mat covered in vomit while being beaten. A photograph found within a WhatsApp text message conversation on a guard's cellphone shows a guard standing over a handcuffed refugee, while pressing his boot into the refugee's neck. Another guard stands nearby, and both guards, grinning, appear to be posing for the photograph.[21] Again, the person who is not allowed to circulate freely is circulated as non-person, objectified by means of sadistic violence, and objectified in the form of a photographic and digital object, which can be passed freely among those with social power. The demarcation between the subjects and objects of global capitalism is reflected in the form of a pornography of violence.

SUBJECTS AND OBJECTS OF GLOBAL CAPITALISM

The "network society" of global capitalism structurally excludes a variety of "others" from the status as free agents in these circuits of communication and exchange. Free-market liberalism promises to constitute social relations as relations of exchange between subjects. But capitalist globalization has been accompanied by new demarcations between those able to claim subject status and those structurally excluded from this status. American power has created hellish new "states of exception," such as Abu Ghraib and Guantanamo Bay, the inmates of which are denied the protections of the liberal state.[22] The aggressive assertion of American "freedom" goes hand in hand with the denial of the status of rights-bearing human subjects to those identified, arbitrarily, as enemies of this freedom.[23] While borders are eroded for the free passage of commodities, they have become increasingly fortified against the passage of human beings, as new walls have been erected around the West Bank and along the US-Mexico border and as hostility to immigrants and refugees has grown in Europe.[24]

Zygmunt Bauman writes that "[t]he pressure to pull down the last remaining barriers to the free movement of money and money-making commodities and information goes hand in hand with the pressure to dig new moats and erect new walls… barring the movement of those who are uprooted"[25] But those excluded from labor and citizenship are frequently drawn into the market as *human commodities*. The circuits of global exchange increasingly incorporate a division between those who exchange and those who are exchanged. Instead of formal equality, wherein the worker is construed as a subject selling his own labor power, we see increasingly those excluded from labor being constituted as *nothing but* objects of exchange. As information networks are celebrated by the "flat world" ideologues of neoliberalism, the new flows of trade and information also involve the constitution of non-persons. As global capitalism produces what Bauman calls human "waste," consigned to structural irrelevance in the globalized economy, the excluded people reduced to this status as non-persons are sucked up in the shadow circuits of the informal or criminal economy that has become an integral feature of economic globalization.[26]

The collapse of the Soviet Union was hailed in the West as the triumph of democratic freedom, understood in the dominant liberal ideology as being inextricably linked with capitalist "free trade." The throwing off of authoritarian rule and the opening of former barriers to trade were presented by the Western media and neoliberal pundits and ideologues as being necessarily twinned forms of liberation from oppression. Not only would those in the Eastern bloc have democratic political freedoms, they would also have the freedoms enjoyed by Western consumers—freedom to choose from amidst an abundance of commodities. However, large numbers of women from former Communist countries have found themselves, on the contrary, to *be* the commodities traded across the porous borders of Europe.

The destruction of Russian society by the neoliberal "structural adjustment" policies of the 1990s threw large numbers of Russians into poverty, while producing stark inequality. At the same time, the collapse of Communism extended the cultural infiltration of Russia and other post-Communist societies by the Western media's consumerist dream factory. The "criminalization of the economy" was fed by the replacement of "socially important goals" with "consumption ideals" in a context in which these ideals remained far out of reach for an impoverished population.[27] Global consumer culture rendered crime attractive as a means to realize otherwise unrealizable consumerist goals. At the same time, the fantasy image of Western consumer affluence was a powerful lure for the victims of this explosion of new criminality, women seeking to escape the deprivation and chaos wrought by neoliberalism on their own societies while attracted by the image of Western luxury propagated by globalized media.

The sexual trafficking of women from Russia and Eastern Europe has exploded since the collapse of Communism. Saltanat Sulaimanova writes that, while there was virtually no human trafficking from the former Soviet bloc region prior to 1991, "since the breakup of the Soviet Union, this phenomenon has reached epidemic proportions."[28] Dennis Altman writes that "The collapse of Communism in Soviet/Eastern Europe has opened up a huge growth in sex work... one estimate in mid-1998 was that half a million women had been brought from the former Soviet states into western Europe for prostitution in the past three years... the Ukrainian government believes that 400,000 Ukrainian women alone have moved into various forms of prostitution since the collapse of the Soviet Union."[29] The rise of human trafficking in this region was a direct result of the imposition of neoliberal structural adjustment and the consequent economic collapse and social disorder that Russia and other former Soviet states underwent in the 1990s. Sulaimanova writes that "Political, economic, and social changes, which occurred after the Soviet Union collapsed, resulted in poverty and unemployment, creating a new pool of women from which traffickers can recruit."[30] In her study of Russian and Eastern European sex workers in Finland, Elina Pentinnen argues that "prostitution has become a means of adaptation and adjustment for women in countries subjected to the transition to a market economy or neoliberalist structural adjustment policies."[31] By the late 1990s, as Maggy Lee notes, the "poverty-ridden countries in Eastern Europe" had become the "fastest growing region" for human trafficking.[32] As well as prostitution, former socialist states have attracted sex tourism and pornography industries.[33]

Trafficked women from former Communist countries constitute a large proportion of the foreign sex workers in Germany. The German government's legalization of prostitution in 2002 has not diminished the problem of trafficking, but it has allowed the creation of so-called mega-brothels in which clients pay a "flat rate" for as long a session with a prostitute as they can keep going. Men often take sexual performance pills in order to prolong these sessions, and prostitutes are forced to service one man after another. The large number of prostitutes working in Germany has driven the price of paid sex so low that Germany has become known to sex tourists as the "Aldi for prostitutes" (a reference to a low-budget supermarket chain).[34]

The vulnerability of women to trafficking is linked to what Lee calls the "feminisation of poverty" in the former Communist countries. Structural adjustment policies in the former USSR were particularly devastating to women's employment, economic position, and social status.[35] Women not only disproportionately became unemployed but were also impacted by the collapse of state provision after the fall of Communism. Trafficking fed off the development of a brutal neoliberal "cancer capitalism" in which social resources were looted by a few, and elites disclaimed any responsibility for the well-being of the rest of society. In this context, the systems of health, education, and state provision that support social reproduction were allowed to collapse.[36]

As women's position in post-Soviet society has deteriorated, the impetus to migration to improve their position or survive is fed by the influx of consumerist media. Movies and television feed a naively idealistic view of the West, which makes it easier for traffickers to lure women through hiring agencies that promise jobs as waitresses, dancers, models, and nannies.[37] Instead, the women find themselves in debt bondage and very often subject to extreme violence, while kept prisoner in squalor. Sultanat Sulaimanova writes that "Trafficked women who do not obey the rules are treated very severely. The corpses of several hundred trafficked women, strangled, shot, or beaten to a pulp, are detected in Europe every year."[38] In the context of the societal chaos wrought by neoliberal globalization, women's aspirations and desire to improve their lives easily backfire on them. Sally Cameron writes:

> Women who are educated, ambitious and aware of their relative position and poverty may be proactive in looking for ways out of their situation and aware of the risks associated with taking up offers of overseas work, but may

still find themselves deceived and becoming the victims of trafficking networks because, ultimately, the power of the individual is extremely limited in the context of the range of options available to them and the strength and control of the trafficking networks.[39]

Neoliberal globalization's combination of the promise of market freedom and the reality of poverty, desperation, and social chaos has, for many women of post-Communist countries, been the jaws of a lethal trap.

In 2012, the International Labor Organization (ILO) put the number of women, men, and children in forced labor at 20.9 million worldwide. Women and girls comprise 55 % or 11.4 million of these modern-day slaves, and the 4.5 million victims of forced sexual exploitation are predominantly female. According to the ILO, "cross-border movement is closely allied with forced sexual exploitation, whereas a greater proportion of victims of non-sexual forced labour are exploited in their home area."[40] According to the United Nations Office on Drugs and Crime, those targeted for sexual exploitation comprise 58 % of all the people trafficked worldwide, and 76 % of the global victims of human trafficking are female.[41]

The global trafficking in human beings shares key features of earlier forms of slave trading, especially its extreme violence.[42] But it is also, Lee argues, "linked to the exponential expansion of possibilities through recent advances in technology, in tandem with the spread of global capitalism and the consequent speed at which capital, bodies and organs can now move around the world."[43] Richard Poulin writes: "Capitalist globalization involves an unprecedented 'commodification' of human beings."[44] Saskia Sassen has written that "The same infrastructure that facilitates cross-border flows of capital, information, and trade is also making possible a whole range of cross-border flows not intended by the framers and designers of the current corporate globalization of economies."[45] Globalization has increased opportunities for the expansion of the size and scope of criminal groups, such that there is "a nearly indecipherable web of nodes and illicit relations" within global organized crime networks.[46] According to Lee, criminal groups "adapted to the pressures and opportunities of globalisation to generate new illicit flows of people, money and goods (including sex trafficking, money laundering, trade in toxic waste and endangered species)," and have themselves globalized with national criminal groups operating transnationally and new transnational criminal networks that are developing.[47] Technologies like mobile phones and the Internet have facilitated communication in criminal networks.[48] According to Phil Williams, "The development of the internet... has led to a close connection between trafficking and pornography, with trafficked women sometimes being exploited for pornography, either en route or in their destination country."[49]

Overlapping legal and illegal flows of persons and money have been facilitated by neoliberal global free trade policies, while the legal movement of people is restricted. Lee writes, "[H]uman trafficking is inextricably linked to the tensions, disjunctures and inequalities associated with globalisation and differential freedom of movement."[50]

People brought to the edge of survival by neoliberal "structural adjustment" or capital flight, yet barred from access to globalization's circuits, who cannot, therefore, move as free agents on the global economy, are moved as illicit human commodities.[51] These new illicit flows and forms of slavery are related to the ways in which neoliberal free trade policies have created new classes of insecure human beings who are not even able to sell their labor. Their very bodies are the commodities for sale. They do not even sell themselves, but *are sold* as slaves for the benefit of others.[52]

According to Williams, "In the final analysis, the trafficking of women and children for commercial sex is a symptom of the growing disorder and breakdown of governance—globally, regionally and nationally—that has characterized many parts of the world since the end of the Cold War."[53] As human beings are thrown into desperation within this global disorder, they are swept up into the global flow of capital *as commodities*.[54] Human trafficking is a highly lucrative trade, estimated at $32 billion, while sex trafficking alone generates between $7 billion and $19 billion annually.[55] The flow of global capital involves the economic exploitation of the global bifurcation of human beings as subjects and objects. Pentinnen argues that, as global capitalism constitutes the subject as the active buyer and seller on the market, it also produces the antithesis of the subject. This is what she calls the "abject," those who are systematically excluded and rendered "socially dead."[56] The exclusion and marginality produced by the global economy become the basis for the extension of the commodification of the human being within globalization's shadow economy. Sociologist Ronaldo Munck writes that "The global flows of money and bodies are equally emblematic of the global market order we live in."[57]

The Human Body as Informational Commodity

The triumphalist post–Cold War rhetoric of liberal freedom in the 1990s was reinforced by the cyberlibertarian image of the Internet as a new realm of freedom in virtual space.[58] The Internet was to be, as Wendy Hui Kyong Chun puts it, "a medium of freedom," liberating users from their bodies and their locations."[59] The Web was associated with globality or non-place corresponding with the global capitalist market, breaking down all local standards. It was expected to "batter down all Chinese walls."

Just as economic globalization created new divisions between those profiting from the flows of capital and commodities and those traded as embodied commodities, this bifurcation is present also in the new flows of information. The "freedom" of information on the Internet enables new modes of commodification of the human being, as trafficked human bodies are marketed for sale through Web sites, and through the explosion of Internet pornography in which the bodies of poor and working-class women and children are transformed into infinitely circulable informationalized commodities.[60]

The contrast between the user or consumer's freedom to buy "services" and the unfreedom of the women who are trafficked and marketed is indicated by Pentinnen's observation about how Finnish men access Russian and Eastern European prostitutes: "Finnish can have access to their hidden neighbors, who are possibly and most likely locked in apartments, by phoning a number posted in a newspaper or on the internet."[61] In 2010, the billboard Web site Craigslist came under scrutiny in the USA for the use of its "Adult Services" page for prostitution and sexual trafficking, including the selling of children for sex. Human trafficking campaigners argued that Craigslist made $36.3 million in one year from the posting of sex advertisements and that the site had become "by far the largest single advertiser of commercial sex in the world."[62]

The Internet's capacity for networking has often meant the increased ability to exploit. In their study of online child pornography, Ian O'Donnell and Claire Milner write that "[t]he digital age has created the potential for abuse on a hitherto unimaginable scale. Within a generation the oft photocopied and much sought after *Lolita* magazine has been replaced by a bewilderingly large and varied catalogue of abuse, which can be accessed via a few commands on a computer keyboard." Child pornography in the 1990s "witnessed a 'return of the repressed' where despite intensive efforts to eradicate the trade... it grew exponentially."[63] The Internet was key to this expansion, facilitating the growth and proliferation of pedophile networks and enhancing their ability to exchange and profit from images of the abuse of children.[64]

Prior to the Internet, arrests for possession of child pornography would tend to unearth a relatively small number of pictures on paper or on tape. This material was expensive, and sharing or exchanging it meant using a postal address and thereby revealing one's location. The Internet made the trade in such images anonymous and instantaneous. The scale of the child pornography trade grew with the expansion of Internet use and access. In 2014, the Internet Watch Foundation found 27,850 Web pages showing child sexual abuse.[65] According to O'Donnell and Milner:

> There is a consensus that the Internet has massively expanded both the supply of, and demand for, this material. A vicious cycle has been initiated whereby the new technologies allow more people to view this material, which in turn stimulates a greater appetite for new images and places more children at risk of exploitation.[66]

The Internet's anonymity itself tempts people into activities they would previously have avoided as too risky and which they might never have known how to access.[67]

O'Donnell and Milner argue that the Internet has allowed the pedophile subculture to "become amorphous and dislocated in a physical sense but virtually united."[68] Some examples give a sense of the globally networked character of pedophile rings exchanging pornography and the centrality of the Internet to their activities. In 2002, European and US law enforcement discovered a cross-Atlantic network of parents who abused their own children and exchanged the images online.[69] In 2006–2007, more than 100 people were arrested in 19 countries in connection with a Web site showing "made to order" child pornography. The site, run by an Italian man who made most of the videos in Ukraine, had at least 2500 customers.[70] In 2011, a police investigation exposed an online pedophile network spanning the UK, the USA, New Zealand, Australia, and Thailand, with 70,000 members.[71] In some cases, pedophiles have used sophisticated encryption methods to hide their online activities.[72] Despite massive police operations netting credit card numbers of those accessing child pornography, criminologist David Wilson predicts that in response, "paedophiles who want to communicate with one another will now have found other ways of doing so. In the fast-moving world of computer and telephone technology, and crime, net-enabled mobile phones have introduced a whole new level by which chat rooms can be accessed and pornographic images traded."[73]

As the Internet has made the supply of images more plentiful, by connecting pedophiles with one another, it has also increased demand. This demand, in turn, fuels further child abuse. This expansion of demand leading to increased child abuse is exacerbated by file-sharing, which is leading to growing "real-time" abuse, whereby videos of ongoing abuse are posted as it occurs. *The Guardian* reports that "[s]ome of the children, police believe, are being abused on a daily basis to provide a constant supply of new computerised material."[74] With the growth in the number of images, more of these images are showing extreme forms of abuse. In 2007, Britain's Internet watchdog, the Internet Watch Foundation (IWF), reported that the number of images of serious child abuse had quadrupled over three years: "In 2003, just 7 % of the web pages investigated... included the highest levels of abuse. [In 2006] the group says that 29 % of all the images that its officers investigated fell under the same classification, marking a fourfold increase in the most disturbing cases." The IWF's chairman, Peter Robbins suggests that "[t]he images appear to be on a trend towards more severity, probably because there is greater demand."[75] In 2012, police cracked an international network which traded pictures including the rape of children, cannibalistic images such as of a toddler in a roasting pan, and online discussions about abducting, murdering, and cannibalizing children. Massachusetts US Attorney Carmen Ortiz said the demand for photos of sexual assaults of very young children, including babies and toddlers, has risen sharply in recent years: "This demand leads to the abuse of children."[76]

Spiraling growth, as new technology facilitates supply and draws in greater demand, fueling the supply and ramping up the extremity of the sexual acts supplied, is a feature of the pornography industry in general, not just of the illegal niche of child pornography. In her research on legal, commercially produced, heterosexual pornography, Gail Dines shows the relationship between growing demand, stimulated by the Internet, the commercial growth of the pornography industry, and the increasing extremity of its content. The most popular form of pornography available today, which has exploded in availability in the last decade, is "gonzo." This has done away with any semblance of plot or stylization and is simply a string of sexual acts. The basic form of gonzo sex is extremely fomulaic: fellatio, penetrative sex, fellatio, ending with the "money shot" in which the man ejaculates on the woman's face. Within this framework, there are variations which also form niche genres of gonzo. For example, Dines lists:

> vaginal, anal, and oral penetration of a woman by three or more men at the same time;
>
> double anal, in which a woman is penetrated anally by two men at the same time; double vagina, in which a woman is penetrated vaginally by two men at the same time;
>
> gagging, in which a woman has a penis thrust so far down her throat she gags (or, in the more extreme cases, vomits);
>
> ass-to-mouth, in which a penis goes from a woman's anus to her mouth without washing; and
>
> bukkake, in which any number of men ejaculate, often at the same time, onto a woman's body, face, hair, eyes, ears, or mouth. In some of these movies, the men ejaculate into a cup, and the 'money shot' is the woman drinking the semen mixture.[77]

These kinds of acts are prevalent and available through the most cursory search for sexual material on the Internet.

Power is integral to pornographic sex. As Dines puts it, "In porn, the man makes hate to the woman, as each sex act is designed to deliver the maximum amount of degradation."[78] The acts (the woman kneeling, being choked, gagging, being ejaculated onto, undergoing and having to appear to enjoy painful penetration) encode domination and the position of the woman as an object.[79] The filming of these scenes, of course, means these acts actually happen—women are being choked, hurt, and made to vomit.[80] The fact that this is a real assault, that the woman is not acting in pain, but *is* in pain, and that it is her expressions of enjoyment that are unconvincing, is what is appealing to porn viewers. What pornography viewers are watching is not fantasy, but real; gonzo porn does not use special effects and leaves nothing to the imagination. Pornography is both the representation of men exerting extreme power over women through physical violence and humiliation and the actual brutalization and humiliation of the women in front of the camera. Pornography markets not merely sex, but sexual cruelty.

The ways in which women are assaulted and degraded are becoming more extreme and elaborate as pornographers seek to differentiate their product from the growing mass of such materials and as consumers of pornography tire of, or become desensitized to, the same scenarios and seek out the novel image that will provide a new kick of sexual excitement.

The commercial logic of the pornography industry is, therefore, toward ever greater violence and domination. Robert Jensen writes, "The more pornography becomes normalized and mainstreamed, the more pornography has to search for that edge. And that edge most commonly is cruelty." Cruelty adds edge because it adds a semblance of human feeling into something that is completely devoid of emotion. It is precisely because it is devoid of emotion that pornography becomes boring so quickly, feeding the quest for novelty-via-cruelty. According to Jensen, "Pornography has to draw on some emotion, hence the cruelty."[81]

Dines describes how men who view pornography are conveyed toward ever more extreme and violent forms of sex. They start to regularly view material that, at first, they found disgusting, but over time become desensitized to this material, and this boredom and the search for the orgasmic fix leads them to even more extreme forms of pornography.[82] Pamela Paul describes this dynamic in the online activity of one pornography user, drawn to images of rape: "Repulsed and terrified by his curiosity, he nonetheless kept clicking back, and soon started to fantasize about rape even when he was not looking at pornography."[83]

The impulsion of the individual pornography viewer toward increasingly extreme material is due also to the fact that this material is becoming more easily available online. The sheer volume of pornography that is available on the Internet creates intense commercial pressure for pornographers to differentiate their product, and they do this by pushing the boundaries of what is deemed too extreme to show. A growing trend in pornography is now testing the strongest boundary—that between adult and child pornography. The gates were opened by a US Supreme Court ruling in 2002 which narrowed the definition of child pornography to those images in which an actual person aged less than 18 years is involved in the making of the pornography. This opened the way for the genre of pseudo-child pornography featuring either computer-generated images or performers who are over 18 years, but who look younger or are, as Dines puts it, "childified."[84]

There is a symmetry between the trajectory toward extremity in the porn industry and in the habits of individual porn users: commercial success depends on satiating individual porn users' quest for exciting novelty. Dines' interviews with incarcerated sex offenders suggest that serial desensitization, due to the sheer availability of online porn, and the search for more extreme porn highs, was a powerful dynamic in their lives, which connected with their sex offending:

> Prior to the Internet, they would regularly use pornography (of adult women) but after the introduction of the Internet, they began to use it compulsively, some of them even losing their jobs because of it. For this group of men, the regular gonzo pornography became boring, and they moved into more violent, fetishistic pornography, often that which looked like overt torture. When this also started to become boring, most of the men moved into child pornography... Most men told me that before becoming addicted to Internet porn, they had not been sexually interested in children.[85]

The speed of circulation and the growth of the market drive exploitation deeper in the production of pornography, toward more violent, degrading, and morally destabilizing content. Just as, in general, the Internet introduces a new freedom for circulation of capital and technologies, spurring the intensified commodification of the world, rapid global circulation through the Web intensifies exploitation in the pornography industry.

A symbiosis has developed between the Internet and pornography. Searching for, and viewing, pornography makes up a large portion of Internet activity, and pornography has been a significant force in the expansion of the Internet. Online pornography use continues to expand: the proportion of Google searches using the word "porn" tripled between 2004 and 2011.[86] Stephen Maddison writes:

> Porn companies pioneered models of online commerce and for much of the 1990s were the only sectors of online media that were making money from charging for online content... Porn companies made significant investments in research and development for security and payment software that they marketed to the rest of the industry, and it seemed that pornography was indeed "the handmaiden of the new technology."[87]

It would be more accurate to say that pornography led the way in harnessing the new technology to commercial monetization. If, as Chun writes, "New technology is a 'carrier'—a new Trojan horse—for pornography," pornography is itself a Trojan horse for capital.[88]

The Internet and pornography share a mode of relating to the world. The subject interacts with a world of images that he controls completely. This world becomes an extension of his own mind. The variety of online pornography gives the search a feeling of "infinite exploration."[89] The Internet allows the porn user to move rapidly through images, searching for the one image that will provide the desired thrill. But this search is propelled by an underlying boredom and dissatisfaction, increasing the more pornography is used.[90]

The human being one encounters in Internet pornography is a cipher. One clicks on the image and stays there as long as it provides interest. As soon as it becomes mundane, one clicks away. That human being's pain, fear, feelings of humiliation, and history (how they came to be in that situation) have no hold on the viewer. To the extent that awareness of the image as a human being in pain breaks through, and the viewer is able to feel empathy, it becomes hard to look at the image as a source of pornographic pleasure. One can escape that painful relatedness by clicking away. However, viewing pornographic images tends to render those images mundane, dulls the initial shock and revulsion from the image, and mutes the capacity for empathy. The more pornography one views, the less one sees the women in the pictures as human beings, the less empathy one feels, the more alone one is in a world of objects.[91]

Paradoxically, however, the viewer of pornography derives pleasure from the fact that it *is* a human being, a woman, that is being degraded and made an object. When the pornography user ceases to experience the image as having a human dimension (a human being dominated and controlled, a human under the total control of the pornography user), the image loses interest. The search for more tantalizing images then takes the pornography user to those more extreme images that initially shock through the violence of what is being done to a human being. The basis for that initial revulsion or empathy—the recognition of humanity—becomes the basis for new pornographic pleasure. The residual humanness of the objectified human being allows sadistic pleasure in the violent annihilation of that humanity. The revulsion is mingled with something else, fascination. Repeated exposure allows the viewer to give play to that fascination; initial revulsion and discomfort is overcome and, for a while, the viewer begins to find new pleasure in those images of total abjection. This lasts until the state of detachment and objectification becomes complete and those images are, in turn, voided of their power to stimulate. The paradox of pornography use is that, since by its very nature it transforms the human being into an object, the means by which it generates sadistic pleasure also rapidly transforms this pleasure into lifelessness and chronic boredom. But this paradox is also what feeds the augmentation of pornography as consumer spectacle—a search for excitement endlessly energized by its own inherent morbidity.

Internet use is a jaded trawling through a world of images, hoping to catch something that gives a momentary glimmer of interest before letting it go and looking for a fresh diversion. Internet users browse through a world that is insubstantial, and has no hold on them. They are engaged in a restless quest for excitation. According to Hubert Dreyfus, the attitude of detached curiosity, which Kierkegaard criticized in relation to the newspaper reader, has reached its apotheosis on the Internet.[92] The Internet gives the "user" access to a world from which they are entirely aloof, which they click away from or turn off at any moment, a world with which they engage without commitment or risk. On the Internet, the world is flattened out as information. The Internet "user" takes in the world as information, and *uses* it as a source of momentary diversion or scandal, before discarding it and moving on.

That uncommitted attitude is frequently coupled with contempt, as displayed by the ubiquitous Internet "trolls" who anonymously post derogatory and often hateful comments on Web sites in response to articles, videos, or comments by other Internet users. The anonymity of the Web is disinhibiting for this kind of aggression, and the contempt and vitriol that is omnipresent in anonymous online discourse is often targeted in an especially intense way against women. There have been well-publicized cases of the abuse of female journalists and writers, with the posting of violent or obscene images and emails or online comments with threats of sexual violence. In 2007, the writer and blogger on computer programming and games, Kathy Sierra, canceled all her speaking engagements after being targeted with death threats and threats of sexual violence, including "fuck off you boring slut ... I hope someone slits your throat and cums down your gob" and the posting online of images of her as a sexually mutilated corpse.[93] The anonymous, detached position becomes one of power.[94]

Detached curiosity is closely related to objectification. If the world is reduced to objects, then this objective detachment is the proper attitude. Only subjects can demand our attention when we want to move on. The total access of the Internet voyeur to a world in which nothing is hidden makes them a subject with limitless objects at their disposal. As Kappeler argues, the stance of the seeing and knowing subject in relation to the seen and known object is a position of power.[95] The Internet, in its anonymity and totality, feeds fantasies of omniscience, and, through this, omnipotence. Online, the world seems open to one's gaze and through that, to one's control.

However, precisely because the online world is infinitely manipulable, it is unable to hold our attention. The rendering of the world accessible by its reduction to information necessarily also represents a deepening objectification of the world and of other people, and hence a loss of aliveness. The very deadness of the informational realm produces chronic boredom as the emotional accompaniment of the Internet user's detached spectatorship. The manipulability of the virtual world that is the source of the Internet user's power is also the source of their frustration, as the world loses substance and interest.

Much of the anger online arises from underlying frustration and boredom. Dreyfus's conservative existentialist critique of the Internet fails to recognize that the detached position of the voyeur is also one of underlying powerlessness, and online sadism is an attempt to claim power in the context of social alienation. The media and Internet open up a world for the human gaze, but the user is still caught in the oppressive relations of capitalism. The control of *images* that the Internet user experiences is a substitute for the lack of control of most individuals over their own lives. The Internet provides a way to release the frustrations of everyday life, to feel power and momentary excitement. But the sense of power that it brings is ultimately illusory.

The Internet user's underlying boredom is symptomatic of the chronic boredom that, as Erich Fromm perceived, pervades contemporary society and which is a feature of the general unaliveness of individuals within modern capitalism. Consumer capitalism works on us through what Fromm called "simple stimuli." Advertising, movies, television, and other media of consumer society target "such drives as sexual desire, greed, sadism, destructiveness, narcissism... The mechanism is always the same: simple stimulation → immediate and passive response. Here lies the reason why the stimuli have to be changed constantly, lest they become ineffective."[96] Fromm suggests that such simple stimuli contrast with interests that call forth an active orientation to the world:

> Such an activating stimulus could be a novel, a poem, an idea, a landscape, music, or a loved person... they invite you, as it were, to respond by actively and sympathetically relating yourself to them; by becoming actively *interested*, seeing and discovering ever-new aspects in your "object" (which ceases to be a mere "object").[97]

The person who is fully alive will be able to engage with the world in a vital way, and will tend to seek out such activating stimuli. In contrast, the alienated, deadened person is unable to muster from within such ongoing, active interest, and therefore feels a need to be constantly stimulated from outside.

It is the alienated person to whom the simple stimuli of consumer society are targeted. But because such stimuli do not provoke a more alive and awake orientation to the world, interest in them rapidly dies, and the consumer always needs to seek out novelty. Even while momentarily activated by some passing amusement, the consumer's underlying state is one of boredom. Fromm wrote about attempts to overcome chronic boredom through alcohol, drugs, or the quest for sexual excitement. But, he also argued that a prevalent response to chronic boredom is anger, cruelty, violence, and destructiveness, which provide easy paths to excitation in contrast with the patience and effort that are required for activating stimuli such as love.[98] The chronically bored person will, therefore, be particularly attracted to spectacles of death and destruction as an escape from their ennui. Such people are, Fromm writes:

> attracted to reports of crimes, fatal accidents, and other scenes of bloodshed and cruelty that are the staple diet fed to the public by press, radio, and television... Yet there is only a short step from passive enjoyment of violence and cruelty to the many ways of actively producing excitement by sadistic or destructive behavior... The bored person often is the organizer of a "mini-Colosseum" in which he produces his small-scale equivalents of the large-scale cruelty staged in the Colosseum.[99]

Today, the Internet functions as society's Colosseum. Devoid of deep interest or meaningful, lasting contact with others, the Internet user clicks in search of excitation through a world which leaves him cold.

This chronically bored, detached curiosity, and the attempt to overcome it through the search for novelty and excitement in the sexual sphere, drives the search for excitement in pornography and the ramping up of the extremity of pornography. In their study of child pornography, O'Donnell and Milner write that

> the Internet allows an unprecedented degree of inquisitiveness, and the danger is of curiosity hardening into deviance. In a Swiss study... [it was] found that two-thirds of men investigated for purchasing child pornography... gave as their motivation 'curiosity', 'fascination' or 'investigation'.
>
> In other words, the Internet *per se* may be a trigger for a significant number of individuals to access child pornography.[100]

The notion of "curiosity" might be a rationalization. However, these authors suggest that we should take it seriously as a way in which people get drawn into the world of child pornography.[101] They suggest that the Internet not only provides opportunities for existing pedophiles, but also draws in those whose "desires might have been different in the precomputer age."[102] Online curiosity alights on child pornography, which a person may never have been able to encounter previously. What begins as curiosity becomes fascination, leading to the quest for new stimuli of that sort, and the person is drawn into deepening involvement in the online pedophile subculture.

But it is worth thinking more about the character of this "curiosity." Fromm's analysis suggests that it is not purely accidental that bored curiosity alights on something unimaginably cruel. The spectator's curiosity is *drawn* to such cruelty as an expression of, and attempt to escape from, their own unalive orientation toward the world. The "escape from boredom" leads to the cruelty of the Colosseum. The attitude of detached curiosity online has a quality of sadism to it. This curiosity is drawn to the Internet's promise of omniscience and omnipotence—one can view whatever one wants, and one can also manipulate these images, storing them, cataloguing them, and thereby controlling the world. The power offered by online omniscience combines with the power relationship shown in the content of the image of the weakest being rendered helpless. Child pornography Web sites that allow viewers to interact with the abuse, giving orders virtually to children to perform sexual acts, allow unseen Internet viewers to experience the total domination of the entirely exposed object of their gaze. In this way, the voyeur realizes detached curiosity as a bearing of power. Detachment is no longer impotence. Instead, the unobserved observer rules over the helpless object, whose hell they coolly oversee.

O'Donnell and Milner observe that child pornography viewers tend to "collect, swap and sort" their images and that they can amass hundreds of thousands of photographs. They write: "The importance of the phenomenology of collecting cannot be overestimated. This can be an integral part of the behaviour, and the reluctance to part with their prized images is one reason why paedophiles are often found in possession of huge numbers of photographs, meticulously filed and cross-referenced." Collections of pornographic material become "central to the collector's life and he is willing to spend considerable time and money on the acquisition of new material." Such collections provide a sense of permanency and continual preoccupation. The collecting of child pornographic images predated the

Internet, but computers have aided the ability to conceal such collections while maintaining easy access. Further, the connectivity of the Internet facilitates the sharing of such collections, which is a way that the pedophile seeks "validation for his efforts."[103] This pattern is evident in the findings of a major police operation in 2014 against child pornography. Some of the approximately 600 devices that police confiscated had libraries of thousands of pornographic images and videos of children. *The New York Times* quotes the Manhattan district attorney saying that the pedophiles collected and exchanged pornographic images "like one might collect and trade baseball cards."[104]

A hoarding orientation seems, therefore, to be an important aspect of child pornography use. O'Donnell and Milner suggest that amassing this material is "a solitary pursuit that can become hugely time-consuming and fill a void in an otherwise empty life."[105] This suggests very strongly the unaliveness of such a person's inner experience and orientation to the world. This unaliveness is expressed in a hoarding orientation in which the relationship to the world is reduced to amassing, storing, and cataloguing objects. This orientation is closely linked to an emphasis on order, as can be seen in the meticulous attention to cataloguing the images. There is a relationship between this focus on the amassing of objects, the emphasis on control and order, and the cruelty that is inherent in the content of the images that such a pedophile is amassing.

Fromm argued that hoarding and sadism are closely linked. In both, the subject renders life ordered and under control, stamping out unpredictability and spontaneity, including the threatening ability of other people to make demands or claims on one's empathy.[106] Philip Jenkins writes that "collectors are seeking a sense of dominance and control over the material. In the case of child pornography, there may also be a sense that the collector is gaining total possession, albeit symbolic, over the child subjects themselves."[107] The exertion of control through hoarding, cataloguing, and secreting pictures combines with fantasies of dominating another human being (targeting children as the most vulnerable and easily controlled). Sadism is expressed in the form of collecting as well as in the content of those pictures.

The gratification of control is also a key dimension of men's attraction to mainstream heterosexual pornography. The content of pornography is about men's control over women's bodies, presenting women's bodies in physically subordinated positions and as objects of manipulation for the purpose of men's erections and orgasms. But this content is twinned with the technological media that allow the viewer fine-grained control. Jensen argues that the eroticism of control is heightened by technology:

> Technology has increased the ability of the viewer to control the sexual experience. The fast-forward button on a videocassette recorder allowed viewers to speed past those portions of the movie that didn't interest them. DVDs offer the same feature, enhanced further by the segmenting of movies by performer or type of sex acts. On many DVDs, one can click to be taken directly to anal penetration, for example.[108]

The networked computer gives even greater control, placing only a click away the concretization of seemingly any fantasy in image.

David Marcus, a California psychologist who treats men with excessive Internet porn use, thinks that the interest in pornography is, at least in part, a response to the increasing lack of control that men feel in their everyday lives as they attempt to balance an increasingly competitive workplace with the maintenance of relationships at home: "Voyeurism offers a certain kind of control."[109] A pornography user quoted by Jensen makes clear this aspect of pornography as a compensatory form of control and how this is provided not just by the material, but also by the technological means that place the images at the disposal of the viewer:

> For me, porn is all about CONTROLLING HUMAN BEINGS, or should I say the ILLUSION of controlling others. That's what got me off. I felt so out of control in my life and from my childhood, that this was something I could control (which women I would see naked or I could hit the pause button and extend a particular image for eternity).[110]

Pornography makes human bodies into objects that can be technologically controlled, and hoarded in collections. Just as many pedophiles amass vast collections of images, cataloguing is a key feature of mainstream heterosexual pornography on the Internet. The pornography user encounters sexual material pre-sorted into a wide variety of categories. As the pornography industry markets to niches of sexual preference, it segments the body and sexual acts into ever more fine-grained categories. The pornography user online, therefore, explores the sexual possibility of the online world through a finely ordered series of categories and subcategories. Chun writes:

If.... video pornography spawned numerous new genres of pornography such as amateur, bondage, and discipline, Internet pornography has expanded the number of categories by several orders of magnitude. The popular pornography search engine penisbot.com, for instance, lists as its "Straight" categories: Amateur, Anal Sex, Asian, Babes, Black, Celebs, Close Ups, Cum Shots, Ethnic, Group Sex, Hardcore, Interracial, Latin, Lesbians, Masturbation, Megasites, Oral Sex, Porn Stars, Products, Public Nudists, Softcore, Teens, Video, and Webcams.[111]

Many of these categories are themselves further differentiated, for example, by race. Roger Pipe notes:

Websites now promised big booties in every possible shade. Like Caucasian women with large butts? You can watch "Big White Asses." If you prefer darker complexioned backsides give "Big Black Asses" a try. If Latinas are more your speed, "Big Latin Asses" can be found. If that is not specific enough, liquid can be brought in to give the gigantic glutes sheen, giving us "Big Wet Asses." If even that won't do, then the wet asses can get an ethnic breakdown treatment as well. One need only add "White," "Black," "Latin," or "Asian" to "Wet" and "Asses" and you open up another rainbow of sexual possibilities.[112]

The human body, and sexual activity, is packaged into a proliferation of consumer niches. This segmentation is a key feature of the intense commodification of the body. It subjects sexuality to a form of capitalist rationalization—sex is pre-sorted, ordered alphabetically for easy searching, and targeted (with advertisements for other porn sites in that genre) to particular market niches. The format of online pornography not only reduces a living person to a body, but also slices and dices these bodies into compartments to suit the niche tastes of pornography consumers.

Pornography dissects human beings into infinitely manipulable and minutely controllable parts. Viewing pornography involves the power to expose, to see and not be seen, and to manipulate. As the body is rendered as image, and the image as information, it becomes a thing that can be stored, catalogued, and viewed at will. But the pornography viewer is also submitting his or her own sexual desire to be packaged, compartmentalized, and channeled into these pre-ordered niche markets. Maddison writes, "[I]n this commercial sector, these diverse and proliferating varieties of porn are in fact assiduously standardized and limited to predictable desires ('teen sluts,' 'painful anal,' 'Asian whores,' 'bareback twinks,' and so on)."[113]

These categories channel the pornography user's sexuality in directions he or she might not previously have explored or wished to explore. Theodore Bach writes, "I do not believe that the growing population of porn categories exists in response to people's antecedent desires. Rather, these categories *create* desires."[114] Even while such categories proliferate and become more finely demarcated, they still entail the reductionist ordering of human sexuality into marketing genres. The sexuality of the pornography viewer becomes increasingly narrow and fetishistic as it is trained into pornography's categories. Pornography reifies human beings, especially women and children, by transforming them into objects for consumption; as it does so, it reifies the sexuality of the pornography user, packaging his or her sexual interests into narrow obsessions. This fetishistic sexuality is the accompaniment of the way in which pornography subordinates sexuality to the fetish of the commodity.

Pornographic Dismemberment

Pornography transforms human bodies and sexual acts into information-image-commodities circulating globally and instantly on the Internet. This commodification of the body, as I have argued, also involves the segmentation of bodies and human desire into marketing categories. Such segmentation, focusing the porn user's gaze and desire on particular body parts, may be seen as a form of dismemberment. Bodies are visually dismemberered in close-up images of breasts, vaginas, penises, and legs. Alan Soble has argued that male sexuality under capitalism is characterized by a "dismemberment syndrome," a tendency to reduce women to body parts for manipulation.[115]

The fragmentation of women's bodies is central to the representation of women in advertising, as Soble notes: "Advertisements in women's magazines (*Cosmoplitan, Vogue, Mademoiselle*) often include photographs not of the whole body of a woman but only of a part of the body... The cumulative message is that a woman is only the sum of her parts."[116] In her documentary series *Killing Us Softly*, Jean Kilbourne points out that "women's bodies are dismembered in ads, hacked apart. Just one part of the body is focused upon." For example, the camera focuses on the midriff, leg, or breast of a female model and the rest of the woman's body and her face are altogether absent from the picture. Advertising images frequently merge women's bodies into commodities such as a beer bottle, a video-game console, or a car. Kilbourne says, "[W]omen's bodies are constantly turned into things and into objects."[117] Pornography is the ultimate expression of this reification and dissection of the female body as the object of gaze.

In its form, pornography is the visual and informational dismemberment of the female body, as bodies and body parts are sorted into categories. In its content, pornography expresses sadistic interest in dismemberment of the female body. This is obviously true of sadomasochistic pornography in which women's arms, legs, and breasts are bound. But another common pornographic image and theme is a woman being forced to accept a penis or dildo that is clearly causing her pain. Popular features of contemporary heterosexual pornography are "double vagina," in which a woman is penetrated vaginally by two men at the same time or "double anal," in which she is similarly penetrated anally.[118] Pornographic Web sites and videos are full of references to vaginas and anuses being "stretched," "ripped," or "gaping." Dines describes this as being particularly characteristic of the genre of "teen" (i.e. pseudo-child) pornography:

> Not surprisingly, throughout these sites, constant mention is made of the teen's small vagina and anus... The men's penises are described as being extra large and thus have the power to "break," "rip," "tear," and "split" her not-yet-mature orifices.[119]

Anal sex is a key feature of contemporary heterosexual pornography, and in Web sites and videos with titles like *Anal Suffering* and *Anally Ripped Whores*, the act is a means of domination and torture of women.[120] Physical and photographic dismemberment are linked when Max Hardcore boasts about the "pile driver" in which "I would gape the girls [*sic*] asses wide open, and provide a clear view for the camera."[121] The excitement provided by such scenes and images lies in the degradation and pain caused to the woman and the prospect of physical damage to the woman's body.[122]

The ripping, tearing, and dismembering of female bodies in pornography go along with the desire to annihilate women as human subjects through degradation. A key message pervading pornography is that women are excrement. They are "dirty," "filthy," or "nasty."[123] A genre that has become prevalent recently is "ATM" or "ass to mouth," in which the penis is withdrawn from a woman's anus and then, without it being washed, the woman (or another woman) fellates it. As Dines notes, the pleasure derived from such pornography must lie in seeing women "totally dehumanized and humiliated."[124] However, such scenes also work to affirm the idea that the women themselves are "filthy." That the women themselves are excrement is signaled in a pornography movie released in 2005 called *Swirlies*. Jensen writes: "At the end of each scene, the man dunks the woman's head in a toilet and flushes. As the company put it, 'Every whore gets the swirlies treatment. Fuck her, then flush her'."[125]

As women are reduced to body parts, dolls, or waste matter, they are transformed from living beings into non-living things. Dines describes a new pornography film being promoted at a 2008 adult video convention: "[I]t featured a young woman being anally penetrated as she knelt in a coffin."[126] This scene is the ultimate expression of pornographic desire—the desire to fuck a woman to death. Necrophilia is entailed by the essence of pornography, which is making the woman into an object or a thing, annihilating her as a human subject. The woman kneeling in a coffin is the representation of pornography's ideal, the entirely objectified woman, and brings out what is entailed in that objectification—that she is now dead meat.

The inherent violence of this drive toward objectification is expressed in the recent popularity of the horror film genre, often labeled "torture porn," movies that revolve around the graphic depiction of the mutilation of bodies, especially those of women. In the 2005 film *Wolf Creek*, two young women and a young man are held captive in the Australian outback and tortured, and the women are killed. In 2005's *Hostel*, and its 2007 and 2011 sequels, young men and women are tortured for the pleasure of paying guests. In *Vacancy* (2007), a man and woman check into a motel only to realize they are on the set of a snuff movie in which they will be tortured and killed if they do not escape. *Captivity* (2007) centers on the abduction and torture of a young magazine cover girl model. In *The Call* (2013), a teenage girl is kidnapped by a killer who surgically scalps his victims for the blonde hair which he fetishizes. The common denominator of such films is the misogynistic sexualization of extreme violence, as Kira Cochrane has pointed out in *The Guardian*:

> The clear logic behind all of these films, TV shows and images appears to be that if a young, good-looking, barely clad woman is sexy while alive, she's even sexier when she's being tortured, or when she's a bloody corpse.[127]

The genre of "torture porn" fits into a more general pattern in contemporary media, in which women are sexualized *as they are being* mutilated and killed. The form of desire that is activated in such images is one that is satisfied by cruelty and death. Its ultimate object is a corpse.

Torture is not incidentally linked to porn but, rather, follows from the underlying relation of pornography, which is objectification. Torture realizes the sadistic desire to turn another human being into a mass of meat over which the sadist has complete control.[128] The sadistic aim of depriving the other of all agency is expressed most fully in the power of life and death, the power to kill the other. So, sadism shades over into necrophilia. The aim becomes, as Fromm puts it, "to transform all that is alive into dead matter... the enemy is life itself."[129]

The object that can be most completely controlled is one that is not alive, but a thing, a device that exists for one's pleasure. Pornographic discourse is full of references to making women into these kinds of objects— "fuck toys," "dolls," and so on. While pornography eroticizes the woman who is used equivalently to an inanimate object, some men substitute mannequins for women. Dines describes a company RealDoll that makes life-sized sex dolls, marketed at pornography expos and on the Web. She was struck by the contrast between pornographic discourse that refers to women as "whores, cunts and sluts" and a message board by RealDoll owners referring to their dolls as "'honey,' 'sweetie,' 'darling,' 'beauty' and 'my love'."[130] It seems that for these men, only something non-living is sufficiently manipulable, possessable, and non-threatening to their own agency that they can allow themselves to "love" it. Their interest in these lifeless bodies becomes a basis for sociality among the men posting on the message board. The relationship of this subculture to pornography is made clear by the fact that on the Doll Forum Web site, men post "porn-like pictures" of their dolls.[131]

There is now at least one company selling robotically animated sex dolls.[132] Journalist David Levy, an expert on computing and artificial intelligence, predicts that "by around 2050," people will be not only having sex with robots but falling in love with them. He goes so far as to say this development is "inevitable," a logical extension of the current market for sex dolls such as the RealDoll brand, vibrators, and plastic vaginas and penises, combined with new developments in computing and robotics.[133] Levy writes about such developments with the enthusiastic spin of popular science and technology writing, acclaiming the benefits of new technology and the ability of the market to satisfy human desire: "People will want better robot sex, and even better robot sex, and better still robot sex, their sexual appetites becoming voracious as the technologies improve."[134] But we might question whether this is to be celebrated, when one considers the substitution of a doll or a robot for a human being as the replacement of an interest in the living with desire for an object that is not alive. Their non-aliveness is what is so appealing about the RealDolls and the robots that Levy predicts will succeed them. Precisely because they are not alive, they can be manipulated, or, in the case of robots, programmed to do the bidding of the human being who is their *user* (in contrast to a relationship with a living *partner*).

Like the sexual interest in an unalive body, there is something close to necrophilia in this phenomenon. A specialized chat room for RealDolls aficionados includes a discussion in which the doll owners attempt to repudiate the parallel between their interests and necrophilia: for example, "*Doll lovers are not to be confused with necrophiles* [original emphasis]. Remember that many doll lovers heat their dolls before using them, and necrophiles like their lovers cold."[135] The desire to animate the doll suggests that there is something unsatisfactory about the non-living object. Sadistic pleasure in turning a *living* human being into an *object* means that the objectified body must be positioned *between* life and death. The animated doll is, in this sense, living dead.

The robotic sex doll is animated, but has no agency. The fact that it only *simulates* life means that it is entirely subject to the will of its owner. It has no needs of its own. As a piece of technology, it can be *programmed*. The sadistic element in the desire for technology is also suggested by Levy's discussion of "technophilia." He writes:

> There are the technophiles, usually programmers, but also those who love pressing buttons to make their gizmos do weird and wonderful things; theirs is a love of control, whether it is control by writing the programs that instruct their computers what to do or the much simpler form of control achieved by pressing the buttons on devices that have already been programmed. And the act of programming has itself been compared to sex, in that programming is a form of control, of bending the computer or the gadget to the will of the programmer, forcing the computer to behave as one wishes—domination.[136]

The desire for control finds its realization in a technologized world, where controllable gadgets substitute for complex and unpredictable reciprocal human relationships. This technological fetish of control finds its sexual expression in the development of the robot as a substitute for the human partner.

Levy's description of technophilia connects with Fromm's discussion of the technical fascination of the "gadgeteer" or "cybernetic man" fostered by corporate capitalism. Fromm writes:

> This new type of man, after all, is not interested in feces or corpses... But he does something much more drastic. He turns his interest away from life, persons, nature, ideas—in short from everything that is alive; he transforms all life into things, including himself and the manifestations of his human faculties of reason, seeing, hearing, tasting, loving. Sexuality becomes a technical skill (the "love machine")... and whatever love and tenderness man has is directed toward machines and gadgets.[137]

Technophilia becomes an expression of necrophilia when gadgets substitute for relationships with living people and the natural world. Cybernetic man channels his death orientation into his love affair with machines.

The devices on which people increasingly focus their attention transmit an endless stream of murders, torture, sadism, and sexual violence. Fromm commented:

> Consider the role that killing plays in our amusements. The movies, the comic strips, the newspapers are full of excitement because they are full of reports of destruction, sadism, brutality. Millions of people live humdrum but comfortable existences—and nothing excites them more than to see or read of killings, whether it is murder or a fatal accident in an automobile race. Is this not an indication of how deep this fascination with death has already become?[138]

The combination of fantasies of dismemberment and destructiveness is encapsulated in the image in Quentin Tarantino and Robert Rodriguez's 2007 film *Grindhouse* of a female character with a machine gun as prosthetic limb. The combined sexualization of mutilation and destructive technology signifies the contemporary unity of technophilia and necrophilia.[139]

Pornography can itself be understood as a sexual relationship that substitutes a non-living object for a living human being. Catherine MacKinnon has called pornography "sex between people and things, human beings and pieces of paper, real men and unreal women."[140] This substitution of the object for the human being is the focus of Melinda Vadas's critique of pornography. She argues that "Within its context of sexual consumption, the pornography used *as* a woman *is* a woman, and not a representation of one."[141] The use of an inanimate object in place of a woman, Vadas argues, entails that women are themselves equivalent to objects. The animation of the pornographic object through its use and the reification of the woman go together.[142]

Rae Langton uses the term "sexual solipsism" to describe the way in which pornography constitutes the user as alone with objects, rather than in interaction with people, in their sexual relations. This is illustrated in the example that Langton gives of a heavy pornography user admitting that he had begun to treat his wife as pornography: "All the while I was thinking either about porn or trying to make her say things she didn't want to say. I was really just using her—she was like a masturbatory accessory."[143] The treatment of things as people and the treatment of people as things are closely interwoven.[144] The substitution of a thing for a woman is an extension of the desire to eliminate the potentially demanding and threatening agency and aliveness from the woman by making her into an object. Both of these impulses represent an escape from life—by sadistically controlling and crushing the woman's vitality, *or*, by the combined necrophile and technophile shift of interest to the object that is not alive. This shift of interest to the non-alive is inherent in pornography, and this is what makes pornography use such a poor substitute for the sexual relationship—the ennui that accompanies it is an expression of its unaliveness. The channeling of desire and interest into something that is dead is also deadening. As sex therapist Mark Schwartz, clinical director of the Masters and Johnson clinic in St. Louis, observes, "A man starts to feel like a computer himself when he realizes that he's dependent on computer images to turn him on."[145]

Just as pornography transforms women into objects, it also renders men as mere robotic penises, devoid of human feeling. As Dines puts it: "Men in porn are depicted as soulless, unfeeling, amoral life-support systems for erect penises."[146] The world of pornography, Dines argues, is "populated by women who are robotic 'sluts' and men who are robotic studs."[147] Sometimes the "robotic studs" are literally machines. Sex machines that provide a phallic attachment with a mechanical thrusting action are marketed with names such as Annihilator, Chopper, Drilldo, Fuckzilla, Hatchet, Intruder, Invader, Stallion, Probe Plus, Thrillhammer, and Trespasser.[148] A genre of pornography—"machine fucking"—has arisen around this.[149] In this, the woman is passive, getting fucked. The subject has become the machine, as an expression of male performativity. In the process, masculinity is integrated with the machine, and the male subject becomes machine-like. Jensen has described how the appeal of pornography, for men, is linked to the way in which it decouples sex from emotion. He reflects that the experience of "watching pornography produces a kind of emotional numbness, a part of which is a process of objectifying myself."[150] The transposing of the male subject into the machine expresses the way in which men are culturally constructed as machines, and encouraged to think about themselves in those terms.[151]

In his classic critique of American culture, *The Pursuit of Loneliness*, Philip Slater observes that the emphasis in modern male sexuality is on "performance and getting a big response from women." As a result, "Most men have difficulty *receiving* pleasure, unless it proceeds quickly to orgasm."[152] While sexual pleasure is focused on the penis and the moment of ejaculation, men's bodies as a whole are desensitized. Soble suggests that this compartmentalized sexuality, oriented toward manipulation, control, and performance, reflects the shaping of male desire by capitalism. In this syndrome, "[a] man sees the female body at rest as an asexual and passive machine, inanimate, cool, inert, not yet 'turned on,' unplugged. His sexual task… is to operate this machine successfully, to transform its potential into kinetic energy."[153] Sex is understood as the meeting not of human beings but of humanoid devices for achieving pleasure as an outcome. It is not surprising that this mechanized sexuality should seek satisfaction in and through machines.[154]

The harnessing of sexual desire to the desire for objects has become basic to capitalist marketing. Capitalism uses women's bodies to generate desire for objects, objectifying women in order to build the consumer's sexual-emotional connection with the object (in that way animating the object). Laurie Penny describes how the display of the body fragments women's bodies into disembodied parts: "[E]verywhere, on book-covers and cereal packets and boxes of sanitary towels, disembodied legs in stilettoed high heels emblematise a cutesy, feminine consumer imperative that edges to replace genuine erotic impulse."[155] Marketing alienates women from their bodies and their sexuality, selling them back an ersatz sexuality attached to the role of consumer, now imagined as fun, adventurous, and sexy even while buying the most mundane products. At the same time, advertisers dangle women's bodies, and body parts, in front of men as a bait and switch, hoping to arouse sexual interest and divert this interest into the product. In auto shows, it is customary to have scantily clad women standing or dancing suggestively next to the automobiles. The woman is made into an object for display and, the suggestion is, for sale, like the car. Her sexuality is appropriated to the car, the car becoming identified as a feminine object to be desired, even while the car is a symbol of phallic potency that promises to make its owner desirable to women like her. In a similar manner, advertisements situate women's bodies next to consumer objects or merge women's bodies with commodities (a beer bottle photographically merged with a woman's body). The woman is rendered as a consumer object. The commodity becomes an object of sexual desire. Pornography is continuous with this—the consumer object itself is the woman reified as image and circulated in magazines, videos, or Web sites. In both advertising and pornography, sexual desire is displaced from the living being onto the commodity. The non-living replaces the living as the object of desire.

The Desire Machine

For the porn consumer, the computer is the medium for their free exploration of sexual desire. But the computer is also the key means of production of late capitalism, used to coordinate and speed-up production and exercise discipline over the workforce.[156] The device that is the gateway to an infinite variety of sexual pleasures is also the device to which office workers are tethered during the working day, imposing boredom, isolation, mental exhaustion, and often painful physical repetition (as in carpal tunnel syndrome). It is hardly surprising that there are many cases of slippage between these two social worlds of the computer. A 2004 survey by the Employment Law Alliance found that one in four workers say they visit pornographic Web sites during office hours or have seen their coworkers do the same.[157] There are numerous cases in which organizations have fired employees for pornography use. In 2002, the Virginia Department of Transportation found employees accessing online pornography for more than two hours daily, resulting in the firing of 15 employees and the resignations of two more. In 2004, Kentucky's state transportation department suspended or fired 43 employees for viewing pornography on office computers. In the same year, an audit manager at the University of Texas Health Science Center in Houston resigned in protest at the lack of action taken over prevalent workplace Internet pornography use, which her investigations had uncovered.[158] In 2010, there was a scandal about the use of Internet pornography by senior employees at the economic regulatory agency, the Securities Exchange Commission. In 2012, the Pentagon cracked down on viewing of pornographic Web sites in the Missile Defense Agency.[159] In 2013, a Freedom of Information request revealed there were 300,000 attempts in the previous year to access pornographic Web sites from the servers of the UK Parliament.[160] Also in 2013, it was reported that the Welsh Government had disciplined

55 staff for viewing pornography at work.[161] Like posting nude pinups or playboy pictures, pornography use may be an exercise of male power, creating a sexualized environment that humiliates and excludes women. But a particularly sexist culture in the workplace need not be behind workers' pornography use. Rather, the temptation to use pornography at work is inherent in the duality of the computer as a device of production and workplace discipline and a medium for fantasies of escape from this discipline.

An article in *The Guardian* describes the isolated United States Army Forward Operating Base Hammer in Iraq, close to the Iranian border. This is where Bradley Manning accessed classified computer files, including the infamous "Collateral Murder" video showing a US Army helicopter gunship crew massacring Iraqi civilians. The description of the base conveys the sheer lifelessness of the place and the ways in which the soldiers stationed there would try to alleviate their chronic boredom:

> Hammer's overriding culture was one of boredom and casual bullying, where bored non-commissioned officers picked on juniors. "They had a saying. 'Shit rolls downhill,'"...
>
> For entertainment, soldiers would download porn to workstations or access footage from Apache helicopters showing civilians being shot at, often through SIPRNet, the classified intelligence network used by the state department and department of defence...
>
> "Soldiers would call it 'war porn' or 'the war channel' or just 'war TV'. It was hypnotic to watch, even when not much was happening, just this lazy overhead view of the world around you. For many soldiers, it was all they ever saw of Iraq."[162]

This context of monotony and meaninglessness is one in which the military hierarchy's anal sadistic character is unfettered—the superiors are "shitting" on their inferiors. The work is boring and the setting equally dreary, "a desolate place built mainly from freight containers." Hierarchy and concomitant bullying exacerbate the feeling of lifelessness. As Manning described it, "I live in a very real world, where deaths and detainments are just statistics; where idealistic calls for 'liberation' and 'freedom' are utterly meaningless."[163] This is to describe an institutional setting of pervasive and systematic cynicism and hopelessness. The computer terminals on which the soldiers were stationed to work were also the source of escape, and presented to the new arrivals as such. The main attractions were sex and death—Internet pornography and real military footage which the soldiers watch as "war porn." Helicopter footage, relayed via the computer network, provided an escape from the enclosure and claustrophobia of the base. The frenetic fantasy worlds of video games provided distraction. Pornography was a similar distraction and escape. But its sexual content is also significant. Viewing pictures and videos of bodies and sex could be understood as an attempt to bring Eros into this place of death. But this culture of death and hierarchy also created its own fantasy world: the pornography of violence—collateral murder as entertainment. In the context of lifelessness, desire becomes intermeshed with destructiveness.

If online pornography use on a military base is an escape from chronic boredom and enforced lifelessness, it seems plausible that its use in the office space of corporate and governmental bureaucracies has a similar quality. The plastic box to which the white collar worker is an appendage, the keyboard that he or she repetitively strokes, the electronic screen which is the source of headaches and eye strain, the electronic space, which the worker fills with monotonous data entry—this machine is also a portal to a collective fantasy world promising total gratification, where a few clicks can summon up whatever they desire.[164]

This is an important way in which the personal computer has become a "universal machine." The computer network is both a tool of production and a medium of exchange. It, thus, embodies the unity of capitalism as freedom or "anarchy" in exchange and despotism in production.[165] The computer binds and disciplines the worker, but it is also a medium of consumption, offering access to the pleasurable expression and fulfillment of desire. Under capitalism, while production is a state of unfreedom for the worker, under the authority of the boss, circulation is the realm of freedom. In everyday life, "free time" is time outside work. Leisure and consumption become the avenues through which we pursue self-expression and construct an individuality that we are forced to suppress while in the workplace.

Advertising appeals to unconscious desire, using sex to manufacture desire for products. As the product is made an object of desire, consumerism becomes an activity in which desire is expressed and made into a force of circulation. The spaces of capitalist production are spaces of repression and subordination under the petty dictates of supervisors and bureaucratic rules. Production is reduced to the monotonous activity of the factory worker, cashier, call-center worker, and office worker. In contrast to, but as a corollary of, repressive production, the activity of consumption offers release. The commodity promises to provide the gratification that is denied in the "9 to 5" workday. For example, the needs of a body that sits in an office chair all week now fuel demand for relaxation therapies and spa products. Utopian leisure is achieved via a week-long vacation in the sun. The body that is an object or resource in production becomes the desiring *subject* in consumption.[166]

The workers are depersonalized in the place of production, or they are forced to assume a standardized corporate identity as representative of the company. In leisure, we are free to shape our identities from a plethora of subcultures, styles, fashions, and niche markets. Sexual identity finds free play in the sex industry's marketplace of desire. Margot Weiss's study of BDSM (bondage, domination, and sado-masochism) subculture makes apparent the ways in which the challenging of sexual codes is facilitated by consumer culture. The practice of sado-masochism requires purchasing a variety of sex toys. Weiss reports that "Spending hundreds and hundreds, or even thousands, of dollars on toys is not unusual" and people arrive at SM events with "toy bags" full of floggers, canes, paddles, crops, bondage devices, and other sex toys. "With its endless paraphernalia," she writes, "BDSM is a prime example of late-capitalist sexuality." In this way, she suggests that the, paradoxically, libertarian emphasis of BDSM culture on the freedom of the individual to realize their sexual fantasies is in tune with the prevailing American capitalist "belief in the 'free,' unfettered market" as an ideology which "locates autonomy in consumption."[167]

However, the commodities that are thrilling or transgressive in the realm of consumption are banal and wearying in production. This is brought out by Mac McClelland's investigative report on the physically exhausting, regimented, "demoralizing and dehumanizing" character of work in warehouses for online retailers. He describes the kinds of objects they spend their days retrieving from shelves and the physical toll it takes on their bodies:

> Amalgamated has estimated that we pickers speed-walk an average of 12 miles a day on cold concrete, and the twinge in my legs blurs into the heavy soreness in my feet that complements the pinch in my hips when I crouch to the floor… to retrieve an iPad protective case. iPad anti-glare protector. iPad one-hand grip-holder device… *And dildos. Really, a staggering number of dildos. At breaks, some of my coworkers complain that they have to handle so many dildos.*[168]

The device that promises the consumer ecstatic pleasure is the source of torment for the warehouse worker who does the carrying and shipping. The consumer's freedom to live out their desires is connected, in a chain of production and circulation of commodities, to the worker's unfreedom. McClelland reports that, in the warehouse, "At lunch, the most common question, aside from 'Which offensive dick-shaped product did you handle the most of today?' is 'Why are you here?' like in prison."[169]

The free expression of their individual sexuality pursued by the BDSM subculture tightly couples with the unfreedom of capitalist inequality and workplace hierarchy. Sado-masochism is built into this hierarchy, as is apparent in McClelland's account of the self-abnegating attitude demanded of warehouse workers:

> Never say that you can't do it... When they ask you why you aren't reaching your goals... Say you'll do better, even if you know you can't... Say you'll try harder, even if the truth is that you're trying your absolute hardest right now, no matter how many times they tell you you're not doing good enough.[170]

Sexual sado-masochism often recapitulates the hierarchies of an unequal society in eroticized form.[171] As sexualized violence is used as a means of control by the American state, Weiss describes BDSM practitioners drawing on the CIA's KUBARK manual on psychological torture methods (an influence on techniques used at Abu Ghraib and Guantanamo Bay) in order to carry out realistic "interrogation" scenes for erotic excitement.[172] The fact that in this subculture men are predominantly the dominants and women the submissives suggests that real-world patterns of hierarchy are being translated into the supposedly separate world of play and fantasy.[173]

It is naïve to expect this space of consumerist fantasy to be able to "transgress" the hierarchies of the broader social world. The splitting off of a private, leisure domain from the "real world" of work is a function of capitalism's division of life between work and leisure, public and private, and its construction of leisure and consumption as compensatory escapes from the demands of an alienated reality. These divides are real in the sense that they structure life, but they are also fictitious, for both sides are conditioned by the totality of capitalist relations. The fantasies of consumer leisure, including its sexual niches, recapitulate the hostile relations of capitalist social reality.[174]

Marx noted in *The Economic and Philosophic Manuscripts* how consumption operates within capitalism as compensation for alienation in work, but also reflects this alienation. When the worker is dehumanized, reduced to an animal state, in repetitive work over which he has no control, he, therefore, "only feels himself freely active in his animal functions—eating, drinking, procreating." These functions of consumption themselves become alienated as they are split off from the rest of human life and treated as the be all and end all: "Certainly, eating, drinking, procreating, etc., are also genuinely human functions. But abstractly taken, separated from the sphere of all other human activity and turned into sole and ultimate ends, they are animal functions."[175] Yet, even in these "animal functions," the individual under capitalism is not truly "at home," since one's "animal" desires are continually manipulated and channeled back into the accumulation process, as they are harnessed to the need to buy products. Internet pornography reduces sex to animal functions, but also seeks to manipulate this "animality." In gonzo, pornography has done away with all "cultural" accoutrements such as plot, and is nothing but animalistic humping. Like the performers, the consumer of pornography is reduced to a body: the aim is nothing but orgasm, an act that when decoupled from any human relationship is, as one porn user puts it, "more like blowing your nose than having sex. A quick physical sensation, bam, you get off."[176]

Yet, while pornography involves this reduction of sexual experience to a simple physical act, the activity of searching Internet pornography is as *disembodied* as contemporary office work. Again, the individual sits at a computer, tapping and clicking, eyes restlessly scanning the screen. Onscreen are the ghostly digital traces of human bodies. It is a primarily a disembodied mental-informational activity in which the body is involved in a secondary way as the porn viewer masturbates. While the fantasy is of sexual freedom, choice, virility, and control, the reality is loneliness. This tragic quality of the solipsism of pornography use is brought out by Mark Schwartz: "The metaphor of a man masturbating to his computer is the Willy Loman of our decade... the completely lonely, isolated man having sex with an imaginary airbrushed woman on a computer screen."[177]

The networked computer is a tool of production, but also offers escape from alienation in the form of fantasy. Thus, the immaterial world of collective fantasy promises to restore the life that is repressed in production and the chronic boredom of everyday life. Life is restored in immaterial form. The mind floats free from the body. This dualism reflects the capitalist division of labor, in which mental and manual labor are sharply divided from one another and arranged hierarchically. Manual work is subordinated to management, which monopolizes decision-making.[178] As a free space of information, virtuality, or pure mentality, the Internet corresponds to capitalism's hierarchy between mental and manual.[179] In this hierarchy, the rewards of mental labor correlate with the degradation of manual labor. Sociologists Charles Derber, William Schwartz, and Yale Magrass write, "Labor reduced to its 'animal' form is the dark side of professionalism as well as capitalism."[180]

The promise of freedom in the immaterial sphere of information is an escape from the corporeal oppression of human beings, and it assumes that oppression as its premise.[181] The virtual world is a technologized version of the religious promise that, while you are oppressed in this world, you can be free in the next. In the case of the Internet, the "next world" is a heaven of desublimation which requires that the body be resurrected in virtual form.[182]

But in this virtual form, the body becomes more perfectly commodified. For example, in the virtual world of the computer game Second Life, the avatars (or virtual personas of the game players) do not have genitals, so players who want to witness their "second selves" in coitus must go to a virtual store where they can buy sexual organs for their avatars. A technology magazine explains: "As with most things, when you buy a penis in Second Life, you get what you pay for you. Free penises are relatively simple with limited functionality. Paid-for-penises come with more options."[183] The body reappears in this immaterial form, but as a commodity, and fragmented in the process. In capitalism's compensatory virtual worlds, human bodies are sucked up into capitalist circulation. But in order to circulate globally and instantly, they lose their quality as bodies, becoming information.

The negation of the body through work discipline in alienated production is mirrored in the negation of the body through informatization in alienated consumption. Underlying consumerist promises of freedom and abundance are the repressive structures of work, hierarchy, and imposed scarcity. Consumption is necessarily attached to production. Intertwined with the desires that consumerism provokes is the desire for liberation from labor, which is something that capitalism cannot fulfill.

What is repressed in capitalism is not sexual desire *per se*. Rather, it is human life itself. In some ways, capitalism is *sexualizing*. This is Marx's point about the worker only being at home in his animal functions. Frustrated as human beings, we are encouraged to seek satisfaction as sexual beings. Our needs are constructed as sexual. Freedom is constructed as sexual freedom. But sexual freedom accompanies and is a corollary of the repression of life. Commercialized sex is offered as an escape from an oppressed and unfulfilled life. The sex addict is never satisfied, and therefore compulsive, because he or she cannot find in sex what has been taken away from life in general.

The sexuality that is harnessed by capital is a *reduction to sex* of a broader range of desires that cannot be met within capitalism. This is why pornified sexuality is always a void, which gives the pornography user a sense of "vertigo" or "endless falling." It is because it cannot deliver the satisfaction that it promises that it has to offer such dizzying variety. Michael Perelman observes that consumerism

> generally fails to provide lasting satisfaction. Instead, the initial pleasure is often fleeting, especially after the consumer sees advertisements for new-and-improved products, or, worse, a neighbor with a better version. Satisfaction rapidly turns into dissatisfaction, creating an emotional emptiness. This emptiness feeds on itself, creating a craving for additional consumption.[184]

The liberation offered by capitalism is always mingled with boredom, subordination, and resentment. Frustrated, alienated sexual desire, harnessed by the spectacle, is, therefore, always mingled with the hatred, anger, and loathing of self and others, that are corollaries of alienated labor and alienated life in a hostile, competitive social order.

The freedom promised by the global market contains within it its opposite—human trafficking as the return of slavery. The free communication of informationalized capitalism is also the reduction of human beings to abstract, informational commodities and the packaging of human bodies and desires within the circuits of capitalist exchange. The pornography user's freedom to browse is the freedom to choose his or her own Colosseum. The form of sexual freedom promoted within capitalism is one that necessarily entails these contradictions. The assimilation of sexuality to the market frees it from traditional moral codes and constraints; the ongoing breaking down of these boundaries allows the expansion of the sex industry. The individual is offered an array of products that operate as simple stimuli, superficially and temporarily arousing sexual interest. Yet, as with commodities in general, this abundance of commodified sex cannot escape what Debord calls the commodity's "essential poverty." This essential poverty "comes to it from the misery of its production."[185]

In pornography, this misery is the brutalization and degradation of human beings whose abuse becomes the circulated image.

Notes

1. Susanne Kappeler, *The Pornography of Representation* (Cambridge: Polity Press, 1986), 50.
2. Kappeler, *Pornography of Representation*, 5–6, 8.
3. Photographs in Mark Danner, *Torture and Truth: America, Abu Ghraib, and the War on Terror* (New York: New York Review Books, 2004), 217–224; Graham, Duncan and Paul Cruickshank, 2009. "Abu Ghraib Abuse Photos 'Show Rape'" *The Daily Telegraph* (May 27), http://www.telegraph.co.uk/news/worldnews/northamerica/usa/5395830/Abu-Ghraib-abuse-photos-show-rape.html; Seymour Hersch, "The General's Report," *The New Yorker*, June 25, 2007, http://www.newyorker.com/reporting/2007/06/25/070625fa_fact_hersh?currentPage=all; Michael Sherer and Mark Benjamin, "Mentally Deranged," *Salon.com*, March 14, 2006, http://www.salon.com/2006/03/14/chapter_9_2/; Steven H. Miles, *Oath Betrayed: America's Torture Doctors* (Berkeley: University of California Press, 2009), 104; Mark Danner, "Abu Ghraib: The Hidden Story," *The New York Review of Books*, October 7, 2004, http://www.nybooks.com/articles/archives/2004/oct/07/abu-ghraib-the-hidden-story/; Richard A. Serrano, "Abused Iraqi Detainees Said to Hold No Intelligence Value," *Los Angeles Times*, August 4, 2004, http://articles.latimes.com/2004/aug/04/nation/na-lynndie4; Scott Higham and Joe Stephens, "New Details of Prison Abuse Emerge," *The Washington Post*, May 21, 2004, http://www.washingtonpost.com/wp-dyn/articles/A43783-2004May20.html
4. Translation of statement provided by Kasim Mehaddi Hilas, Detainee #151108, reprinted in Danner, *Torture and Truth*, 242–243.
5. Translation of statement provided by Abdou Hussain Saad Faleh, Detainee #18470, reprinted in Danner, *Torture and Truth*, 230.
6. Anonymous detainee statement, reprinted in Danner, *Torture and Truth*, 248.
7. Danner, *Torture and Truth*, 18.
8. Danner, *Torture and Truth*, 19.
9. Kappeler, *Pornography of Representation*, 154.
10. George W. Bush, "President Bush Addresses the Nation," September 20, 2001, reprinted in *The Washington Post*, http://www.washingtonpost.com/wp-srv/nation/specials/attacked/transcripts/bushaddress_092001.html

11. Joanna Bourke, "Torture as Pornography," *The Guardian*, May 6, 2004, http://www.guardian.co.uk/world/2004/may/07/gender.uk. See also De Clarke, "Prostitution for Everyone: Feminism, Globalization and the 'Sex' Industry," in *Not For Sale: Feminists Resisting Prostitution and Pornography* ed. Christine Starke and Rebecca Whisnant (Melbourne: Spinifex Press, 2004), 149–205, on 205.
12. Bourke, "Torture as Pornography"; Danner, *Torture and Truth*, 45.
13. Al Jazeera, "Storm over Israeli 'Abuse' Photos," *Al Jazeera*, August 17, 2010, http://www.aljazeera.com/news/middleeast/2010/08/2010816164542801123.html; Diaa Hadid, "Eden Abergil Facebook Pictures: Israeli Soldier's Photos Cause Outrage," *The Huffington Post*, May 25, 2011, http://www.huffingtonpost.com/2010/08/16/eden-abergil-facebook-pic_n_683816.html; Jean Shaoul, "Facebook Postings of Abuse of Palestinians Highlight Polarisation of Israeli Society," *World Socialist Web Site*, August 25, 2010, http://www.wsws.org/en/articles/2010/08/isra-a25.html
14. Hadid, "Eden Abergil."
15. Hadid, "Eden Abergil."
16. Simon McGregor-Wood, "Israeli Soldier Belly Dances Around Palestinian Woman," *ABC News*, October 6, 2010, http://www.abcnews.go.com/international/israeli-soldier-belly-dances-palestinian-woman/story?id=11802427
17. Jonathan Glover, *Humanity: A Moral History of the Twentieth Century* (London: Pimlico, 2001), 341.
18. Glover, *Humanity*, 37.
19. Khatib, quoted in Hadid, "Eden Abergil."
20. Kappeler, *Pornography of Representation*, 50–51.
21. Christoph Dreier, "'Abu-Ghraib-like' Torture of Refugees Exposed in Germany," *World Socialist Web Site*, October 1, 2014, http://www.wsws.org/en/articles/2014/10/01/mist-o01.html; Jenny Hill, "German Police Probe Abuse at Burbach Asylum Center," *BBC News*, September 29, 2014, http://www.bbc.com/news/world-europe-29408172; "Criminals are at Work in Refugee Homes," *The Local*, September 30, 2014, http://www.thelocal.de/20140930/germany-shocked-and-ashamed-over-refugee-photo
22. Giorgio Agamben, *State of Exception* (Chicago: University of Chicago Press, 2005); Judith Butler, *Precarious Life: The Powers of Mourning and Violence* (London: Verso, 2004), 50–100.
23. This continues under the Obama administration. See Glenn Greenwald, "Another Guantánamo prisoner death highlights Democrats' hypocrisy," *The Guardian*, September 11, 2012, http://www.guardian.co.uk/commentisfree/2012/sep/11/guantanamo-prisoner-death-democrats

24. Wendy Brown, *Walled States, Waning Sovereignty* (New York: Zone Books, 2010).
25. Zygmunt Bauman, *Globalization: Its Human Consequences* (Cambridge: Polity Press, 1998), 93. See also Maggy Lee, *Trafficking and Global Crime Control* (London: Sage, 2011), 152.
26. Zygmunt Bauman, *Wasted Lives: Modernity and its Outcasts* (Cambridge: Polity Press, 2004); Lee, *Trafficking and Global Crime Control*, 152.
27. S.P. Glinkina, quoted in Nikos Passas, "Global Anomie, Dysnomie and Economic Change: Hidden Consequences of Neoliberalism and Globalization in Russia and Around the World," *Social Justice* 27(2): 16–44, on 29.
28. Saltanat Sulaimanova, "Trafficking in Women from the Former Soviet Union for the Purpose of Sexual Exploitation," in Karen Beeks and Delia Amib eds., *Trafficking and the Global Sex Industry* (Lanham, MD: Rowman and Littlefield, 2006), 61–75.
29. Dennis Altman, *Global Sex* (Chicago: University of Chicago Press, 2001), 108. Trafficking of women from Tajikistan to the Gulf States and Russia is discussed in Gustavo Capdevila, "Globalization Leads to Slavery," *Asia Times*, August 23, 2001, http://www.asiatimes/com/c-asia/CH23Ag03.html
30. Sulaimanova, "Trafficking in Women," 61.
31. Elina Pentinnen, *Globalization, Prostitution and Sex-Trafficking: Corporeal Politics* (London: Routledge, 2008), 25–26.
32. Lee, *Trafficking and Global Crime Control*, 48.
33. Gail Kligman and Stephanie Limoncelli, "Trafficking Women after Socialism: From, To, and Through, Eastern Europe," *Social Politics: International Studies in Gender, State and Society* 12(1) (Spring 2005): 118–140, on 122.
34. Quotation from Nisha Lilio Piu, "Welcome to Paradise: Inside the World of Legalized Prostitution," *The Telegraph*, March 5, 2014, http://s.telegraph.co.uk/graphics/projects/welcome-to-paradise/. See also "Unprotected: How Legalizing Prostitution has Failed," *Spiegel Online*, May 30, 2013, http://www.spiegel.de/international/germany/human-trafficking-persists-despite-legality-of-prostitution-in-germany-a-902533.html
35. Lee, *Trafficking and Global Crime Control*, 51.
36. Sulaimanova, "Trafficking in Women," 63.
37. Sulaimanova, "Trafficking in Women," 62, 64–65.
38. Sulaimanova, "Trafficking in Women," 69. See also Phil Williams, "Trafficking in Women: the Role of Transnational Organized Crime," in Sally Cameron and Edward Newman eds, *Trafficking in Humans: Social*,

Cultural and Political Dimensions (Tokyo: United Nations University Press, 2008), 126–157, on 142–145.
39. Sally Cameron, "Trafficking of Women for Prostitution," in Cameron and Newman, *Trafficking in Humans*, 80–110, on 87.
40. ILO 2012 Global Estimate of Forced Labour: Executive Summary (International Labor Organization, Geneva, Switzerland: 2012), http://www.ilo.org/wcmsp5/groups/public/@ed_norm/@declaration/documents/publication/wcms_181953.pdf. See also ILO Global Estimate of Forced Labor: Results and Methodology (International Labor Organization, Geneva, Switzerland: 2012), 16, http://www.ilo.org/wcmsp5/groups/public/—ed_norm/—declaration/documents/publication/wcms_182004.pdf
41. United Nations Office on Drugs and Crime, Global Report on Trafficking in Persons 2012 (Vienna: United Nations Office on Drugs and Crime, 2012), 10, 25–26, 36, http://www.unodc.org/documents/data-and-analysis/glotip/Trafficking_in_Persons_2012_web.pdf
42. Williams, "Trafficking in Women," 145.
43. Lee, *Trafficking and Global Crime Control*, 4.
44. Richard Poulin, "Globalization and the Sex Trade: Trafficking and the Commodification of Women and Children," *Canadian Woman Studies* 22 (3/4) (2004): 38–47, quoting 38.
45. Saskia Sassen, "Two Stops in Today's New Global Geographies: Shaping Novel Labor Supplies and Employment Regimes," *American Behavioral Scientist* 52 (3) (November 2008): 457–496, on 459. See also Saskia Sassen, "Women's Burden: Counter-Geographies of Globalization and the Feminization of Survival," *Nordic Journal of International Law* 71 (2002): 255–274, 255; Lee, *Trafficking and Global Crime Control*, 50; Rey Koslowski, "Economic Globalization, Human Smuggling, and Global Governance," in David Kyle and Rey Koslowski eds., *Global Human Smuggling: Comparative Perspectives* (Baltimore: The Johns Hopkins University Press, 2001), 337–358, esp. 338–339; Alfred E. Eckes, *The Contemporary Global Economy: a History Since 1980* (Chichester, UK: Wiley-Blackwell, 2011), 220–223, esp. 220.
46. L. Shelley and J. Picarelli, quoted in Lee, *Trafficking and Global Crime Control*, 23.
47. Lee, *Trafficking and Global Crime Control*, 23–24, quoting 23; Cameron and Newman, "Structural Factors," 28; Amelia Hill, "Girls of Six Sold into Sex Slavery," *The Observer*, December 17, 2000, http://www.theguardian.com/uk/2000/dec/17/childprotection.society
48. Sally Cameron and Edward Newman, "Structural Factors in Human Trafficking," in Cameron and Newman eds, *Trafficking in Humans*, on 26.

49. Williams, "Trafficking in Women," 126.
50. Lee, *Trafficking and Global Crime Control*, 6.
51. Williams, "Trafficking in Women," 127. See also Phil Williams ed., *Illegal Immigration and Commercial Sex: The New Slave Trade* (London: Frank Cass, 1999).
52. Williams, "Trafficking in Women," 130.
53. Williams, "Trafficking in Women," 155.
54. Ronaldo Munk, *Globalization and Social Exclusion: A Transformationalist Perspective* (Bloomfield, CT: Kumarion Press, 2005), 90–91. See also Kevin Bales, *Disposable People: New Slavery in the Global Economy*. (Berkeley: University of California Press, 1999).
55. United States Department of State, *Trafficking in Persons Report 2008* (June 2008), 34, http://www.state.gov/documents/organization/105501.pdf
56. Pentinnen, *Globalization, Prostitution and Sex Trafficking*, 20–21, see also 56–57.
57. Munk, *Globalization and Social Exclusion*, 94; see also Ursula Biemann, "Remotely Sensed: A Topography of the Global Sex Trade," *Feminist Review* 70 (2000): 75–88.
58. Langdon Winner, "Cyberlibertarian Myths and the Prospects for Community," *ACM SIGCAS Computers and Society* 27 (3) (September 1997): 14–19; PJ Rey, "The Myth of Cyberspace," *The New Inquiry*, April 13, 2012, http://thenewinquiry.com/essays/the-myth-of-cyberspace/; Richard Barbrook and Andy Cameron, "The Californian Ideology," *Science as Culture* 6 (1) (1996): 44–72.
59. Wendy Hui Kyong Chun, *Control and Freedom: Power and Paranoia in the Age of Fiber Optics* (Cambridge, MA: MIT Press, 2006), 37–38. Cf. Sadie Plant, *Zeroes and Ones: Digital Women and the New Technoculture* (New York: Doubleday, 1997).
60. Pentinnen, *Globalization, Prostitution and Sex-Trafficking*, 45–46.
61. Pentinnen, *Globalization, Prostitution and Sex-Trafficking*, 73.
62. Amanda Kloer, "Craigslist Makes $36 million from illegal sex ads," *Change.org*, April 26, 2010, http://humantrafficking.change.org/blog/view/craigslist_makes_36_million_from_illegal_sex_ads; Liz Goodwin, "Craigslist Founder Rendered Speechless by CNN's Sex Trafficking Questions," *Yahoo! News*, http://news.yahoo.com/craigslist-founder-rendered-speechless-cnn-sex-trafficking-questions-155002984.html; Steve Turnham and Amber Lyon, "Sold on Craigslist: Critics Say Sex Ad Crackdown Inadequate," August 4, 2010, http://www.cnn.com/2010/CRIME/08/03/craigslist.sex.ads/; Amir Attaran, "Sex Slaves in Canada," *Literary Review of Canada* (December 2010), http://reviewcanada.ca/magazine/2010/12/sex-slaves-in-canada/

63. Ian O'Donnell and Claire Milner, 2007. *Child Pornography: Crime, Computers and Society* (Cullompton, Devon, UK: Willan Publishing), 28–29.
64. O'Donnell and Milner, *Child Pornography*, 55–56.
65. "The Internet Watch Foundation (IWF) Identified Twice as Many Child Sexual Abuse Webpages This Year Compared to Last Year," Internet Watch Foundation, December 11, 2014, https://www.iwf.org.uk/about-iwf/news/post/399-the-internet-watch-foundation-iwf-has-identified-twice-as-many-child-sexual-abuse-webpages-this-year-compared-to-last-year. Accessed January 5, 2015.
66. O'Donnell and Milner, *Child Pornography*, 54.
67. O'Donnell and Milner, *Child Pornography*, 54.
68. O'Donnell and Milner, *Child Pornography*, 28.
69. Oliver Burkeman, "Parents Charged in Paedophile Ring," *The Guardian*, August 9, 2002, http://www.guardian.co.uk/world/2002/aug/10/childprotection.usa?INTCMP=SRCHMc
70. David Batty, "100 Arrests Hit World Paedophile Ring," *The Guardian*, November 5, 2007, http://www.guardian.co.uk/world/2007/nov/05/ukcrime.internationalcrime?INTCMP=SRCH; Williams, Rachel, "Police Act over 'Made-to-Order' Child Videos," *The Guardian*, November 6, 2007, http://www.guardian.co.uk/uk/2007/nov/06/ukcrime.children?INTCMP=SRCH.
71. Karen McVeigh, "Police Shut Down Global Paedophile Network in Operation Rescue" *The Guardian*, May 11 (2011), http://www.guardian.co.uk/society/2011/mar/16/global-paedophile-ring-smashed?INTCMP=SRCH
72. "Police Swoop on International Paedophile Ring," *The Guardian*, July 2, 2002, http://www.guardian.co.uk/technology/2002/jul/02/internetnews.childprotection?INTCMP=SRCH
73. David Wilson, "Missing the Real Danger to Children," *The Guardian*, August 22, 2003, http://www.guardian.co.uk/society/2003/aug/22/childrensservices.comment?INTCMP=SRCH. See also S.A. Mathieson, "Image Control," *The Guardian*, September 7, 2005, http://www.guardian.co.uk/technology/2005/sep/08/onlinesupplement.insideit?INTCMP=SRCH; Rosie Cowan, "100 Children Saved from Paedophiles," *The Guardian*, April 14, 2004, http://www.guardian.co.uk/society/2004/apr/15/childrensservices.childprotection1
74. Audrey Gillan, "Race to Save New Victims of Child Porn," *The Guardian*, November 4, 2003, http://www.guardian.co.uk/society/2003/nov/04/childrensservices.childprotection?INTCMP=SRCH
75. Bobbie Johnson, "Worst Child Abuse Images Quadruple Online in Three Years, Says Watchdog," *The Guardian*, April 17, 2007, http://www.theguardian.com/technology/2007/apr/17/news.frontpagenews

76. Denise Lavoie (Associated Press), "Vast International Child-Porn Network Uncovered," *ABC News*, August 4, 2012, http://abcnews.go.com/US/wireStory/vast-international-child-porn-network-uncovered-16928881
77. Gail Dines, *Pornland: How Porn has Hijacked our Sexuality* (Boston: Beacon Press, 2010), xviii–xix; see also Robert Jensen, *Getting Off: Pornography and the End of Masculinity* (Cambridge, MA: South End Press, 2007), 57.
78. Dines, *Pornland*, xxiv–xxv.
79. Dines, *Pornland*, xxv–xxvi.
80. Jensen, *Getting Off*, 101.
81. Jensen, *Getting Off*, 76.
82. Dines, *Pornland*, 93–94; see also Pamela Paul, *Pornified: How Pornography is Damaging our Lives, our Relationships, and our Families* (New York: Henry Holt and Co., 2005), 88, 227–229; Norman Doidge, "Brain Scans of Porn Addicts: What's Wrong with this Picture?" *The Guardian*, September 26, 2013, http://www.theguardian.com/commentisfree/2013/sep/26/brain-scans-porn-addicts-sexual-tastes
83. Paul, *Pornified*, 228.
84. Dines, *Pornland*, 142–143. See also "Children are the Pornography Industry's Next Goal" (interview with Gail Dines, March 2008), *CitizenLink*, June 14, 2010, http://www.citizenlink.com/2010/06/14/children-are-the-pornography-industry%E2%80%99s-goal/. Accessed August 13, 2012.
85. Dines, *Pornland*, 94.
86. "At a XXX-roads," *The Economist*, October 1, 2011, 64.
87. Stephen Maddison, "Online Obscenity and Myths of Freedom: Dangerous Images, Child Porn, and Neoliberalism," in Feona Attwood, *Porn.com: Making Sense of Online Pornography* (New York: Peter Lang, 2010), 17–33, on 26–27.
88. Chun, *Control and Freedom*, 12–13.
89. Porn user, quoted in Paul, *Pornified*, 76.
90. Pamela Paul, *Pornified*, 83–84.
91. Rae Langton, *Sexual Solipsism: Philosophical Essays on Pornography and Objectification* (Oxford: Oxford University Press, 2009).
92. Hubert Dreyfus, *On the Internet* (London: Routledge, 2009), 78–79. See also Søren Kierkegaard, "The Present Age" in idem, *The Present Age and Of the Difference Between a Genius and an Apostle*, trans. Alexander Dru (New York: Harper and Row, 1962), 33–86, esp. 39.
93. Joan Walsh, "Men who Hate Women on the Web," *Salon.com*, March 31, 2007, http://www.salon.com/2007/03/31/sierra/; See also Tim

Adams, "How the Internet Created an Age of Rage," *The Guardian*, July 23, 2011, http://www.guardian.co.uk/technology/2011/jul/24/internet-anonymity-trolling-tim-adams; Vanessa Thorpe and Richard Rogers, "Women Bloggers Call for a Stop to 'Hateful' Trolling by Misogynist Men," *The Observer*, November 6, 2011, http://www.theguardian.com/world/2011/nov/05/women-bloggers-hateful-trolling; "Creepy Crawlies: The Internet allows the Malicious to Menace their Victims," *The Economist*, April 20, 2011, http://www.economist.com/node/18584386; Jaron Lanier, *You are Not a Gadget* (New York: Vintage Books, 2011), 60–61.
94. Martha C. Nussbaum, "Objectification and Internet Misogyny," in Saul Levmore and Martha C. Nussbaum eds, *The Offensive Internet: Pivacy, Speech, and Reputation* (Cambridge, MA: Harvard University Press, 2010), 68–87.
95. Kappeler, *Pornography of Representation*, 57–58.
96. Erich Fromm, *The Anatomy of Human Destructiveness* (New York: Holt, Rinehart and Winston, 1973), 240–241.
97. Fromm, *Anatomy*, 239.
98. Fromm, *Anatomy*, 242–245.
99. Fromm, *Anatomy*, 248.
100. O'Donnell and Milner, *Child Pornography*, 54.
101. For curiosity as an explanation for mainstream heterosexual pornography use, see Paul, *Pornified*, 30.
102. O'Donnell and Milner, *Child Pornography*, 54.
103. O'Donnell and Milner, *Child Pornography*, 87–88. On collecting practices in child pornography use, see also Max Taylor and Ethel Quayle, *Child Pornography: an Internet Crime* (Hove, East Sussex, UK: Routledge, 2003), 148–170.
104. Marisol Bello and Yamiche Alcindor, "Police Chief, Rabbi Among 71 Nabbed in Porn Bust," *USA Today*, May 22, 2014, 1; Joseph Berger, "71 Are Accused in a Child Pornography Case, Officials Say," *The New York Times*, May 22, 2014, A22.
105. O'Donnell and Milner, *Child Pornography*, 87.
106. Fromm, *Anatomy*, 291, 293. See also Erich Fromm, *The Escape from Freedom* (New York: Henry Holt and Co., 1969), 155–158.
107. Philip Jenkins, *Beyond Tolerance: Child Pornography on the Internet* (New York: New York University Press, 2003), 103.
108. Jensen, *Getting Off*, 115.
109. Quoted in Paul, *Pornified*, 35.
110. Quoted in Jensen, *Getting Off*, 115. Capital letters in original.
111. Chun, *Control and Freedom*, 106–107.
112. Roger T. Pipe, "Something for Everyone: *Busty Latin Anal Nurses in Leather and Glasses*," in Monroe ed., *Porn*, 193–203, on 200.

113. Maddison, "Online Obscenity," 27.
114. Theodore Bach, "Pornography as Simulation," in Dave Monroe ed., *Porn – Philosophy for Everyone: How to Think with Kink* (Malden, MA: John Wiley and Sons, 2010), 52–65, on 62. Emphasis in original.
115. Alan Soble, *Pornography: Marxism, Feminism and the Future of Sexuality* (New Haven: Yale University Press, 1986), 56, see also 61.
116. Soble, *Pornography*, 57.
117. Quoting and giving examples from *Killing Us Softly 4: Advertising's Image of Women* (Northhampton, MA: Media Education Foundation, 2010).
118. Dines, *Pornland*, xviii.
119. Dines, *Pornland*, 152.
120. Jensen, *Getting Off*, 59; Dines, *Pornland*, xxi.
121. Quoted in Dines, *Pornland*, 71.
122. Dines, *Pornland*, xxv–xxvi.
123. Jensen, *Getting Off*, 121, 125–126.
124. Quoted in Dines, *Pornland*, 69. See also Jensen, *Getting Off*, 59–60.
125. Jensen, *Getting Off*, 126.
126. Dines, *Pornland*, xvii.
127. Kira Cochrane, "For Your Entertainment," *The Guardian* (G2), May 1, 2007, 4–7, quoting 5–7.
128. See Fromm, *Anatomy*, 288–290.
129. Fromm, *Anatomy*, 348.
130. Dines, *Pornland*, 75.
131. Dines, *Pornland*, 77.
132. Vicki Larson, "Can Loving a Robot Lead to Divorce?," *The Huffington Post*, December 20, 2011, http://www.huffingtonpost.com/vicki-larson/robots_1_b_1150679.html
133. David Levy, *Love and Sex with Robots: The Evolution of Human-Robot Relationships* (New York: Harper Collins, 2007), 22, 215, 242–253.
134. Levy, *Love and Sex*, 310.
135. Quoted in Patricia Pulham, "The Eroticism of Artificial Flesh in Villiers de L'Isle Adam's *L'Eve Future*," *Interdisciplinary Studies in the Long Nineteenth Century* 7 (2008) 12. Available online at: http://www.19.bbk.ac.uk/index.php/19/article/viewFile/486/346
136. Levy, *Love and Sex*, 127–128.
137. Fromm, *Anatomy*, 350.
138. Fromm, *The Heart of Man*, 58–59. See also Philip Slater, *The Pursuit of Loneliness: American Culture at the Breaking Point* (Boston: Beacon Press, 1990), 37.
139. See also Mark Dery, *Escape Velocity: Cyberculture at the End of the Century* (New York: Grove Press, 1996), 225.

140. Catherine Mackinnon, *Only Words* (Cambridge, MA: Harvard University Press, 1993), 109; quoted in Langton, *Sexual Solipsism*, 315.
141. Melinda Vadas, "The Manufacture-for-use of Pornography and Women's Inequality," *Journal of Political Philosophy* 13 (2005): 174–193, on 186; quoted also in Langton, *Sexual Solipsism*, 352.
142. Langton, *Sexual Solipsism*, 352–353.
143. Quoted in Langton, *Sexual Solipsism*, 23. See also Jensen, *Getting Off*, 111.
144. Cf. Langton, *Sexual Solipsism*, 354.
145. Quoted in Paul, *Pornified*, 105.
146. Dines, *Pornland*, xxiv.
147. Dines, *Pornland*, xxiv. See also Laurie Penny, *Meat Market: Female Flesh Under Capitalism* (Winchester, UK: Zero Books, 2011), 12.
148. Levy, *Love and Sex*, 257; Mimi Marinucci, "What's Wrong with Porn?" in Monroe ed., *Porn*, 130–139, on 136.
149. e.g. http://www.fuckingmachines.com. See Marinucci, "What's Wrong," 136. See also Katharine Mieszkowskie, "Battlebots in the Bedroom," *Salon.com*, February 12, 2002, http://www.salon.com/2002/02/12/sexbots/
150. Jensen, *Getting Off*, 113.
151. Jane Caputi, *The Age of Sex Crime* (Bowling Green, Ohio: Bowling Green State University Popular Press, 1987), 142; Chris Hables Gray, "Man Plus: Enhanced Cyborgs and the Construction of the Future Masculine," *Science as Culture* 9 (3): 277–299.
152. Slater, *Pursuit of Loneliness*, 87–88.
153. Soble, *Pornography*, 60.
154. O'Donnell and Milner, *Child Pornography*, 34–35.
155. Penny, *Meat Market*, 9–10.
156. See, for example, Phil Taylor and Peter Bain, "'An Assembly Line in the Head': Work and Employee Relations in the Call Centre," *Industrial Relations Journal* 30(2) (1999): 101–117.
157. Paul, *Pornified*, 29–30; Stephanie Armour, "Technology Makes Porn Easier to Access at Work," *USA Today*, October 18, 2007, http://www.usatoday.com/money/workplace/2007-10-17-porn-at-work_N.htm
158. Paul, *Pornified*, 35.
159. Daniel Wagner, "SEC Porn Probe: Staffers Watched as Economy Porn as Economy Crashed," *Huffington Post*, April 23, 2010, http://www.huffingtonpost.com/2010/04/23/sec-porn-probe-staffers-w_n_548931.html; Dino Grandoni, "Missile Defense Agency: Porn Watching Employees Called out by Boss," *Huffington Post*, August 2, 2012, http://www.huffingtonpost.com/2012/08/02/missile-defense-agency-porn_n_1733572.html

160. Philip Landau, "Pornography at Work: Grounds for Dismissal?" The Guardian, September 4, 2013, http://www.theguardian.com/money/work-blog/2013/sep/04/pornography-work-dismissal-workplace-rights; "Parliamentary Attempts to Access Online Pornography Revealed by FOI Request," The Guardian, September 3, 2013, http://www.theguardian.com/technology/2013/sep/03/parliamentary-network-pornography-websites-figures
161. Landau, "Grounds for Dismissal"; "Government Staff Disciplined for Accessing Pornography," Workplace Law, January 14, 2013, http://www.workplacelaw.net/human-resources/news/45616/government-staff-disciplined-for-accessing-pornography
162. Maggie O'Kane, Chavala Madlena, and Guy Grandjean, "Bradley Manning: The Bullied Outsider Who Knew US Military's Inner Secrets." The Guardian, May 27, 2011, http://www.guardian.co.uk/world/2011/may/27/bradley-manning-us-military-outsider
163. Quoted in O'Kane, Madlena, and Grandjean, "Bradley Manning."
164. "Working Hard? Or Hardly Working?" EuropeanCEO, April 25, 2013, http://www.europeanceo.com/home/featured/2013/04/9120/
165. Karl Marx, Capital, Volume One (New York: Vintage Books, 1977), 477.
166. See also Londa Singer, Erotic Welfare: Sexual Theory and Politics in the Age of Epidemic (New York: Routledge, 1993), 35–37.
167. Margot Weiss, Techniques of Pleasure: BDSM and the Circuits of Sexuality (Durham, NC: Duke University Press), 14, 107, 121. See also Singer, Erotic Welfare, 36–37.
168. Mac McClelland, "I was a Warehouse Wage Slave," Mother Jones (March/April 2012), http://www.motherjones.com/politics/2012/02/mac-mcclelland-free-online-shipping-warehouses-labor. Emphasis added.
169. McClelland, "Wage Slave."
170. Advice given by a warehouse worker, quoted in McClelland, "Wage Slave."
171. cf. Weiss, Techniques of Pleasure, 148–149.
172. Weiss, Techniques of Pleasure, 20–21; Walter Pincus, "Iraq Tactics have a Long History with U.S. Interrogators," Washington Post, June 13, 2004, http://www.washingtonpost.com/wp-dyn/articles/A37340-2004Jun12.html;
Laura Melendez-Pallitto and Robert Pallitto "Psychologists and Torture: Then and Now," Foreign Policy in Focus, March 1, 2012, http://www.fpif.org/articles/psychologists_and_torture_then_and_now
173. Weiss, Techniques of Pleasure, 178; Deborah Cameron and Elizabeth Frazer, The Lust to Kill: Feminist Investigation of Sexual Murder (Cambridge: Polity Press, 1987), 175–176.
174. Weiss, Techniques of Pleasure, 17–19.

175. Karl Marx, *Economic and Philosophic Manuscripts of 1844* (New York: International Publishers, 1964), 111.
176. Quoted in Paul, *Pornified*, 98.
177. Quoted in Paul, *Pornified*, 105.
178. On the subordination of the body of the worker, see Michael Perelman, *The Invisible Handcuffs of Capitalism: How Market Tyranny Stifles the Economy by Stunting Workers* (New York: Monthly Review Press, 2011), 93.
179. See also Zygmunt Bauman on the "'bodylessness' of power in its mainly financial form": Zygmunt Bauman, *Globalization: The Human Consequences* (New York: Columbia University Press, 1998), 18–26, quoting 19.
180. Charles Derber, William A. Schwartz, and Yale Magrass, *Power in the Highest Degree: Professionals and the Rise of a New Mandarin Order* (Oxford: Oxford University Press, 1990), 103; quoted also in Annalee Newitz, *Pretend We're Dead: Capitalist Monsters in American Pop Culture* (Durham: Duke University Press, 2006), 82.
181. Of course, information flows are not "immaterial": Richard Maxwell and Toby Miller, *Greening the Media* (Oxford: Oxford University Press, 2012); David Naguib Pellow and Lisa Sun-Hee Park, *The Silicon Valley of Dreams: Environmental Injustice, Immigrant Workers, and the High-Tech Global Economy* (New York: New York University Press, 2002).
182. Margaret Wertheim, *The Pearly Gates of Cyberspace: A History of Space from Dante to the Internet* (New York: W.W. Norton and Co., 1999); David F. Noble, The Religion *of Technology: The Divinity of Man and the Spirit of Invention* (New York: Penguin, 1999), 158–159; Bauman, *Globalization*, 19.
183. "Getting 'the special equipment'!" *APC*, February 20, 2008, http://apcmag.com/the_special_equipment.htm; see also Tim Guest, *Second Lives: a Journey Through Virtual Worlds* (New York: Random House, 2007), 182–183.
184. Perelman, *Invisible Handcuffs of Capitalism*, 274.
185. Debord, *Society of the Spectacle*, 69.

CHAPTER 5

The Tyranny of Negative Freedom

FREEDOM AS REACTION

Negative freedom was the ideological rallying call of the bourgeoisie's historically progressive period, when it overthrew the economic and political power of the landed aristocracy and gave birth to modern liberalism. Liberal philosophers asserted the moral primacy and autonomy of the individual and advocated the market and representative democracy as forms of association that allowed *freedom from* externally imposed authority. Only those relations of obligation and authority entered into voluntarily by the individual could have legitimacy. This negative conception of freedom, rooted in classical liberalism, is especially ideologically powerful in America, where it not only is the primary language of justification for the legal protection of private property but also is ideologically identified with the character of the nation itself. American society exemplifies the point made by Erich Fromm, that negative freedom is not merely a political doctrine but is a social condition and mode of being.[1]

Fromm argued that it is a condition that cannot be sustained. The uncertainty and isolation that accompany negative freedom are psychologically unbearable. The individual who is free in this way will, therefore, be spurred to escape into social forms that provide shelter from the uncertainty and isolation that necessarily accompany negative freedom.

Therefore, Fromm argued, it is necessary to move from the negative freedom of the isolated, anti-social individual to the positive freedom of the social individual. Instead of freedom from interference, this is the freedom to realize oneself as an individual *in and through* one's existence within society and species, that is, as a social being and a human being.

In his classic, *Escape from Freedom*, Fromm writes:

> [F]reedom has a twofold meaning for modern man: that he has been freed from traditional authorities and has become an "individual," but that at the same time he has become isolated, powerless, and an instrument of purposes outside of himself, alienated from himself and others; furthermore, that this state undermines his self, weakens and frightens him, and makes him ready for submission to new kinds of bondage. Positive freedom on the other hand is identical with the full realization of the individual's potentialities, together with his ability to live actively and spontaneously. Freedom has reached a critical point where, driven by the logic of its own dynamism, it threatens to change into its opposite.[2]

For Fromm, negative freedom presented two dialectical possibilities. Either the opposition between freedom and security would be transcended via the social transformation toward the higher synthesis represented by positive freedom, or the insecurity entailed by negative freedom would spur escape into submission to fascism or the growth of more subtle forms of authoritarianism within bureaucratic consumer society.

The unsustainability of negative freedom may be clearly seen in America, where this ideology is most embedded in political discourse and in everyday life. In America, negative liberty is currently the key discourse of political reaction. It has a nostalgic and kitsch quality to it. Freedom from constraint seems today to be prized not so much for what one can do with it, but rather as a protection against the uncertainty that comes with social change. "Freedom from" is sought less as freedom from authority than as freedom from disaster. Negative freedom today manifests itself as a flight from uncertainty toward sources of ontological security. Symbols of negative freedom, especially the gun and a fetishized Constitution, serve as sources of security of the self for lumpen and frightened elements of America's middle class. The economic and political system they defend produces the insecurity that drives them more and more desperately to wave the banner of negative freedom.

The Tea Party movement emerged to oppose what they saw as a deeply threatening expansion of the role of government, manifested in the Troubled

Asset Relief Program (TARP) bank bailouts begun under the Bush administration in 2008 and continued by the Obama administration's economic stimulus plan (American Recovery and Reinvestment Act), and in Obama's healthcare reforms. For the Tea Party, the quasi-Keynesian stimulus policies of the Federal Reserve and the attempt by government to reorganize healthcare smacked of "socialism," a term that, to them, is highly pejorative.

At Tea Party rallies, placards bear slogans such as "Obamunism," "Freedom vs. Obama," "Obama = Socialism. Socialism = Evil." Journalist Ed Pilkington writes that at a Tea Party rally in the late summer of 2009, "[t]he protesters vented their spleens over a wide range of targets, from conservative staples such as perceived high taxes and big government, through President Barack Obama's plans to reform health care, to more extreme portrayals of Obama as a terrorist or Hitler figure. The depiction of the administration as socialist or communist was a unifying theme."[3] One Tea Party protestor told a journalist, "My concerns are about the health care bill, and the direction it takes us is toward communism, quite frankly."[4] The conservative Republican candidate Rick Santorum put at the forefront of his 2012 primary campaign the idea that personal liberty needed to be defended against the healthcare reforms. He told his audience in Steubenville, Ohio, on the night of the crucial "Super Tuesday" primary elections that there was "one particular issue that to me breaks the camel's back with respect to liberty in this country, and that is the issue of Obamacare… Ladies and gentlemen, this is the beginning of the end of freedom in America." Santorum presented Obama's healthcare regulations and reforms as a move that would make every individual dependent on the state and, therefore, controlled by the state: "Once the government has control of your life, then they've got you."[5]

As its symbol, the Tea Party adopted the Gadsden flag, a naval standard dating from the Revolutionary war.[6] It bears the image of a rattlesnake and the words, "Don't Tread on Me." The slogan encapsulates the doctrine of negative freedom. The Republican politician Dick Armey, whose organization FreedomWorks played a key role in funding and shaping the Tea Party, summarizes its political ethos by saying, "The Tea Party movement is asking to simply be left alone."[7]

The Tea Party's conception of freedom entails a sharp distinction between public and private. In order to illustrate the conflict between "liberty" and "big government," Armey recounts an exchange that has entered "Washington folklore," between Republican Senator Phil Gramm and a "woman representing the education establishment." Gramm asserted

"There is no one in Washington who knows and loves my children as much as I do." To this, the member of the "educational establishment" replied, "I take exception to that Senator Gramm. I believe I do." Gramm's response was "Oh yeah? What are their names?"[8] The political meaning of the anecdote lies in its contrast between the private realm of the family and an intrusive, impersonal public bureaucracy. Liberty means maintaining the boundaries between the private sphere and public authority. It implies that love and care are properly bounded within the family. Relations in public between families and between individuals should be contractual, market relations. These public relations are evacuated of care: in the market, I am not my brother's keeper.

Disavowal of responsibility of one individual for another was the key meaning of the rant by trader and CNBC market commentator Rick Santelli, which is widely regarded as the opening shot of the Tea Party movement. Attacking the Obama administration's mortgage relief program, Santelli shouted, "This is America! How many people want to pay for your neighbor's mortgages that have an extra bathroom and can't pay their bills?" The bailout of homeowners would move America closer to the socialism of Cuba, he alleged. American freedom, for Santelli, meant preserving the market. This was to be a revolt of the capitalists: "We're thinking of having a Chicago Tea Party in July, all you capitalists. I'm organizing."[9]

In order to stabilize itself after the 2008 stock market collapse, American and global capital has required the pay out of trillions of dollars to the banks by the federal government and Federal Reserve. So, currently, capital takes ideological cover behind the notion of laissez-faire, which, if actually applied, would cause the system to collapse. The function of laissez-faire as ideological cover is tied to the social-psychological hold of the doctrine, especially in America. The "naturalness" of individual freedom—the facile idea that the individual under capitalism is free unless and until the state steps in—is tied to the market's occlusion of productive cooperation, that is, to commodity fetishism. This occlusion is particularly pathological today as the globality and complexity of economic and social life contrast so sharply with privatist individualism upheld by bourgeois ideology. The now anachronistic ideology of liberal individualism supports the immense accumulation of power in corporations, the reduction of democracy to a hollow shell, and the degradation of public life. Freedom from human interference means the domination of human beings by inhuman systems and forces.

"Don't Tread on Me"

Capitalism produces both complex interdependency and atomization. The production of goods depends on global supply chains, the complex organization of corporate bureaucracies, complex financial instruments, and regulatory apparatuses. But the market also atomizes us as individuals, since each of us sells ourselves as a commodity on the labor market, in competition with everyone else, and satisfies our needs through the purchase of goods for private (individual and family) consumption. The market produces an anti-social sociality, which only connects individuals by holding them apart. The atomized existence of individuals as buyers and sellers on the market is the model for negative freedom. As our lives are increasingly globally interconnected and dependent on complex systems, we are trapped in the freedom of the solitary monad.[10]

Christopher Caudwell points out that negative freedom, by pitting the freedom of the individual against their dependence on others, is not only isolating but also ultimately primitivist. He notes that bourgeois intellectuals tend to "suppose that man is more free, more at liberty, the more he is free from the pressure of culture, consciousness, and social organisation." Carried to the "logical conclusion," Caudwell argues, this conception "means that the only beings with real liberty are the unconscious brutes." He writes:

> Thus to the bourgeois, civilisation seems damned by its premises and there is no hope in this life of attaining freedom. All organisation, all consciousness, all thought eventually seems to the bourgeois intellectual the corruption or inhibition or repression of the completely free natural man; but this natural man is an anthropoid ape, for man without society is a brute.[11]

The anti-social character of the prevailing conception of freedom explains the prevalence of fantasies of escape. The doctrine of negative freedom makes social existence a loss to the individual. It implies that the more highly developed and complex the society, the less free the individual.

Every social advance, therefore, intensifies the desire to escape. The market draws on this desire and transforms it into fuel for consumerism. Philip Slater points out the privatizing and isolating dynamic of consumerism: "We seek a private house, a private means of transportation, a private garden, a private laundry... An enormous technology seems to have set itself the task of making it unnecessary for one human being ever to ask anything of another."[12] Vacations are sold as relief from modern life, and from other people. The desired destination is "unspoilt" by other tourists. The ultimate ideal is total privacy, an island to oneself. Only the super-rich are able to fulfill such solipsistic fantasies. Ted Turner, the businessman who started CNN, owns two million acres in Montana and New Mexico, and presents himself as an environmentalist since he keeps much of this land as a wildlife reserve. Jon Wiener writes: "Turner's motto seems to be 'Hell is other people.' He's taken extraordinary and expensive measures to keep his neighbors away from his land... It's hard to escape the conclusion that Turner's utopia is a land without people."[13] Wealth allows one to divorce oneself from society, and this ability to detach oneself becomes the indicator and reward of success.

The more money a person has, the more totally they are able to cultivate the illusion of existing apart from society. The money that mediates one's sociality is also one's barrier against other people. While bourgeois thought constructs an ideal freedom that is at odds with all the tendencies of the modern world, this impossible freedom is made attainable by money, which releases its possessor from the "bonds" of sociality (masking the alienated sociality that is presupposed by the money relation). The darker side of this escape from sociality is that the rich are increasingly worried about being the targets of violence by the dispossessed. An article in the *Wall Street Journal* describes how the elite react to a growing sense of hostility from below by "keeping a lower profile, hiring $230,000 guard dogs, and arming their yachts, planes and cars with military-style security features."[14]

Mounting societal problems, exacerbated by privatist escapism, produce an overwhelming sense of individual precariousness—the fear of falling into destitution with no one to help. This combines with a sense of the more general precariousness of social order itself. Individualist ideology assumes that people are motivated entirely by their own self-interest, and therefore any breakdown of law and order will lead to a brutal struggle of all against all.[15] A society that is dominated by private interests and unable to plan for the common good is directionless and prone to crisis, haunted by horrors of economic collapse, ecological disaster, and sudden descent into war. This sense of fragility reflects the real weakness of the social fabric in a society of competitive consumers. But, it is continually magnified by a sensationalistic and violence-obsessed media that focuses on natural disasters, epidemics, terrorism, and crime in ways that increase anxiety and undermine resilience.[16]

Some Americans have organized their lives around these anxieties, engaging in active preparation for the collapse of society. In the 1990s, "survivalism" was associated with the militia movement, expressing extreme right-wing hostility to the Clinton administration, often mingled with apocalyptic religious ideas or belief in a coming race war. While the militia movement has declined, survivalism has become more diffused. "Prepping" discards the explicit racist and religious paranoia of extreme survivalism and instead focuses on the practicalities of self-reliance. Journalist Paul Harris writes:

> Unlike the 1990s survivalists, preppers come from all backgrounds and live all over America. They are just as likely to be found in a suburb or downtown loft as a remote ranch in the mountains. Prepping networks, which have sprung up all over the country in the past few years, provide advice on how to prepare food reserves, how to grow crops in your garden, how to hunt and how to defend yourself.[17]

A sensationalistic National Geographic television show, *Doomsday Preppers*, is devoted to the phenomenon:

> Doomsday Preppers explores the lives of otherwise ordinary Americans who are preparing for the end of the world as we know it... And with our expert's assessment, they will find out their chances of survival if their worst fears become a reality.[18]

Survivalism and prepping are highly individualistic. Philip Lamy writes, "The motto of the survivalist might as well be, 'God helps those who help themselves.' Survival may not [be] in the hands of the savior but in the preparations of the individual."[19] The emphasis on individual, rather than collective action, is reinforced by the authorities' messages about disaster preparedness. When agencies such as the Federal Emergency Management Agency and the CDC, for example, remind Americans to ready their own "earthquake kit" or "preparedness kit," the message is that survival will be a matter for the individual and family, rather than a collective response by communities.

Prepping is an expression of what Zygmunt Bauman calls "liquid fear." He argues that a "diffuse, scattered, unclear" type of fear is particularly characteristic of the psyche of atomized individuals in a world in which social bonds have become frail and in which individuals are acted on by global forces that are unpredictable, seemingly uncontrollable, and hard to comprehend.[20] Tom Martin, who runs the American Preppers Network states, "Millions of people now have the mindset that they want to be prepared for something, but don't know what to call it."[21]

A *Newsweek* article describes how survivalist culture has become more and more mainstream:

> Lisa Bedford is what you'd imagine of a stereotypical soccer mom… But about a year ago, Bedford's homemaking skills went into overdrive. She began stockpiling canned food, and converted a spare bedroom into a giant storage facility. The trunk of each of her family's cars got its own 72-hour emergency kit… Then, for the first time in her life, Bedford went to a gun range and shot a .22 handgun. Now she regularly takes her two young children, 7 and 10, to target practice. "Over the last two years, I started feeling more and more unsettled about everything I was seeing, and I started thinking, 'What if we were in the same boat?'," says Bedford, 49.[22]

Bedford admits that being "a newsaholic" fuels her anxieties. American television news is a sensationalized and superficial cascade of crime and disaster, providing little to no analysis, contextual background, or intellectual tools to weigh the importance of each event. Being a "newsaholic" means exposure to a stream of horrors, or a series of audiovisual assaults on one's nervous system. Struggling to make sense of the unrelated items, one could very easily do so by treating them as portents of disaster. In response to a non-specific feeling of anxiety, the response is to hoard and prepare for any eventuality.

Bedford's response to her anxieties is continuous with middle-class suburban privatism. (It takes a modicum of financial security in the present to stock up for future disaster.) The impossible task of being ready for any eventuality gains warrant from the American middle-class individualistic ethos that one should, at all costs, avoid needing the assistance of others. Journalist Jessica Bennett writes that "what it all boils down to, at least for the preppers, is self-reliance."[23] Just as Americans have to face personal calamities, such as joblessness, illness, and bankruptcy, alone, they must also face the apocalypse as individuals.

Apocalyptic culture is pervasive in contemporary television and film, and there is a genre of books dedicated to disaster and post-apocalyptic scenarios.[24] There is a sense of wish fulfillment about this, informed by anti-urbanism and the idea of rural America as the "heartland" where true American values are to be found. In the 2007 film version of *I am Legend*, diverging drastically from the original book plot, the protagonist escapes from the city to a compound of survivors in the countryside. Slavoj Žižek notes that the film establishes an "opposition between a destitute New York and the pure eco-paradise of Vermont, a gated community protected by a wall and security guards."²⁵ This kind of apocalyptic wish fulfillment of a return to rural simplicity derives from the negative conception of freedom, which implies that the advancement of social organization can only be a trajectory toward unfreedom. This view also has a basis in real social experience in capitalist society: the loneliness of atomized individuals, the bewilderment of precarious workers, and the powerlessness and subjection experienced at work. These features of the experience of capitalist everyday life contribute to the subterranean fantasy of collapse of this order, out of which the individual would emerge self-reliant and dignified. An anti-social conception of freedom, in which one is most free outside society, leads to a culture that wills the destruction of society.

Gun Ownership and Self-Ownership

In order to protect their homestead, the prepper must be ready to deal with other survivors, in a raw Hobbesian war of all against all. The National Geographic program features preppers stockpiling weapons. For example, "Megan Hurwitt furthers her skills with a firearm, as defense is a serious concern with most preppers. Here she practices with an AR-15."²⁶ In its enthusiasm for firearms, prepping draws on the idea, deeply rooted in America, of the gun as the primary tool and symbol of self-reliance.

In the 1976 Western movie, *The Shootist*, gunfighter John Bernard (J.B.) Books, played by John Wayne, famously says, "I won't be wronged, I won't be insulted, and I won't be laid a hand on. I don't do these things to other people, and I require the same from them."²⁷ The gun is the ultimate guarantee of the inviolability of the person, and in this way has come to have, in America, special significance as an object associated with negative freedom. On the Internet, one can find numerous photographs of guns and gun paraphernalia, with engravings of the Gadsden rattlesnake and the slogan "Don't Tread on Me."²⁸ Joshua Horwitz and Casey Anderson write, "It would be difficult to exaggerate how thoroughly the 'guns equal freedom' message has been incorporated into everything having anything to do with gun rights organizations and their cause."²⁹ National Rifle Association (NRA) President Charlton Heston calls personal gun ownership the "First Freedom." NRA Executive President Wayne LaPierre asserts that gun ownership affirms "America's traditional bedrock values of self-reliance, self-defense, and self-determination."³⁰

In this discourse, guns are the primary check on the over-encroachment of state power on the freedom of the individual.³¹ The individual self-reliance put forward by the gun rights lobby also meshes with free-market ideology (as well as the direct interest of the gun industry in preventing tighter regulation). LaPierre has asserted, "Only the NRA energizes the powerful pro-freedom voting bloc, resulting in election outcomes good for both American gun rights and for American business. Candidates who support the Second Amendment... [are] typically pro-business people who fight for free-market issues, from tort and estate tax reform to immigration policy and the global war on terror."[32]

The case for "gun rights" in America taps deeply into what C.B. Macpherson calls the philosophy of "possessive individualism," which underpins liberal negative freedom. The demand for freedom from interference has been warranted by the idea that the individual has property not only in their material possessions, but also in their person. Individuals are "regarded as proprietors of themselves"; one has "proprietorship of one's own capacities." This ownership of one's person underlies the individual's negative freedom: "freedom from the wills of others... is a function of proprietorship of one's person."[33]

According to the right-wing libertarian philosopher Robert Nozick, self-ownership means "each person as having a right to decide what would become of himself and what he would do, and as having a right to reap the benefits of what he did." [34] For Nozick, any redistributive action by the state—taking one individual's property via taxation to give to another individual in the form of welfare—is as unjustified as slavery. The only form of state that is justifiable, according to Nozick, is a minimal one that protects the negative liberty of self-owning individuals by preventing them from stealing from, or killing, one another.[35] The doctrine of the minimal state is reflected in the view of the Tea Party that the extension of welfare amounts to tyranny. The political theory of possessive individualism, pitting individual freedom against the interventionist state, is a key element in the ideological framework within which gun ownership is currently legitimized in America.

The ideal of a gun-owning citizenry in contemporary America is linked not only to a theory of politics, but also to a conception of social order. According to the right-wing libertarian Congressman and presidential candidate, Ron Paul, "an armed society truly is a polite society." He justifies this assertion by asking rhetorically, "[W]hy would the worst shootings consistently happen in gun-free zones such as schools?... [A]ggressive, terroristic shootings like this are unheard of at gun and knife shows, the antithesis of a gun-free zone.... Even if you don't like guns and don't want to own them, you benefit from those who do."[36] This view of social peace as an accomplishment of the balance of force is a logical outcome of a Hobbesian abstract individualism in which human beings are driven purely by self-interest. On this view, individuals are held in check only externally. The individual's freedom and security from encroachment by other individuals is bought by force of arms. The view that security can come only from force led Hobbes to regard social order as deriving from the absolute ruler as Leviathan. Fearful of the absolutist state, however, American libertarians argue that individuals must take responsibility for their own security through private gun ownership. The clear logic of this position is that everyone must be armed.

However, the scenario of a society made up of armed individuals, ever vigilant against each other's latent threat of violence, looks like the collapse of modern civil society.[37] In 2008, a Texas school district voted to allow teachers to carry a concealed handgun into the classroom. The district's superintendent said, "We have a lock-down situation, we have cameras, but the question we had to answer is, 'What if somebody gets in? What are we going to do?'"[38] In an armed society, especially in the American situation of a society that is both armed and atomized, there is the omnipresent possibility of an armed assailant whom one must be ready to fight.[39]

The resultant sense of insecurity becomes further justification for the right to bear arms. According to LaPierre and James Jay Baker, one ought to have a gun in the house because no one else can effectively protect you from criminals. You can rely on the police only "to… draw chalk marks around your body."[40] Of course, the proliferation of guns means that a criminal is more likely to be armed with a gun. And, as Horwitz and Anderson point out, the gun lobby's legislative influence has created obstacles to police action against gun crime.[41]

The availability of guns in the USA is a key factor in its high homicide rate. More than 30,000 Americans die by gunshot every year. Approximately 11,000 of these are homicides.[42] In the USA, approximately two out of every three homicides are committed with guns.[43] However, as Richard Wilkinson and Kate Pickett show, the high level of economic inequality is also a key underlying cause of America's extraordinarily high levels of violence. Inequality produces violence because it is itself a form of structural violence. A key motivator for violence is the attempt to maintain dignity and self-respect, and inequality is, for those disadvantaged, a continual humiliation which crushes self-respect. This makes a violent response to additional threats to the self more likely.[44]

Economic insecurity, powerlessness, and the availability of guns also combine with the hegemonic construction of masculinity, emphasizing unemotionality, control, physical strength, and an anti-social individualist conception of autonomy. The anomic violence of contemporary America is the outcome of a contradiction between an individualism that emphasizes (especially for men) being in control and being self-reliant, in a situation in which the individual is never in control and is acted on by arbitrary authority at work and by the vagaries of market forces (in which consolations of solidarity are increasingly unavailable). Isolation, emotional and psychological rigidity, insecurity, and meaninglessness combine with the availability of guns, the media's glorification of violence, and the cultural fetish of the gun as a source of power and freedom.[45] The irrationality of violence in America, seen especially in mass shootings that now regularly punctuate the news, is, at least in part, a product of the bewilderment of Americans whose freedom and self-reliance is continually undermined by forces that they cannot identify. In America, as Fromm writes, "Instead of overt authority, '*anonymous*' *authority* reigns… [I]n anonymous authority both command and commander have become invisible. It is like being fired at by an invisible enemy. There is nobody and nothing to fight back against."[46] Seemingly at random, Americans take aim at each other, in a desperate attempt to shoot down the source of their all-pervading anxiety.

George Zimmerman's shooting of the black teenager Trayvon Martin in Florida in 2012 exemplified the interplay between insecurity and violence in American life. While predominantly framed in the media and political discourse as a racial killing, it is better understood as a crime rooted in America's social crisis.[47] There is no evidence that Zimmerman, registered on the voter roll as a Hispanic and a Democrat, had consistently racist attitudes. For example, at a public meeting he condemned local police for engaging in a cover up after a white police lieutenant beat Sherman Ware, a black homeless man.[48] However, on his MySpace social media account, Zimmerman wrote the following about Manassas, Virginia, where he used to live:

> I don't mind driving around scared to hit Mexicans walkin on the side of the street, soft ass wanna be thugs messin with peoples cars when they ain't around (what are you provin, that you can dent a car when no ones watchin) don't make you a man in my book. Working 96 hours to get a decent pay check, getting knifes pulled on you by every Mexican you run into.[49]

The last sentence is revealing. Zimmerman views himself as a hard worker, doing the right thing, but as embattled by social disreputables—in this case identified as "Mexican." Zimmerman was an insurance underwriter, who hoped he would find a career in law enforcement or criminal justice. But, he had also worked as a security guard, as well as at CarMax used-car dealers and at a previous insurance company.[50] In 2009, when he moved to the Retreat at Twin Lakes, a gated community where he would later shoot Martin, he was working at a pressure-washing company. He was on the cusp between white-collar and blue-collar jobs. The Retreat was built in 2004, and advertised as "resort"-style living, at the height of America's housing bubble. By the time of the shooting, the community had gone into economic decline. Many of the townhomes had been foreclosed and their original owners evicted. Of the neighborhood's 263 townhomes, 40 now stood empty, and more than half of the residents were now renters, since owners had moved out and leased the properties in order to cover their mortgage payments. This made for a more transient population. Zimmerman had moved in as a renter in 2009 and had soon begun phoning 911 to report what he saw as suspicious or anti-social behavior such as a car driving with no headlights, a motorcycle doing wheelies, a loose pit bull.[51]

Zimmerman saw himself as a protector of the community and was increasingly obsessed with reporting outsiders.[52] During the time he lived there, he made 48 calls to emergency and non-emergency police numbers.[53] There had been a number of burglaries in the community, despite signs on many of the front lawns advertising the homes' alarm systems. After three burglaries in the summer of 2011, a civilian employee of the police department had visited the community to advise on setting up a neighborhood watch group, and Zimmerman had introduced himself as neighborhood watch coordinator, appointed by the president of the homeowners association, and he volunteered to be captain. It was also in the wake of the summer burglaries that Zimmerman's 911 calls began to focus more on black males. Martin fit Zimmerman's personal profile of a "suspicious individual," and as the teenager milled around the streets while his father visited his girlfriend, Zimmerman trailed him in a car and then on foot, armed with a gun.

Zimmerman's behavior manifests the defensive privatism of American middle-class life, a privatism growing more paranoid as its material conditions deteriorate. Its context was a gated community, set up to wall insiders off from outsiders; but now with a transient population, the insiders and the outsiders could not be so easily distinguished. In this context, Zimmerman, himself one of the newer renters and economically precarious, dedicated himself to maintaining the boundaries of the community, and thereby to securing, if only in his own mind, his own middle-class respectability. However, while fixated on threats from outside, he himself became the threat, further eroding any sense of trust or cohesion within the community. Such is more broadly the fate of America's culture of middle-class possessive individualism, standing behind alarm systems and guns, but powerless against economic forces that perpetually threaten security, and periodically shocked by apparently inexplicable atrocities that intensify the sense that it is not only outsiders, but everyone and anyone who must be guarded against.

An unequal and competitive individualist society, setting individuals against one another, undermines solidarity, and encourages both crime and the fear of crime.[54] The lack of solidarity also shapes punishment. Unequal societies are less likely to see offenders as fellow human beings who can be rehabilitated. Instead, they are written off, locked up with the key thrown away, as in the "Three strikes and you're out" law in California, which can result in life imprisonment for non-violent offenses.[55] America, with the highest incarceration rate in the world, exemplifies how possessive individualism is accompanied by a massive emphasis on punitive state power as a means of external control.[56]

Declining state spending on welfare and education has been accompanied by vast increases in spending on law enforcement and prisons. US penal state spending "has nearly doubled as a percentage of civilian government spending over the past fifty years and now stands at 15 percent of the latter."[57] This increased punitiveness, however, cannot provide real security when crime is generated by the social order itself.[58] So, despite this growth of the penal state, many Americans feel that their best security is their own gun. If, in a violent society in which guns are prevalent, insecurity about crime is assuaged by the ownership of a gun, attempts by government to limit gun ownership will appear to be taking away this bulwark of personal security. Government then appears to be in cahoots with the criminals, undermining the citizens' personal safety. Within this culture of suspicion, American life seems to be spiraling inward, focusing on private space protected by gates and guns.

The Weight of Dead Generations

LaPierre invites America's gun owners to imagine themselves as the brave Minutemen resisting the tyranny of King George III:

> When the ragtag band of Massachusetts farmers stopped General Gage's Redcoats at the foot of Concord Bridge, they weren't fighting for an obscure idea in some philosopher's dusty textbook. They were fighting for the only right that guarantees the others... the only freedom that could allow them to fight for freedom at all. The right to keep and bear arms is our first freedom.[59]

This rhetoric is an escape from the modern world into a mythologized past. While it draws on the past, this kind of language is a denial of historicity. In the fetishism of the Constitution and of the American Revolutionaries, time is petrified.[60]

The notion of the Constitution as an unchanging bedrock fits with a conception of freedom as an inherent property of the individual, existing outside of and prior to all social relationships. As an inherent property, abstracted from society, freedom does not change. However, society changes, increasing in complexity, interdependence, globality, and diversity. The disjunction between unchangeable freedom and a changing society feeds paranoia. The growth of the state (which is, in fact, oppressive, because it is so geared toward repressive functions) is inexplicable on possessive individualist terms. The American right-wing explains it as the result of a conspiracy between elites and the underclass, making the government the embodiment of all forces buffeting the middle-class individual.

Freedom is conceptualized as a possession, a thing to be hoarded. It must be held, as LaPierre puts it, "intact." He writes:

> We must declare that there are no shades of gray in American freedom. It's black and white, all or nothing... Freedom is not negotiable or malleable. And there is no temporary suspension of freedom. Once on loan, you never get it back.
>
> American freedom is the most precious way of life the world has ever known. The quality of freedom our ancestors bought with their blood is not ours to squander. Individual freedom is the essence of what America is all about, and it must remain intact. The true patriot is the American who supports the sanctity of American freedom as defined by the Bill of Rights.
>
> In the months and years ahead, every American must stand unflinchingly for the individual personal freedoms guaranteed in the Bill of Rights that make our nation, the United States of America, the finest nation in all mankind. Only then can we pass the torch of freedom to the next generation, unequivocally endorsed well into this millennium and beyond.[61]

LaPierre conceptualizes freedom as something absolute and unchangeable. Its immutability is given material form in the Bill of Rights, a sacred document, which, in turn, sanctifies this freedom. This freedom, once established, is not subject to change. It must be preserved to be handed unchanged down to the generations. Freedom, in this way, embodies the past and is the sacred inheritance of the past. LaPierre presents freedom as the product of past sacrifice or "blood." This ancestral sacrifice creates a debt: what is "bought with their blood is not ours to squander." Freedom, in this way, takes the character of money: "Once on loan, you never get it back." It is a check that has been "endorsed," and this endorsement is written in the blood of ancestors. This sheds light on the NRA slogan, "Freedom is not free." In this context, the slogan is suggesting not only that one has to work to maintain freedom but also that this inheritance of freedom constrains new generations to preserve it, since it is "not ours" but belongs to the past, the Founding Fathers, those who died in the Revolution. In LaPierre's language, freedom is associated with the past, with blood spilt, with the dead, and with that other embodiment of the past, money.

LaPierre's reification of freedom in terms of money is integrally related to the way in which right-wing libertarianism conceptualizes freedom *as* property. Political theorist G.A. Cohen has argued that this right-wing libertarianism, represented in political theory by Nozick, is first and foremost a defense of property.[62] Cohen interprets Nozick's view as follows:

> According to the thesis of self-ownership, each person possesses over himself... all those rights that a slaveholder has over a complete chattel slave... A slaveholder may not direct his slave to harm other (non-slave) people, but he is not legally obliged to place him at their disposal to the slightest degree... So, analogously, if I am the moral owner of myself, and, therefore, of this right arm, then, while others are entitled, because of *their* self-ownership, to prevent it from hitting them, no one is entitled, without my consent, to press it into their own or anybody else's service.[63]

The negative freedom of the individual, therefore, rests on a property right in oneself. Property is so fundamental to Nozick's thinking that it is also the essence of what is meant by self. Cohen writes:

> Note that what is owned, according to the thesis of self-ownership, is not a self, where 'self' is used to denote some particularly intimate, or essential, part

of the person... The term 'self' in the name of the thesis of self-ownership has purely reflexive significance. It signifies that what owns and what is owned are one and the same, namely, the whole person.[64]

So at the root of free-market libertarianism is an understanding of the self, entirely in terms of property. The individual is nothing other than what the individual owns. I *am* my own property.

The notion of freedom that stems from this equation of the self with property is also focused on property. This prioritization of property right is evident from the fact that free-market libertarianism cannot account for the unfreedom that people endure at work and in the labor market. While the worker can be said to be self-owning, since they sell their labor for a wage, workers are unfree because they *must* work for a capitalist. "Fine freedom," Engels rightly scoffed, "where the proletarian has no other choice than that of either accepting the conditions which the bourgeoisie offers him, or of starving, of freezing to death, of sleeping naked among the beasts of the forests!"[65] Under this basic compulsion, workers are radically unfree. Nozick's defense of self-ownership leads him to defend capitalist relations in which propertyless people are forced to work for a capitalist.[66] Cohen, therefore, argues that "Nozick cannot claim to be inspired throughout by a desire to protect freedom, unless he means by 'freedom' what he really does mean by it: the freedom of private property owners to do as they wish with their property."[67] The doctrine of self-ownership equates the self, and its freedom, with property.

The reification of freedom as property is closely coupled with, and underpins, LaPierre's association of freedom with the past, the dead, and money. Among America's gun enthusiasts, this reified freedom finds its *totem* in the gun as an object associated with death.[68] Heston famously said that the government would have to pry his guns from his "cold dead hands." He used the line in the run-up to the 2000 Presidential election, saying:

> I'm here because I love my country and I love this freedom... It dawned on me that the doorway to all freedoms is framed by muskets... So as we set out this year to defeat the divisive forces that would take freedom away, I want to say those words again for everyone within the sound of my voice to hear and heed, and especially for you Mr. [Al] Gore: From my cold dead hands![69]

The slogan was such a success with the NRA membership, that Heston repeated it at every NRA convention he attended, and on the occasion when he announced his retirement as head of the organization.[70] In Heston's battle cry, freedom becomes an attitude of unwavering commitment, stubbornness, and the grim refusal to let go. Freedom is identified with the dead hand clutching, hoarding, even in death, its prized possession. The free individual is imagined in *rigor mortis*.

This image of the free man as dead man expresses the reification fundamental to the conception of freedom as self-ownership. Fromm noted how deeply capitalist culture frames the sense of self, and understanding of freedom, in terms of "having." He thought it characteristic of bourgeois culture that

> [p]ersons are transformed into things; their relations to each other assume the character of ownership. "Individualism,"… means, in the negative sense, "self-ownership," the right—and the duty—to invest one's own energy in the success of one's own person.[71]

This conception of the self, Fromm stressed, is not a recondite feature of political theory, but rather is part of the experience of self within a society organized around the production and exchange of commodities.

Capitalist relations, Fromm observed, shape the sense of self such that "the ego is felt as a thing we each possess, and… this 'thing' is the basis of our sense of identity."[72] In a society based on property ownership, we define ourselves through what we own and we come to relate to ourselves as property:

> In the last analysis, the statement "*I* [subject] have *O* [object]" expresses a definition of *I* through my possession of *O*. The subject is not *myself* but *I am what I have*. My property constitutes myself and my identity. The underlying thought in the statement "I am I" is "*I am I because I have X*"—X equalling all natural objects and persons to whom I relate myself through my power to control them, to make them permanently mine.[73]

If the self is defined as property, the relationship with the rest of the world must also be one of possession. This means that the individual relates to all people and things as objects to be possessed. Fromm observes:

> In the having mode, there is no alive relationship between me and what I have. It and I have become things, and I have *it*, because I have the force to make it mine. But there is also a reverse relationship: *it has me*, because my sense of identity, i.e., of sanity, rests on my having *it* (and as many things as

possible). The having mode of existence... makes *things* of both object and subject. The relationship is one of deadness, not aliveness.[74]

The self becomes just another object, and objects can be lost.

So the *having* relation necessarily produces insecurity and fear.[75] If one's very self is understood in terms of possession, then in a volatile world, not only one's job and one's savings, but one's very personhood and identity are at risk. The defense of self, and of freedom, is implicated in the defense of what one possesses. So one has the right to defend what one possesses, by violence if need be. Libertarian philosopher Murray Rothbard argues that, "If, as libertarians believe, every individual has the right to own his person and property, it then follows that he has the right to employ violence to defend himself against the violence of criminal aggressors."[76] Self-ownership is, therefore, not only a defensive, but a violently defensive, orientation.

If one adopts this possessive conception of self and freedom, then other human beings are always a potential threat. They might steal, or defraud one of, one's property. But, more fundamentally, other living human beings always have the potential to impinge on the boundaries of the self and thereby threaten the shell of negative freedom. A reified negative freedom, denying interdependence with others, and threatened by change, is at odds with aliveness. You are most free in this negative sense if you can prevent anything from impinging on you. Therefore, freedom may be affirmed through the destruction of beings or forces that threaten to impinge on the self. The gun functions as the guarantee of boundaries of the self from a world that is perceived as full of threats.

Fear and Freedom

The link between negative freedom and the capacity for violence is explicit in the rhetoric of rock star and gun rights activist Ted Nugent. In a 2010 NRA advertisement urging supporters to register to vote, Nugent declares himself to be "cocked, locked, and ready to rock, doc, celebrating freedom everyday."[77] In Nugent's worldview, freedom is threatened by unpalatable "others." Hillary Clinton, he has said, is a "toxic cunt" and a "two-bit whore for Fidel Castro" and her "very existence insults the spirit of individualism in this country."[78] If one's individual freedom can be threatened by the "very existence" of certain kinds of people, the security of one's freedom is linked to the gun as an instrument that guarantees one's ability to annihilate these existential threats. At an NRA convention in 2005, he declared his philosophy as follows: "Remember the Alamo! Shoot'em!... To show you how radical I am, I want carjackers dead. I want rapists dead. I want burglars dead. I want child molesters dead. I want the bad guys dead. No court case. No parole. No early release. I want 'em dead. Get a gun and when they attack you, shoot'em." At a concert in 2007, Nugent embarked on a rant against the liberals in the executive branch: "Obama, he's a piece of shit. I told him to suck on my machine gun. Hey Hillary,' he continued, 'You might want to ride one of these into the sunset, you worthless bitch." According to *Rolling Stone*, "Nugent summed up his eloquent speech by screaming 'freedom'!"[79]

The gun, bestowing the power to annihilate the threatening other, preserves the boundaries of the self against being swallowed up by the world. Holding the gun, one is assured that one is powerful, and that one will never have to depend on anyone else or open oneself to anything outside of oneself. Through its power to destroy what is external, the gun holds the self, and its autonomy, intact.

However, anxiety must always return as the inevitable accompaniment of a freedom that splits the individual off and isolates him or her. Fromm writes, "The individual finds himself 'free' in this negative sense, that is, alone with his self and confronting an alienated, hostile world."[80] The corollary of negative freedom is "ontological insecurity." The radical psychiatrist R.D. Laing coined this term to describe the experience of the schizophrenic, for whom the boundedness and stability of the self and the permanence of external reality could not be taken for granted. Sociologist Anthony Giddens has extended the scope of Laing's concept, arguing that this kind of insecurity becomes characteristic of human experience in late modern societies. Tradition no longer provides sure solutions to ethical questions of how we should live and no longer provides fixed standards of what we can expect from others. Global forces of capital, science, and technology impinge continually on everyday life, destabilizing and opening up for question what had been taken for granted, producing the vertiginous sense that there is no firm ground, and that everything is in flux.[81] Ontological insecurity is linked to Kierkegaard's conception of dread as a diffuse anxiety with no specific, identifiable source. As Giddens notes, Kierkegaard regarded this anxiety as arising within "the possibility of freedom."[82] Fromm also saw Kierkegaard's discussion of dread as foreshadowing what would come to be the characteristic human experience of the twentieth century: "the helpless individual torn and tormented by doubts, overwhelmed by the feeling of aloneness and insignificance."[83]

It is freedom *in the negative sense* that, Fromm argued, produces this diffuse anxiety. Capitalism frees the individual from traditional and communal bonds, remaking individuals as free agents operating on the market, but simultaneously isolating them and stripping their existence of meaning apart from perpetual accumulation and consumption. Capitalism enables, and forces into being, a new mobility of goods and people, but the psychic corollary of this for the individual is the feeling of being cast adrift. "The new freedom," writes Fromm, "is bound to create a deep feeling of insecurity, powerlessness, doubt, aloneness, and anxiety."[84]

American right-wing politics celebrates the freedom that is produced by capitalism and the market. But, alongside the assertion of this freedom, this politics also involves the search for sources of ontological security. A bumper sticker responds to the Obama election campaign slogan of "Hope and Change" with the line "I'll keep my Guns, my Freedom, and my Money. You can keep the change."[85] Negative freedom becomes freedom from social and political change. The idea of an unchanging Constitution serves as a foundation of ontological security. There has long been a tendency in America to sanctify the Constitution, and even to regard it in explicitly religious terms as divinely inspired. The fetishization of the Constitution as a source of unquestionable and invariant values and truths is a key element of the libertarianism of Ron Paul and of the outlook of the Tea Party. The emphasis on fiscal discipline, whether cast in terms of balanced budgets or the idea of a return to the gold standard, also represents a search for boundaries against chaos and flux, and resonates deeply with a psychology of self-discipline and continence.

The tension between freedom and the search for security is particularly strong for the middle class. The mentality of the middle class is conditioned by its position between the large-scale owners and controllers of capital, or the senior managerial class, and the working class. Their social and economic position above the "lower-classes" is vitally important to the middle-class sense of self, and it means that they feel that they have a great deal to lose. Their sense of self is deeply informed by possessive individualism, since it is their possessions (their home, whatever savings they have managed to build up, their business if they are self-employed) that maintain their distance from the proletariat and give them their sense of pride in their own independence. However, they are also tormented by their subordinate position in the class hierarchy, in relation to the wealth and power of people above them, which they may not understand very well. The middle-class individual admires and envies those with more money than they do, who have the material objects and status to which the middle class aspires, and, most importantly, who seem to be free of the financial worries that bedevil middle-class life. But, the middle-class person also feels that they are somehow neglected and hard-pressed by those who run things, who seem to them to be more concerned about the well-being of those at the bottom than about the hardworking middle. And there is, along with admiration and envy, a current of disdain for the perceived decadence of the people at the top.

There is a feeling of insecurity and threat from above and below. Caudwell's description of the petite bourgeoisie of early twentieth-century Britain still has relevance:

> Functionally it is exploited, but because it is allowed to share in some of the crumbs of exploitation that fall from the rich bourgeois table, it identifies itself with the bourgeois system on which, whether as bank manager, small shopkeeper or upper household servant, it seems to depend. It has only one value in life, that of bettering itself, of getting a step nearer the good bourgeois things so far above it. It has only one horror, that of falling from respectability into the proletarian abyss which, because it is so near, seems so much more dangerous. It is rootless, individualist, lonely, and perpetually facing, with its hackles up, an antagonistic world… More and more the petty bourgeois expression is that of a face lined with petty, futile, bewildered discontent.[86]

This could describe the angry faces mouthing confused slogans at Tea Party rallies. The difference is the American ideology of classlessness, whereby the category "middle class" is applied much more broadly than in Britain. This ideology makes it harder for America's petite bourgeoisie to identify what it is below them in the social order. Their understanding of this is highly racialized: ethnic minorities provide the key image of the "undeserving poor."

Caudwell emphasizes the lack of solidarity between members of the petite bourgeoisie. They are competing with one another, each striving for individual ascension of the societal ladder. One sees this also with today's American middle class. Their solutions to their problems are primarily individualist. For example, instead of challenging educational inequality, they try to move to the neighborhoods with the best schools.[87] But, as worsening economic conditions make their individualistic competitive struggle more intense and more futile, they become increasingly angry and flustered. Their individualistic outlook prevents them from understanding social conditions, so they look for more direct targets, and usually fix their ire on those below them, namely, the ethnic minorities or the undeserving poor. In the petit bourgeois mind, these groups epitomize what happens if one is without the inner discipline of the striving, hardworking individualist. Their contempt for these classes is proportionate to the level of fear that they feel about their own inability to live up to the harsh demands of the social climb.[88]

Libertarianism, and the more ideologically diffuse Tea Party movement, are rooted in the worldview of the petite bourgeoisie. The Tea Party has predominantly middle-class appeal. According to a CBS News/*New York Times* survey in 2010, a total of 56 % of Tea Party supporters had an annual income of more than $50,000 and 20 % more than $100,000.[89] Paul Street writes that the Tea Party base "is distinctly petit-bourgeois, relatively comfortable, comparatively educated. It includes a particularly large number and outsized percentage of solidly middle class professionals (I met a remarkable number of dentists and insurance agents in my research) and small business owners... along with an outsized component of reasonably well off retired folks."[90] Theda Skocpol and Vanessa Williams write that, while their contacts in the Tea Party included professionals, "the plurality seemed to be small business owners, often in fields like construction, remodeling, or repair... A fair number of others worked in technology, insurance, or real estate."[91] Skocpol and Williamson create an intimate portrait of this milieu:

> The homes of Tea Partiers we visited are modest in size and peppered with family pictures and mementos. These domiciles were not the professionally decorated, oversized pseudo-mansions so prevalent among America's well-to-do business chieftains and elite professionals.

The typical Tea Partier family, they write, "is not suffering economically, but it is not rolling in wealth, either."[92]

Beyond the specific class milieu of the Tea Party, the movement also draws on the broader ideological appeal of the image of the small independent producer and of "Main Street" as the classless locale of "the American way of life." Ron Paul, in particular, weaves his petit bourgeois origins into a just-so story supporting values of family, hard work, thriftiness, and economic independence:

> My first job, and that of my brothers, was to assist my dad in a small dairy run out of our basement. Even at the age of five, the incentive system was instilled in me. Our job was to make sure all the glass bottles, which had been hand washed, were clean. It was bad for business if a customer saw a black spot in the middle of a milk bottle. For each dirty bottle we found as we removed them from the conveyer belt and placed them into a wooden case, we were rewarded a penny... This experience taught me the importance of working, and the value of a penny. My parents did not believe in allowances, but I was a natural saver, even in my early years.... My dad... [understood] the value of hard work, savings, and even a penny.[93]

Paul presents his political defense of liberty, self-reliance, and limited government as directly deriving from common-sense values nurtured in the setting of a small family business.

However, Paul's penny-pinching philosophy is also directly related to the economic insecurity of this petit bourgeois setting. A profile in the *New York Times* emphasizes how hard economic times shaped Paul's outlook:

> His parents married two days before the crash of 1929. He was reared on nightmarish stories of currency that proved worthless, told by relatives whose patriarch had fled Germany in the dark of night when his debts were about to ruin him. Hard times, and fear of worse, were constants in Ron Paul's boyhood home.[94]

Paul inherited from his parents an "instinctive conservatism that viewed Franklin Delano Roosevelt and Harry S. Truman as villains and blamed Democrats for getting America into wars." He was influenced by a school janitor who vented against bankers as "the source of our problems," while Paul helped him with painting work.[95] But, the anti-banker element of Paul's thought is targeted specifically at the Federal Reserve, as a combination of big government and the power of elite bankers, and as a Progressive Era expansion of the functions of central government.[96] Alongside the threats of big government and big banks, his small-business background ingrained opposition to organized labor. He recounts how his father was forced to pull his milk trucks off the road for fear of being attacked by union strikers. Union power, Paul concludes, is violence, whether backed by physical force or "legal force."[97] Paul champions the position of the idealized self-reliant small-holder against organized power above and below.

The politics of the Tea Party similarly tap into the insecurities of the middle class. Robert Horwitz writes, "The political subjectivity which the

Tea Party appeals to—and, in turn, produces—is the victimized, dictated-to, predominantly white middle."⁹⁸ Tea Party ideology expresses the idea that there is an alliance between the undeserving poor and governmental elites, and that the respectable middle class is caught in between these forces.⁹⁹ Skocpol and Williamson argue that it is axiomatic among Tea Partiers that it is wrong to redistribute wealth "from productive taxpayers like themselves to people who have not earned their way." They quote one Tea Partier saying, "I would prefer that the moocher class not live off my hard work." Skocpol and Williamson suggest that "mooching" is a keyword that focuses Tea Partiers' grievances.¹⁰⁰ Tea Party activists tend to be older, many around retirement age, and are "deeply suspicious" of younger generations, whom they regard as having lost the work ethic, a view that connects with their more general sense of decline of social values and standards.¹⁰¹ Tea Partiers' class consciousness is highly racialized. Predominantly white, they imagine moochers as black or Hispanic: "Tea Partiers have negative views about all of their fellow citizens; it is just that they make extra-jaundiced assessments of the work ethic of racial and ethnic minorities". They also "regularly invoke illegal immigrants as prime examples of free-loaders."¹⁰² If the undeserving poor is perceived to consist of racial minorities, then apparent elite sympathy for minorities, manifested in "liberal" multiculturalism, gives Tea Partiers a sense of encirclement on all sides.¹⁰³ According to Skocpol and Williamson, "educated elites… are seen by Tea Partiers as allied with freeloading groups."¹⁰⁴ This alliance between the "establishment" and the poor pushes out the middle, the average citizens, who are the new "outsiders."¹⁰⁵

Tea Partiers regard themselves as representing the decent, ordinary Americans caught in between multitudinous forces threatening both freedom and order. Rand Paul describes them as "concerned and worried average citizens."¹⁰⁶ In his *Tea Party Handbook*, a text full of highly charged sloganizing and paranoid conflations, Arizona Tea Partier Charly Gullett tosses out a list of the groups he thinks were mobilized to vote for Obama: "[S]uch diverse constituencies as illegal immigrants, drug addicts, environmental wing nuts, pro-abortion groups, wealthy liberal elites, global warming alarmists, academic terrorists, animal rights activists, uninformed independents, unhappy Republicans, and anarcho-pacifist-anti-war flute hippies to name a few." Against these, the Tea Party represents "[f]amilies, soldiers, farmers, musicians, small business owners, factory workers, ranchers, plumbers, everyday folks who have been inspired to stand up against the onslaught of political terrorism."¹⁰⁷ This decent, true America of the hardworking little people, now under threat, is imagined in a romanticized, nostalgic way.

Armey writes of his youth in which he and his father would drive "through countryside dotted with painted barns straight from a Norman Rockwell canvas." It was in this sort of setting that he learnt his "commonsense values." However, at college he found these were "militantly rejected" by "an elite who existed in government offices and college faculty lounges and who were hostile to the universal values of the American people."[108] The Tea Party, in Armey's words, pits itself against "the political establishment" and "the political intelligentsia… the gatekeepers and message experts and focus group gurus."[109] Rand Paul told a Tea Party audience that "[t]he establishment in their high rise penthouse laughs at you, they laugh at us."[110] But, despite the reference to penthouses suggesting luxurious living, he does not identify the establishment as the wealthiest. For example, he lists the multimillionaire business magazine publisher Steve Forbes as someone who helped him take on the Republican Party "establishment." Paul uses the term "establishment" primarily to refer to the "political class" in Washington and the media. It means for him, the "establishment media and government."[111] Skocpol and Williamson note that "While the business community gets a free pass, Tea Party activists are very concerned about liberal cultural elites, who they believe scorn most Americans."[112] In his *Tea Party Manifesto*, Joseph Farah writes that "our major cultural institutions, which represent unelected, unaccountable, elite power centers—the major media, the entertainment industry, the major foundations, academia, the government education establishment, among others—are promoting bigger government and less freedom."[113]

These anxieties fix on Obama who seems to embody the breakdown of order by blurring boundaries.[114] Skocpol and Williamson describe the Tea Party image of Obama as "a secret Muslim, a foreigner, a Socialist, a Communist, a Nazi—or maybe all of the above! … President Obama is somehow outside or beyond comprehensible categories." As a Harvard intellectual and Chicago community organizer, Obama embodies the Tea Party's fears of elite-underclass collusion. Skocpol and Williamson write, "Tea Party members connect Obama and his administration and political allies directly with those deemed undeserving—not just with African-Americans but also with illegal immigrants and criminals."[115]

Tea Partiers' experiences and perceptions of economic uncertainty, cultural chaos, and political loss of control combine into a sense of foundations being undermined and of staring into the abyss. Skocpol and Williamson write that "In the highly emotional telling of many Tea Partiers, the ballooning federal deficit merges into a general sense of a coming collapse for America." Expressing fears of coming economic meltdown, wiping out savings and wealth, the Tea Party worldview merges with the culture of "prepping." Skocpol and Williams describe a couple living in a "pristine retirement community in exurban Phoenix" who have armed themselves, have a safe full of ammunition, and have been transferring their assets into silver and stockpiling food. "For this charming and friendly older couple," they write, "Tea Party politics inextricably mixes relatively routine political engagement with extraordinary efforts to save America and themselves in a looming end-of-the-world scenario."[116]

As I have argued, the insecurity manifested in "prepping" is an expression of the experienced fragility both of self and of social order among possessive individualists. Since the security of the self is tied to *having*, the threat of the loss of material wealth is also a threat to the individual's ontological security, or feeling of security in his or her own existence. Possessive individualism magnifies these feelings of insecurity also by undermining social solidarity as a basis for mutual aid and as a support for the self. It spurs withdrawal from society into a hostile privatism, undermining society's capacity for mutual assistance and collective action.

The Tea Party outlook seems characterized less by individualism than by sheer egoism. This accounts for some of the apparent inconsistencies in Tea Partiers' political thinking. While sharing generally anti-government and pro-free-market ideas with Ron Paul, they are not consistently libertarian.[117] Skocpol and Williamson show that the Tea Party's rank and file tend not to oppose government programs such as Medicare, from which they themselves benefit. But, they are virulently opposed to the extension of such government assistance to younger generations and to government programs targeted at assisting low-income people.[118] This seeming inconsistency can be understood as an expression of egoism. The egoist cannot consistently follow a political doctrine (such as libertarianism) because their basic question is, as Street and Anthony DiMaggio have put it, "*what's in it for me?*"[119]

During a Republican Primary debate in Myrtle Beach, South Carolina, Ron Paul was met with boos when he said, "[I]f another country does to us what we do others, we're not going to like it very much. So I would say that maybe we ought to consider a golden rule in—in foreign policy."[120] The booing makes sense when one understands this displeasure as an extension of egoism to the particular group with which the individual identifies—the American nation. The egoist does not recognize the validity of the golden rule as a political principle, and does not universalize the value they place on their own freedom and well-being. Journalist George Monbiot has noted this aspect of egoism at play among those claiming to be "libertarian" today. Libertarians who bitterly oppose environmental regulation or the restraint of exploitative practices by banks, he argues, violate the universalistic implication of the doctrine of negative liberty, which requires that individual freedom be restrained when it impinges on the freedom of others. This requirement was acknowledged by Isaiah Berlin who noted, "[N]o man's activity is so completely private as never to obstruct the lives of others in any way. 'Freedom for the pike is death for the minnows'." But, according to Monbiot, it seems to be ignored by today's right-wing libertarians who "assert their freedom to pollute, exploit, even—among the gun nuts—to kill, as if these were fundamental human rights. They characterise any attempt to restrain them as tyranny. They refuse to see that there is a clash between the freedom of the pike and the freedom of the minnow."[121] The Tea Party are adamantly opposed right to consistently universalize their precepts speaks to the root of their thinking in egoism. This is a worldview derived from brute self-interest, appealing to both individual and group narcissism, and implacably hostile to taking the view of the other.

The Tea Party represents the paradox of organized egoists, an attempt to construct a political program on the basis of a self-interest that refuses to universalize. The predominant orientation is one of hostility and suspicion toward others. Skocpol and Williamson observe that, while Tea Partiers are "extra-jaundiced" in their judgment of racial and ethnic minorities, they "have negative views about all of their fellow citizens."[122] Mark Lilla notes that the new populism represented by the Tea Party is individualist in the extreme, verging toward solipsism: "It appeals to petulant individuals convinced that they can do everything themselves if they are only left alone, and that others are conspiring to keep them from doing just that."[123] This anti-social individualism is reminiscent of Caudwell's observation about the mutually antagonistic, even paranoid, quality of petit bourgeois individualism:

> It is the peculiar suffering of the *petit bourgeoisie* that they are called upon to hate *each other*. It is not impersonal things or *outside* classes that hurt them and inflict on them suffering and poverty, but it appears to be other members of their own class. It is the shopkeeper across the road, the rival small

trader, the family next door, with whom they are actively competing. Every success of one *petit bourgeois* is a sword in another's heart. Every failure of one's own is the result of another's activity. No companionship, or solidarity, is possible. One's hatred extends from the workers 'below' that abyss always waiting for one, to the successful *petit bourgeois* just above one whom one envies and hates.[124]

Since the conditions of petit bourgeois life tend to undermine solidarity even within their class, it takes a powerful sense of external threat to spur them to act together. Then, outward hostility can overcome their privatism, mutual distance, and antagonism.

In the case of the Tea Party, this external threat was President Obama, who became, for them, as Skocpol and Williamson put it, "virtually the Devil incarnate."[125] Under this threat, individual narcissism could be extended to group narcissism, galvanizing a sense of shared identity and interest based on sameness. Tea Partiers, therefore, identify and find common ground with those like them, namely, those who are white, of retirement age, and are relatively affluent, and are suspicious of those they see as different, namely, those who are young, belong to ethnic minorities, and are poor. In domestic politics, their group narcissism means demonizing these other groups and programs that might benefit them. However, they overlook these social divisions when, looking out beyond the USA to the world, they extend their group narcissism to the nation, pitted against external threats (whether immigration or Islam). Waving the flag, and other symbols of American patriotism, at Tea Party rallies, expresses this kind of nationalistic group narcissism. It is this group narcissism that galvanizes the Tea Party's egoists into a movement.

Group narcissism also protects and reinforces the individual egos of the movement's members. It expresses an attempt to anchor selfhood in we-identity and a search for a solution to ontological insecurity. The movement from individual to group narcissism is a flight from an untenable individualism, one that necessarily generates isolation, insecurity, and fear.[126] But the pathology of individual narcissism is also present in group narcissism, which is a defensive and partial belonging, clinging onto symbols such as the flag, angrily rejecting difference, and reproducing subordination to more powerful entities, for example, the billionaires who bankroll the movement. Both the individualism and the (group-narcissistic) solidarity prove illusory. The "little people" railing against big government are the jingoists who support military spending and wars that expand the size of government, and that lead to spiraling war and terrorism that produce further insecurity. The same little people prove convenient pawns for billionaire political manipulators like the Koch brothers, and the deregulatory neoliberal policies they promote exacerbate social inequalities. In turn, the socio-economic ladder becomes steeper and more slippery; the struggle for credentials, jobs, and standing in the social hierarchy intensifies; and the antagonistic character of life in capitalist society sharpens. Generalized insecurity becomes more and more the order of the day.[127]

America's petit bourgeois egoists are bewildered and angry about the growth of government. However, they fail to understand that the enlargement of the state is not separate from the individualism that they promote. Precisely because individuals' freedom has the potential to interfere with that of others, a society of competitive individuals requires a higher authority to provide order in this anarchy. This was, of course, Hobbes' justification for Leviathan. If civil society pits individuals and private interests against one another, as increasingly complex interdependencies develop between these hostile, private agents (with increasingly advanced technology and economic organization), this requires increasingly manifold and far-reaching forms of regulation to ensure fairness, safety, and transparency in these interactions. A society of individuals set against one another looks to the state to provide order, and the more complex that society the more demands are placed on the state. So, development within this conflictual paradigm necessarily spurs the growth of state power.

The federal government appears to the petit bourgeois American to be very far from a neutral regulator or arbiter. Rather, it seems to be the instrument of obscure "elites" who have captured it and use it for their own purposes. But again, the individualists are unable to understand the moment of truth in this, because they cannot understand the nature of social power in capitalist society. It is certainly true that the American state is no neutral arbiter. It is an inherently *capitalist* state, captured by large corporations and manipulated through a political system in which money is the primary medium of power.[128]

The power of the state is deeply integrated with the concentration of economic power in oligopolistic or monopolistic corporations. While libertarians rail against the government's distortion of the competitive market, they fail to see how competition itself leads to monopoly, as small enterprises are pushed out of the market or bought up by the larger players. While monopolies are anti-competitive, they arise from the dynamics of competition. George Orwell said, "'[F]ree' competition means for the great mass of people a tyranny probably worse, because more irresponsible, than that of the State. The trouble with competitions is that somebody wins them."[129]

The libertarians, however, regard economic power arising within the market as beyond question. Ron Paul's view is that the size of government invites its manipulation: "If there were less to buy through influencing campaigns, there would be a lot less incentive to invest so much in the process." However, he defends the idea that corporate financing of political campaigns is constitutionally protected "free speech."[130] The fantasy is that economic power has no bearing on the character, and indeed on the size, of the state. Indeed, economic power is not conceptualized as power—it is "spontaneous order," a miraculous process of mutual adjustment.[131] Only the state is identified with power, and the state seems to grow, driven by its own internal dynamic, or by the power-drive of the political elites. Against the growth of the state, its opaqueness, and lack of responsiveness to ordinary people, the libertarians call for unleashing the market. But, in advanced capitalism, this amounts to the call to unfetter the most powerful economic interests. So, the Tea Party is funded by the Koch Brothers, who have a clear economic interest in loosening regulation over their petroleum, chemical, plastics, paper, and commodities trading businesses.[132] In the Tea Party, the minnows work to secure the freedom of the pikes. They fail to see how, by doing so, they exacerbate their own insecurity. Skocpol and Williamson note that the primary beneficiaries of Tea Party-inspired policies are "the super-rich fat cats who have manipulated Tea Party activism with such glee."[133] As social forces and institutions become ever larger and ever more complex, the petit bourgeois libertarians become increasingly angry and defensive, retreating further into their fantasy idyll of self-reliance and the free market.

The Search for Foundations

Right-wing political discourse in America explicitly champions a rugged individualism, in which individuals are supposed to take responsibility for themselves and rely on nothing but their own capacities. However, this individualism is accompanied by the search for sources of ontological security, or bulwarks against change and disintegration. This is a key function of the "constitutional reverence" and literalism that are features both of Tea Party ideology and of the libertarianism of Ron Paul. In his

Tea Party Manifesto, Farah writes that America has "lost its moral bearings and constitutional moorings."[134] The Constitution is conceptualized as an anchor against the forces of social change. For Paul, the Constitution is a standard to which he wants to "rally and recall our people."[135] Liberty, reified in the Constitution, becomes, as Paul puts it, "a fundamental bedrock of our country."[136]

Skocpol and Williamson observe that a "constantly restated reverence for the country's founding documents" is central to Tea Party ideology. They describe how the founding documents, the Constitution, the Bill of Rights, and the Declaration of Independence are "woven into the warp and woof of Tea Party routines," available at their stalls, quoted and referenced on placards, T-shirts, and even jewelry and continually invoked in the movement's political discourse.[137] The Tea Partiers admit no ambiguity in the Constitution, insisting on its literal interpretation. Armey told a rally, "If you don't understand the Constitution, I'll buy you a dictionary."[138] The Constitution is brandished as a means to banish ambiguity from politics. Ron Paul repudiates any governmental measure not explicitly provided for in the Constitution.[139] The transformation of the Constitution into a sacred, unquestionable source of value and meaning often takes explicitly religious form. Christine O'Donnell, who, with Tea Party support, campaigned for a Senate seat in Delaware, expressed a view of the Constitution as a "covenant" based on "divine principles," depicting it as America's equivalent of the "Hebrew scriptures."[140] Skocpol and Williamson note that many Tea Partiers who are evangelical Christians translate their approach to Bible study to their reading of the Constitution. Cleon Skousen's *The Five Thousand Year Leap*, which gives a Biblical explanation for the US Constitution and the founding of the US, is a favorite among Tea Partiers.[141]

Constitutional fetishism is an attempt to freeze time, and is therefore the denial of historicity. Jill Lepore calls the Tea Party's insistence on the incontrovertible truth of the Constitution "anti-historical." She writes: "In antihistory, time is an illusion. Either we're there, two hundred years ago, or they're here, among us."[142] Making the Constitution a sacred text and sanctifying the "Founding Fathers" are ways of denying historical transformation.[143] The notion of the Constitution as an unchanging source of meaning and values has particular appeal for people who feel overwhelmed by social change. Former Oklahoma Congressman Mickey Edwards has described a sense of cultural disorientation among older Tea Party supporters:

They don't know how to work the computers; now everyone's texting... All of a sudden it wasn't just that people were gay, now they're getting married. All the things you grew up with, all the biases you had and believed were accurate, all the ways your daily life worked are being challenged. You don't have to be a racist to look at: there's a black president, there's a woman speaker, it doesn't look the same.[144]

There is also the fact that the kinds of middle-class jobs that many Tea Party activists have are being threatened by changes in technology and economic organization. An article in *Forbes* notes that "rule-based jobs like accounting and many intermediation-type jobs (travel agent, bank teller, even some stock brokers) can now be replaced by computers."[145] It is likely that these economic shifts, even if not fully understood, contribute to a sense of unease in this class layer.

The telescoping of the temporal distance from the American Revolution to the present world is linked also with Tea Partiers' desire to turn back the clock in their own biographies, as they romanticize the America of their childhoods. According to Skocpol and Williamson, "When Tea Partiers talk about 'their rights,' they are asserting a desire to live again in the country they think they recall from childhood or young adulthood. Their anger evinces a determination to restore that remembered America."[146] Since change is entropic, eroding an order that was more perfect in the past, the fetishized Constitution offers timeless order.[147] The Constitution appears a stable reference point, holding things in place and establishing boundaries.

Money is a particular focus for fears of overflowing and loss of control. Debt is a central issue for the Tea Party. Rand Paul writes that as the Tea Party began to "gather forces from every direction.... [t]hey all came with one grievance foremost in their mind—the national debt. This problem... had set off brushfires in the minds of millions of Americans across the country."[148] In 2011, Tea Party-affiliated Congressional Republicans blocked a measure to raise the federal government's debt ceiling, an act that led the rating agency Standard & Poor's to downgrade the credit rating of US government bonds.[149] Republican Congressional leader Eric Cantor (closely associated with the conservative candidates swept into Congressional office by the Tea Party in 2010) asserted that the debt ceiling was an "existential" question for fiscal conservatives.[150] The mission statement of Tea Party Patriots reads, "The impetus for the Tea Party movement is excessive government spending and taxation. Our mission is to attract, educate, organize, and mobilize our fellow citizens to secure public policy consistent with our three core values of Fiscal Responsibility, Constitutionally Limited Government and Free Markets."[151]

The issue of public debt combines concerns about an endlessly expanding government with insistence on social discipline. Right-wing discourse on fiscal prudence and austerity focuses on welfare spending and "entitlements" as the causes of the federal budget deficit. The Tea Party are adamantly opposed to addressing deficits through raising taxes. Rand Paul notes that TEA in the title of their movement is often said to stand for "Taxed Enough Already."[152] For the Tea Party, as for libertarians, the problem of deficits points to the need for shrinking the state and imposing austerity measures, cutting back social programs. The imposition of fiscal discipline becomes a means for imposing social discipline, rolling back welfare and insisting on the responsibility of the individual to work. In April 2010, when Republican Senator Jim Bunning blocked the extension of unemployment benefit, and Senate Democrat Jeff Merkley pleaded with him to drop his objection, Bunning answered, "Tough shit."[153] As an image of retention, this could not be more vivid.

The image of a bloated, uncontrollable state combines with ideas about morality and the self. Rand Paul writes that his fundamental message is "a message of fiscal sanity. It's a message of limited constitutional government and balanced budgets."[154] These themes of institutional and social order (sanity, limits, balance) are articulated through homilies about family morality: "The Paul kids were always taught the value of a dollar. We were expected to work hard and were never given money without earning it... The Pauls never were extravagant, we always shopped at Sears or JC Penney and wore inexpensive tennis shoes."[155] Public debt and the over-expanding state are traced, by the Tea Party, to the lack of discipline that marks the "moochers" in society. Tea Partiers regard individual discipline, shown in working and saving, as requiring the reinforcement of morality. In this way, social conservatism connects with fiscal conservatism.

Ron Paul especially combines constitutional fetishism with fetishism of metal coinage as unchanging sources of value—timeless political values and non-corroding economic value. Inflation, caused by the printing of paper money, is a key pre-occupation. Paul advocates return to the gold standard and argues that gold-based currency is required by the US Constitution. He writes, for example, "Accepting the principle of free markets, sound money, and private property and recognizing that the welfare-warfare state is incompatible with our Constitution would go a long way to solving our economic crisis."[156] He himself has been buying gold since Nixon's flotation of the dollar in 1971, and he continues to invest heavily in precious metals.[157] Along with the Constitution, a dollar "as good as gold" functions in Paul's thought as a source of ontological security, a bulwark against the erosion of values.[158]

As noted above, Tea Party balanced budget rhetoric tends to focus on welfare or "entitlement" spending as the major cause of deficits and as the target for cuts. Ron Paul is certainly more consistent in his critique of "big government" and is an opponent of wars that he regards as key drivers of the expansion of federal government power. However, Paul recognizes that his views on this are unpopular among many conservatives. He notes that conservatives are frequently "uncritical" of military spending, and writes, "Too many times, I've seen how the conservative agenda of cutting government gets overtaken by this ideological attachment to unlimited military spending."[159] The contradiction is glaring in the Tea Party, which, Street and DiMaggio argue, incorporates key features of America's broader "culture of national militarism."[160] According to Street, "Tea Party Republicans hold up the right-militarist, interventionist, and force-projecting end of the foreign policy opinion spectrum."[161] While opposing welfare, the Tea Party supports the controlling, punitive, and aggressive functions of the state, especially toward the groups they perceive as irresponsible or threatening. Skocpol and Williamson write that, in contrast to their hostility to state regulation of business, Tea Party members "took a very different view of the use of government powers to police disfavored groups with whom they do *not* identify… When it comes to law enforcement, Tea Party members support strong governmental authority, even at the expense of budgetary constraint."[162]

In terms of Pierre Bourdieu's distinction between the "left hand of the state," which serves social rights in welfare, education, and public health, and the "right hand of the state" represented by the ministries of finance and budget and the coercive apparatuses of police and military, the Tea Party supports the right hand while attacking the left hand.[163] The "minimal state" that these types of libertarians would leave in place would primarily consist of police and military functions. Rand Paul says that "[n]ational defense is the most important thing we do in Washington."[164]

The contrast between the left hand and right hand of the state is often imagined in gendered terms. The left hand is the "nanny state." Obama's healthcare proposals represent, as Gullet puts it in his *Tea Party Handbook*, "Mama-care health control."[165] One Tea Party supporter expressed her attitude toward the welfare state by saying, "As the independent teenagers say to their hovering, smothering parents, so we the people say to the social agencies: 'Bug off. Get off our backs, damn it.'"[166] In this kind of conservative politics, the caring, feminine-associated functions of the state are conceptualized as smothering and infantilizing. Yet, the patriarchal, aggressive, and repressive operations of the state in law enforcement and the military are respected and adamantly supported.

This dualistic stance toward the state can be understood in relation to negative freedom and the possessive-individualistic conception of self, which involves a denial of human interdependence. The caring functions of the state impinge on the boundaries that possessive individualism establishes around the self. If the self exists by virtue of being bounded from other selves and from the external world, dependency (especially on a more powerful entity) threatens the dissolution of these boundaries and the collapse of autonomous selfhood. In the worldview of possessive individualism, caring represents an existential threat. This is true of being cared for. It is also true of caring for others, since empathy requires emotionally or imaginatively taking the view of the other. To care means opening oneself to the pain and suffering of others, an experience that can be difficult and ambivalent. Insisting that others' problems are their own fault and therefore their own business, allows one to remain closed to their experience, therefore preserving the separateness of one's own experience and the boundedness of one's self.

The aggressive operations of the state do not similarly threaten boundaries of the self. The aggressive operations of Bourdieu's right hand of the state can be conceptualized as, to quote Dana Villa, the "'daddy state'—the state that fights, that decides who is friend and who is enemy."[167] Here, state action attacks, represses, and excludes. If the individual identifies with state violence against troubling others (whether Muslim terrorists, criminals, ethnic minorities, or the poor), then state aggression can extend the individual's own aggressive impulses. The identification with state force reinforces the individual's own armoring of their self against the ambivalence provoked by recognition of the experiences and needs of other selves.

The extreme individualism of the sort deeply ingrained in American cultural ideology, and manifested most clearly politically in libertarianism, denies the social existence of the individual, the fact that individuals are necessarily attached to others within a web of social relations.[168] The more that this kind of individualism is realized, in social atomization and privatized modes of living, the more it is bound to give rise, correspondingly, to longing for the *social* dimensions of human experience that have been repressed. Slater argues that American culture, organized around the value of individualism, "deeply and uniquely" frustrates human desires that aim at overcoming the isolation of the ego—the desire for community, cooperation, and "the wish to share responsibility for the control of one's impulses and the direction of one's life." [169] American culture is deeply and irrationally hostile to manifestations of these desires. But, these frustrated desires become more internally powerful the more they are repressed. In his *Tea Party Manifesto*, Farah asserts the need to struggle against "mankind's innate desire to collectivize and rebel against God's order."[170]

The repressed desire for collectivity finds expression in Tea Partiers' identification with the right hand of the state. The desire for community is manifested in patriotic identification with the nation; with symbols of collective identity such as the flag, with manifestations of power and authority (especially the military); and in demands for police repression of "irresponsible" or "undeserving" *outsider* groups such as illegal immigrants, ethnic minorities, and protesting youth. Ron Paul's conundrum as to why his fellow conservative "individualists" so rarely agree with his anti-militarism, therefore, has the following answer: that the narrow individualist ideology that they share with him is fundamentally constricting of the breadth of human desires and needs. Conservatives are attracted to collectivist patriotic symbolism and to authority structures of the military and law and order precisely as vehicles for their suppressed longing for collectivity. The contradictory character of the Tea Party as a strongly nationalistic and xenophobic movement with racist currents, whose supporters drape themselves in patriotic symbols, while claiming to represent individualism and opposing the "authoritarianism" of government healthcare, must be understood in relation to the inevitable psychological contradictions that arise within individualism.[171]

The Constitution and gold function as sources of meaning and value that appear to resist time and human imperfection. The defenders of negative freedom are watchful against the imposition of personal authority. Against this threat, they look to impersonal mechanisms to mediate the private actions of individuals. The key impersonal mediating mechanism is the market. Armey expresses an article of faith in libertarianism, and more broadly in neoliberalism, when he outlines "Armey's Axiom number one: 'The market is rational and the government is dumb'."[172] Ron Paul is similarly enamored of what he calls "the magnificence of the market economy."[173] The market is, to use the title of David Friedman's libertarian manifesto, "the machinery of freedom."[174] The very impersonality of the market, the absence of human control and intervention, is supposed to guarantee the freedom of the individual agents whose action the market mediates. Paul's stance on the role of money in politics exemplifies the way in which he treats market outcomes as unquestionable. He is against regulating how much money individuals or corporations can invest in the political process. The spending of money on political campaigns is, in his view, not a manifestation of unequal power to manipulate the political process, but is free speech. If there is a market in political influence, that is no different from a market in political journalism.[175]

Just as the outcomes produced through the market are unquestionable, so Paul also treats technology as a brute fact when he writes that "Gun-control advocates tell us that removing guns from society makes us safer. But that is simply an impossibility. The fact is that firearm technology exists. It cannot be uninvented."[176] For Paul, technology develops in response to market demand. It is one side of the interaction of supply and demand, and to ban a technology like handguns or assault weapons would be an illegitimate intervention. Where there is no government intervention, there is freedom and spontaneous order.

The problem, however, is that direct personal domination is not the only form of unfreedom. These mechanisms themselves—the market, money, technology—are forms of domination that can be more oppressive, because they are more all-pervading and harder to throw off. Tom Palmer, a right-wing libertarian, associated with the Cato Institute, writes, "Embracing free-market capitalism means embracing *the freedom to change*, to innovate, to invent. It *means accommodating change* and respecting the freedom of others to do as they please with what is there. It means *making place for new technologies...*"[177] Palmer's unintentional logic is that the entrepreneur's power to effect technological changes necessarily burdens society with "accommodating" that "change." We *must change* in order to accommodate the capitalist's freedom *to change*—to change the world, and to change us with it. The possessors of capital have the freedom to mobilize money as power on the market, but this becomes the unfreedom of all others, who encounter the movements of money and technology as impersonal forces beyond their control.

The deep sense of frustration, just below the surface of American life, arises from powerlessness in the face of impersonal domination: recessions, the wiped-out retirement plan, the foreclosed home, the financial chaos driven by increasing financial complexity and the power of large banks, the worries about medical bills, the stress of the job and the fear of losing it, the closure of the factory, environmental deterioration, and the increasingly hollowness of democratic institutions. There is pervasive cynicism and hopelessness in the face of the power of money to influence the political process and the operations of government. Anxiety is provoked by horrendous, "inexplicable" crimes such as mass shootings that are occurring with greater frequency (and each time the authorities' expression of shock is more perfunctory).[178] One might temporarily blame individuals, but without much satisfaction. The criminal was caught and put away, but the next day a similarly "incomprehensible" gun crime is on the television news. The new supervisor is not much better than the old one, and both are only doing what is required by the higher-ups, the shareholders, and ultimately "the competitive environment in this industry."

Treating the market and technology as unquestionable, and state intervention as tyranny, the doctrine of negative freedom makes social problems, and the inequities of economic power, impossible to confront or address in any kind of systematic way. While, perhaps, freer from personal domination, we are more and more subject to domination by complex systems.[179] Attempts to identify the source of impersonal domination feed the paranoias of right-wing populism.[180] This paranoia is also drawn on by the state and mobilized in support of its violence. Ideas about "Reds under the bed" or the domino theory of Communist takeover have their counterpart today in the supposedly ubiquitous threat represented by Al-Qaeda terrorism. The "war on terror" is a war against an enemy that can never be located or even clearly defined. This shadowy, diffuse enemy becomes the ideal object on which to project aggression rooted in the diffuse frustrations that arise within an impersonal, marketized, and bureaucratic order.[181] But this war also becomes the perfect justification for the growth of the state, and for the blanketing of state power in secrecy.[182]

As the secret state grows, the form of government becomes increasingly conspiratorial. And in the "war on terror," we are subject to ever more impersonal, bureaucratic, and technological domination, for example, having to acquiesce to full body scans at airports and ubiquitous electronic surveillance. But ubiquitous control is warranted by ubiquitous threat. Only a vast, sprawling, and secretive state can meet the diffuse threat of contemporary terrorism, or, rather, the amorphousness of contemporary fear. This state draws sustenance from, manipulates, and further provokes the anxieties of atomized individuals. Ron and Rand Paul express horror at this enlargement of the state. But they fail to see how these systems of oppression are connected with the "free-market" individualism that they advocate.[183] The collapse of American democracy evident in the growth of an invasive secret state bears out the way in which negative freedom, as a partial and incomplete form of freedom, necessarily negates itself. What Caudwell wrote in the 1930s continues to be true today: "Bourgeois liberty at once gives rise to bourgeois coercion."[184]

Beyond Negative Freedom

The politics of the Tea Party and the contemporary American right wing exemplify how the liberal doctrine of negative freedom has become defensive and reactionary. The theory of negative freedom is constructed around a fiction of the autonomous atomic individual. This notion of the individual is always a fiction, because it denies the inherent sociality of human nature and the interconnectedness of individuals within a social community. It is a fiction that was useful and progressive in the early development of capitalism when it provided the ideological framework for the liberal bourgeois revolt against aristocratic power. However, the rise of monopoly capitalism rendered this ideology of individualism and negative freedom an increasingly nostalgic view, at odds with the tendencies being produced by the very market forces that the ideology promoted and legitimized.[185] The confusion of today's lumpen petit bourgeoisie about the nature of the system, which they stubbornly defend in the name of individual freedom, can be seen in their mobilization in the name of free markets against the state bailout of the finance sector, while they provide jingoistic support for the military–industrial complex. They are totally mystified as to the deep and inherent interconnections between the state, imperialism, and finance within what they see as "the free market."[186] As it becomes increasingly divorced from, and at odds with, the technocratic-managerial system of advanced capitalism, for which it provides an ideological smokescreen, the ideology of negative freedom comes to be most shrilly defended by reactionary groups threatened by social changes that they perceive as marginalizing them.

The notion of a bounded and autonomous individual, the centerpoint of the conception of negative freedom, is increasingly contradictory. Within today's monopolistic media culture, it is clear that consumer desire is far from purely individual and spontaneous, but is carefully manipulated and continually stimulated by advertising. Desire is shaped by culture, and today that culture and the desires that it promotes are carefully orchestrated for the purpose of generating and renewing demand for the continual ramping up of commodity production. The advertising industry grew rapidly over the course of the mid-to-late twentieth century.[187] What is new today is not only the creation of new media venues for advertising, especially the Internet, and the sophistication of the penetration of existing media by advertising (e.g. the manipulation of news by corporate public relations), but also the expansion of information gathering on the ideas and preferences of the population. The ability of corporations to see into the souls of individuals enhances their ability to manipulate those souls through advertising messages which are increasingly targeted at individual tastes and lifestyles. Surveillance by private corporations, as well as the state, has expanded through new means of information gathering, such as the social networking site Facebook. This surveillance is combined with the increasing ability to target advertising at the individual through the same types of media. Individual desire is open to both inspection and manipulation.[188] Far from being an autonomous agent, the individual becomes, rather, a node in the circulation of capital. The individual flying the "Don't Tread On Me" flag fails to realize that his or her very thoughts are imprinted with the footprints of others. The current dominant ideology maintains the fiction of negative freedom, while the supposed subject of this freedom is increasingly evanescent. Fromm's diagnosis in *Escape from Freedom* retains its accuracy: "The cultural and political crisis of our day is not due to the fact that there is too much individualism but that what we believe to be individualism has become a hollow shell."[189]

We lack both truly autonomous individuality and true community. While not autonomous, we face our troubles alone. We must sink or swim as individuals in the swells and currents of what Bauman calls "liquid life." The individual is the bearer of risk, and must choose the best options and navigate the problems of unemployment, medical insurance, loans, and so on. But, this devolution of responsibility to individuals, their aloneness in their own precariousness, does not entail autonomy. With the end of the traditional company pension, individuals are supposed to be responsible for managing their own retirement fund and, therefore, free to invest in whatever portfolio they want. But they are not free from the worry about how to survive in old age. Rather, this worry is intensified as they struggle to make ends meet in the present, and find their retirement preparations slipping behind. People feel anxiety and helplessness, and they hope for some piece of luck that will come along and put things right. They are at the mercy of fate. All the while, their underlying fear of the future is preventing them from enjoying life, from participating in activities that might connect them to a community, from doing what they love. This is the syndrome of the student who graduates from college loaded with debt. The student as free-choosing "customer" is enslaved to debt and must take, and try to hold, the job that offers the best pay and benefits, even if it is not the life to which he or she truly aspires. The autonomy of the individual on the market here is only apparent. Individuals are more fundamentally oppressed by impersonal forces such as bills, loan repayment demands, and the vagaries of the job market. In the job that they do not love, but are forced into by insecurity, they are oppressed by the crushing routine, the need to subordinate their feelings and personality, and to be polite and accepting. Their oppression is not only impersonal; economic forces constitute the *force* behind the personal authority of the boss.

Negative freedom has become a trap, in which freedom turns into unfreedom and individualism turns into subordination to the corporations and the state. If negative freedom, the freedom of the atomized individual, negates itself by subjecting the individual to powerful external forces which they do not control, overcoming this and moving toward a truer form of freedom means bringing these external forces under control, thereby negating their character as external and inhuman. Positive freedom represents a higher synthesis in which modern individual freedom is not negated but maintained while the antipathies of individual versus individual and individual versus collective are overcome.[190] Fromm argues that it requires, therefore, historical movement toward a new kind of individuality and a new kind of sociality. "Capitalism has created [the] premise" for this new sociality, Fromm argues, by making possible "a future of abundance, in which the fight for economic privileges is no longer necessitated by economic scarcity."[191] But capitalism blocks the realization of this potential.

Negative freedom has degenerated into unfreedom precisely because it has been undermined by the increasing scope and power of social organization and technological means for social coordination. The advances in organizational and technological power that threaten negative freedom also have the potential to produce new forms of global sociality, coordination, and planning, and new forms of democratic, cultural, and social relations between individuals. Today, however, with the increasing domination of the Internet by corporate monopolies and communication technologies distorted into a global net of state surveillance, these new forms of interconnectedness take alienated form as they are translated into new forms of domination and control. Corporate and state power undermine negative freedom, while blocking the necessary historical development toward a new sociality capable of sustaining positive freedom.

The ideology of negative freedom has become defensive, destructive, and hostile *even to recognizing* realities such as climate change, which pose problems to which it can offer no solution.[192] The remaining power of the idea of negative freedom is the ideological stasis that reflects the enforced political stasis of a dysfunctional and destructive capitalism. Negative freedom has become the domination of human beings by objects and forces beyond their control. Negative freedom today is the remnant of bourgeois liberalism, now thoroughly reactionary and rotten. The ecological and social destruction waged in its name, and the individual fear and rage that it produces, are manifestations of a decaying social order.

Notes

1. The distinction between negative and positive freedom is most often associated with Isaiah Berlin's lecture "Two Concepts of Liberty," delivered in 1958. But Fromm made the distinction in his 1941 book *Escape from Freedom*. See Berlin, "Two Concepts of Liberty," in idem, *Four Essays on Liberty* (New York: Oxford University Press, 1970), 118–172; Fromm, *Escape from Freedom* (New York: Henry Holt and Company, 1969). Tim Gray writes that the distinction between these two concepts of liberty "has been implicit, if not always explicit, in political thought since the Ancient Greeks": Gray, *Freedom* (Houndsmill, Basingstoke: MacMillan, 1991), 7.
2. Fromm, *Escape from Freedom*, 269.
3. Ed Pilkington, "Barack Obama Denounced by Rightwing Marchers in Washington," *The Guardian*, September 13, 2009, http://www.theguardian.com/world/2009/sep/13/barack-obama-denounced-washington-march; Joel Kovacs, "Obama Slammed: Chains We Can Believe In," *WND* April 15, 2009, http://www.wnd.com/2009/04/95135/; Ewen McAskill, "Obama Faces Re-election Hurdle as Health Reforms go Before Supreme Court," *The Guardian*, November 14, 2011, http://www.theguardian.com/world/2011/nov/14/obama-supreme-court-healthcare-bill
4. "Rep. Protesters Yelled Racial Slurs," *CBS News* March 20, 2010, http://www.cbsnews.com/stories/2010/03/20/politics/main6318517.shtml

5. Rick Santorum's Super Tuesday speech (full transcript, video), March 6, 2012, http://www.washingtonpost.com/blogs/election-2012/post/rick-santorums-super-tuesday-speech-full-transcript-video/2012/03/06/gIQAdPhrvR_blog.html. Accessed March 8, 2012. For a socialist critique of Obamacare, see Kate Randall, "Obamacare Lies Exposed," *World Socialist Web Site*, November 12, 2013, https://www.wsws.org/en/articles/2013/11/12/pers-n12.html
6. "Conservative Anti-Government Protesters Appropriate Historic US Flag," Guardian.co.uk, Deadline USA Blog, September 14, 2009, http://www.guardian.co.uk/world/deadlineusa/2009/sep/14/print
7. Dick Armey and Matt Kibbe, *Give Us Liberty: A Tea Party Manifesto* (New York: William Morrow, 2010), 67.
8. Quoted in Armey and Kibbe, *Give Us Liberty*, 71. The exchange is recounted also in http://www.nationalreview.com/articles/227383/presidents-say-darndest-things-c/jay-nordlinger
9. Rick Santelli, quoted in Armey and Kibbe, *Give Us Liberty*, 19–20.
10. See Michael Perelman, *Manufacturing Discontent: The Trap of Individualism in Corporate Society* (London: Pluto Press, 2005), 1.
11. Christopher Caudwell, *The Concept of Freedom* (London: Lawrence and Wishart, 1965), 123–124.
12. Philip Slater, *Pursuit of Loneliness: American Culture at the Breaking Point* (Boston: Beacon Press, 1976), 11.
13. Jon Wiener, "'Hell Is Other People': Ted Turner's Two Million Acres," in Mike Davis and Daniel Bertrand Monk, *Evil Paradises: Dreamworlds of Neoliberalism* (New York: The New Press, 2007), 199–206, quoting 204–205.
14. "Why the Rich Fear Violence in the Streets," *The Wall Street Journal*, July 6, 2011, http://blogs.wsj.com/wealth/2011/07/06/why-the-rich-fear-violence-in-the-streets/
15. Denis Duclos, *The Werewolf Complex: America's Fascination with Violence*, trans. Amanda Pingree (Oxford: Berg Books, 1998), esp. 119, 141.
16. Bill Durodié, "Fear and Terror in a Post-Political Age," *Government and Opposition* 42(3) (2007): 427–450, esp. 436–439. See also Kathleen Tierney, "Disaster Beliefs and Institutional Interests: Recycling Disaster Myths in the Aftermath of 9-11," in Lee Clarke ed., *Terrorism and Disaster: New Threats, New Ideas (Research in Social Problems and Public Policy*, Volume 11) (Emerald Publishing, 2003), 33–51. Henry Giroux, *Stormy Weather: Katrina and the Politics of Disposability* (Boulder: Paradigm Publishers, 2006), 50–54; Rebecca Solnit, *A Paradise Built in Hell: The Extraordinary Communities That Arise in Disaster* (Penguin, 2010), esp. 236–237.

THE TYRANNY OF NEGATIVE FREEDOM   249

17. Paul Harris, "US 'Preppers' Are Ready to Fend for Themselves Come What May," *The Guardian Weekly*, February 19, 2010, 3. See also Richard G. Mitchell Jr., *Dancing at Armageddon: Survivalism and Chaos in Modern Times* (Chicago: The University of Chicago Press, 2002).
18. http://channel.nationalgeographic.com/channel/doomsday-preppers/. Accessed February 16, 2012.
19. Philip Lamy, *Milennium Rage: Survivalists, White Supremacists and Doomsday Prophecy* (New York: Plenum Press, 1996), 89.
20. Zygmunt Bauman, *Liquid Fear* (Cambridge: Polity Press), 2.
21. Harris, "US 'Preppers'."
22. Jessica Bennett, "Rise of the Preppers: America's New Survivalists," *Newsweek*, December 27, 2009, http://www.newsweek.com/rise-preppers-americas-new-survivalists-75537
23. Bennett, "Rise of the Preppers."
24. "Survival in Popular Culture: *Falling Skies* Review," June 22, 2012, *Urban Survivalist Blog*, http://urbansurvivalistblog.com/survival-in-popular-culture-falling-skies-review/. Accessed February 11, 2014.
25. Slavoj Zizek, *Living in the End Times* (London: Verso, 2011), 64.
26. "Prepper Weapons and Survival Strategies Pictures – Doomsday Preppers – National Geographic Channel," http://channel.nationalgeographic.com/channel/doomsday-preppers/prepper-weapons-survival-strategies-pictures/. Accessed February 16, 2012.
27. Quoted in Clancy Sigal, "America's Endless Romance with Guns," *The Guardian*, February 20, 2011, http://www.theguardian.com/commentisfree/cifamerica/2011/feb/20/gun-crime-arizona-shooting
28. For example, a limited edition Smith and Wesson Model 629-6 .44 Magnum, http://www.armslist.com/posts/2057969/asheville-north-carolina-handguns-for-sale–smith-and-wesson-629-6–don-t-tread-on-me—engraved (accessed January 1, 2015); 1911 Colt .45ACP, http://www.armslist.com/posts/99537/ohio-handguns-for-sale–1st-edt–colt-1911–don-t-tread-on-me- (accessed November 8, 2015).
29. Joshua Horwitz and Casey Anderson, *Guns, Democracy, and the Insurrectionist Idea* (Ann Arbor: University of Michigan Press, 2009), 23.
30. Wayne LaPierre, *Guns, Freedom and Terrorism* (Nashville, TN: WND Books, 2003), 29 (for Heston quote), and 196. See also Scott Melzer, *Gun Crusaders: The NRA's Culture War* (New York: New York University Press, 2009), 29.
31. Horwitz and Anderson, *Guns, Democracy, and the Insurrectionist Idea*, 1–2.
32. LaPierre quoted in Horwitz and Anderson, *Guns, Democracy, and the Insurrectionist Idea*, 40.

33. C. B. Macpherson, *The Political Theory of Possessive Individualism: Hobbes to Locke*. Oxford: Oxford University Press, 1962, 264–265.
34. Robert Nozick, *Anarchy, State, and Utopia* (New York: Basic Books, 1974), 171.
35. Jonathan Wolff, *Robert Nozick: Property, Justice and the Minimal State* (Cambridge: Polity Press, 1991), 10.
36. Ron Paul, *Liberty Defined: 50 Essential Issues that Affect Our Freedom* (New York: Grand Central Publishing, 2011), 145.
37. See also Firmin DeBrabander, *Do Guns Make Us Free? Democracy and the Armed Society* (New Haven: Yale University Press, 2015).
38. "Texas School District to Let Teachers Carry Guns," *Reuters*, August 16, 2008, http://www.reuters.com/article/2008/08/16/us-texas-guns-idUSN1538661720080816
39. See also David Ingram and Patricia Zengerle, "NRA Offensive Exposes Deep Divisions on Guns," *Reuters*, December 21, 2012, http://www.reuters.com/article/2012/12/22/us-usa-guns-nra-idUSBRE8BK0S520121222; Alina Selyukh, "Longtime Gun Lobby Ally to Lead Plan for Armed Guards at Schools," *Reuters*, December 21, 2012, http://www.reuters.com/article/2012/12/21/us-usa-guns-nra-hutchinson-idUSBRE8BK18P20121221; Ian Urbina, "Locked, Loaded, and Ready to Caffeinate," *The New York Times*, March 7, 2010, http://www.nytimes.com/2010/03/08/us/08guns.html; Richard C. Paddock, "Facing Gun Issue, Starbucks Throws Up Its Hands," *Aol News*, Mach 3, 2010, http://www.aolnews.com/nation/article/facing-gun-issue-starbucks-throws-up-its-hands/19381679?sms_ss=email; Rob Walker, "Crossfire," *The New York Times*, March 26, 2010, http://www.nytimes.com/2010/03/28/magazine/28FOB-consumed-t.html?_r=0
40. Wayne LaPierre and James Jay Baker, *Shooting Straight: Telling the Truth about Guns in America* (Washington DC: Regnery Publishing, 2002), 63. See also Jennifer Carlson, *Citizen-Protectors: The Everyday Politics of Guns in an Age of Decline* (Oxford: Oxford University Press, 2015).
41. Horwitz and Anderson, *Guns, Democracy, and the Insurrectionist Idea*, 219.
42. Jonathan M. Metzl and Kenneth T. MacLeish, "Triggering the Debate: Faulty Associations between Violence and Mental Illness Underlie US Gun Control Efforts," *Risk and Regulation* 25 (Spring 2013), 8–9, on 8; "Gun Crime Statistics by US State: Latest Data," *The Guardian*, December 17, 2012, http://www.theguardian.com/news/datablog/2011/jan/10/gun-crime-us-state; "Assault or Homicide," Center for Disease Control and Prevention, http://www.cdc.gov/nchs/fastats/homicide.htm. Accessed 5, 2015; Ray Sanchez, "Death and Guns

in the USA: The Story in Six Graphs," *CNN*, October 3, 2015, http://www.cnn.com/2015/10/03/us/gun-deaths-united-states
43. Richard Wilkinson and Kate Pickett, *The Spirit Level: Why More Equal Societies are Almost Always Better* (London: Allen Lane, 2009, 132, 137. See also Jeffrey Rieman, *The Rich Get Richer and the Poor Get Prison: Ideology, Class, and Criminal Justice* (Boston: Allyn and Bacon, 1998), 31–33.
44. Wilkinson and Pickett, *The Spirit Level*, 133–137. See also Rob Reiner, *Law and Order: An Honest Citizen's Guide to Crime and Control* (Cambridge: Polity Press, 2007), esp. 75.
45. Mark Ames, *Going Postal: Rage, Murder and Rebellion* (Brooklyn, NY: Soft Skull Press, 2005), 10, 18; Douglas Kellner, *Guys and Guns Amok: Domestic Terrorism and School Shootings from the Oklahoma City Bombing to the Virginia Tech Massacre* (Boulder: Paradigm Publishers, 2008), esp. 90–95; Kevin Martinez and David Walsh, "Shooting Rampage in Santa Barbara, California, Leaves 7 Dead," *World Socialist Web Site*, May 26, 2014, http://www.wsws.org/en/articles/2014/05/26/sanb-m26.html; James Brewer, "A New Wave of School Shootings and Other Violent Acts," June 20, 2013, *World Socialist Web Site*, http://www.wsws.org/en/articles/2014/06/20/shoo-j20.html; David North, "The Columbine High-School Massacre: American Pastoral… American Beserk," *World Socialist Web Site*, April 27, 1999, http://www.wsws.org/en/articles/1999/04/colo-a27.html; Kate Randall, "School shooting in Connecticut leaves 27 dead, including 20 children," *World Socialist Web Site*, December 15, 2012, https://www.wsws.org/en/articles/2012/12/15/conn-d15.html
46. Fromm, *Escape from Freedom*, 166. Emphasis in original.
47. See "The Killing of Trayvon Martin and Racial Politics in America," *World Socialist Web Site*, April 5, 2012, http://www.wsws.org/en/articles/2012/04/pers-a05.html; Patrick Martin, "Obama, Race and Class," *World Socialist Web Site*, July 22, 2013, https://www.wsws.org/en/articles/2013/07/22/pers-j22.html
48. "Tape Showed Zimmerman's Anger over Black Man's Beating," *CNN Justice*, May 24, 2012, http://www.cnn.com/2012/05/24/justice/florida-teen-shooting/; Ashley Hayes, "Witnesses Tell FBI that George Zimmerman is No Racist," *CNN Justice*, July 13, 2012, http://www.cnn.com/2012/07/12/justice/florida-teen-shooting/index.html
49. Quoted in Hayes, "Witnesses Tell FBI."
50. "Who is George Zimmerman?," *CBS Miami*, March 26, 2012, http://miami.cbslocal.com/2012/03/26/who-is-george-zimmerman/; Mattew Lysiak and Helen Kennedy, "George Zimmerman Lost Job as Party Security Guard for Being Too Aggressive, Ex-co-worker Says," *New*

York Daily News, March 29, 2012, http://www.nydailynews.com/news/national/george-zimmerman-lost-job-party-security-guard-aggressive-ex-co-worker-article-1.1053223#ixzz36A9ZEZIN; Jeff Weiner, "Trayvon Martin: New Photo, Details of George Zimmerman's Employment," *Orlando Sentinel*, March 23, 2012, http://articles.orlandosentinel.com/2012-03-23/news/os-trayvon-martin-george-zimmerman-job-20120323_1_robert-zimmerman-source-new-details

51. Lane DeGregory, "Trayvon Martin's Killing Shatters Safety within Retreat at Twin Lakes in Sanford," *Tampa Bay Times*, March 24, 2012, http://www.tampabay.com/news/humaninterest/trayvon-martins-killing-shatters-safety-within-retreat-at-twin-lakes-in/1221799
52. See also Carlson, *Citizen-Protectors*, 161.
53. Amy Green, "Zimmerman's Twin Lakes Community was On Edge Before Trayvon Shooting," *The Daily Beast*, March 28, 2012, http://www.thedailybeast.com/articles/2012/03/28/zimmerman-s-twin-lakes-community-was-on-edge-before-trayvon-shooting.html
54. Robert Reiner, *Law and Order: An Honest Citizen's Guide to Crime and Control* (Cambridge: Polity Press, 2007), 13–16; Steve Hall, Simon Winlow and Craig Ancrum, *Criminal Identities and Consumer Culture: Crime, Exclusion and the New Culture of Narcissism* (Willan, 2008); Edward Leyton, *Hunting Humans: The Rise of the Modern Multiple Murderer* (New York: Carroll and Graf, 2001), 350.
55. Wilkinson and Pickett, *The Spirit Level*, 153; Ruth Wilson Gilmore, *Golden Gulag: Prisons, Surplus, Crisis, and Opposition in Globalizing California* (Berkeley: University of California Press, 2007), 108, 112; Henry Giroux, "Racial Injustice and Disposable Youth in an Age of Zero Tolerance," *Qualitative Studies in Education* 16 (4) (2003): 553–565.
56. Gilmore, *Golden Gulag*, 52; Perelman, *Invisible Handcuffs*, 257–258. Cf. Andrew Gamble, *The Free Economy and the Strong State: The Politics of Thatcherism* (Houndmills, Basingstoke: MacMillan Education, 1988).
57. Hannah Holleman, Robert W. McChesney, John Bellamy Foster and R. Jamil Jonna, "The Penal State in an Age of Crisis," *Monthly Review* 61 (2) (June 2009), 1–17, on 3.
58. Rieman, *The Rich Get Richer*, 12–18.
59. LaPierre, *Guns, Freedom and Terrorism*, 204.
60. Jill LePore, *The Whites of Their Eyes: The Tea Party's Revolution and the Battle over American History* (Princeton: Princeton University Press, 2010).
61. LaPierre, *Guns, Freedom and Terrorism*, 210–211.
62. G. A. Cohen, "Self-Ownership, World Ownership, and Equality," in idem, *Self-Ownership, Freedom, and Equality*. Cambridge: Cambridge University Press, 1995, 67–91, quoting 67–68.

63. Cohen, "Self-Ownership, World Ownership, and Equality," 68. Emphasis in original.
64. Cohen, "Self-Ownership, World Ownership, and Equality," 68–69.
65. Friedrich Engels, *The Condition of the Working Class in England* (1845), https://www.marxists.org/archive/marx/works/1845/condition-working-class/ch05.htm
66. G. A. Cohen, "Illusions about Private Property and Freedom," in John Mepham and David-Hillel Ruben eds., *Issues in Marxist Philosophy*, Vol. IV. Hassocks: Sussex, 1981; Cohen, "Robert Nozick and Wilt Chamberlain," in Cohen, *Self-Ownership*, 19–37, esp. 34–36.
67. Cohen, "Self-Ownership, World Ownership, and Equality," 90.
68. Lamy, *Millennium Rage*, 72.
69. Quoted in Horwitz and Anderson, *Guns, Democracy, and the Insurrectionist Idea*, 21.
70. http://en.wikipedia.org/wiki/I%27ll_give_you_my_gun_when_you_take_it_from_my_cold,_dead_hands. Accessed on September 20, 2015.
71. Erich Fromm, *To Have or To Be?* (London: Continuum [1976] 1997), 59.
72. Fromm, *To Have or To Be?*, 59.
73. Fromm, *To Have or To Be?*, 63. Emphasis in original.
74. Fromm, *To Have or To Be?*, 63–64. Emphasis in original.
75. Fromm, *To Have or To Be?*, 89.
76. Murray N. Rothbard, *For a New Liberty: The Libertarian Manifesto*. New York: Collier Books, 1978, 114.
77. "Uncle Ted Triggers the Vote," *Youtube*, uploaded August 16, 2010. http://www.youtube.com/watch?v=R6YWqnq5T3A&feature=related. Accessed February 21, 2012.
78. Michael Roberts, "Ted's World," *Denver Westword*, July 27, 1994, http://www.westword.com/1994-07-27/music/ted-s-world/. Accessed February 21, 2012. See also Matt Gertz, "NRA Spokesman Ted Nugent's Top 10 Inflammatory Comments," *MediaMatters for America*, February 15, 2012, http://mediamatters.org/mobile/blog/201202150010
79. Nugent, quoted in Horwitz and Anderson, *Guns, Democracy, and the Insurrectionist Idea*, 42–43. See also Elizabeth Goodman, "Ted Nugent Threatens to Kill Barack Obama and Hillary Clinton During Vicious Onstage Rant," *Rolling Stone*, August 24, 2007, http://www.rollingstone.com/music/news/ted-nugent-threatens-to-kill-barack-obama-and-hillary-clinton-during-vicious-onstage-rant-20070824.
80. Fromm, *Escape from Freedom*, 150.
81. R. D. Laing, *The Divided Self: An Existential Study in Sanity and Madness* (London: Tavistock Publications, [1960] 1969), 40–64; Anthony Giddens, *Modernity and Self-Identity: Self and Society in the Late Modern*

Age (Stanford: Stanford University Press, 1991), 36–55; Susie Scott and Charles Thorpe, "The Sociological Imagination of R. D. Laing," *Sociological Theory* 24 (4) (2006): 331–352; Charles Thorpe and Brynna Jacobson, "Life Politics, Nature and the State: Giddens' Sociological Theory and *The Politics of Climate Change*," *The British Journal of Sociology* 64 (1) (March 2013): 99–122.

82. Søren Kierkegaard quoted in Giddens, *Modernity and Self-Identity*, 47.
83. Fromm, *Escape from Freedom*, 132. See also Roger A. Salerno, *Landscapes of Abandonment: Capitalism, Modernity, and Estrangement* (Albany, NY: State University of New York Press, 2003), 68.
84. Fromm, *Escape from Freedom*, 61–63.
85. http://www.amazon.com/Keep-Guns-Freedom-Money-Change/dp/B0084SCL66; http://patriotdepot.com/ill-keep-my-guns-and-freedom-bumper-sticker/. God and Religion can also be inserted into the slogan, e.g. http://www.zazzle.com/you_can_keep_your_change_car_bumper_sticker-128745869261518938. See also the country song by Hank Williams Jr. "Keep the Change," https://www.youtube.com/watch?v=2iRReHtq_dk. Accessed November 8, 2015.
86. Christopher Caudwell, "H.G. Wells," in idem, *Studies in a Dying Culture* (New York: Dodd Mead & Co., 1938), 73–95, quoting 77–78.
87. Hilary Levey Friedman, *Playing to Win: Raising Children in a Competitive Culture* (Berkeley: University of California Press, 2013).
88. Barbara Ehreneich, *Fear of Falling: The Inner Life of the Middle Class* (New York: Pantheon Books, 1989), esp. 15.
89. Horwitz, *America's Right*, 169. Horwitz also notes that many Tea Party supporters "are or were small business owners": ibid., 170.
90. Paul Street, "Tea Party Republicans are Petit-Bourgeois Militarists," *ZSpace*, December 27, 2011, http://www.zcommunications.org/tea-party-republicans-are-petit-bourgeois-militarists-by-paul-street. Accessed February 24, 2012. See also Paul Street and Anthony DiMaggio, *Crashing the Tea Party: Mass Media and the Campaign to Remake American Politics* (Boulder: Paradigm Publishers, 2011), 47–48, 50; Paul Street and Anthony DiMaggio, "What 'Populist Uprising?': Facts and Reflections on Race, Class, and the Tea Party 'Movement,' Part 1," *ZNet*, April 23, 2010, http://www.zcommunications.org/what-populist-uprising-pt-1-by-paul-street. Accessed February 24, 2012.
91. Theda Skocpol and Vanessa Williamson, *The Tea Party and the Remaking of Republican Conservatism* (Oxford: Oxford University Press, 2012), 23.
92. Skocpol and Williamson, *The Tea Party*, 23.
93. Ron Paul, *End the Fed* (New York: Hachette Book Company, 2009), 212.

94. David M. Halbfinger, "Ron Paul's Flinty Worldview Was Forged Early," *The New York Times*, February 6, 2012, pp. A1, A15, quoting A1.
95. Halbfinger, "Ron Paul's Flinty Worldview," A15.
96. Paul, *End the Fed*.
97. Paul, *Liberty Defined*, 302.
98. Horwitz, *America's Right*, 172.
99. Horwitz, *America's Right*, 171.
100. Skocpol and Williamson, *The Tea Party*, 66.
101. Skocpol and Williamson, *The Tea Party*, 24, 66.
102. Skocpol and Williamson, *The Tea Party*, 69, 71.
103. Joseph Farah, *The Tea Party Manifesto: A Vision for American Rebirth* (Washington, DC: WND Books, 2010), 83–84.
104. Skocpol and Williamson, *The Tea Party*, 80.
105. Paul, *Tea Party Goes to Washington*, 12.
106. Rand Paul, *The Tea Party Goes to Washington* (New York: Center Street, 2011), 11.
107. Charly Gullett, *Tea Party Handbook: A Tactical Playbook for Tea Party Patriots* (Prescott, AZ: Warfield Press, 2009), 12.
108. Armey and Kibbe, *Give Us Liberty*, 3. See also Neil Gross, "The Indoctrination Myth," *New York Times*, March 3, 2012, http://www.nytimes.com/2012/03/04/opinion/sunday/college-doesnt-make-you liberal.html?_r=3&scp=1&sq=The%20Indoctrination%20Myth%22&st=cse. Accessed March 15, 2012.
109. Armey and Kibbe, *Give Us Liberty*, 20.
110. Paul, *Tea Party Goes to Washington*, 7.
111. Paul, *Tea Party Goes to Washington*, 11, 13, 68, 81; see also 74.
112. Skocpol and Williamson, *The Tea Party*, 79–80. See also Street and DiMaggio, *Crashing the Tea Party*, 102.
113. Farah, *The Tea Party Manifesto*, 20.
114. Christopher S. Parker and Matt A. Barreto *Change They Can't Believe In: The Tea Party and Reactionary Politics in America* (Princeton: Princeton University Press, 2013), esp. 190–217.
115. Skocpol and Williamson, *The Tea Party*, 78–79.
116. Skocpol and Williamson, *The Tea Party*, 77.
117. Skocpol and Williamson, *The Tea Party*, 34–40; Street and DiMaggio, *Crashing the Tea Party*, 66.
118. Skocpol and Williamson, *The Tea Party*, 63–68.
119. Street and DiMaggio, *Crashing the Tea Party*, 15. Emphasis in original.
120. Ron Paul, quoted in "Ron Paul's Golden Rule," *RT*, January 18, 2012, http://rt.com/usa/news/golden-rule-paul-war-099/. Accessed March 11, 2012.

121. Berlin, "Two Concepts of Liberty," 124; George Monbiot, "This bastardised libertarianism makes 'freedom' an instrument of oppression," *The Guardian*, December 19, 2011, http://www.guardian.co.uk/commentisfree/2011/dec/19/bastardised-libertarianism-makes-freedom-oppression. Accessed March 11, 2012.
122. Skocpol and Williamson, *The Tea Party*, 69.
123. Mark Lilla, "The Tea Party Jacobins," *The New York Review of Books*, May 27, 2010, http://www.nybooks.com/articles/archives/2010/may/27/tea-party-jacobins/. Accessed March 15, 2012. See also in Kate Zernike, *Boiling Mad: Inside Tea Party America* (NY: Times Books, 2010), 61
124. Caudwell, "H.G. Wells," 78–79. Emphasis in original.
125. Skocpol and Williamson, *The Tea Party*, 28.
126. Erich Fromm, *The Anatomy of Human Destructiveness* (New York: Holt, Rinehart and Winston, 1973), 204.
127. Richard G. Wilkinson, *The Impact of Inequality: How to Make Sick Societies Healthier* (New York: The New Press, 2005).
128. Jim Rutenberg, "How Billionaire Oligarchs are Becoming their Own Political Parties," *New York Times Magazine*, October 17, 2014, http://www.nytimes.com/2014/10/19/magazine/how-billionaire-oligarchs-are-becoming-their-own-political-parties.html; Patrick Martin, "US Midterm Elections Dominated by Corporate Cash," *World Socialist Web Site*, October 21, 2014, http://www.wsws.org/en/articles/2014/10/21/elec-o21.html
129. George Orwell, "Review of *The Road to Serfdom* by F. A. Hayek, *The Mirror of the Past* by K. Zilliacus," in *As I Please, 1943–1946* (Jaffrey, New Hampshire: David R. Godine, 2000), 117–119, on 118.
130. Paul, *Liberty Defined*, 29.
131. Paul, *Liberty Defined*, xii.
132. Street and DiMaggio, *Crashing the Tea Party*, 69.
133. Skocpol and Williamson, *Tea Party*, 204.
134. Farah, *Tea Party Manifesto*, 40.
135. Paul, *Revolution*, 67.
136. Paul, *Liberty Defined*, xii.
137. Skocpol and Williamson, *Tea Party*, 48.
138. Armey, quoted in Zernike, *Boiling Mad*, 67.
139. See Paul, *Revolution*, 49.
140. O'Donnell (from a *Newsweek* article) quoted in Street and DiMaggio, *Crashing the Tea Party*, 116.
141. Skocpol and Williamson, *Tea Party*, 51; Street and DiMaggio, *Crashing the Tea Party*, 68; Horwitz, *America's Right*, 176; LePore, *The Whites of Their Eye*, 16. See also Vincent Crapanzano, *Serving the Word: Literalism in America from the Pulpit to the Bench* (New York: New Press, 2001).

142. Jill Lepore, *The Whites of Their Eyes*, 8, 15.
143. Daniel Lazare, *The Frozen Republic: How the Constitution is Paralyzing Democracy* (New York: Harcourt Brace and Co., 1996), esp. 29–30, 79, 88, 157.
144. Mickey Edwards, quoted in Zernike, *Boiling Mad*, 59.
145. Jeffrey Dorfman, "Middle Class Jobs are Disappearing and the Fed is the Culprit," *Forbes*, June 7, 2014, http://www.forbes.com/sites/jeffrey-dorfman/2014/06/07/middle-class-jobs-are-disappearing-and-the-fed-is-the-culprit/
146. Skocpol and Williamson, *Tea Party*, 75.
147. Street and DiMaggio, *Crashing the Tea Party*, 14.
148. Rand Paul, *The Tea Party Goes to Washington*, 10.
149. "America's Debt Ceiling: No Normal Party," *The Economist*, July 5, 2011, http://www.economist.com/blogs/freeexchange/2011/07/americas-debt-ceiling-0 (accessed March 15, 2012); "United States Debt Ceiling Crisis," Wikipedia, http://en.wikipedia.org/wiki/United_States_debt-ceiling_crisis. Accessed March 15, 2012.
150. Alex Altman, "Eric Cantor, the GOP's Hard-Line Lieutenant, Sways Debt Talks," *Time*, July 11, 2011, http://swampland.time.com/2011/07/11/eric-cantor-the-gops-hard-line-lieutenant-sways-debt-talks/
151. Quoted in Bruce E. Levine, *Get Up, Stand Up: Uniting Populists, Energizing the Defeated, and Battling the Corporate Elite* (White River Junction, VT: Chelsea Green Publishing, 2011), 35.
152. Rand Paul, *The Tea Party Goes to Washington*, 10.
153. Arthur Delaney, "Jim Bunning Repeatedly Blocks Unemployment Benefits Extension, Tells Dem 'Tough Shit'," *The Huffington Post*, April 28, 2010, http://www.huffingtonpost.com/2010/02/26/jim-bunning-repeatedly-bl_n_477910.html Rand Paul expresses support for Bunning's position, in *The Tea Party Goes to Washington*, 71–72.
154. Rand Paul, *The Tea Party Goes to Washington*, 3.
155. Rand Paul, *The Tea Party Goes to Washington*, 27.
156. Paul, *Liberty Defined*, 171.
157. Halbfinger, "Ron Paul's Flinty Worldview," A15.
158. Quoting Paul, *Liberty Defined*, 201.
159. Paul, *Liberty Defined*, 176. See also Horwitz, *America's Right*, 182.
160. Street and DiMaggio, *Crashing the Tea Party*, 14; see also 66–67.
161. Street, "Tea Party Republicans are Petit-Bourgeois Militarists."
162. Skocpol and Williamson, *Tea Party*, 57. Emphasis in original.
163. Street and DiMaggio, *Crashing the Tea Party*, 13; Pierre Bourdieu, *Acts of Resistance: Against the New Myths of Our Time* (Cambridge: Polity Press, 1998), 1–2; Pierre Bourdieu, "The Invisible Hand of the Powerful,"

in idem, *Firing Back: Against the Tyranny of the Market 2*, trans. Loic Wacquant (London: Verso, 2003), 26–37, on 34–35.
164. Rand Paul, *The Tea Party Goes to Washington*, 132.
165. Gullet, *Tea Party Handbook*, 35, 50.
166. Anne Bowker, letter to Donald Warren (University of Michigan sociologist), quoted in Zernike, *Boiling Mad*, 50.
167. Villa, *Public Freedom*, 10.
168. Slater, *Pursuit of Loneliness*, 13.
169. Slater, *Pursuit of Loneliness*, 8.
170. Farah, *Tea Party Manifesto*, 113.
171. On authoritarianism and racism in the Tea Party, see Street and DiMaggio, *Crashing the Tea Party*, 77–99, 103.
172. Armey and Kibbe, *Give Us Liberty*, 61. On markets and freedom, see also Horwitz, *America's Right*, 38.
173. Paul, *Liberty Defined*, xvii.
174. David Friedman, *The Machinery of Freedom: A Guide to Radical Capitalism* (New Rochelle, NY: Arlington House, 1978).
175. Paul, *Liberty Defined*, 29.
176. Paul, *Liberty Defined*, 144–145.
177. The complete last sentence is: "It means making place for new technologies, new scientific theories, new forms of art, and new identities and new relationships": Tom G. Palmer, "The Morality of Capitalism," in idem ed., *The Morality of Capitalism: What Your Professors Won't Tell You* (Ottowa, Illinois: Jameson Books, 2011), 1–12, on 11. Emphases added.
178. Mark Follman, "Yes, Mass Shootings are Occurring More Often," *Mother Jones*, October 21, 2014, http://www.motherjones.com/politics/2014/10/mass-shootings-rising-harvard
179. Slater, *Pursuit of Loneliness*, 48.
180. See Chip Berlet and Matthew N. Lyons, *Right-Wing Populism in America: Too Close for Comfort* (New York: The Guilford Press, 2001).
181. Slater, *Pursuit of Loneliness*, 52. See also Simon Clarke and Paul Hoggett, "Empire of Fear: the American Political Psyche and the Culture of Paranoia," *Psychodynamic Practice* 10 (1) (2004): 89–106.
182. Glenn Greenwald, *No Place to Hide: Edward Snowden, The NSA, and the U.S. Surveillance State* (New York: Metropolitan Books, 2014).
183. It is indicative of this contradiction that Ron Paul's largest donor is involved in the *business* of expanding state surveillance: "Ron Paul Wants to Abolish the CIA: His Largest Donor Builds Toys for it," *The Nation*, February 23, 2012, http://www.thenation.com/article/166421/ron-paul-wants-abolish-cia-his-largest-donor-builds-toys-it; Ashlee Vance and Brad Stone, "Palantir: The War on Terror's Secret Weapon," *Bloomberg Businessweek Magazine*, November 22, 2011, http://www.businessweek.

com/magazine/palantir-the-vanguard-of-cyberterror-security-11222011.html; Brad Johnson, "ChamberLeaks: Military Contractors Palantir and Berico Under Scrutiny," *ThinkProgress*, March 19, 2011, http://thinkprogress.org/economy/2011/03/19/144160/chamberleaks-berico-palantir/?mobile=nc
184. Caudwell, *The Concept of Freedom*, 70.
185. See also James O'Connor, *Accumulation Crisis* (New York: Basil Blackwell, 1984), 231–232.
186. John Bellamy Foster and Fred Magdoff, "Monopoly-Finance Capital," in Foster and Magdoff, *The Great Financial Crisis: Causes and Consequences* (New York: Monthly Review Press, 2009), 63–76; John Bellamy Foster, *Naked Imperialism: The U.S. Pursuit of Global Dominance* (New York: Monthly Review Press, 2006).
187. Stewart Ewen, *Captains of Consciousness: Advertising and the Social Roots of Consumer Culture* (New York: McGraw Hill, 1976); Paul Baran and Paul Sweezy, *Monopoly Capital: An Essay on the American Economic and Social Order* (New York: Penguin, 1966), 117–144, esp. 120, 122–123; Robert W. McChesney, John Bellamy Foster, Inger L. Stole, and Hannah Holleman, "The Sales Effort in Monopoly Capital," *Monthly Review* 60 (11) (April 2009): 1–23.
188. Robert Scheer with Sara Beladi, *They Know Everything About You: How Data-Collecting Corporations and Snooping Government Agencies are Destroying Democracy* (New York: Nation Books, 2015); Robert Booth, "Facebook Reveals News-Feed Experiment to Control Emotions," *The Guardian*, June 29, 2014, http://www.theguardian.com/technology/2014/jun/29/facebook-users-emotions-news-feeds
189. Fromm, *Escape from Freedom*, 269.
190. Fromm, *Anatomy*, 226.
191. Fromm, *Escape from Freedom*, 269.
192. Naomi Oreskes and Erik M. Conway, *Merchants of Doubt: How a Handful of Scientists Obscured the Truth on Issues from Tobacco Smoke to Global Warming* (New York: Bloomsbury Press, 2010), 248–249.

INDEX

A
Abergil, Eden, 156–7
abstraction, 25–6, 81, 100, 110, 119, 136–7, 190, 192
  abstract labor as, 14
  the individual/individualism as, 11, 215, 219
  money as, 16, 18, 30, 65
abstract labor, 14, 19, 57, 80
abstract life, 57–9, 64–8, 72–3, 80, 83–4n.19
Abu Ghraib, 154–8, 189
acceleration, as destructive, 63, 129–33
  and economic crisis, 134–5
  technological, 97, 98–101, 105–8, 110–12, 122, 124, 138–9
Adam, Barbara, 64
advertising, 9, 21, 24, 26, 59, 75, 118, 131, 135, 163, 171, 176, 177, 184–5, 187, 192, 244–5
Afghanistan, 131
Age of Spiritual Machines (Kurzweil), The, 98, 100
A.I. (Kubrick and Spielberg), 61, 78
Aldiss, Brian, 93
algae, 61, 78

alienation, 2, 10–14, 46n.126, 171. *See also* labor
  of the body, 113, 117, 191
  and consumerism, 23, 30, 189–90
  as living death, 3, 18–21, 22
  Moravec's conception of, 79, 123–4
  of nature, 56, 80
Amazon phone, 24–5
amphibian decline, 60, 61
anal character, 22, 186, 238
animals, technologization of, 58, 64, 66, 69–71. *See also* extinction
Ansell-Pearson, Keith, 120
anxiety, 3, 9–10, 28, 30, 32–6, 54, 123, 132, 210–12, 216, 223–5, 231, 233, 237, 243, 245–6. *See also* dread
AquAdvantage salmon, 67
Armey, Richard Keith "Dick", 207, 230, 236, 241
Army, of the United States, 129–30, 154–5
artificial intelligence, 68–70, 79, 94, 96, 107, 110, 112, 113, 117, 123, 126–7, 129, 131, 180. *See also* robotics

262 INDEX

artificial life, on a dead planet, 55, 80–2
   as technoscientific field, 67–8
ATryn, 70
Atwood, Margaret, 54, 55

B

Bahro, Rudolf, 5–6, 12
Baker, James Jay, 215
Bank of England, 27
Barrow, John, 127
bats. *See* white nose syndrome
Bauman, Zygmunt, 9–10, 31–3, 158, 204n.179, 211, 245
BDSM (Bondage Domination and Sado-Masochism), 188–9
bees, made into device, 70. *See also* Colony Collapse Disorder
Beijing Olympics, 78
being, *versus* having, 4, 5, 17–18, 22, 32, 36, 222–3, 231
Belfort, Jordan, 29
Berlin, Isaiah, 232, 247n.1
BioBrick. *See* synthetic biology
body, the, alienation of, 83–4n.19, 117
   as commodity, 162, 166, 175–8, 184–5
   escape from, 80, 106–7, 128, 191
   and nature, 11, 13
   objectification of, 175
   reduction to, 14, 30, 179, 190
   surveillance of, 243
   as technology, 104, 113–14, 117, 126, 130, 184
   of worker, 20, 30, 36, 188, 190, 204n.178
boredom, 23, 123, 167–9, 171–3, 185–7, 190, 192
Borgmann, Albert, 21, 23
Boston Dynamics, 69–70, 129, 148n.194

Bourdieu, Pierre, 239, 240
Bowring, Finn, 58
Boyd, William, W. Scott Prudham, and Rachel Schurman, 57
Boyle, Daniel "Danny", 33
Brooks, Rodney, 59, 69–70, 97
Bunning, James Paul David"Jim", 238
Bush, George W., 16, 33, 77, 155, 207

C

Cameron, Sally, 160
Cantor, Eric, 237
Capital (Das Kapital), 14, 56. *See also* Marx, Karl
capital, as alienated labor, 10, 121–2
   concentration of, 58
   as dead, 2–3, 12–13, 19, 138–9
   and declining rate of profit, 27, 136
   financial, 7–8, 76, 133–4, 208
   globalization of, 132, 161–3, 168, 224
   human, 118
   as moving contradiction, 95–6
   and needs, 15, 21, 27
   self-replicating, 75–6, 81, 102–3, 128, 135–7
   subsumption by, 13–14, 19, 55–7, 59, 65, 81–2, 129
   as vampire, 3, 20, 27, 56, 82 *See also* Marx, Karl
Carnegie Mellon University, 68, 70
Caudwell, Christopher, 17, 209, 226, 244
Center for Disease Control, 33, 211
Central Intelligence Agency, 25
chemical pollution. *See* pollution
child abuse, 163–5, 173
Chun, Wendy Hui Kyong, 163, 168, 175–6
class, 1, 2, 19, 28, 29, 33, 36, 46n.126, 134, 138, 139,

145n.127, 163, 206, 212, 217–19, 225–30, 232–4, 237
climate change, 5–7, 15, 54, 60–3, 77–8, 81, 132, 229, 247
Clinton, Hillary, 223
cloning, 70–1, 111
Club of Rome, 76
Cohen, G. A., 220–1
Colony Collapse Disorder, 61
commodity fetishism. *See* fetish
Commoner, Barry, 64–5
Communism, 139
  fear of, 207, 230, 243
  Soviet and Eastern European (Stalinism), 95, 158–61
Constitution, of the United States of America. *See* fetish
consumerism, 6, 9, 21, 23, 25, 28–32, 94, 118–19, 159, 177, 184–5, 187–92, 209–10, 225, 244–5
Cookson, Clive, 73, 75
Cooper, Melinda, 76, 81
Craigslist, 163
cybernetic man. *See* marketing character
cybernetic religion, 120, 122, 129
cyborg, 104

D
Danner, Mark, 155
Dawkins, Richard, 101
Dawn of the Dead (Romero), 29, 30
Daybreakers (Spierig Brothers), 27
Debord, Guy, 6, 9, 26, 32, 37, 95, 122, 128, 192
De Chardin, Teilhard, 127–8
Defense Advanced Research Projects Agency, 97, 141n.17
deforestation, 54, 62, 63
De Grey, Aubrey, 106, 143n68
depression, 23
Dery, Mark, 106–9

device paradigm. *See* Borgmann, Albert
Dick, Philip K., 53, 55, 80
DiMaggio, Anthony, 231, 239
Dinello, Daniel, 54
Dines, Gail, 165–7, 178–80, 183
diversity, 3, 13, 19, 26, 55, 60, 62, 63, 65, 68–9, 219
Do Androids Dream of Electric Sheep? (Dick), 53
dread, Kierkegaard's concept of, 30, 224. *See also* anxiety
Drexler, Eric, 75, 78–9, 81, 96, 97, 100–2, 107–8, 111, 114–15, 120–1, 135, 140n.13
Dreyfus, Hubert, 170–1
drones, 25, 130–1
Dyer-Witheford, Nick, 96

E
ecology, 11, 76, 80
  and artificial life, 68–9, 80, 108, 111, 135
  destruction of, 1, 6, 10, 52, 56, 60–6, 97, 132, 139, 210, 247
  economic crisis, 8–9, 27, 76–7, 108, 134–5, 139, 149n.205, 210, 216, 239
economic growth, 78, 80, 99, 107, 111, 115, 116, 128, 132, 133, 139, 165, 168
Economist, The, 8, 18, 24, 60, 73
Edmundson, Mark, 28
Edwards, Marvin Henry "Mickey", 236–7
egoism, 231–3
Electronic Benefit Transfer card. *See* food stamps
Ellul, Jacques, 55
end of history, 1, 95, 99, 114, 128, 138–9

Endy, Drew, 73
engineering, 58, 101, 110, 118, 123. *See also* genetic engineering, geoengineering, science, Taylorism
Engines of Creation (Drexler), 75–6, 78, 96
England, Lynndie, 154
Escape from Freedom (Fromm), 206, 245. *See also* Fromm, Erich
escape velocity, 106–7, 109
eternal present, 94, 114, 138
exterminism, 5, 12
extinction, 6, 54, 60–6, 109

F

Facebook, 97, 156, 245
Farah, Joseph, 230, 236, 241
fascism, 4, 206
fear, of crime, 218
　of falling, 227–8
　liquid, 9–10, 33, 211
　of Obama, 230. *See also* anxiety, dread
feces, 22, 26, 154, 182
fetish, of commodities, 3, 19–21, 30–2, 121–2, 133, 136–7, 177, 208, 238–9
　of gun, 213–14, 216
　sexual, 168, 177, 179, 181
　of US Constitution, 206, 219, 225, 236–8
Feuerbach, Ludwig, 121
financial crisis. *See* economic crisis
Financial Times, The, 73, 75, 76, 78
fish. *See* overfishing
food stamps, 9, 32
Forbes, Malcolm Stevenson "Steve" Jr., 230
Fordism, 24, 74. *See also* post-Fordism
Forster, E. M., 9

Foster, John Bellamy, 58, 64, 65, 139
freedom, positive and negative. *See* Fromm, Erich
Fromm, Erich, on abstraction, 26
　and affluent society, 133
　on anonymous authority, 216
　criticism of, 46n.126
　on escape from freedom, 205–6
　on having, 22, 32, 119, 174, 222–3
　on individualism, 245
　interpretation of Marx, 2, 22
　on marketing character/ cybernetic man, 23–6, 118–20, 129, 131, 145n.127, 181–2
　on necrophilia, 4–5, 21, 180
　on negative freedom, 3, 205, 224–5, 244–7, 247n.1
　on simple stimuli, 23, 171–3
　on zombies, 23
frozen arks, 66
Fukushima, 6, 132
Fukuyama, Francis, 1, 100

G

Gadsden flag, 207, 213
genetic engineering, 54–5, 58–9, 66–7, 70–1, 76, 100
geoengineering, 7, 77, 81
Giddens, Anthony, 224
Glavin, Terry, 63, 65–6
global warming. *See* climate change
Glover, Jonathan, 156–7
Golumbia, David, 118
Google Glass, 24–5, 47n.147
Gore, Albert Arnold "Al" Jr., 62, 221
Graner, Charles, 154
Green Revolution, 63, 76–7
Gregg, Melissa, 22
Grindhouse (Rodriguez and Tarantino), 182

Gullett, Charly, 229
guns, crimes and deaths by, 214–18, 243
  and prepping, 34, 212
  as symbol, 23, 182, 206, 213–14, 216, 221, 223–5
  as technological commodities, 242

H
Hamlet(Shakespeare), 128
Hansen, James, 62
Harman, Chris, 132
Harris, Paul, 211
Helmreich, Stefan, 68
Heston, Charlton, 213, 221
history/ historicity, 12, 97, 98–9, 101, 104, 107–9, 115–16, 120, 126, 131, 137–9, 151n.222, 169, 219, 236–7
  and natural history, 12, 60, 66, 99, 109. *See also* end of history
hoarding, 5, 22, 34, 174, 222
Hobbes, Thomas, 213, 215, 234
homelessness, 15, 19, 31, 216
Horwitz, Joshua and Casey Anderson, 213, 215
Horwitz, Robert, 228–9
human trafficking, 159–63, 192
Hurricane Katrina, 19, 33

I
I am Legend, film, (Francis Lawrence), 53, 212
idol. *See* fetish
immortality, 79, 100, 106, 112–16, 120, 121, 127, 138
imperialism, 1, 6, 37, 131–2, 154–7, 244

individualism, 9, 28, 29, 108, 115, 116, 118, 208, 214–16, 218, 222–3, 225, 231–5, 240–1, 244–6
inequality, 2, 107–8, 124, 125, 159, 189, 215, 226
Internet, the, 23, 24, 162, 163–77, 185–91, 213, 245, 246
Iraq, 6, 130, 131, 154–6, 186
iRobot, 70, 131
Israel, 156–7

J
Jackson, Jeremy, 60
Jenkins, Philip, 174
Jensen, Robert, 167, 175, 179, 183
Jha, Alok, 73
Jones, Richard, 75
Joy, Bill, 54, 100

K
Kali, 129
Kappeler, Susanne, 153–5, 157, 170
Kasire, Thomas, 153–4
Kelly, Kevin, 98, 105, 106, 150n.217
Khatib, Ghassan, 157
Kierkegaard, Søren, 170, 224
Kilbourne, Jean, 177–8
Knight, Tom, 72
Koch, Charles G. and David H., 234, 235
Korea, 21
Kurzweil, Ray, 75, 79–81, 97, 99, 110–11, 115, 120–1, 135, 140n.13, 146n.142
  business activities of, 134
  on life extension, 113–14
  the Singularity, 96, 103–5, 122–3, 127–8
  Singularity University, 96
  and US military, 129–31

L

labor, alienated, 5, 10, 12–14, 18–21, 27, 30, 36, 46n.126, 56–8, 117–8, 121–2, 188–9, 192
- as historical force, 137
- market, 94, 135, 158, 209, 221
- mental *vs.* manual, 190–1
- replacement of by machines, 102–3, 105, 124–5, 131, 191
- slave, 20, 29, 53, 161–2, 192

Laing, R. D., 224
Langton, Rae, 183
LaPierre, Wayne, 213–15, 219–21
Latham, Rob, 28
Leadbeater, Charles, 105, 137
Lee, Maggy, 159
Lepore, Jill, 236
Levy, David, 180–1
Lexus, 59, 75
liberalism, 1, 158, 205, 208, 214, 244, 247
- American liberals, 224, 229, 230
- neo-liberalism, 7–8, 95, 157–63, 234, 241

libertarianism, 97, 110, 135, 144n.110, 163, 188, 214–15, 220–1, 223, 225, 227, 231, 232, 234–5, 238–42
life extension. *See* immortality
Lilla, Mark, 232
living dead, 1–3, 19, 21, 27–30, 35, 37, 65–6, 82, 129, 181
Loman, Willy, 190

M

MacKinnon, Catherine, 182
Macpherson, C. B., 214
Maddison, Stephen, 168, 176
Marcus, David, 175
Marcuse, Herbert, 95, 133
marketing character. *See* Fromm, Erich

market, the, 4, 17, 20, 25–6, 36–7, 94, 95, 101, 103, 105, 121, 125, 128, 131, 133, 135–6, 139, 158, 162–3, 168, 176, 180, 208, 216
- and freedom, 3, 161–2, 188, 192, 206, 209, 214, 221, 225, 241–2, 246
- and monopoly, 234–5, 244
- and self, 23, 221
- stock market, 27, 134

Martin, Tom, 211
Martin, Trayvon, 216
Marx, Karl, 1–22. 27, 56–8, 76, 82, 95, 121–2, 136–9, 191
- vampire metaphor of, 27, 56

masculinity, 183, 216
Massachusetts Institute of Technology, 69, 72, 73, 97, 131
Matrix, The (Wachowski Brothers), 53
McClelland, Mac, 188–9
McCray, W. Patrick, 79
McMurty, John, 7
McNally, David, 27
memes, 101
Merkley, Jeff, 238
Mészáros, István, 10, 138
military, 5–6, 10, 37, 132, 139, 154–7, 186–7, 233
- expenditure, 7
- support for, 239–41, 244
- technology, 69–70, 101, 129, 130–1

Minutemen, 218
Monbiot, George, 232
money, 10, 15–16, 18, 19, 20, 25, 26, 31, 32, 35–6, 65, 75, 76, 119, 135, 158, 161, 162, 165, 168, 173, 210, 220, 221, 225–6, 234, 242–3
- for bank bailout, 9, 134, 207, 208, 244
- as feces, 22, 225, 237–8

INDEX

laundering of, 8, 161
time as, 18
Mooney, Pat, 63
Moravec, Hans, 68, 79, 81, 96, 97, 99, 100, 102–3, 106, 108–11, 115–17, 120, 123–9, 135–7, 140n.13, 141n.17
Munck, Ronaldo, 162

N

nanotechnology, 54, 59, 67, 76, 78–80, 82n.4, 96, 97, 99–101, 104, 108, 111, 113, 115, 121, 130
bionanotechnology, 59, 74–5
narcissism, 23, 24, 171
group, 232, 233
National Rifle Association, 213–14, 220, 221, 223–4
necroculture, 2–3
necrophilia, 2, 4, 23, 179–82
Neocleous, Mark, 21
Nestlé, 76
networks, 9, 23, 24, 93, 99, 105–6, 114, 133, 135, 156–8, 161–5, 186–7, 190, 211, 245
New Economy, the, 98, 105, 134, 149n.205
Nexia Biotechnologies, 70
Night of the Living Dead (Romero), 29
Nixon, Richard, 239
Noble, David F., 97, 103
Nozick, Robert, 214, 220–1
Nugent, Ted, 223–4

O

Obama, Barack, 34, 194n.23, 207, 208, 224, 225, 229, 230, 233, 239
ocean, the, 6, 15, 37, 54, 60–1, 63, 77, 78

O'Donnell, Christine, 236
O'Donnell, Ian and Claire Milner, 163–4, 172–4
Omega Point. *See* De Chardin, Teilhard
ontological security/ insecurity, 206, 224–5, 231, 233, 235, 239
Oryx and Crake. *See* Atwood, Margaret
overfishing, 6, 60–1

P

Palantir Technologies, 97, 258n.183
Palestine, 156–7
Palmer, Tom, 242
Paul, Pamela, 167
Paul, Rand, 229, 230, 237–9, 243
Paul, Ron, 97, 214, 225, 227–8, 231, 235–6, 238–9, 241, 258n.183
Pearce, Fred, 77–8
pedophilia, 164–5, 173–5. *See also* child abuse, pornography
Penny, Laurie, 184
Pentinnen, Elina, 159, 162, 163
petite-bourgeoisie (middle class), 28, 36, 212, 217–19, 225–9, 232–5, 237, 244
Pipe, Roger T., 176
pollution, 6, 15, 54, 60, 61, 64, 77, 78, 80, 105
pornography, and alienation, 171–2, 184, 189–92
anal sex in, 178
categories in, 175–8
child, 163–5, 167–8, 172–4, 178
collecting, 173–5, 200n.103
dismemberment in, 177–8, 182
internet, 163–77, 185–91
market, 163, 168, 175–7, 180, 184, 188, 192
and military, 186–7

pornography (*cont.*)
  necrophilia and, 179–83
  rape in, 154, 165, 167
  as structure of representation, 153–7, 177–9
  and technology, 175, 180–1, 183–4
  torture in, 153–7, 168, 178–80, 182
  use at work, 185–7
Pornography of Representation, The. *See* Kappeler, Susanne
post-Fordism, 94
post-human, 68, 110. *See also* techno–futurism, transhumanism
Postone, Moishe, 138, 150n.212
preppers. *See* survivalism
privatism, 212, 217, 231, 233
prostitution. *See* human trafficking
Proudhon, Pierre-Joseph, 137
psychoanalysis, 2, 22

R
Ray, Thomas, 67–8
Reagan, Ronald, 28
RealDolls, 181
recession. *See* economic crisis
reification, 55, 57, 75, 80, 81, 122, 136–7, 139, 177–8, 182, 185, 220–3. *See also* alienation, fetish
Rice, Anne, 28
Rikowski, Glenn, 21
Roberts, Callum, 60
robotics, 53–4, 58–9, 67–70, 74, 76, 82n.4, 93–4, 96, 100, 102–3, 108–9, 124, 126, 129–31, 180–1, 183. *See also* artificial intelligence
Rockwell, Norman, 230
Rodriguez, Robert, 182
Romero, George, 29, 33
Roosevelt, Franklin D., 228
Rosa, Hartmut, 94–5
Rose, Nikolas, 73
Rothbard, Murray, 223
Russia, 7–8, 159–60, 163, 195n.29. *See also* Soviet Union

S
Sachs, Jeffrey, 77
sado-masochism, 23, 171, 173, 174, 180, 182, 188–9. *See also* BDSM
Saint-Simon, Henri Comte de, 103
salmon. *See* AquAdvantage
Santelli, Rick, 208
Santorum, Rick, 207
Schumpeter, Joseph, 96
Schwartz, Mark, 183, 190
science, 2, 7, 11, 54–5, 57–81, 100, 108, 110, 119–22, 127, 180, 224
science fiction, 9, 53–4, 82n.4, 93–4, 105, 106, 131
Scorsese, Martin, 29
Second Life, 191
Seeman, Nadian, 74–5
self, alienation of, 13, 14, 24–5, 118, 145n.127, 187–8, 190, 192
  and group, 233
  and having, 4, 22–3, 28, 32, 119, 210, 222–3, 225, 231, 238
  and inequality, 215
  narcissism, 113–14, 119
  pleasure in loss of, 14, 29–30, 106, 125–6
  security of, 224–6, 231, 240
  self-consciousness, 11–12, 31
  self-ownership, 213–14, 220–3
  and species being, 16–17, 206
  technologization of, 114–15, 117, 126
  torture and, 155
selfie stick, 24
sexual trafficking. *See* human trafficking
Shootist, The (Don Siegel), 213

Sierra, Kathy, 170
Singularity, the. *See* Kurzweil, Ray
Skocpol, Theda and Vanessa Williamson, 227, 229–33, 236, 237, 239
Skousen, Cleon W., 236
Slater, Philip, 189, 209, 241
slavery. *See* human trafficking, labor
Soble, Alan, 177, 184
social death, 31, 162
soil erosion, 54, 62–4
Southwood, Ivor, 94
Soviet Union, the, 99, 158, 159
space, outer, 69, 79, 81, 97, 102, 107–8, 111, 126, 131
spectacle, 9, 21, 27, 32, 37, 94, 95, 128, 132, 135, 156, 169, 172, 192
    Debord's concept defined, 26, 128
speculation. *See* capital, financial
state of exception, 158
state, the, 158, 207–8, 214, 219, 234–5, 238–41, 243–6
    as capitalist, 234
Street, Paul, 227. *See also* DiMaggio, Anthony
subsumption, formal and real. *See* capital
Summy, Ralph, 7
"Supertoys Last All Summer Long," (Aldiss), 93–4
Supreme Court, United States, 167
surveillance, 1, 70, 243, 245, 246
    self-surveillance, 113
survivalism, 34–6, 210–13, 231
Symbrion Project, 69
synthetic biology, 58–9, 71–3
synthetics, 6, 65

T

Tarantino, Quentin, 182
Taylorism, 71
Tea Party, 206–8, 214, 225–44
technocracy, 103, 110, 244
techno-futurism, 59, 68, 75, 79, 81, 82n.4, 96–7, 105–6, 115–17, 120, 128, 131–8, 140n.13. *See also* transhumanism
technological determinism, 98–106, 109, 115, 119, 130, 133, 137–9, 242
television, 1, 9, 14, 23, 24, 28, 160, 171, 172, 211, 212, 243
Terminator, The (James Cameron), 53
terrorism, 33, 34, 155, 207, 210, 214, 229, 234, 240, 243
Thiel, Peter, 97, 258n.183
Thompson, E. P., 5–6, 12
Thoreau, Henry David, 124
"Three Strikes and You're Out" law, 218
time, cycles/rhythms, 64–5, 99, 113, 114, 116
    historical, 138
    linear, 97, 99, 100, 103, 114–16, 120, 123, 128, 129, 138–9
Tipler, Frank, 127
Titanic syndrome, 10
transhumanism, 68, 104, 106, 121, 138. *See also* techno–futurism
Truman, Harry S., 228
Turner, Ted, 210

U

Ukraine, 164
Unmanned Aerial Vehicles. *See* drones
USSR. *See* Soviet Union

V

Vadas, Melinda, 182
vampires, 27–9
    Marx's metaphor of, 3, 20, 27, 56, 82

Veblen, Thorstein, 103
Venter, Craig, 71, 78
Virilio, Paul, 130–3, 139, 147n.180, 149n.205

W
Walking Dead, The, television series, 1, 34
Walsh, David, 29
war, 1, 2, 5–7, 9, 37, 70, 129–32, 186–7, 210, 211, 234
 of all against all, 213
 on terror, 131, 132, 214, 243
Warhol, Andy, 94
waste, 3, 5, 6, 22, 55, 56, 64, 65, 111, 158, 161, 179
Wayne, John, 213
Weber, Max, 18, 22
WhatsApp, 157
white nose syndrome, 61
Whole Foods Market, 32
Wiener, Jon, 210
Williams, Hank Jr., 254n.85
Williamson, Milly, 28
Williams, Phil, 162

Wolf of Wall Street, The. *See* Scorcese, Martin
working class, the, 36, 46n.126, 134, 138, 163, 225. *See also* labor

Y
Youtube, 156

Z
Zerzan, John, 124
Zimmerman, George, 216–18
Žižek, Slavoj, 95, 146n.142, 212
zombie, as anxiety, 30, 33, 36–7
 apocalypse, 34
 as capital, 27, 30
 as consumer, 29
 film and television, 1, 29, 33
 folklore, 29, 48n.169
 Fromm on, 23
 as gun-range targets, 34
 as mass, 29
Zombie Economics (Desjardins and Emerson), 34–6
Zombie walks, 29–30
Zoological Society of London, 60

The manufacturer's authorised representative in the EU is Springer Nature Customer Service Centre GmbH, Europaplatz 3, 69115 Heidelberg, Germany. If you have any concerns regarding our products, please contact ProductSafety@springernature.com

Printed and bound by CPI Group (UK) Ltd, Croydon, CR0 4YY
23/03/2026
02076458-0003